A System of Ambition?

British Foreign Policy 1660–1793

2nd edition

"He declaimed against the system, and said let us call it anything but a system of peace; let us say it is a system of ambition, of vain glory, to see the offspring of the immortal Chatham, intriguing in all the courts of Europe, and setting himself up as the great posture-master of the balance of power, as possessing an exclusive right to be umpire of all, and to weigh out, in patent scales of his own, the quantity of dominion that each power shall possess."

(Richard Brinsley Sheridan, opposition MP attacking William Pitt the Younger, 12 April 1791, Cobbett's *Parliamentary History*, vol. 29, 213–14)

A System of Ambition?
British Foreign Policy 1660–1793
2nd edition

Jeremy Black

SUTTON PUBLISHING

First published in 1991 by Longman

This edition first published in 2000 by
Sutton Publishing Limited
Phoenix Mill · Thrupp · Stroud · Gloucestershire GL5 2BU

Copyright © Jeremy Black, 2000

British Library Cataloguing in Publication Data
A catalogue record for this book is available from the British Library

ISBN 0 7509 2278 8

*Cover illustration: The Duke of Marlborough at the fall of Lille, 1708;
tapestry woven by Judocus de Vos, Blenheim Palace, Oxfordshire
(photograph Bridgeman Art Library, London)*

Typesetting and origination by
Sutton Publishing Limited.
Printed in Great Britain by
Redwood Books, Trowbridge, Wiltshire.

CONTENTS

ACKNOWLEDGEMENTS

I would like to acknowledge the support of the British Academy, the Leverhulme Foundation, the Staff Travel and Research Fund of Durham University, the University of Exeter, and the Wolfson Foundation in conducting the archival research upon which this work is based. I would like to thank Her Majesty the Queen, the Duke of Bedford, the Marquess of Bute, Earl Fitzwilliam and the Wentworth Woodhouse Trustees, the Earl of Harrowby and the Trustees of the Harrowby MSS Trust, Earl Waldegrave, Lady Lucas and John Weston-Underwood for permission to consult their collections of manuscripts. I benefited greatly from the comments of Matthew Anderson and Philip Woodfine on drafts of the first edition and of Grayson Ditchfield on a draft of the second edition. Richard Harding also helpfully commented on a section of the latter. Welcome opportunities to outline and discuss ideas developed in this book were provided by invitations to give lectures at the Anglo-American conference, the Institute of Historical Research, the Naval War College at Newport, Harvard, the University of Boston, Augusta State University and the Triangle Institute for Security Studies.

June 1999

LIST OF ABBREVIATIONS

AE CP	Ang. Paris, Ministère des Affaires Etrangères, Correspondance Politique Angleterre. (Also Allemagne, Autriche etc.)
AST	Turin, Archivio di Stato, Lettere Ministri Inghilterra.
BL Add	London, British Library, Additional Manuscripts.
BL Eg	London, British Library, Egerton Manuscripts.
BL Stowe	London, British Library, Stowe Manuscripts.
BN NAF.	Paris, Bibliothèque Nationale, nouvelles acquisitions françaises.
Bayr. London	Munich, Bayerisches Hauptstaatsarchiv, Gesandtschaften London.
Beinecke	New Haven, Beinecke Library.
Bod.	Oxford, Bodleian Library.
CRO	County Record Office.
CUL	Cambridge, University Library.
Chewton	Chewton Mendip, Chewton House, papers of James, 1st Earl Waldegrave.
EHR	*English Historical Review*.
Farmington	Farmington, Connecticut, Lewis Walpole Library.
Grafton	Bury St Edmunds, West Suffolk Record Office, Grafton papers.
HJ	*Historical Journal*.
HL LO.	San Marino, California, Huntington Library, Loudoun papers.
HL MO.	San Marino California, Huntington Library, Montagu papers.
HL ST, STG	San Marino California, Huntington Library, Stowe papers.
MS	Mount Stuart, island of Bute, papers of 3rd Earl of Bute including those formerly in Cardiff.
NeC	Nottingham University Library, Clumber papers.
NLS	Edinburgh, National Library of Scotland.
PRO FO	London, Public Records Office, Foreign Office papers.
PRO SP	London, Public Records Office, State papers.

Polit. Corresp.	*Politische Correspondenz Friedrichs des Grossen* (46 vols, Berlin, 1879-1939).
RA CP	Windsor, Royal Archives, Cumberland papers.
WW	Sheffield Public Library, Wentworth Woodhouse papers.
WU	Iden Green, Mill St House, papers of Edward Weston.

PREFACE

Foreign policy was a central concern in Britain between 1660 and 1793. It affected and interested not only those involved in government and politics, but also all those influenced by economic and religious developments. War and taxation, which owed much to war and foreign policy, played a major rôle in the economy. Religion and the succession were intimately involved with foreign policy until 1746. Foreign policy was not only important; it also provides a means by which the operation of Britain as a state, a political system in which pressures, interests and views interact, can be considered. Indeed, the importance of foreign policy ensures that it is an especially appropriate means to this study.

By 1793 Britain was a much more powerful state than she had been in 1660, her dominions in both hemispheres far more extensive, her public finances far stronger. This growing strength and territorial expansion led some foreign commentators to present Britain as a threat, her goals ambitious, her diplomacy manipulative, all centred on a bid for maritime and colonial hegemony outside Europe and for diplomatic predominance on the Continent. The latter part of this charge was echoed in 1791 by Sheridan, an opposition MP as well as a great playwright, at the time of the Ochakov crisis – an attempt by the ministry of William Pitt the Younger to employ diplomatic pressure and the threat of naval force in order to determine the outcome of the struggle between Russia and Turkey in the Balkans. He attacked what he presented as 'a system of ambition, of vain glory'. Was he correct? Or was British policy much more a matter of shifts and expedients, a response to unexpected crises and alarming developments in an unpredictable international system? It is one of the central aims of the book to throw light on that question.

In a work of this length devoted to such a large topic there has necessarily been a process of selection. I have sought to concentrate on relationships between domestic circumstances and foreign policy and on episodes of choice over policy. It is important to appreciate that choices existed, that policy was not structurally determined, that contingencies and the views of individuals were of consequence. I have also used original quotations extensively. They indicate the rich variety of sources that exists for the subject and hopefully capture the flavour of contemporary opinion. Documents of course present problems: they were intended to persuade and can mislead. However, it is necessary to overcome the all-too-common division between monographs based on archival sources and written for the specialist and general works which are often schematic. This book is offered in the conviction that general works are most valuable if they are securely based on as wide a mastery of the archival sources as is possible. These sources enable one to grasp the uncertainties of the past and the rôles of chance and perception, and to restore a human perspective to an historical imagination too often dominated by impersonal forces. If that can lead to greater difficulties in posing and answering questions of the relationships between change and continuity, the short term and the long term, it is appropriate to point out that history is not an unbroken mirror reflecting our views, but a fractured glass with pieces missing or opaque and a general pattern that is difficult to distinguish, and impossible to do so to general satisfaction.

For Bruce Coleman
A good friend and a respected colleague.

INTRODUCTION

The danger of any summary of foreign policy is the tendency to create a schematic impression. Major events, or rather events that appear full of importance and consequence in hindsight, necessarily provide the chronological structure of such a summary, dictate the emphases and thus appear to occur as a result of preceding such events. A shortage of space produces an emphasis on order and policy, causes and results, as opposed to disorder and confusion. In the domestic context, decision-making processes are simplified and pressures are said directly to cause policies. The ambiguity of influence is replaced by the need to attribute cause briefly, and, in the text, the balancing equivocations of subordinate clauses and the passive tense are replaced by the staccato of active assertion. A process of aggregation eases the difficulties of lengthy explanation. Policy, the government, mercantile influence, Parliament, public opinion are presented as clear and distinct activities, influences and bodies whose conscious interaction determined events. This culminates in the understandable use of countries as a shorthand term for complex or confusing processes of decision making. Even when greater definition is used in describing the British situation, it is understandable that foreign states are presented crudely as France or Austria etc., ignoring the various processes and opinions through which foreign policy was formed. In addition, it is all too easy to present a simplistic description of the international system, and/or a misleading schematic account of its operation.

The relationship between institution or group and opinion is another vexed problem, especially when it is necessary to consider the rôle of public opinion. Furthermore, there is a strong tendency to consolidate and reify ideas that can, for example, be described as isolationist or interventionist, blue water or continental. In practice, the nature and influence of such ideas altered considerably and require continual reassessment in any wide-ranging scholarly study, but space rarely permits this. In addition, it is necessary to be cautious in suggesting that policies arose or events happened because of ideas. It is important to explain the process by which these ideas were influential.

To assert that the reality of the period was in fact one of confusion is not simply to draw a contrast between the theoretical nature of institutions and their actual operation, which was frequently a matter of patronage and rival policies. In this period the idea of distinct institutions, with defined responsibilities and comprehensive records, whose relationships can be ascertained, is inappropriate. As will be discussed elsewhere (pp. 72–7), the formal mechanism for the execution of foreign policy – the offices of the Secretaries of State for the Northern and Southern Departments and, from 1782, the Foreign Office – played a variable rôle in its formulation. Diplomacy was indeed under the control of the relevant institutions, and the use of secret missions or confidential correspondences outside the diplomatic and Secretarial structure was relatively limited, more so in the eighteenth century than the seventeenth. However, the formulation of policy, the formal and actual responsibility of the Crown and its chosen ministers, was not generally determined in a rigid or clearly defined institutional structure, and this has important consequences for the value of the surviving sources (pp. 6–10). An important exception lies in those periods when the monarch was abroad, when a confidential and frequent correspondence was carried on with the ministers left in London. This was less the case under William III, who tended to keep his English ministry in the dark and showed little more confidence in individual ministers, than under George I and II, between 1716 and 1755. The correspondence between the Secretary of State accompanying George and the Secretary or acting Secretary who remained in London survives in State Papers Regencies, offering a valuable guide to the formulation of policy.

Having sketched briefly some of the problems that arise in offering a synoptic survey, one must note that all of the difficulties can be found in this text. There is no compensation for a shortage of space but, more seriously, there is no language that can be offered which will free the text from the ambiguities and expectations aroused by terms such as 'policy'. Having undertaken detailed archival research and published on topics in the entire period from the 1680s until 1793 this author is more than conscious of what has been lost through compression and synopsis, especially the world of choice in uncertainty that affected decisions.

At the outset, it is also important to underline the importance of this topic. At the close of the twentieth century, the British Empire increasingly seems both distant and irrelevant, but the latter view is wrong. First, the imperial experience was important to the development of Britain as a state and society. Secondly, it was very important to the wider question of the rise of the West. If the 'Rise of the West' is one of the meta-narratives of world history over the last half-millennium, it is the case that more attention has been devoted to the linked questions of when/how/why Rise?, rather than which West? Yet the latter was important. Would the Rise of the West have occurred or followed another path had there been a different West?

Domestic conditions and changes affected the cultural suppositions that moulded the use and choices of power. An understanding of Europe as fluid in its development, in terms of relations between and within European states, can be seen as important in terms of structures, priorities and ideas. The forms of governments and structures of politics and administration that enabled societies to mobilise and control resources, both for relations with the non-West and more generally, were not fixed. Secondly, the priorities for the use of resources were not fixed. Thirdly, the ideas that influenced relations with the non-West were culturally conditioned and affected by developments within Western societies.

What does this mean? To take the case of Britain, the deployment of regular troops from the 1750s to assist the East India Company in India involved choice and reflected particular priorities and ideas that had not been present twenty years earlier. Similarly, but here within the trans-oceanic European world, with the attempt in 1763–75 to increase the contribution of Britain's American colonies to imperial resources. These attitudes and ideas can be seen as more important than the mechanics and techniques of force and as necessarily open to counterfactual speculation.

If France had beaten Britain during their protracted conflict for much of the period 1688–1815 then this would have greatly affected the struggle of the West versus the Rest. Why? France after all had oceanic and trans-oceanic interests and ambitions of her own. It was unclear which power would prevail in North America until the failure of the French attempt to regain Québec in 1760. In 1750, France was more powerful than Britain in India. France put as much effort as Britain into Pacific exploration. She was also energetic in trying to develop links in South-East Asia, Persia, the Turkish empire and West Africa. Allied with Spain, the third most powerful naval power, France, the second most powerful, was able to challenge the most powerful, Britain, on a number of occasions. Furthermore, after 1815, France again took a path of trans-oceanic expansion, and successfully so, first in North and West Africa and then in Indo China and Madagascar.

Thus, had France beaten Britain it is at first glimpse unclear why this should have made a difference to the extension of European power; although the nature of that power would have been different. A French-dominated trans-oceanic world would have looked to Catholicism, civil law, French culture and language, and a different notion of representative government and politics to that of Britain. Furthermore, after the French Revolution, there would have been a different racial politics, one that can in part be glimpsed by considering official French attitudes to ethnicity over the last half century. Martinique and Guadeloupe, for example, are currently part of metropolitan France in a way that none of Britain's trans-oceanic colonies ever became.

Yet, had France beaten Britain, the trans-oceanic situation would have been very different. This was due to geopolitics, priorities, and assumptions about the international system. The geopolitics were that France was both a maritime and a European continental power, unlike Britain even when ruled by the Electors of Hanover, as it was in 1714–1837. French geopolitics led to clashing priorities, for example in 1778 when France could have intervened in the War of the Bavarian Succession, rather than the War of American Independence, and priorities, of course, are a matter that immediately invite counterfactual speculation, as they did for contemporaries. In 1756 and 1805, the British feared that the French would invade England or Ireland; instead the French turned elsewhere, as they also did with most of their forces when invasion attempts were mounted on the British Isles in 1708 and 1796–8.

Priorities owed something to resources and a sense of the possible, especially in the case of invasion plans. They also reflected ideas, in this case the dominance of European conceptions in French geopolitical thought; and, more specifically, concern with dynastic and landward aggrandisement until the mid eighteenth (and territorially from the 1790s also); and anxiety about the impact in Europe of the rise of other land powers, the Habsburgs from the early sixteenth century, and Russia and Prussia also from the early eighteenth.

Furthermore, more generally, French society was not dominated by an ethos of commercial strength and maritime destiny, the ethos that was the prelude to territorial ambitions in South Asia, Africa and the Pacific. The spatial composition of French power was that of inland France. The landed nobility was crucial in Valois and Bourbon France, and the role of land in elite identity was underlined under Napoleon by his reliance on a new service aristocracy who were provided with estates. The nobility were far more interested in the army than the navy, in the land, rather than trade or empire. These values affected French society as a whole. The loss of Canada to Britain in 1760 and Louisiana to Spain in 1763 was criticized in mercantile circles in the Atlantic ports, but had only limited impact elsewhere, not least because they were seen in fashionable circles as barren and profitless. Aristocratic families had scant presence in French North America.

The values of aristocratic power were important to French policy-making and diplomacy. Trade was not the most resonant symbol of national identity. Louis XIV was no Peter the Great, keen to develop and sustain a navy and to move the capital to the coast, while Louis XV lacked the Emperor (ruler of Austria) Charles VI's ostentatious commitment to trading companies, and Louis XVI failed to match Charles III of Spain's interest in the colonies and trade. There were choices in French foreign policy. Policy-makers put Europe first, and were able to maintain their leading position in Western Europe, but not to gain a comparable one in the expanding European world. Had France been the dominant Western power, then it is likely that the resources of the trans-oceanic world would have been employed to further European ambitions. For example, France's long-standing interest in European allies, such as Bavaria, Poland, Sweden and Turkey, might have led to a more sustained intervention in Central and Eastern Europe. The attempt in 1741 to reorder Central Europe that led French troops to St. Polten and Prague might have been given greater force. So also with the attack on Prussia in 1757. Further east, the expeditionary force sent to Danzig in 1734 and the squadron dispatched to the Baltic in 1739 could have been part of a stronger effort to help Poland and Sweden against Russia. When, in 1783, Vergennes, the French Foreign Minister, negotiated peace with Britain it was not in order to pursue plans in India but rather to better oppose Russian aggrandizement in the Crimea.

A stronger France might have avoided revolution: greater success could have encouraged obedience and respect for the political system and monarch. That, however, might not necessarily have left France freer to pursue international ambitions outside Europe. Instead, it might have encouraged a more assertive, even hegemonic, stance within Europe. This counterfactual is important because the period 1789–1842 was very much the 'tipping point' in South and East Asia. During that period, the Turks, Marathas, Gurkhas, Burmese, Chinese and Mysore were all defeated, as was the Egyptian fleet. European territorial gains included Singapore, Aden, Karachi and Hong Kong, all gained by Britain. Promising political and military developments in the defeated powers were cut short or seriously curtailed. To suggest that in some way there would have been no expansion had France not Britain been the leading European power is implausible. The British bombarded Algiers in 1816, but the French occupied it in 1830. They also established themselves in the Marquesas and Tahiti in 1842 and Gabon in 1844. However, the pace and extent of European overseas expansion would probably have been less had France been the prime European power, whether it had had a Revolution or not. This might well have given other non-European powers, including, but not only, those listed above, a vital opportunity to consolidate politically, to develop militarily, and to acquire Western industrial technology by trade and investment, rather as Latin America and later Japan did.

Did then Britain have to win? For geographical, cultural and political reasons, France was different to Britain as an economy, a society and a state. When the Count of Broglie arrived in London as French ambassador in 1724 he was astonished by the apparently innumerable quantity of shipping in the Thames. Structural limitations have a role, not least because the character of French political culture affected the perception of options. Rulers living in Versailles were much less exposed to the dynamic forces of European economics and overseas activities than a government and Parliament located in London, a growing centre of world trade. This affected, but did not determine, policy choices, resource availability, and international responses. Louis XIV could have devoted more resources to trans-oceanic activity in the 1660s and 1670s. He could have sought to prevent Anglo-Dutch co-operation in 1689–1713, either by making more of an effort earlier to retain Dutch support, or by thwarting William III of Orange's invasion in 1688, or by providing more assistance to the Irish thereafter. Greater effort could have been put into sustaining and strengthening the promising French positions in India and North America in the early 1750s. Possibly the promise of 1783–6 – expanding trade, alliance with Spain and the Dutch, an isolated Britain, and moves towards peaceful reform within France – could have been developed. Maybe, despite his aggressiveness, Napoleon could have maintained the Tilsit agreement, successfully incorporated Iberia, peaceably or by conquest, into his system, and then forced Britain to terms.

If in 1815 Britain was the strongest state in the world, the situation had been very different seventy years earlier, as Jacobite forces under Bonnie Prince Charlie advanced on Derby, out-manoeuvring the armies sent to defeat them, and the British government feared a supporting French invasion of southern England. If by 1815 Britain was the dominant military power in India, in 1746 the British had lost Madras to the French. In the 1780s, and again in the late 1790s, British politicians had worried about France's global and Middle East ambitions, especially in the Indian Ocean. There had been fears that the French would overthrow the British in India, as they had earlier done in North America.

Was it the French victory at Minden in 1759 or in the Mediterranean in 1798, or Napoleon's triumphant entry into London in 1805 that put paid to the idea that France's geopolitical position was such that she could be the dominant power on the landmass of Western Europe, but would fail to be the leading European colonial and maritime power? To buy peace in each case, Britain had to return colonial gains, as she had also done in 1748. In each case France was able to assert her position in the world, both in her own right and in conjunction with her allies, especially Spain. The claims of domestic and foreign critics that particular aspects of French society and the French state made them less likely to prevail over more mercantile, tolerant and populist Britain seemed redundant.

France of course did not triumph in these campaigns, but the fancy outlined above directs attention to the question whether her failure was inherent or the product of contingency and chance. Those who are inclined to emphasise resources and their mobilisation will tend to see failure as inherent, while the proponents of choice and policy will be more cautious. In particular, Napoleon's exploitative and insensitive treatment of his allies compromised France's position within and outside Europe. More generally, focusing on diplomatic failures makes sense of the contrast between long-term 'structural' characteristics and the very varied fates of Britain and France as great powers.

Britain, therefore, did not have to win. *Ex-post facto* determinism is totally inappropriate in this case, and British ministers of the period had no confidence in the eventual outcome. This remained the case until Napoleon's failure in Russia in 1812. After that, there were still strong fears in 1813, and even as late as early 1814, that he might divide his opponents and settle, in particular, with Austria, leaving a situation in which France was more powerful than was to be the case after the Peace of Vienna. Austria distrusted Russia and Britain and would have liked to retain a strong France, while the Russians sought a strong France in order to balance Britain. Napoleon's instinctive refusal to accept limits wrecked such schemes, but either would have had serious implications for Britain's position and might therefore have lessened her postwar trans-oceanic expansion. This would have been particularly the case if France had then been able to support non-European opponents of British expansionism, and if she had sought to do so.

The issue of whether, and with what consequences, Britain could have been beaten by France can be linked to the question of whether and with what affects Britain could have developed differently as a state and society. This is not a foolish question, but was a counterfactual posed throughout the period from the 1530s. There was a sense of precariousness about religious, ecclesiastical, dynastic, institutional and political settlements, not only within England but also in the other parts of the British Isles and with reference to the relations between these parts. Furthermore, these disputes did not take place in isolation. Instead, foreign, especially French, Spanish and Dutch, intervention, was frequent. As a consequence, developments within Britain were played out in a wider international context and, thus, had consequences for European power politics and for the position of Britain and other countries in the global system.

A comparison between Britain and Poland is instructive, not least because both were linked in personal unions with German principalities: Britain with Hanover from 1714 and Poland with Saxony from 1697. George I's accession in Britain in 1714 was followed by a civil war in 1715–16 as those of James II (1685) and William III (1689) had been, while in Poland the Saxon rulers, Augustus II and Augustus III, gained the throne through violence. However, the civil wars in Britain after 1637–51 were swiftly over, especially in England, and, although England and Britain were bitterly divided in the 1640s and 1680s, Britain acted like a major power in the 1650s and 1690s. There was an elective character to the Williamite position and the Act of Settlement (1701), as there was to Polish kingship. Possibly the important difference was that in Britain the Jacobites were not able to prevent William III and the Hanoverians from winning parliamentary support, whereas in Poland the political and constitutional system did not work to the benefit of the Saxons. Indeed, Jacobitism helped to preserve a measure both of Whig unity and of Whig-royal cohesion.

Earlier, Britain parted from a more general European trajectory because the monarchs were defeated in the late 1630s, 1640s and 1688, thus obliging opponents to consider new political, constitutional, ecclesiastical and dynastic arrangements. None of these defeats were inevitable, and all were reversible, as was to be shown by the restoration of the Stuart dynasty (and much, but by no means all, else) in 1660. A second Stuart restoration after 1688 at the behest and with the help of France would have had much impact on British policy, not least by leaving an unpopular, Catholic dynasty and its political supporters dependent on France. Was such a second restoration possible? That question can be focused by looking at the closest chance, the Jacobite invasion and rising of 1745. Again there are the two dimensions of counterfactualism, to adopt a simple typology, first, the specific, in this case military, in which the possibility of different developments is constrained by the context of a particular conjuncture, much of which can be recovered and assessed within the prime Western tradition of historical research, namely empirical positivism. Secondly, there is the wider context, that of possibilities stemming from a conjuncture that in fact worked out differently. In this case, they relate most interestingly to the possibility that a new political settlement in 1745 would have altered Britain's position in the world, and thus the West, not only with regard to geopolitical alignments but also with reference to the nature of public culture, economic interest and social dynamics.

The Jacobites had an important advantage in 1689, 1708 and 1745 that stemmed from British foreign policy. France was then at war with Britain and planned to assist the Jacobites. French intervention raises the comparison with the American War of Independence. In the latter, the British crucially lost control of the sea, most obviously off the Chesapeake in 1781, but also off New York in 1778 and Savannah in 1779. During the American war, the French had no other military commitments bar war with Britain. Crucially, despite her Austrian alliance, France did not get involved in the War of the Bavarian Succession of 1778–9. International relations were not set in a rigid pattern. It was entirely possible that France would have made more of an effort to assist the Jacobites and no effort to help the Americans.

The historical purchase of such counterfactuals is weak, however, for neither corresponds to the Whiggish teleology that is so powerfully established in Western public culture and intellectual life. The argument that counterfactuals throw light on situations by returning us to the uncertainty of the past is of scant interest to those in the present who lack such uncertainty, and it thus undermines a major role of history as the assertion and support of public myth. This is seen both with eighteenth-century Britain and with American independence. The argument that Britain could have become Jacobite or that American independence was not inevitable, or might have been compromised, with, for example South Carolina, Georgia and the Floridas remaining under the Crown, is a fundamental challenge to powerful suppositions. Yet each was possible and both would have interacted with, indeed were episodes in, the struggle between Britain and France. Thus they contributed to the character and power of the leading power of the West, with all the possibilities that this entailed for changing the identity of that power and thus its relationship with the non-West.

It is a long way from Derby on 5 December 1745 to the East River on the night of 22 August 1776, when the British fleet could have blocked Washington's retreat from Long Island, let alone to British troops storming the Mysore capital at Seringapatam on 4 May 1799 or defeating the Marathas at Assaye on 23 September 1803, but maybe the distance and difference were not that great. Had the Jacobites succeeded, then it is unclear whether the imperial relationship with the

Protestant American colonies would not have been sundered in 1746. If not, it is still likely that suspicion of and hostility to British rule would have been greater and that the revolution would have occurred earlier. A Jacobite British state overshadowed by France might not have been able to mount an effective counterthrust to such a revolution, although so much would have depended on French attitudes, not least because the French would still have been in control of Canada. Had the French acted in 1746, or subsequently, to impose Stuart control then another counterfactual offers, one that is of major importance for American history. French-backed Stuart control might have led to a much more arduous independence struggle, and one that was far more revolutionary in character because it would have been necessary to mobilise national resources and energies to a greater extent than was done in 1775–83. The obvious comparison is with the French Revolution.

A Stuart Britain could be seen as more likely to lead to co-operation with France and thus to diminishing rivalry within the West and to increasing the force available for the pursuit of policies either in Europe or against non-Western powers. A Stuart Britain with its stress on legitimism, Catholicism and conservatism, would presumably have been bitterly opposed to a Revolutionary and Napoleonic France, so that revolutionary change in France would have sundered the link between Britain and France but done so when Britain was relatively less powerful in the world and less united than was in fact the case for Britain in 1793. This might have made French intervention in Britain in support of radical options, such as Irish independence or politico-social revolution in England, Scotland and Wales, more likely to succeed. Conversely, there might have been no revolution in France but, instead, one against the Stuarts in Britain.

The global implications can be crudely enumerated:

Option 1   Radical France and Radical Britain.
Option 2   Conservative France and Conservative Britain.
Option 3   Conservative France and Radical Britain.
Option 4   Radical France and Conservative Britain.

Terms such as conservative and radical of course conceal many differences and numerous tensions. Furthermore the history of the period 1500–1945 reveal conflicts between conservative powers and also (for example the First Dutch War) between radical counterparts. Nevertheless, it is possible to see a mutual need in the case of options 1 and 2, especially 2, a Stuart regime dependent on French support. As already suggested, the energies of such a league might well have been concentrated on ambitions and anxieties in the European or Western world. In North America, the British and French devoted more effort to conflict with each other than with the native population. In the absence of such conflict, they might well have sponsored more expansion at the expense of the latter.

Yet, it is also possible to tease out a different global trajectory. Would an alliance of Britain and France as conservative or radical powers have made a major difference and, if so, more or less so had they been conservative or radical? Could the co-operation they were to display against the Turks in 1827, or against Russia in the Crimean War of 1854–6, or in China in 1860, when the two powers occupied Beijing, have been seen earlier. The Anglo-French alliance of 1716–31 had had scant global impact, because both powers were then focused on European enmities, but the situation, thereafter, could well have been very different, not only because of the opportunities presented by expansion in India and the Pacific, but also because of the greater resources made available by sustained demographic and economic expansion from the 1740s.

The most exciting idea is that of two radical states, both benefiting from early industrialisation, setting out to expand their power but possibly doing so with what was, at least in terms of the age, more progressive ideas. This might have led not to the emphasis on territorial control and landed values discerned by Christopher Bayly in his account of British expansion in 1780–1830 (Bayly 1989), but, rather, to a stronger emphasis on commercial growth. It is difficult to feel confident on this head. France under the Third Republic was scarcely a benign imperial power, but the prospect of a very different character to the imperialism of the two leading Western maritime powers is worth considering. It re-focuses attention on the why question. Why the West should wish to extend its power, and what power meant in this context are both worth considering. We are in the realms of cultural construction, but those also are open to counterfactual scenarios and analysis. Looked at in this light; because Western political dominance did not have to take the forms it did it was always changeable, even reversible. As this book hopes to show, there was nothing inevitable about Britain's rise to be the leading world power.

PART ONE
DIPLOMACY AND DOMESTIC PRESSURES

CHAPTER ONE

INTRODUCTION AND THE SOURCES

INTRODUCTION

Domestic circumstances set the parameters for diplomatic conduct, but the extent to which they determined the development of policy should not be exaggerated. It is very tempting to offer a multi-angled analysis in which policy is seen to result from these circumstances, and this is a strength of schematic treatments that relate economic strength, financial resources, political circumstances and diplomatic policy. In such an analysis the rôle of Parliament is central, for parliamentary support unlocked the financial resources of the state and enabled public discussion of policy in which Parliament played a major rôle; its constitutional and political functions and more specific parliamentary interventions helped to ensure that diplomatic policy was formulated in accordance with the wishes of Parliament and the dictates of parliamentary management. Commercial interests are commonly seen as playing a major rôle in this relationship, and thus a connection can be suggested between Parliament's function as guarantor and supporter of a system of public finance that enabled the tapping of national, especially commercial, wealth for government finances, particularly the costs of war, war-debt and foreign policy, and parliamentary determination to ensure that this policy fostered commercial interests.

Clearly there was a dynamic relationship between resources, Parliament and policy, but any detailed analysis of the last would suggest that considerable caution is required in discussing domestic influences. Explanations stressing diplomatic considerations can also be advanced for the episodes commonly cited as evidence of the significance of domestic pressure (Black 1988a). There is indeed a hitherto neglected tension latent in recent work on the domestic background of British foreign policy, one that leads to a somewhat disaggregated analysis. The stress on domestic resources and their mobilisation by political action differs from the recent emphasis on the power and significance of monarchs after, as well as before, the Glorious Revolution of 1688. Economic power and financial strength were indeed important in the international relations of the period 1660–1793, but their influence should not be exaggerated (Black 1990d). They were more important in periods of conflict than in peace time diplomacy, and in this context it is worth noting that British governments were singularly unwarlike after 1731, despite the growing wealth of the country and the increasing financial strength of the state. They were neutral in the War of the Polish Succession (1733–5), driven unenthusiastically to the War of Jenkins' Ear with Spain (1739), unwilling to get involved militarily in the early stages of the War of Austrian Succession (1741), and concerned to protect North American frontiers rather than to launch a war that would drive France from Canada (1754). Thereafter, British governments unsuccessfully sought to prevent a continental war (1755–6) and to avoid hostilities with Spain (1761), launched a police operation in the Boston area in 1775 that led to war with France (1778), Spain (1779) and the United Provinces (1780), and avoided war with Spain in 1790, with Russia in 1791, and with France in 1792. British diplomacy was commonly designed to avoid war rather than to prepare for it, a situation to which strategic vulnerability and military weakness contributed. Economic strength and financial resources did not generally become central issues until conflicts had begun, and it was then that parliamentary support and management, and domestic political attitudes and developments, were crucial.

In other periods policy was conducted with less reference to these attitudes and developments. This could pose political problems with Parliament, as William III discovered in 1701 when his negotiations with Louis XIV were criticised, and it was especially serious in wartime. Abroad with George II in 1743, Lord Carteret, the Secretary of State for the Northern Department, aroused first the ire of his ministerial colleagues, concerned about the difficulties of defending his policies in Parliament, and then their determination, eventually successful, to press George to dismiss him; 'the coffee house joke is that Lord Carteret was looking over the map and by some accident the ink fell down and blotted out England, since which he has never thought of it' (BL Add. 51417, 17 Aug.). Dangerous during periods of political instability, when the debate over foreign policy was often most bitter, such an attitude was far more common in peace- time. One of Carteret's most bitter opponents, his co-Secretary of State, the Duke of Newcastle, followed an active foreign policy in the years after the War of the Austrian Succession, despite pressure from his brother, Henry Pelham, the First Lord of the Treasury, to heed the financial cost of his policy.

Discussion of the burgeoning economy, and of the power of the government to raise money provides little guidance to policy choices. Instead, it is necessary to address the views of monarchs and ministers, and to recognise the extent to which policy was often reactive, a response to actions on the part of other rulers. The diplomatic agenda was made unpredictable by the central rôle of dynastic events – the births, marriages and deaths that ensured that so many wars arose from disputed successions – and by the general absence of firm alliances. This helped to produce a volatility in international relations in which much depended on the personal views of a small number of individuals. They had to consider domestic resources and political circumstances, but these were not the only considerations and pressures. For British monarchs, security was uppermost in most of the period: their own position as rulers in Britain and the security of possessions overseas. A discussion of monarchical views therefore leads to a stress on problems and dangers, and on a reactive attitude that makes it difficult to advance the suggestion that policy was consistent.

This does not mean that foreign policy can be approached only in terms of 'what one clerk said to another', but it does ensure that in assessing the views of monarchs and ministers it is necessary to appreciate that their agenda was not always determined by domestic considerations and that when these considerations were important, as with the Jacobite challenge to Georges I and II, they were not necessarily influential as a result of domestic political pressures from within the political system. Foreign policy could appear disjointed to contemporaries and this led to crises when diplomatic and military commitments appeared to bear little relation to what were commonly understood to be national interests, as in the confrontation with Russia in 1791, the Ochakov crisis. However, what is striking is the extent to which monarchs and ministers were generally free to pursue the policies they felt most appropriate, especially in peace-time and if they had no commercial or colonial consequences. As a result, it is necessary to devote more space to the views of the rulers than to the position of Parliament, and it is important to examine critically the notion of a parliamentary foreign policy. Nevertheless, the public debate over policy was important, as were mercantile interests.

It is not easy to offer a coherent account of foreign policy that relates domestic circumstances to diplomatic developments, in part because much of the necessary detailed research has not been undertaken, but also because there was no neat pattern of influences and policies. Instead, there were varied pressures, the impact of which was generally episodic, and in understanding them it is necessary to consider what factors the clerks, and certainly their superiors, cited. It is also important to appreciate that foreign policy was sometimes within the domestic political arena, but often not. To approach it solely from the diplomatic angle would be misleading, but so equally would be a stress both on domestic parameters, if they are seen as determinants of policy, and on the political context and politicisation of policy. Important differences of opinion over policy reflected clashing ministerial views on diplomatic strategy as much as those of rival political groups or parties. The two could be related, but it is necessary to underline the extent to which the public and political (as opposed to ministerial) debate over foreign policy varied in its extent and its intensity. Britain was not a political system operating in accordance with rigid guidelines. There was much in the constitution and in the political culture of the period that was inconstant or ambiguous, and the formulation, execution and discussion of foreign policy reflected this.

THE SOURCES

The study of diplomatic history in both Britain and continental Europe was essentially a development of the second half of the nineteenth century. The period from then up to about 1930 was the golden age of diplomatic history, with the publication of numerous books and articles and the editing of large collections of documents. In Britain the subject shared a position of eminence with that type of constitutional history which Bishop Stubbs had handed down to mankind. In much of continental Europe there was less material for, and interest in, constitutional history, and the study of diplomatic history predominated, often from a nationalist perspective and adopting a determinist approach predicated on the inevitability of the development of particular nation states. However, the interwar years saw attention in both Britain and the Continent focus increasingly on socio-economic topics and this has been more clearly the case since 1945, most obviously in France and Italy. As a result, the preoccupations and methods adopted by the diplomatic historians of the late nineteenth century remained for long without serious challenge and it is only in recent years that this situation has altered.

The study of foreign policy in the late nineteenth century was the study of diplomatic records, the instructions dispatched to diplomats, the reports they wrote and the memoranda they exchanged. Ambassadors then still played a mjor role as agents of foreign policy. Foreign policy was regarded as a matter of diplomatic negotiation and there was little concern about the debate over policy within particular countries. Instead countries were treated like units, and there was an assumption that national interests had been clear and obvious. This reflected the views then current about the conduct of contemporary international relations. Diplomacy was seen as a 'rational' activity conducted by relatively autonomous Foreign Offices with distinct bureaucratic practices. These institutions were regarded as largely independent in an administrative sense. This matched the assumption that foreign policy was substantially divorced from domestic politics, the clear pursuit of national interest of the former contrasting with the vagaries and compromises, to diplomatic historians usually trivial or disastrous, of the latter. Diplomatic history was generally a cool subject, devoid of passion and ideology, and based on a secure and copious documentation. There was a close relation between diplomatic history and the development of national archives. Interest in the subject played a rôle in the growth of the latter and several distinguished diplomatic historians were archivists by training and/or profession.

The diplomatic history written in the late nineteenth and early twentieth centuries was very important and its continued value can be seen by the number of references to it made in modern works. However, in recent years there have been changes in the subject that have clear archival implications.

The older type of diplomatic history can be described, unfairly, as reading the respective series of two states, such as *Correspondance Politique Angleterre* and State Papers France, and then meshing them together, rather as a card- dealer joins two halves of a shuffled pack. The diplomatic papers were commonly regarded as providing a coherent and complete explanation of the subject. The modern shift has been clearly marked in the attempt to understand more fully the processes constituting the formation of policy, and correspondingly there has been a move away from a near-total reliance on the diplomatic records towards an attempt to supplement these sources. In short, the study has moved from the execution to the formation of policy, from the discrete and clear-cut study of the actions of a number of diplomats to the less focused consideration of a range of pressures.

The modern position can be summarised as follows. In order to appreciate foreign policy it is necessary to consider not only diplomacy but also domestic history, and the relationship between domestic developments and debates, and foreign policy. It is important not to treat the international system as the sum of the diplomacies of the various European powers, nor to present foreign policy in a monolithic interpretation in which the actors are the 'British', the 'French' and others. Instead, it is clear that policy options were debated and that these debates were not concerned simply with diplomatic options. Rather, the debates about foreign policy were intertwined with struggles over power, patronage and domestic politics. This process was encouraged by the fact that the formulation and execution of foreign policy was generally not the job of a distinct bureaucratic institution unrelated to the strife of domestic politics.

The consequence for scholars of this development is that it is no longer acceptable to write accounts based solely upon the diplomatic archives and relating simply to the questions to which a study of them gives rise. It is necessary to consult a far wider range of sources, from the private papers of ministers, officials and diplomats to documents relating to the public discussion of policy. The latter classes of documents are clearly far removed in archival terms from diplomatic papers, but the position with regard to the private papers of ministers, officials and diplomats involved in the conduct of policy varies greatly between the major European archives.

In Britain a sharp distinction is made between official diplomatic correspondence and relevant private correspondence, and they are essentially cared for by different institutions and located in separate archives. Diplomatic papers are the responsibility of the Public Records Office, while private papers are held in a variety of archives, both national and local, ranging from the largest individual holder, the British Library, to county records offices, municipal and university libraries and private individuals. The government retained copies of instructions to diplomats and of the reports of the latter, and these served as the state papers. In the eighteenth century, it was common for ministers and officials to retain possession of whatever papers they chose and no distinction was made in the case of sensitive and secret material. It was very rare for an individual's papers to be searched on his retirement or death, and though this happened with the 3rd Earl of Sunderland in 1722, the Sunderland papers in the Blenheim collection, now in the British Library, contain a mass of official documentation. It is often the case that documents in private hands are drafts or copies of material held in the Public Records Office. This is true for example of many of the papers of James, 1st Earl Waldegrave, British ambassador in Paris in 1730–40, whose papers are still held by his descendants.

However, it is also often the case that material which is clearly in the public domain exists solely in private hands. The papers of Edward Weston, who was an under-secretary in 1729–46 and 1761–4, contain official memoranda on British foreign policy for which no copies exist in the Public Records Office.

Eighteenth-century intercepted diplomatic correspondence provides a good example of this general problem. Foreign diplomatic correspondence was regularly intercepted by the British government, and there is, accordingly, a relevant documentary series in the Public Records Office, SP 107. Unfortunately this series was badly damaged by being held in a leaking building in the nineteenth century, and by the failure of eighteenth-century ministers to return official papers. Intercepts can therefore be found in the private papers of several ministers and diplomats, such as Sir Robert Walpole and the 3rd Earl of Sunderland.

There has been an increased interest in aspects of the history of international relations that require a broader coverage of the available documentation. In particular an interest in the mood of international relations has often displaced the study of particular negotiations. The general attitudes held by ministers and diplomats have been increasingly regarded as topics in their own right and ones that are of crucial significance for the history of foreign policy. Important studies include Michael Roberts' *Splendid Isolation 1763–1780* (Reading, 1970) and Stephen Baxter's 'The Myth of the Grand Alliance in the Eighteenth Century' in P.R. Sellin and Baxter, *Anglo-Dutch Cross-Currents in the Seventeenth and Eighteenth Centuries* (Los Angeles, 1976).

Even if more conventional diplomatic history is being written, it is necessary to examine a wider range of sources than in the past. The traditional method of approaching bilateral relations has been to examine the correspondence between diplomats in the respective countries. However, it is increasingly clear that to follow this method is to adopt too narrow an approach. In the eighteenth century powers often preferred to negotiate through an intermediary or through high-ranking diplomats of their own who might be accredited to a third party. Thus, envoys in the leading European diplomatic centres, The Hague, Paris and, to a lesser extent, Vienna, were often entrusted with negotiations (Black 1986e). Prominent diplomats, such as Sir Robert Walpole's brother Horatio, envoy in both Paris and The Hague, were regarded as being more reliable as negotiators. Therefore an approach to bilateral relations based simply on bilateral sources is inappropriate. This is obviously the case for periods when states lacked the relevant diplomatic representation, but it is also, more generally, a feature of eighteenth-century international relations.

The use of intermediates, usually the envoys of friendly powers, was also significant. For example, in the summer of 1729, the Austrians sought to negotiate a settlement of their differences with George II. A certain amount of material on this theme can be found in the reports of Count Philip Kinsky, the Austrian envoy in London, who followed George to Hanover. However, the crucial Austrian approach was to have been made by a more influential diplomat, Count Seckendorf. He sought permission to go to Hanover, but this was refused by George. Vital information on this approach can be found in the letters of the intermediary he used, his friend General Diemar, the Hesse-Cassel envoy accredited to George II, which are held in Staatsarchiv in Marburg.

To tackle either similar topics to those that interested scholars in the past or newer ones of greater interest today, it is necessary to consult more volumes of diplomatic material and to be able to browse more widely than was common for past scholars. One of the most famous British scholars of the great age of diplomatic history, Sir Richard Lodge, worked in very few archives and consulted a surprisingly narrow range of documents for his *Great Britain and Prussia in the Eighteenth Century* (Oxford, 1923) and *Studies in Eighteenth-Century Diplomacy 1740–1748* (London, 1930). The latter was based on the Newcastle papers in the British Library, material in the Public Record Office, and on the papers of the 4th Earl of Sandwich. Significant collections then available in the British Library were neglected, foreign archives were ignored and, aside from the Sandwich papers, relevant material outside London was overlooked. A good modern comparison is Ragnhild Hatton's biography of George I, published in 1978 and in large part a history of international relations during the reign of that monarch. This was based on a wealth of archival material from both Britain and abroad.

Use of Continental archives is crucially important, because negotiations were frequently conducted by foreign diplomats in London and, in addition, their reflections on British policy and politics can provide valuable information on the operations of British foreign policy and the perception of Britain that influenced foreign responses. The instructions sent to foreign diplomats in London can also throw light not only on attitudes and policy towards Britain, but also on how these were influenced by British actions and domestic politics. This is of considerable importance in the debate over the relative importance of domestic and diplomatic considerations in British foreign policy, which cannot be separated from the question of how they affected the policies of other powers, for, in studying British foreign policy, it is inappropriate to present the other powers as passive or untutored in their responses.

It is similarly important to present a careful account of domestic debates. An emphasis on government sources can lead to a failure to understand contemporary debates on state interest. In essence, opposition views are presented from outside, and treated as ridiculous and/or inconsequential. This is exacerbated by the sources that are employed. The archival basis for re-creating the perceptions and views of opposition politicians is often limited, certainly in comparison with those of their ministerial counterparts. There is a great temptation to turn to the public politics of the opposition, their statements in print and representative assembly. This is helpful, but partial, and risks the danger of caricaturisation. Futhermore, these sources are not always as clear as they seem. It is necessary to have a deep understanding of the conventions of parliamentary and newspaper discussion and the facts affecting the surviving record before using these sources. For example, to appreciate William Pitt the Elder's parliamentary speeches, it is important to understand the reporting problems, and also to appreciate the political strategies motivating the expression of his views on military policy and international relations and the way in which these views responded to specific conjunctures, the latter more of domestic politics than of the international systems. In addition, ministerial sensitivity, or lack of it, to the prejudices and reservations of the wider political (taxpaying) elite is very hard to measure; although it was surely present in Walpole's foreign policy in the early 1730s.

A failure to appreciate the domestic debate is related to a more general difficulty with assessing policies: a neglect of external or internal implications can lead not only to a failure of explanation, but also to one of evaluation. These limitations create a problem in judging British interventionism in Continental politics. Reference to new sources, questions and methods underlines the tentative nature of much apparently definitive work on foreign policy.

CHAPTER TWO

THE CROWN

A marked feature of recent work on foreign policy in this period has been a tendency to stress the role of the Crown. As yet, however, this work has not been pulled together to produce an overall impression of this role and there has been no balanced account of the political importance of the Crown in post-Revolution Britain. As ever the principal theme is one of variety. The monarchs, Charles II (1660–85), James II (1685–8), William III (1689–1702), Anne (1702–14), George I (1714–27), George II (1727–60) and George III (1760–1820), had different views and followed various methods in seeking to obtain their ends. However, a consistent theme was provided by the political importance of their views and the consequent role of these views in the public debate over foreign policy.

William III, George I and George II had considerable authority as European rulers in their own right. They were experienced, competent in languages, well travelled and very knowledgeable in European affairs. This made a big difference to the authority of the Crown in foreign policy.

Monarchs played a central role in the formulation and execution of foreign policy. They saw all important papers, both instructions to diplomats and their reports, so that if individual envoys wished to keep the ruler in the dark they were obliged to write separate and secret letters to ministers. Envoys who sought to pursue policies of which monarchs disapproved were dismissed, reprimanded or ignored, as were Robert Trevor at The Hague in 1746 and Henry Legge at Berlin in 1748. Similar treatment was meted out to Secretaries of State who appeared critical or unreliable, Charles, Viscount Townshend being demoted from the Secretaryship of the Northern Department in December 1716 because of his unwillingness to support George I's Baltic policy. The monarchs saw the Secretaries of State regularly, saw British diplomats before they went on their missions, and saw foreign diplomats accredited to them relatively often. They therefore had opportunities to direct foreign policy. The question of how effectively they did so cannot be answered simply, as rulers were in part guided by the advice they received and also because their personal interests varied. Colonial questions in general excited little royal concern prior to 1760, whereas, in contrast, Continental power politics were of continual concern. While Britain played a major and active role in these, the views of the monarch were of importance not only to his ministers but to foreign commentators. In 1751, Frederick II of Prussia correctly doubted that Henry Pelham, the First Lord of the Treasury, would be able to restrain George II from negotiating the subsidy treaties that he sought in order to bolster his diplomatic schemes.

> I hope Pelham maintains his position, but I fear that when George II goes to Hanover he will be able to lead the Duke of Newcastle further than the British ministers would like him to go and that, once the decision has been taken, these ministers will be obliged to applaud it. (*Polit. Corresp.* 8,538)

Constitutionally, the ruler was the most powerful force in the formulation and execution of foreign policy. The Crown appointed, paid, promoted and dismissed British diplomats and had powers of war and peace and authority to negotiate, sign and break treaties. Foreign diplomats were accredited to the monarch. These powers were not free from criticism, Sir William Yonge, the Secretary-at-War, telling the Commons in 1739:

> I have often heard that, according to the old maxim of our constitution, the king is invested with the sole power of making peace and war; but, from the late conduct of some gentlemen in this House, I begin to doubt whether this ought to be allowed as a maxim in our constitution. There are some amongst us who, of late years, have taken upon them to prescribe to his majesty not only when, but how he is to make both peace and war. (Cobbett, 1806–20: XI, 155)

Fearing that Britain would have to surrender colonial gains in order to secure a French withdrawal from Hanover, the leading London opposition newspaper, the *Monitor*, claimed in its issue of 23 September 1758: 'As the crown is, by the Act of Settlement, restrained from making war in favour of a foreign state without consent of Parliament: by parity of reason no part of a British conquest or dominion ought to be given back to an enemy, upon any other consideration than in exchange for some place or privileges to be restored to the British crown.' However, in 1763 the Electorate was evacuated as part of a contentious settlement in which colonial gains were restored. Nevertheless, the constitutional authority of the monarch in the field of foreign policy was not essentially a prime subject of political controversy. British political society was fundamentally monarchical and the republican interlude of 1649–1660 had underlined this. The political nation had been grateful for the return of the Stuarts in 1660.

The major constitutional change came with the Act of Settlement of 1701, which was both a reaction against what was generally felt to be William's neglect of English political opinion, Parliament, and most of his English ministers in the 1690s, and an expression of concern about the prospect of a new foreign dynasty. William's wife, Mary, the elder daughter of James II's first marriage, had had no children and had died in 1694. Her sister, Anne, had had numerous children, but they had all died in childhood and the most long-lived, the Duke of Gloucester, died in 1701. The Act provided for the succession of the Electoral house of Hanover, descendants of the German marriage of James I's daughter, but stated that, after their succession, no war should be fought for the defence of interests that were not British without parliamentary consent, and that this consent should also be required before the monarch could leave Britain. The latter clause was repealed before George I's accession, and he and his son visited Hanover on fifteen occasions during their reigns – in 1716, 1719, 1723, 1725, 1729, 1732, 1735, 1736, 1740, 1741, 1743, 1748, 1750, 1752 and 1755 – without having to seek approval from Parliament or from their English ministers, many of whom were unhappy about their long absences. In 1727, George I died on his way to Hanover. George III, however, never went to the Electorate, a practice that contributed to his enjoying greater popularity than his two predecessors.

The provision that no war could be fought for non-British interests without parliamentary approval was not reversed, and was in theory a major restriction of royal power, for the Hanoverians, especially George I and George II, were greatly concerned about their Electorate and, understandably, sought to direct British foreign policy to its support. However, not once was this parliamentary control driven home, for the Act of Settlement, like the role of Parliament in general, essentially raised the issue of parliamentary management and the more general point of the power, rather than the authority, of the monarch in the political system. In January 1744, Richard Tucker suggested to his brother John, an opposition MP, that if the motion for subsidising Hanoverian troops was carried, as in fact it was to be, 'I think the Nation were as good desire the administration to determine among themselves what is necessary and not give gentlemen the trouble of leaving their houses to cloak their measures with the ceremony of a consultation or giving advice' (Bod. MS. Don. c. 106 f. 134). The *Monitor* complained on 18 November 1758 that 'bad ministers, without applying to Parliament, have agreed to take part in the defence of foreign dominions, under false pretences of British interest, and then found means to secure a majority in both houses'.

The issue of royal power can be approached from a number of angles. Comparatively, the rulers of Britain might appear weak by European standards, especially if the point of the comparison is, as it often was to contemporaries, the power of the Bourbons of France. George II certainly compared his power unfavourably with that of Louis XV (McCann 1984: 149). This supposed contrast of royal power can then serve to exemplify the difference between Britain and the Continent, and this difference can be used to explain particular features of British political conduct. There has been some attempt to argue that Britain was not different, that it was instead an *ancien régime* society (J.C.D. Clark 1985), although this is not a view that commands universal assent. Part of the problem is the common assumption that there was essentially one type of *ancien régime* society in Europe and therefore that by noting points of similarity or difference, the case for or against Britain being such a society can be established. In practice, the keynote of European development was one of diversity, and of political and constitutional developments affected by chance, especially in the form of the crucial dynastic variables of birth, marriage and death, international adversity and particular domestic characteristics. Louis XV (1715–74) did not exercise the same control as his great-grandfather Louis XIV (1643–1715), Earl Waldegrave reporting from Paris in 1740: 'as to His Christian Majesty, it is more for form's sake that we wait on him than anything else, for with regard to public affairs, our seeing him or not is much the same' (PRO SP 78/223 f. 138). The shape of Europe and the sense of what was typical looked different from Madrid, Munich and Moscow, and that diversity needs to be extended to include Britain, instead of imagining that British developments were in some way unique. Britain in 1660 was a multiple kingdom of three separate political units, Scotland, Ireland, and England and Wales, that had recently experienced a serious and successful rebellion against royal authority and where traditions of contractualism and representation had produced a political system in which representative assemblies, Parliaments, had distinct powers and functions. Although the recent episode of republicanism was exceptional, the central characteristics of British political life were not. Indeed, the reaction against disorder and innovation, not least republicanism, in part enhanced the practice of loyalism and hierarchical traditions in British life. Far from Britain being seen as different, there were many who were convinced in 1660–88 that she was following a common European pattern towards stability and the enhanced monarchical control that was subsequently to be described as absolutism.

Clearly royal authority received a serious blow in 1688–9 and the subsequent position of monarchs was to be weaker for three reasons. First and most important, the so-called 'Glorious Revolution', like the abolition of monarchy in 1649, was rendered incomplete by the survival of a claimant, or pretender, to the throne. William did not wish to wipe out the male line of the Stuarts. James II was his uncle and his father-in-law; a trial would have been impossible, and James's flight to France was encouraged and abetted by William in order to remove an embarrassing obstacle to the coup he wished to engineer, by which he translated his successful invasion into the change of monarch he had promised he was not seeking (R. Beddard 1991). However, James maintained his claim to the throne and was succeeded in this by his son, 'James III', in 1701. The male Stuart or Jacobite (after the Latin *Jacobus* for James) claim was a fundamental threat to British stability until 1746, the year when George II's younger son, the Duke of Cumberland, defeated James II's grandson, Charles Edward, Bonnie Prince Charlie, at Culloden, ending not only the '45, the Jacobite rising that had begun the previous year, but also all serious prospect of domestic armed support for the Jacobite cause (G.H. Jones 1954).

The extent of Jacobite support between 1689 and 1746 and the seriousness of the threat posed are both matters of controversy, though historians have tended to devote their efforts to the former question, largely examined in a domestic context, without adequately dealing with the more complex issue of the extent of the threat, a problem that demands an evaluation of the international situation (Cruickshanks 1979, 1982; Cruickshanks and Black 1988: 142–60; McLynn 1981; Colley 1982; Black 1988c). This question is considered elsewhere (pp. 85–6) but it can be seen as a significant question mark against the continuation of the political order. Precisely for that reason, however, it helped to bind the order to the monarch, as most politicians who had any prospect of office were wary about the prospect of a Jacobite and Catholic return, particularly as it would probably have to be brought about through violence, especially after 1714 when it was clear that the succession would not revert to the male Stuart line after the death of Anne. Such politicians perforce found themselves in a difficult position when they came to consider the policies of William III, and especially George I and George II, that were recognisably designed to further their personal views. This increased those monarchs' room for political manoeuvre. At the same time, Jacobitism reduced the monarch's room for manoeuvre by tying him to the Whigs.

The second weakening of royal authority that flowed from the events of 1688–9 was brought about by the consequences of war. Two linked abrupt changes have been discerned as stemming from the Revolution. The first is a supposed shift from compliance towards France, which is commonly held to have characterised the restored Stuart monarchy, to marked opposition to her. The second serves as both proof and consequence of the first. It is the shift from peace to war. England had last fought France in 1627–9 and had not taken part in a European conflict since the Third Anglo-Dutch war in 1672–4. In contrast, between 1689 and 1713, England was at war with France in the Nine Years' and Spanish Succession wars, a precarious peace pertaining only in 1697–1702. The two wars were costly in men and money and the economic and financial burdens they created became a political issue, as the conduct and purposes of the conflicts had been throughout their course. After 1714 what was feared most was a return to the pressures of the recruiting officers. War caused numerous deaths as well as severe problems for agriculture, labour shortages, higher taxes, borrowing and interest rates, and an increase in the number of families on poor relief.

When William III invaded England, war had already broken out in western Europe, with Louis XIV's invasion of the Rhineland, the French siege of Philippsburg beginning on 27 September 1688. Louis was not seeking a major conflict, but, instead, hoped, through deterrent action, to secure a favourable settlement of two disputes in the Rhineland, over the Palatinate and Cologne. Arguably the basis existed for negotiations over the winter of 1688-9, the period when military operations were traditionally suspended, though Louis was not noted for his willingness to yield points. William made no effort to negotiate with Louis, which was scarcely surprising as the purpose of the expedition by the childless prince was not dynastic aggrandisement but immediate benefit in European power politics. News of his success was promptly followed by reports of English participation in attacks on France. Indeed, Sir Robert Holmes had reported in early November 1688 that William's fleet was designed for an attack on the French Channel coast rather than on England (BL Add. 63780 ff. 17,26). Louis was correct to argue that William's invasion would be a great obstacle to peace (AE CP Allemagne 323 f. 56), because, in place of the territorial compromises that had characterised the two previous western European wars, William sought a non-negotiable gain. The Emperor and ruler of Austria Leopold I's subsequent hope that William would permit a succession by James II's son, thus settling the issue of the British succession, was misplaced.

As in other European states, war forced monarchs to turn to financial grants from representative assemblies and these grants required political co-operation and, frequently, concessions. The major concessions were not constitutional but related to political management: the employment of ministers who could create a working majority in a political system with only inchoate parties. A number of constitutional changes can be traced to the parliamentary exigencies of war finance, including, most significantly, the Triennial Act of 1694. This required a parliamentary election at least every three years, a measure designed to limit the prospect of the Crown employing the tools of management, particularly patronage, to create a lasting working parliamentary majority, which, it was feared, might challenge the liberties of the population and, more prosaically, hinder politicians' room for manoeuvre. The possibilities of a standing parliament were indicated in Ireland, where elections only followed the accession of a monarch and where stable management could lead to quiescent sessions.

War, therefore, limited the authority and power of the Crown, a lesson of Tudor and Stuart statecraft and a position that was fairly general throughout Europe. And yet the situation was more complex. It was not so much that wartime concessions could be reversed, the Triennial Act for example being replaced by a peacetime Septennial Act in 1716, which enabled George I and his Whig ministers to delay the election due in 1718 until 1722 with, for them, beneficial consequences, but that the picture of parliamentarians inexorably seeking to use wars and their control over war finance to limit royal authority is a false one. Britain was at war for much of the period after 1688: 1689-1697, 1702–13, 1718–20 (the War of the Quadruple Alliance), 1739–48 (the War of Jenkins' Ear and the War of the Austrian Succession), 1754 (officially 1756)–1763 (the Seven Years' War), 1775–83 (the War of American Independence) and 1793–1801 (the war with revolutionary France). These years did witness domestic political defeats for monarchs, especially in the field of management. George I was forced to end the Whig split by offering Walpole and Townshend office in 1720; George II was obliged to part with Walpole in 1742, Carteret in 1744 and 1746, and to accept the rise of Pitt the Elder; George III lost Lord North in 1782 and Shelburne in 1783. The longest fruitful combinations of Crown and ministerial parliamentary management, the Walpole ministry, the Pelhamite system and the North ministry, all collapsed under the strain of war.

Monarchs were not always kept fully informed. Sarah Marlborough's comment on George II – 'It is said, His Majesty is much offended at this proceeding with Spain, but I won't answer for the truth of that report. For I can't imagine by what means His Majesty will be rightly informed of it' (Beinecke, Osborn Shelves, Stair Letters no. 22) – could be dismissed as gossip in opposition circles, but, shortly afterwards, Horatio Walpole wrote from his diplomatic mission at The Hague to an under-secretary promising to continue a confidential correspondence 'on condition that my letters shall not be sent with the packet to Kensington' (Farmington, Weston Papers vol. 12, 3 July 1739).

However, major politicians sought to win the co-operation of the Crown, not to limit its power. There was general satisfaction, indeed a considerable measure of complacency in Whig circles, about the Revolution settlement, in so far as the constitution was concerned, and critics of disturbing features in the political system tended to blame ministerial corruption rather than royal activity. There was, of course, a separate, though linked, Jacobite critique, but that had little influence in political circles, especially after the institution of one-party Whig government following the accession of George I in 1714. The tendency to blame ministers, rather than the Crown, was hardly novel, the evil minister having been a persistent theme of political diatribe and a central problem of constitutional thought for centuries. It was accentuated by the annual meeting of Parliament, and consequently the increased stress on parliamentary management; the focusing of patronage on parliamentary votes; the need for foreign rulers, who spent considerable time abroad and were unsure of domestic politics, to rely on British managers, rather as local expertise directed control towards parliamentary 'undertakers' in Dublin; and the prominence of a number of these managers. In this respect the position of Sir Robert Walpole, parliamentary manager from 1720 until 1742 and clearly first minister from the mid 1720s, was crucial. An adept manager, he epitomised patronage and, to his critics, corruption for a generation of politicians, and his unprecedented ability to survive a change of monarch, the accession of George II in 1727, helped further to focus attention on management of the Commons. Walpole enjoyed the confidence of the Crown, and was, in effect, leader of the Whig party, head of the ministry, and parliamentary leader in the most important and contentious house, the Commons. The role of management has to be seen alongside the relative brevity of parliamentary sessions and the degree to which the role of Paliament was essentially reactive: the ministry still took the initiative.

Although it would be inaccurate to suggest that George I and George II were able to follow their own policies while political tension was focused on their first ministers, especially Sunderland, Walpole and Carteret, this was true to a certain extent, especially if their policies did not involve cost. Whereas the policies of Charles II and James II linked domestic fears with crucial questions of foreign policy, those of George I and George II were less threatening, even if no more popular. Given the extraordinary agitation in 1742–3 over the subsidising of Hanoverian troops (Birke and Kluxen 1986: 33–50), it would scarcely be accurate to suggest that royal views on foreign policy were depoliticised, but there is an obvious contrast between Charles II's secret negotiations with Louis XIV preparatory to their joint attack on the Dutch in 1672 and George I's attempt in 1719–20 to create a European coalition to drive the Russians from their recent Baltic conquests, or George II's attempt in 1750–3 to procure the election of the Habsburg heir, the future Joseph II, as king of the Romans and, therefore, next Emperor.

Both of the latter steps could be and were presented as measures that were not in Britain's interest, though ministerial apologists disagreed. Each instead, especially the former, could be seen as designed to further Hanoverian views, and yet neither was particularly controversial because they were not central to British political debate. War had weakened Stuart monarchs because doubts about their domestic intentions led politicians to seek to use the opportunities that parliamentary control over war finance presented to curtail their power. As, among the groups with parliamentary influence, these anxieties were less strong in the case of the Hanoverians, they, in turn, were freer to pursue their policies, and wars had a less detrimental consequence for their power, even though they could affect their choice of political manager. The Hanoverians were very different from the Stuarts in that their attitudes and policies did not rouse fears about religion, with all the capacity for engendering tension that these possessed.

The third reason why the position of monarchs was to be weaker after 1688–9 was the specific constitutional changes encapsulated in the phrase 'Glorious Revolution'. These cannot really be separated from those changes that the war caused, though if they are, it can be noted that the constitutional power of the monarch, in so far as it affected foreign policy, was not dramatically limited. There was no English equivalent to the Scottish 'Act anent peace and war' of 1703, which removed from the monarch the right to declare war without the consent of the Scottish Parliament. The previous year, the Scottish Privy Council had declared war on France while Parliament was not sitting, a necessary step in light of the unpopularity of war with France in Scotland, a country with which she had strong commercial ties.

It remained the case in England after the Revolution that the power of the monarch in foreign policy was greater in combination with Parliament, because, even if a ruler had no wish to engage in war, the confrontational nature of international relations required an ability to deploy armed force for which the prospect of gaining and sustaining parliamentary funds was crucial, while the foreign perception of English politics remained a crucial factor in English strength. Thus, Louis XIV, by giving Charles II subsidies on the condition that he did not call Parliament, in effect removed the possibility of significant initiatives by England, while James II's failure to adapt his policies to the arithmetic of parliamentary support ensured that he was obliged to follow a cautious diplomatic line. However, James's foreign policy demonstrates a recurrent theme – the danger of adopting any monocausal explanation. It could equally be suggested that international circumstances made the adoption of a cautious line desirable.

CHARLES II: A DIPLOMACY FOR ENGLISH ABSOLUTISM?

The intentions of Charles II (1660–85) have been a subject of sustained scholarly debate (Hutton 1986, 1989), but there is little doubt that his foremost objective was not to lose the throne or expose himself to prolonged domestic turmoil. This was particularly important in 1678–81 when the Popish Plot and the Exclusion Crisis, an attempt to prevent the succession of childless Charles's avowedly Catholic brother James Duke of York, threatened to lead to civil war. In his earlier years, however, Charles had been willing to initiate or co-operate with more adventurous policies. The most controversial was his alliance with Louis XIV in 1670, the Treaty of Dover, and his subsequent participation in Louis's attack on the Dutch in 1672, a policy that contrasted with Charles's lack of enthusiasm for the Second Anglo-Dutch war. The Treaty of Dover represented not only a new diplomatic alignment but also a prospectus for dramatic change in England. Charles undertook to convert himself to Catholicism and Louis promised to help him with a force of 6000 if this led to rebellion or disorder. Such an agreement was not a condition for alliance with Louis; other Protestant rulers, such as Frederick William of Brandenburg-Prussia (1640–88), did not make such promises, which were anyway dangerous in a kaleidoscopic diplomatic world where secret agreements, such as that of Charles, could limit options and betray their parties to blackmail.

Charles's commitment revealed his wish to use his personal position to alter the situation, including his own circumstances. In this, he was similar to his brother James II, who also sought to engineer domestic changes, and, though to a lesser extent, to William III, George I and George II, who wished to secure changes abroad with the assistance of

British strength. Charles and James's task was more difficult because of the great immediacy of domestic circumstances and the visceral forces that anti-Catholicism inspired. The prime ideological commitment of the majority of the population was anti- Catholicism. And yet in the previous two decades there had been two Anglo-Dutch wars (1652–4, 1665–7) and a war with Spain (1655–9), from 1657 as an ally of France. English policy was less fixed than a stress on hostility to France and to Catholicism might suggest.

There was no shortage of contemporaries willing to criticise Louis XIV in Parliament, the press and in private. Growing military power, especially at sea, increasing commercial strength and a more forceful if not aggressive diplomatic attitude made France appear more threatening (J.R. Jones 1966: 67–84). The boldness of French action during the War of Devolution (1667–8), when the French overran much of the Spanish Netherlands (modern Belgium), helped to make France the central issue in foreign policy and the prime topic of public discussion, a position from which it had displaced Spain and the United Provinces, though the parliamentary debates about the increasing power of France were not very serious until the mid 1670s. The note of widespread English hostility to France had been sounded by numerous commentators including French diplomats, such as Cominges in 1663. Four years later, Charles II admitted to a French envoy, concerned about the prospect of parliamentary agitation in favour of Spain and against France, that it would be necessary to display the advantages England could gain from France (AE CP Ang. 89 f. 114). His attempt to make the United Provinces the centre of English animosity once more failed, though some regarded the Dutch rather than the French as England's main enemy until after the Third Dutch war. The French alliance of 1670 was widely unpopular within the political nation, both because it was seen as cause and effect of pernicious domestic designs on the part of Charles, and because the scale of initial French success in 1672 and the broadening of the war in 1673 to include a French attack on Spain presented the threat of France overrunning the Low Countries (Boxer 1969; Haley 1958, 1986).

The need for an English response to Louis's expansionism became an issue both in ministerial politics and in parliamentary debate, the two ultimately focusing on the person of Thomas Osborne, Earl of Danby, who sought to create an understanding between Crown and Parliament that would ease parliamentary management, on the basis of opposition to Louis. There were, however, cogent reasons for arguing that Louis's position was not as threatening to England or the rest of Europe as some suggested, and therefore that Charles's unwillingness to oppose him was not as dangerous to national interests, in whatever fashion those were to be understood. In April 1675, Sir Edward Dering noted in his parliamentary diary:

> Sir Thomas Littleton began a set speech against the growing greatness of the French, how dangerous and formidable he was, what enlargement he had made of his empire in Flanders, Germany, Alsace, the Franche Comte and elsewhere, now threatening all Sicily, but concluded that he did not say this to engage us in a war with France, but only to forewarn us, that we might not at least lend our own hands to raise him so high. Secretary Williamson said . . . that . . . the King of France was in no such grandeur as was apprehended . . .

The following month, Dering informed the Commons that 'the Dutch have recovered all their own, both strength and vigour and are able to put the French upon the defensive' (Bond 1976: 64–5). It was not only possible to debate the nature of French intentions and strength in 1675, but the debate was complicated by its relationship to, indeed location in, that over the succession, the constitution and religion. The intervention of foreign powers in English politics increased this relationship, making it impossible to present a debate about English foreign policy in the abstract. James, Duke of York sought French support to bolster his position. At one level, English politics became a battleground of foreign powers, French influence opposed by that of Spain and of William of Orange. Statements attacking supposed French schemes emanated from the partisans of the latter; discussion of English foreign policy was political in its nature and intentions. Although both Spain and the Emperor were also opposed to Louis in the Dutch war (1672–8), it was William who played the principal rôle in inciting English opposition to Louis and to Charles's supposed favour to him, and thus the international dimensions of Charles's policy were increasingly presented from a Protestant perspective, even though from 1673 Louis's principal goal was a Catholic power, Spain.

Charles had not envisaged that the attack upon the United Provinces would turn into a long war that would expose his foreign policy to continuing domestic criticism, while abroad he found himself allied to a ruler who did not enjoy a monopoly of military success. However, though the initial French advance of 1672 had suggested that the Dutch war would be quicker and more successful than the War of Devolution, with concomitant benefits for Louis's ally Charles, the military and diplomatic situation abruptly deteriorated for France and, unlike in the previous war, she was unable to negotiate an acceptable peace speedily, the talks that were held at Cologne in 1673 proving abortive. Far from slavishly sticking to Louis, a course of action that the domestic situation made improbable, Charles was willing to abandon him and make peace in 1674.

The end of his grand design had a comparable effect to George II's failure to create a successful anti-Prussian coalition in the War of the Austrian Succession (1740–8); the last twelve years of both reigns were spent by both monarchs, each essentially tired, in seeking to prevent the situation from deteriorating and in trying to avoid dependence on their ministers. In each case, their position was initially complicated by the reversionary interest, the expectations and fears engendered by the heir to the throne, but whereas George II's eldest son, Frederick Prince of Wales, who had acted as a focus of political opposition, predeceased his father in 1751, James II, though only three years younger, was to survive his brother by sixteen years.

Had James had only daughters, and had they been brought up as Protestant and married to Protestants, as happened with the children of his first marriage, Mary and Anne, then the situation might have been less threatening, especially if he had not been too healthy. However, James was both healthy and in 1673 had married a young Italian Catholic princess, Mary of Modena, with the support of Louis XIV. He was not to have a healthy son until 1688, but this could not be predicted in the 1670s and the fears aroused by the prospect of a Catholic line complicated Charles's position for the rest of his reign. Concerned about the possibility that Danby, Lord Treasurer 1673–9, would succeed in bringing England into the anti-French camp (Haley 1958) and keep it there, Louis helped to overthrow him by providing Ralph Montagu, a rival who had been ambassador in Paris, with secret correspondence. Revealed in the Commons by Montagu, this showed Danby's opportunism in seeking French funds in return for neutrality at the same time as he was pressing Parliament for money for an anti-French policy. The Commons began impeachment proceedings against Danby in December 1678, leading Charles to dissolve Parliament the following month. Danby had to resign in March 1679.

By parting with Danby and the Cavalier Parliament, Charles was forced to begin the search for a new system of parliamentary management, at the same time as widespread suspicion of his and his heir's intentions made this impossible on acceptable terms. Domestically, 1679-82 were years of short- lived expedients on Charles's part and it is scarcely surprising that his foreign policy was both similar and essentially designed to assist these expedients. In his last years, after the Exclusion Crisis was over, he fulfilled the conditions of Louis's agreement of 1681 to grant subsidies in return for Parliament not sitting. A pensioner of France, albeit a poorly paid one, Charles was, however, simply being subsidised to do what he would have done anyway. He had no wish to associate or compromise the reimposition of order and Tory reaction of these years with an active foreign policy. The Peace of Nymegen (1678–9) had brought a fitful peace to western Europe and, though Louis endangered it by his seizure of territories along France's frontier in his *réunion* policy and broke it by briefly attacking Spain, it was no more plausible for Charles to oppose him than it was for other rulers constrained by domestic problems and other international commitments. Charles's last years should not, however be understood as the consequence of any overall policy that was pro-French abroad and absolutist at home. Whatever the situation in 1670–4, in 1681–5 Charles was primarily concerned with helping to restore an acceptable domestic stability, not creating a new order, and the events of 1678–81 had shown him that, however much Louis might appear to be undermining international stability, the domestic consequences of opposing him were unacceptable. Internal weakness, not craven support for France, was the keynote of the last years of Charles's foreign policy.

JAMES II: A PROTÉGÉ OF LOUIS XIV?

Though James as Duke of York sought the support of Louis, it would be misleading to suggest that he acted simply in response to French interests. Instead, James sought to create a position in which it would be credible for him to receive French support. The fundamental basis of this policy in the latter stages of the Franco-Dutch war was French moderation in the conduct of the war and the peace negotiations. As France, by this period, was substantially fighting Spain and the Emperor, this did not entail James urging restraint on Louis in order to help the Dutch. James was convinced that French restraint would make it easier for Charles to preserve his domestic position and that the absence of it would lead Charles to oppose Louis in order both to quieten domestic political opinion and to obtain money from Parliament. In July 1676, he warned Courtin, the French envoy, that Louis must demonstrate that he sought peace (AE CP Ang. 119 ff. 69–70); the following year, he pressed Courtin on the need to stop Anglo-French disputes in the Channel over striking the flag, a sign of naval predominance that the English government expected, because refusal to do so inflamed opinion in England. By the summer of 1677, James's fears about the deteriorating Spanish position in the Spanish Netherlands, and his anger at Louis's unwillingness to offer conciliatory peace terms, led him not only to abandon his support for Louis, but also to show increasing favour to Danby's scheme for bonding Crown and people in French blood. The marriage of his elder daughter Mary to William of Orange in November 1677, sent a clear message about a possible change of policy by England. As it was swiftly followed by the death of James's newborn son, the Duke of Cambridge, the marriage also had clear implications for the English succession. It was followed by the presentation to Louis of a set of proposals, agreed by Charles, James and William, which would have led to France ceding more of her conquests than she had hitherto offered to do. Louis instead offered an armistice, which Barrillon, the French envoy, presented to Charles as a clear sign both that France was not out to conquer Flanders and that Louis was determined to allow Charles to show English opinion that he heeded Charles's view (AE CP Ang. 127 ff. 20–4). Charles and James were unimpressed, fearful that France would still overrun the Spanish Netherlands and increasingly interested in seeking the domestic political benefits of confrontation with Louis (Haley 1958), at a time when a strong anti-French coalition existed in western Europe. James was especially eager and showed considerable interest in commanding in Flanders against the French. He saw war with France as a solution to his domestic unpopularity, and an obvious demonstration that anti-Catholic polemic was inaccurate. Thus James was aligned with William at the same time that in the spring of 1678 the French attempted to intrigue with parliamentarians in order to prevent any war with France.

From the outbreak of the Popish Plot foreign policy took a decided second place to domestic problems for James, as they did for Charles. He was displeased with William's attempt to intervene in the Exclusion Crisis and grateful that French support allowed Charles to dispense with Parliament. However, like Charles, he was not an enthusiastic supporter of Louis's policies in western Europe, the principle victims of which were Catholic powers, especially Spain; just as French relations with Pope Innocent XI had deteriorated sharply over Louis's determination to control the church in France.

If James's views on French foreign policy were variable prior to his accession, this situation did not cease when he became king. He both renewed existing treaties with the Dutch in 1685 and appealed to Louis for regular subsidies. James sought to retain this mixed inheritance, which gave him greater flexibility, offering him more options and, in particular, allowing him to avoid being dependent either on France or on Parliament, which would have been compatible with neither his interests nor his dignity. Sensible from the domestic point of view, this policy was also reasonable in diplomatic terms. Louis was no more nor less reliable as an ally than most other rulers in this period, but that was little recommendation to any dependence on him. French diplomatic pressure on James not to align with other powers indicated that alliance with Louis would entail a position of dependence in which England would be unable to develop links elsewhere and to respond to events (AE CP Ang. 156 ff. 25–6, 33-4, 37, 40, 58–9). Rather than surrendering his capacity for diplomatic initiatives, James sought to maintain links with Louis by stressing common interests, not least in 1685 the supposed co-operation of the French Protestants, the Huguenots, with the Duke of Monmouth, Charles II's illegitimate son who rebelled against James, both allegedly supported by Protestant powers (AE CP Ang. 156 ff. 40 2, 46, 70). He also suggested to Barrillon in the autumn of 1685 that it was unnecessary for him and England to choose between Louis and his opponents. In part, the reasons James advanced were plausible. Pointing out that Austria and Spain were not in a state to break the Truce of Regensburg (1684), which had brought an uneasy peace to western Europe, he suggested that even when Austro-Turkish hostilities ended, Leopold I would not lightly begin a war with France. James continued with the unrealistic statement that he would be able to block such a project, as Leopold would not attempt it without consulting and seeking to engage James in what was entirely opposed to his designs and interests (AE CP Ang. 156 f. 39). James discerned correctly that England could play a major rôle in any serious conflict and that the continental powers were therefore interested in English politics, but he was mistaken in assuming that this would necessarily accord with his views and he arguably exaggerated the significance of England to the major European powers, a mistaken path in which he followed his grandfather, James I. Possibly the rapid suppression of Monmouth's rising in July 1685 increased James's confidence about his international position excessively. William of Orange's support for James during the rising, which contrasted with Louis's decision to refuse to provide a subsidy, suggested that foreign powers would not meddle in English domestic politics in an unfriendly fashion. The success of the 1685 general election and the prorogation of Parliament in November appeared to close a major sphere of foreign intrigue.

James thus followed an independent policy and sought to keep both England and Europe at peace. If in September 1685 he declared that he would openly support France if Spain broke the Truce of Regensburg and, the following January, he rejected Spanish pressure to renew the 1680 defensive treaty, stating that it would be neither advantageous nor necessary, and that Louis seemed in favour of peace, James repeatedly pressed Louis in late 1685 to recognise William's right to the principality of Orange, recently annexed by France (AE CP Ang 156 ff. 62–3, 158 ff. 72–3). If in 1686 James's interests were identified more closely with those of Louis, he did not display a willingness to co-operate with France comparable to those of Cromwell in the late 1650s and Charles II in 1670–3. Instead, James wanted peace to enable him to pursue domestic schemes, avoid the difficulties that calling Parliament might bring, and evade the problems of commitment that war on the Continent would entail. Reports that James wished in alliance with Louis to attack the Dutch in 1687 were inaccurate. In fact, that spring James sought to persuade William to support the repeal of anti-Catholic legislation. James did not believe it necessary to align with Louis in order to further his domestic ends; indeed, as in 1677–8, he thought that this might make matters more difficult, by arousing domestic and foreign opposition.

James's room for diplomatic manoeuvre was narrowed by William's growing unwillingness to keep out of English domestic affairs. Most monarchs encountered problems with the reversionary interest, the standing question mark against all policies. For James the position was complicated by the fact that the reversionary interest was based abroad, enjoyed an independent international position while having experience of playing a rôle in English politics, and represented Protestant aspirations in England more obviously than the monarch himself. In 1687, James became convinced that William was seeking to form a Protestant League. However, his response was not a slavish adherence to Louis, but rather advice to him to moderate his policies and, in particular, settle his differences with other Catholic rulers (AE CP Ang. 162 ff. 129, 141; 165 f. 83). Believing that war would serve the interests of his domestic rivals, James was uncertain how best to avoid it, other than by resisting public identification with Louis, and he misunderstood the nature of the developing international crisis in 1688.

Aware that William was seeking to enlist allies against Louis, including crucially the leading Catholic ruler, Leopold I, James was unsure about the attitude he ought to adopt towards Louis. He feared that close support would encourage other rulers to oppose him, while Louis's pressure in 1688 for expansion of the English fleet could be seen both as justifying accusations of joint Anglo-French schemes against the United Provinces and as a possible cause of heightened tension. James's attitude to naval preparations, at a time of increased Dutch naval activity, was as aggravating to the French as his refusal to commit himself to them diplomatically. Unhappy about James's general approach towards international relations, Louis, nevertheless, offered his assistance in order to repel any Dutch invasion. Neither wishing to commit himself, nor believing it necessary, James's misunderstanding of William's schemes led him to respond in an equivocal fashion to Louis's offer.

Hence James was far from being a client of the French. His representation thus during his reign owed much to propaganda. That he was forced into the rôle of French client after William's invasion encouraged his presentation in this way subsequently and a consequent rewriting of his political career, consistency being intertwined with polemic. The widespread belief that no Catholic monarch could support national interests, however defined, helped to encourage a negative assessment of James as did the absence of any public knowledge of his differences with Louis. James's Catholic interests did dominate his foreign policy, but not in the fashion that was generally believed. Far from leading him to support Louis in the hope that that would elicit French backing for his domestic schemes, James tried to avoid an identification that would compromise these schemes. At the same time, he followed a foreign policy that sought to encourage the maintenance of peace and the continuance of acceptable relations with as many rulers as possible, especially the Catholics opposed to Louis. They had to be prevented from supporting any hostile action by William for, without their support, William's options would be political, not military, and James's prorogation of Parliament had narrowed these options. James, however, was unlucky in that, whereas the western European crisis in Charles's last years had been resolved by the Truce of Regensburg, freeing Charles from the problems of the international arena, that of 1688 over Cologne and the Palatinate was not settled peacefully. Instead widespread antipathy to Louis allowed William to obtain from other rulers significant assistance, support and acceptance of the invasion that the birth of an heir to James appeared to make necessary (J.R. Jones 1972; Miller 1978; Black 1989a).James was unlucky, but the unpredictable nature of European diplomacy did not defeat him alone. Louis found he had begun a war that was to be longer and less successful than anticipated, while William's attempts from 1697 to settle the problems of western Europe diplomatically were to be defeated by Leopold's obduracy and the last wishes of a sub-normal king of Spain.

WILLIAM AND ANNE: RIVALS TO AND PEACEMAKERS WITH LOUIS

William III (1689–1702) was a warrior king, a ruler who not only was at war for much of his reign but also took an active rôle in conflict. As

Captain General of the United Provinces, he had played a major rôle in the war of 1672-8, capturing Bonn in 1673, fighting the battles of Seneffe (1674) and Cassel (1677) and besieging Maastricht (1676) and Charleroi (1677), and he led the invasion of England in 1688. In 1690, William led the forces sent to drive James II and his French and Irish troops from Ireland, defeating James at the Boyne. In 1691, William commanded the Allied army in the Netherlands for the first time, and he fought a largely inconclusive battle at Steenkerk (1692), before being defeated at Neerwinden (1693). In 1694, William counter-attacked, capturing Huy and in 1695 Namur. Alongside his active military rôle, William also played a crucial part in creating and maintaining an anti-French coalition. From 1689–90 on, he held a meeting or congress of the representatives of the Allies every winter at The Hague.

Of all the European rulers, William was Louis's most persistent opponent. He had a strong conviction of a European community, critically of *both* Catholics and Protestants, that was threatened by the power and ambition of Louis. William argued that only through opposing Louis could the liberty of Europe, defined in terms of the integrity and independence of the European powers both large and small, be preserved. The Treaty of the Grand Alliance of 1701 referred to the danger that a Bourbon France and Spain would seize 'the empire over all Europe' in order 'to oppose the liberty of Europe'; the Dutch declaration of war of 1702 warned of the danger of Louis's 'universal monarchy'. Those of the political nation who were not loyal to James II felt obliged to follow William in this direction. Having been manoeuvred into swallowing the succession of William and Mary, they were scarcely going to demur at the obvious consequence of war with France. French support for the opponents of the new establishment in Ireland made conflict with Louis appear less of a foreign interest. However, William's personal determination to defeat Louis ensured that the English political nation was faced by the same problem that had confronted their Dutch counterparts in the last years of the Dutch war. Neither group wanted the long war they had become engaged in, but in the United Provinces it was easier to circumvent the bellicose intentions of William, who was not the sovereign, and whose coup in the province of Holland in 1672 had not been followed by any constitutional revolution. Despite his opposition to separate negotiations with Louis, which he correctly feared would destroy the anti-French alliance, enable Louis to obtain more favourable terms by picking off his opponents individually and make the creation of a new alliance to police the peace more difficult, the States General signed a separate peace in August 1678. Aware that the peace was made, William, nevertheless, attacked the French army, leading to the battle of Saint-Denis. In 1684, William was also thwarted when he failed to bring Dutch support to the assistance of Spain, which had been attacked the previous year by France. In England, in contrast, it was harder to oppose William's war. Despite considerable financial and economic burdens (D.W. Jones 1988), it was not England which negotiated first with Louis, as it might well have done had it been fighting France as an independent member of the coalition. William's very position was a bar to peace, as he insisted on French recognition of his royal title as a condition of any treaty.

If William's conduct of the war, with scant consultation of his English ministers, led to serious criticism, that was even more the response to his post-war diplomacy. The failure to defeat Louis in the Nine Years' War led William to welcome the opportunity to negotiate in the late 1690s a settlement by which conflict would be avoided over the Spanish succession by partitioning the inheritance (Roosen 1987). Had the Partition Treaties agreed in 1698 and 1700 by William and Louis been in fact negotiated by James and Louis then it is likely that contemporary and subsequent English commentators would have criticised them bitterly for their territorial concessions to France. By the First Partition Treaty of October 1698, the Dauphin, Louis XIV's heir, was to gain Naples and Sicily, both of which were ruled by the King of Spain, and some minor additional Italian and Spanish territories, leading to a major addition to French strength. By the Second Treaty of 1700, the Dauphin would additionally gain Lorraine. The crucial Anglo-French negotiations were conducted on the English side by William in London and the United Provinces and, in Paris, by Hans Willem Bentinck, Earl of Portland, a Dutch favourite who had virtually settled the peace terms of 1697 and was sent as ambassador to Paris in 1698. The partition negotiations led to an upsurge of parliamentary criticism of William, essentially because in a political situation in which conventions of behaviour were slowly adapting to the consequences of annual parliamentary sessions, and thus to an enhanced rôle for parliamentary leadership and management, William continued not only to follow his own views and ignore those of others but also to underrate the importance of domestic political management (Baxter 1966).

The consequent political crisis, encapsulated in the title of the Act of Settlement, 'an Act for further limitation of the Crown and for better securing the rights and liberties of the subject' (1701), did not, however, fundamentally alter the basis of foreign policy, because the creation of a permanent parliamentary standing committee, as used in some other European states, was neither desired nor attempted. If there was therefore no administrative representation of parliamentary influence, the political effect was also limited. It has been argued that developing party cohesion allowed politicians to 'storm the closet', to insist on one-party governments, rather than the mixed ministries favoured by William and Anne (C. Roberts 1983, 1985: 107–248). Such a system in theory should have produced parliamentary control by obliging the monarch to accept an executive representing majority opinion in Parliament. However, in practice, royal power was enhanced by the limited rôle of Parliament (see pp. 44–61) and by the absence of party unity. This enabled monarchs to decide through which politicians they wished to try to govern, and obliged politicians to seek royal support. Thus, under Anne, both the Whigs and the Tories were divided and the monarch was not only able but obliged to play a considerable rôle in manipulating these divisions for the sake of coherent government.

Anne (1702–14) has been recently vindicated as an able and independent monarch, less dependent on her courtiers than had been hitherto believed (Gregg 1980). As she had no domestic programme of change, she was a relatively uncontroversial figure and indeed political criticism in her reign was centred on ministers, not monarch. Anne followed William III in sustaining the Grand Alliance created to fight Louis, and, like William, realised that a compromise peace would have to be negotiated, though the greater rôle of her ministers in the negotiations, especially Robert Harley, Earl of Oxford, and Henry St John, Viscount Bolingbroke, led to their views being criticised. Anne lacked the independent political position that William had enjoyed as stadtholder of most of the Dutch provinces. However, not only did she not travel (and thus negotiate with scant ministerial oversight abroad), as William had done and George I and II were to do, but her rôle in negotiations in London was far smaller. In foreign policy, Anne was important less for her distinct views than for her willingness to support ministers with particular opinions. Her sense in 1709–10 that the War of the Spanish Succession (in which Britain was engaged 1702–13) was unpopular and that the vital war goals had been obtained played a major rôle in weakening the Whig ministry. Conversely, she supported their Tory successors in their contentious task of negotiating a peace settlement and was willing to create twelve new Tory peers in 1711 in order to ensure that the peace preliminaries passed the Lords.

THE HANOVERIAN CONNECTION 1714

The most obvious qualification of the thesis that the Revolution of

1688 led a Protestant Britain into opposition to France, indeed a second Hundred Years War, was not the partition diplomacy of 1698–1700, nor the Anglo- French rapprochement of 1713–14 following the Peace of Utrecht (Mckay 1971), but the alliance between the two powers between 1716 and 1731 and the subsequent care to avoid conflict until 1743. This, like much of British diplomacy in the period 1714–60, can be traced in large part to the interests of the Crown as Electors of Hanover and, though to a lesser extent, to their dynastic position in Britain. Hanover was vulnerable, the Hanoverian succession was contested; the defence of both was pressed by George I (1714–27) and George II (1727–60).

The extent to which the Hanoverian succession affected British foreign policy is a contentious question that depends upon the credence attached to ministerial expressions of concern about Jacobitism. It was argued by contemporaries, and has been suggested subsequently, that such fears were deliberately expressed in order to unite the Whigs, discredit the notion of a loyal opposition and bind the monarch to the Whigs. In the case of Sir Robert Walpole it has been claimed that concern about Jacobitism played a rôle in his support for British neutrality in the War of the Polish Succession (1733–5). Jacobitism indeed could clearly be exploited by foreign rulers seeking to intimidate Britain (Black 1985a: 138–59).

However, it is difficult to show that George I and George II were consistently influenced in their views on foreign policy by a desire to secure their succession. This was clearly important in 1714–16, but, once that immediate crisis was passed, the issue became less important. The crisis consisted of a combination of an insurrection in England and Scotland, the '15, and the prospect of French support on behalf of the rebels. The French were influenced by a conviction that George I and the Whig ministers he appointed to replace the Tories would fulfil their criticism of the Peace of Utrecht of 1713 by destroying the Tory rapprochement with France, recreating the wartime Grand Alliance, and possibly taking hostility to France to the point of war. The Whigs did indeed seek to restore relations with Austria and the Dutch, but George I's concern about the Great Northern War (1700–21), a Baltic conflict in which Hanover was involved, helped to push Britain towards France, a process aided by the death of Louis XIV in 1715, the fears of the Duke of Orléans, regent for the infant Louis XV, about a challenge from the new king's uncle, Philip V of Spain, and French caution in providing support for the Jacobites. Once the Anglo-French alliance of 1716 had been negotiated, the Hanoverian succession became a less serious issue in foreign policy. The defeat of the '15 demonstrated the strength of the new dynasty, and George I and his ministers were inhibited neither from opposing Philip V and Charles Xll of Sweden in 1717–19 by their willingness to support Jacobitism, nor from confronting the Austro-Spanish Alliance of Vienna in 1725–7.

Hanover was a different matter. The Electorate, a tract of territory in north-west Germany, mostly between the Elbe, the Weser and the Harz mountains, was a weak military power lacking strong fortresses or readily defended frontiers. In 1739, its army of 21,000 was outnumbered four times by that of Prussia. In January l751, Frederick II told the French envoy in Berlin that if war broke out he would invade Hanover in order to capture the Electoral treasury and that if he failed he would impose, under threat of burning everything, a massive daily levy until the treasury was delivered. Two months later the Prussian foreign minister said that, in the event of war, Prussia would use a conquered Hanover as a source of supplies.

Hanover was a recent state, the product of the uniting of two major branches of the House of Brunswick, and benefited from the weakness of the major non-German power in the area, Sweden, the Baltic concerns of the second-ranking such power, Denmark, and the number of weak territories in the region, especially the prince-bishoprics of Münster, Paderborn and Hildesheim. However, Hanover had one powerful neighbour, Brandenburg-Prussia, while the opportunities for territorial gain at the expense of Sweden presented by the collapse of her power after Charles XII's defeat by Peter I (the Great) of Russia at Poltava (1709) were followed by a westward movement of Russian strength and, in 1716, by a collapse of agreement among the rulers opposed to Charles, which led to a marked deterioration in relations between George and Peter.

Hanover was thus exposed to the potential enmity of two of the rising European powers, Prussia and Russia, a challenge to which George I responded by seeking the alliance of France. This introduced what was to be a cause of considerable tension in British foreign policy. For Hanover, the principal threats were eastern and central European land powers – Russia (1716–31), Prussia (1726–55) and, though in a less immediate fashion, Austria (1720s). Security required an attempt either to obtain alliances that would neutralise the threat or to reach an acceptable settlement of differences. The central problem, in contrast, as far as most British politicians were concerned, was Bourbon strength and intentions. The focus of this threat varied and, from the 1740s, was increasingly to be seen as centred on colonial competition. However, in so far as allies were believed to be helpful in confronting the Bourbons, it was increasingly the case that the reliance on Austria and the United Provinces, which had characterised anti-Bourbon discussion and diplomacy from the 1670s, was supplemented or replaced by a desire to gain the support of the rising powers of Prussia and Russia.

Neither George I nor George II was particularly interested in colonial affairs and, for them, France and Spain constituted part of a European system whose pivot should be the defence of Hanover, rather than part of a maritime and colonial system. These different opinions lay at the root of political controversy over foreign policy in the period 1714–60. This was more complex than that created by the Continental interests of William III, because William's concerns were focused on France, the prime threat to the independence of the United Provinces and, in his eyes, to the European system. Conversely the controversy was less serious than that inspired by Charles II's views.

Dynastic interests always had a political cost. Such costs were accentuated in the case of personal unions. There was a danger that the views of constituent units would be poorly handled, due to insensitivity, a lack of understanding, and pressures arising from the interests either of other units or of the unifying hand represented by the monarch. In the case of such unions, there was a stronger likelihood of a conflation of representation, particularism, proto-nationalism and xenophobia.

The representation might be organised in very different ways – the British Parliament or Polish Sejm were not like the Hanoverian Council of Ministers – but, in each case, there was a distancing of the ruler, creating political and governmental problems, pressures, and expectations. Tension arose over foreign policy and the distribution of the profits and costs of power. Although Hanover was a source of troops, the Hanoverian link gravely weakened Britain as an international force, because, like its counterparts in Poland and Sweden, it was unpopular, and challenged the practice of crown-elite co-operation on which successful politics depended. Jacobitism was also a dangerous weakness. Conversely, the defeat of Jacobitism greatly strengthened the British monarchy, making possible a reconceptualisation of the domestic political situation such that the identity and ability of the monarch became less central and the Hanoverian issue less serious.

Hanoverianism in British foreign policy was criticised by contemporaries, but there was a counter-argument that the British had perforce to accept a European role, whatever their rulership, that, in short, the Hanoverian connection was not the cause of interventionism. Both the connection and British interventionism had to respond to a rapidly changing international system.

The views of George I and George II were most contentious in the late 1710s, with regard to Russia, and in 1740–55, especially 1740–8, with regard to the Prussia of Frederick II (the Great). In both cases, this led to political disputes in Britain as some ministers contested the royal interpretation of British interests (Owen 1973; Hatton 1982). These criticisms have received insufficient attention, as the non-interventionalist tradition of ministerial thought, to adopt a description that is not intended to suggest a false coherence or, indeed, isolationism, has generally been considered in light of Walpole and Henry Pelham, First Lord of the Treasury 1743–54, who both cited domestic, particularly financial, reasons, rather than with reference to informed criticisms arising from views on the international situation. By their very nature, the sources, which rarely include detailed accounts of council meetings, do not provide sufficient material to permit a sustained account of criticisms of Hanoverian concerns from within government, and there has been a tendency to stress the often relatively uninformed views of political opponents.

However, it would be misleading to regard criticism of Hanoverian concerns as simply a feature of xenophobia that was adapted to contemporary political concerns and opportunities. There were intelligent reasons for doubting the wisdom of diplomatic initiatives and commitments arising essentially from the Hanoverian connection. This was certainly the case with opposition to Peter I during the reign of George I. Though a case was advanced that the Russian gain of Sweden's former eastern Baltic possessions, Estonia, Ingria and Livonia, was a threat to British commercial interests in the Baltic, it is clear that, whatever the supposed threat from Russia, it was not in Britain's interest to play the leading rôle in creating or sustaining an anti-Russian alliance of weak and divided powers. In addition, Russian economic growth was to be a fruitful basis for expanding British trade. As a result of hostility to Russia, Britain was drawn into support of Denmark and meddling in Swedish politics, but neither power could contribute materially to Britain's international situation (Black 1988b) . Furthermore, a pact was created from 1726 of Austria, Prussia, Russia and Saxony, none of which had serious points in dispute with Britain, but all of whom were hostile until 1731, essentially as a consequence of the Hanoverian connection.

The detrimental consequences of this connection stemmed not from the Electoral government but from royal concerns arising from Hanover. It is misleading to see Hanover as a united force, for the Hanoverian ministers were divided and, at times, unhappy with the Elector's views (BL Add. 35410 f. 252). In 1763, the Hanoverian envoy in Vienna revealed divisions over policy towards neighbouring Osnabrück to his

French counterpart (AE CP Autriche 295 ff. 241–2). However, the Elector was unaffected by any equivalent to Parliament and was well placed to give consistent direction to Hanoverian policy.

The views of George I and II as Electors are difficult to chart fully, because neither monarch wrote much and Hanoverian diplomatic material was substantially destroyed by bombing in World War II. However, it appears to be the case that, while George I was most concerned about Russia, not least because of the marriage of members of Peter's family to the Dukes of Holstein-Gottorp and Mecklenburg, both of whom had disputes with him, George II was more worried about Prussia. Under Frederick William I (1713–40), the Prussian army appreciably increased in size, and, whereas Frederick William's relations with his uncle and father-in-law, George I, though not always close, were generally respectful, those with his cousin and brother-in-law, George II, were poor. George II sought to breathe fresh life into the Hanoverian-Prussian dynastic relationship by arranging the marriage of a daughter to the Prussian heir, the future Frederick II, and of Frederick Prince of Wales to a Prussian princess, a scheme initially envisaged by George I, but in 1730 this fell victim to differing diplomatic views and Frederick William's violent suspicion of George II. George II's independent links to Crown Prince Frederick further aroused Frederick William's fury when the prince sought to escape in 1730, and, for the rest of the decade, relations remained poor. These poor relations angered a number of British diplomats who believed that a Prussian alliance was necessary for Britain, including Walpole's brother and principal foreign policy advisor Horatio Walpole, but, despite their hopes that an alliance could be negotiated, a number of disputes arising from Hanoverian interests kept the rulers, and therefore the powers, apart. In 1738, Horatio Walpole wrote to his protégé Robert Trevor, the envoy at The Hague:

> What should hinder the kings of England and Prussia from being intimately well together, not their interests, but their humours . . . little views founded on jealousy etc. I could go on and sketch out a noble plan for opposing the power of the House of Bourbon; if the great interest of the whole was to take place of humour, brigues and pitiful notions, but Providence only can make the proper disposition in the hearts of his Viceregents to answer so good and great an end. (Aylesbury CRO, Trevor papers vol. 15, 24 Oct.)

It was scarcely surprising that British ministers were not terribly concerned about what were to them essentially unimportant Hanoverian interests, such as the fate of the German principality of East Friesland, the succession to which was contested by Hanover and Prussia, while they were worried that another German succession dispute, the Jülich-Berg question, would lead in 1738 to a Prussian invasion of Hanover. Indeed, on a number of occasions, George II obtained British diplomatic support, and, as in 1729, the prospect of military assistance, for the protection of Hanover. The hiring of Hessian troops was specifically for the purpose, and, in the face of domestic criticism and references to the Act of Settlement, British ministers were obliged to argue that Hanoverian needs arose from her exposure as an associate of Britain in cases that stemmed from British policies (Black 1989c: 41–54). This was a cost of royal support for the Whigs, but, arguably, in the 1730s, it was not as serious as it had been earlier. The prospect of a major conflict placing Hanover as the advance guard of an Anglo-French coalition attacked by Austria, Prussia or Russia disappeared in 1731, when the Second Treaty of Vienna was negotiated with Austria, and, in subsequent diplomatic realignments, Prussia became isolated, while Anglo-Russian relations eased with the commercial treaty of 1734. George II and his ministers hoped that the accession in 1740 of Frederick II, who had been given money by George in the 1730s, would improve the situation, and had it done so and good Anglo-Hanoverian-Prussian relations begun, then it is probable that Hanover would have been both secure and not an issue in British public debate. However, Frederick chose to follow an independent course, repaying his uncle's money. It had been somewhat naive to imagine that Frederick would wish to tie himself to Britain, since 1739 at war with Spain with the prospect of France coming to Spain's assistance. As a result, it is necessary to be careful of excessively attributing the failure to improve relations with Prussia to Hanoverian disputes.

Bereft of Prussian assistance, George II had no military prospect of resisting a threatened French invasion of Hanover in 1741, and he was obliged to accept a neutrality convention that led him to vote for the French candidate for the Imperial throne. This measure, entered into strictly in an Electoral capacity, was nevertheless disliked by his British ministers who correctly feared that Electoral measures would be interpreted as affecting British conduct both at home and abroad. The convention hindered British attempts to create a pro-Austrian alliance, while in Britain it was viewed as evidence of a ministerial failure to defend national interests, especially when, allegedly as a result of a secret clause, that did not, in fact, exist, the British fleet failed to prevent Spanish forces designed to attack Austrian Italy from landing in Italy.

Neutrality was probably the best option for Hanover. There was a long tradition of German princes being neutral in major disputes and, militarily, the Electorate was no more able to defend itself in 1741 than it had been in 1729 or 1716. Indeed, an obvious feature of most

German principalities was that they did not take part in the increase in military strength that characterised the leading powers, a group that Prussia was able to join only with considerable difficulty. If Britain's capacity as a major power was limited by the absence of a large army, Hanover was not protected, as Britain was, by insularity and a navy. Having failed in 1741 to create an effective alliance that could prevent Frederick from gaining Silesia from Austria, there was no doubt of George II's second-rank status in northern Germany, and that was simply demonstrated when Fredrick gained East Friesland on the death of the last prince in 1744, a measure that George futilely complained about for years.

Neutrality suited neither George nor his British ministers. Both devoted the years from 1741 until 1755 to an attempt to recreate the Grand Alliance which was, however, confused in purpose between opposition to France, the principal British goal, and hostility to Prussia, the view of George and increasingly of Austria. The contribution of Hanover to this policy waned. It served as a means for conducting anti-Prussian negotiations that George knew would not please his British ministers, but, more directly, it was in large measure the Hanoverian minister Münchhausen who encouraged the Duke of Newcastle in 1748 to intervene actively in German politics.

The year 1748 was in many respects one of possibilities, as were most years of peace treaties, with refocusing of alliances and possibilities of new relations with former enemies. In 1748, the French foreign minister Puysieulx sought better relations, Henry Legge was sent to Berlin to seek an understanding, and Britain and Austria disagreed over the progress of the peace negotiations. By the end of the year the choice had clearly been made for Vienna rather than Berlin and, over the next two years, Newcastle elaborated the Imperial Election Scheme which was designed to be a keystone of a new Anglo-Austrian system of collective security. If this reflected Hanoverian views and interests, it did not, however, sufficiently allay fears that Prussia or France would attack the Electorate. In February 1751, the French foreign minister observed that, thanks to Hanoverian vulnerability, Frederick II had no need to fear George II. These fears helped to put British diplomacy on the defensive, as in 1753 when a Prussian attack was anticipated, and in 1755–6, as conflict with France became more serious, fears about Hanover led to a change in the direction of British policy. It was concern about a French or French- sponsored Prussian attack on Hanover that led George II, then on his last visit to the Electorate, to respond favourably to discussions with Frederick through his Brunswick relatives.

If Hanover led to the Anglo-Prussian Convention of Westminster of January 1756, which guaranteed their respective possessions and German neutrality, that was intended to supplement, not replace treaties with Austria and Russia. It was the Electorate that reaped the failure of this diplomatic strategy when, in 1757, French forces overran it. Frederick, attacked by Austria, Russia and Sweden, could not defend Hanover as well.

Newcastle observed in January 1757, 'His Majesty [George II] chooses to confine his present attention to the defence of Hanover only' (BL Add. 32870 f. 22). The Duke of Cumberland with an army of Hanoverians and other German forces, the 'Army of Observation', was, however, defeated at Hastenbeck (26 July 1757), and, on 8 September, the outnumbered and out-manoeuvred Cumberland signed the Convention of Klosterseven, disbanding his army and leaving the French in control of Hanover. Lord Chancellor Hardwicke had written the previous month of 'a misfortune happening to His Majesty by the part he has taken as Elector in an English cause' (BL Add. 35417 f. 16). Like the neutrality convention of 1741, Klosterseven revealed the limited value to Hanover of her ruler's great-power diplomacy. The emptiness of such a policy without significant military force had been displayed. Though George II had benefited from and fostered the willingness of Carteret and Newcastle to support an active continental diplomacy that entailed the creation of an international system that would guarantee Hanover, the weakness of both policy and arrangements had been revealed in 1756–7. Hanover's value in great-power diplomacy lay in her vulnerability and her consequent use by other states to affect British policy.

GEORGE III 1760–93: A HEART TRULY BRITISH OR A HANOVERIAN *SECRET DU ROI?*

Hanoverian weakness was not the only important background to George III's views. He also, at least initially, lacked the emotional attachment to and concern about the Electorate that had influenced his grandfather, George II, and his great-grandfather, George I, with their birth, education and youth there, their frequent visits and their German affections. Though George III (1760–1820) also had a German wife (though not a mistress), he never visited the Electorate, before or after his accession. There is no doubt of his early determination to repudiate the policies and methods of his grandfather, and this was markedly revealed in his willingness to break with Frederick II, a ruler for whom he revealed neither respect nor affection, without securing the alliance of another power that might guarantee Hanover.

One obvious difference between George III and his grandfather was his greater concern for domestic British politics. Particularly in his last years, the elderly George II, while still determined to resist ministerial appointments that he disliked, was nevertheless essentially prepared to leave politics and government to his ministers. George III, in contrast, wished to overthrow a system that he believed had corrupted and divided British political life. He was not prepared to accept dictation from Newcastle or Pitt the Elder. It was not unusual for an accession to lead to a dramatic change in political fortunes, as in 1714 (though not 1727), and George was able both to create a new ministry around his favourite, the 3rd Earl of Bute, in 1762 and to end the Seven Years' War. However, the new political arrangement proved fragile, in large part because of Bute's failure of nerve and resignation in 1763. This was followed by a period of ministerial instability, mainly because of the King's refusal to give his full support to the Grenville (1763–5) and Rockingham (1765–6) ministries.

As the prime topic in European diplomacy in this period – the Polish election of 1764 – was not one that greatly concerned Britain, it was possible for both George and his ministers to feel that their concentration on domestic affairs was not having too serious a consequence for foreign policy. There are suggestions of specific royal views, not least on the vexed question of whether to concentrate on improving relations with Austria or Prussia, but the King focused on domestic and colonial issues, and there is little sense of any royal determination to direct policy matching that of George II. George was presumably responsible for pressure on Prussia in 1763 to stop recruiting violently in Mecklenburg-Schwerin, to whose Duke he was related (BL Stowe 257 f. 107), but this was a minor issue. Three years later, the Earl of Albemarle blamed the replacement of the Rockingham ministry by that of Chatham on George's concern for Hanover:

> You will stare and perhaps shake your head, when I tell you it was by the advice of his German ministers. The King of Prussia, tired of soliciting England for the arrears due to him, informed the Hanoverian ministers that unless he was paid (or indemnified by some part of America), and immediately, that he would seize upon the Duchy of Lunenbourg and immediately. This so alarmed Munchhausen that he sent an express to the King with his alarms, and saying at the same time that no man could deal with the King of Prussia but Mr Pitt, that he had a confidence in him, and a diffidence in all his Majesty's ministers. This determined the King so suddenly, and so unexpectedly to send for Mr Pitt.

Newcastle was rightly sceptical (WW R1-692, 694), and it is clear that Hanoverian concerns played a less central rôle than they had done in the previous decade. They were superseded by imperial concerns.

The first major shift that George considered was a rapprochement with France in 1772, in face of the aggressive action of Austria, Prussia and Russia in co-operating to force Poland to accept the First Partition. Though worried about the unprovoked despoliation of a neutral, George and his ministers were not so much concerned about the fate of Poland which, as in 1733 and 1764, when there had last been royal elections, was seen as a distant country that contributed little to the balance of power, as about the possibility that, singly or collectively, the partitioning powers would sooner or later move on to fresh prey. Irrespective of their gains, there was no doubt that their co- operation represented a radical shift in international relations. The reasons why a counter-agreement with France was not negotiated are examined elsewhere (pp. 239–41), but one factor that is difficult to assess was the effect on George of the vulnerability of Hanover to Prussian attack. As in the late 1720s, Hanover would be in the forefront of any war. The importance of such military considerations is open to discussion, but the possibility that a dispute might erupt into a major war was ever present. Six years later, in 1778, opposition to Austrian gains at the expense of Bavaria led to the Austro-Prussian War of the Bavarian Succession.

Hanover was not really in a position to take part in such conflicts but George, as Elector, displayed from the late 1770s a growing interest in German politics. To a considerable extent, this stemmed from his opposition to change in the Empire, a sentiment that most German rulers shared and which helped to perpetuate the Imperial political system at a time when in most of Europe, including Poland, attempts were being made to strengthen central government. Just as George I, in the early 1720s, had opposed the efforts of the Emperor Charles VI to stress the authority of Imperial courts over disputes between German rulers, and George II had sought to stop Frederick II's invasion of Silesia and the development of two- power Austro-Prussian preponderance in the Empire, so George III was concerned about the attempt by the Emperor Joseph II (sole Austrian ruler 1780–90), the intended beneficiary of the Imperial Election Scheme in the 1750s, to increase Austrian power within the Empire. Generally happy to see Austria strong in Italy and eastern Europe (as Electoral Prince, George I had fought for Austria in Hungary), the Electors of Hanover were deeply concerned about Austrian power and the use of Imperial authority in the Empire. In 1757, George II had pressed the Bavarian envoy on the need for concerted action to preserve German liberty (Bayr. London 233, 7 Jan.). In the 1770s, antagonism between Austria and Hanover led the latter towards Prussia, and, during the War of the Bavarian Succession (1778–9), George, as Elector of Hanover, adopted a pro-Prussian position. Austria hoped for French support.

The Bavarian succession dispute appeared to provide proof of widely circulating rumours about Joseph's intentions, and from then, until he became involved in the winter of 1787–8 in the Russo-Turkish war that had begun the previous summer, Joseph was clearly a central problem for George. This Hanoverian interest clashed with his British ministers' wish to break the Austro-French alliance and improve Anglo-Austrian relations in order to counteract French diplomatic predominance in western Europe. The British wish was unrealistic, as they had little to offer the Austrians, and Joseph II, whose disparaging view of Louis XVI was matched by his opinion of George III, had no intention of exchanging his fragile French alliance for agreement with Britain. Such an exchange would lead to closer Franco–Prussian relations and would expose his possessions in Italy and the Austrian Netherlands in the event of war (Black 1990h).

However, it was understandable that British ministers should blame their failure in part on George III's hostility as Elector to Joseph. This hostility led George to support closer relations between Hanover and Prussia, thus creating a rival focus of diplomatic activity and speculation and, eventually, the basis for the negotiation of an Anglo-Prussian treaty in 1788. George's concern about Joseph was enhanced by the latter's success in having his youngest brother elected successor to the ecclesiastical states of Cologne and Münster. When these had last been contested, in 1761, George had betrayed little interest, a reversal of the policy of his Hanoverian predecessors, but the prospect of one of the two leading German powers gaining control of a hitherto weak neighbour of Hanover appeared to limit further the Electoral position. Both Hanover and Prussia opposed the elections, though without success. They were equally concerned in 1784–5 by the revival of Joseph's interest in the acquisition of Bavaria, this time by exchange with the Austrian Netherlands. This proposal did not accord with traditional British interests. There had been concern during the War of the Spanish Succession that an independent state in the former Spanish Netherlands would be excessively vulnerable to French control. However, in the mid 1780s British ministerial doubts about Joseph's intentions took second place to a determination to win his alliance, a determination that had already led to the offer of support for the opening of the Scheldt to improve the trade of Antwerp, in express defiance of international treaty. Ironically the opening of the river was to be one of the specific reasons for the outbreak of war between Britain and revolutionary France in 1793.

The clash between British and Hanoverian intentions came with the formation of the *Fürstenbund* (League of Princes) in 1785, an anti-Austrian alliance based on the co-operation of Hanover, Prussia and Saxony. The reasonable attempt by British ministers to disclaim responsibility impressed neither Joseph nor his Russian ally Catherine II (Blanning 1977). Both became convinced that British policy was being directed by George III to Hanoverian ends, and this interpretation was sustained in 1787 by the conviction that the British envoy in Constantinople, Sir Robert Ainslie, had been responsible for inciting Turkey to declare war unexpectedly on Russia (Black 1984b). In January 1786, Fox told the Commons that he found it difficult to avoid smiling at Pitt's arguments about the *Fürstenbund*:

> . . . as it was obvious that the regency of Hanover ought neither to form laws nor enter into any treaties which might prove injurious to Great Britain consequently it behoved the ministers of this country to have prevented their entering into any alliances which might involve serious consequences to the interests of England. (Cobbett 1806-20: XX, 1019–20).

In 1788–9, Joseph's attitude during the Regency Crisis, a period of constitutional uncertainty and political instability provoked by a temporary breakdown in George III's health, further exacerbated his relations with George after the latter's recovery, for Joseph had attempted to intervene in the government of Hanover (Blanning 1989).

It would be misleading to suggest either that George's personal interest was restricted to issues relating to Hanover or that the British ministers were so united in their views that a clear contrast existed between them and George. Contemporaries were certain that George was less convinced of the possibilities of Anglo-French friendship in 1786-7 than Pitt, and more inclined to adopt a harsher line towards revolutionary France in 1790-2. The evidence for both these points is not completely satisfactory, though clearly George had views on important issues. However, it is also apparent that the ministers had contrasting opinions. If Pitt was enthusiastic about the prospect of the Eden Treaty of 1786 serving as the basis of a lasting Anglo-French friendship, Carmarthen, the Foreign Secretary, was very sceptical about French intentions. Similarly, Lord Chancellor Thurlow was allegedly more critical of revolutionary France than Pitt (Black 1994). It is too easy to think in terms of rigid divisions, such as Crown versus ministry, Hanover versus Britain. There were instead finer lines of agreement and difference, hesitations in policy and ambiguities in opinion, a political, especially governmental, world in which royal influence continued to be of great importance, though generally more dependent on and responsive to domestic and international circumstances and personal skills than on the constitutional position. Nevertheless, this survey of foreign policy suggests that it is possible to understand much through the perspective of royal interests and initiatives. There were, though, important omissions and it is worth noting that a chapter on the Crown and foreign policy has relatively little to say about colonial and commercial issues. If these are stressed, then the rôle of the monarch appears less central, at least prior to the struggle for American independence. The Hanoverian connection brought little benefit for British commerce and mercantile interests. Colonial and commercial issues, however, certainly played a major part in parliamentary discussion of foreign policy.

CHAPTER THREE

PARLIAMENT AND FOREIGN POLICY

> The old proverb says, 'Fare no better, or fare no worse, he rules the roost that carries the purse'. Money must be got and the House of Commons alone can give it.
>
> (Charles Delafaye, former Under-Secretary, 1761, W. U.)

Once the nature of foreign policy and of the political debates it gave rise to are appreciated, then it becomes increasingly difficult to present Britain as possessing obvious interests, interests that could be defended and financed by Parliament without question. It also becomes increasingly difficult to present a set of policies as the natural agenda for furthering national interests. Rather than defender of national interests against royal wishes, Parliament's rôle becomes that of definer of often shifting partisan views as national interests. Thus, the increased discussion of foreign policy in Parliament, especially from 1701, can be presented as reflecting a new set of political circumstances and perceptions that encouraged and necessitated such a process of definition. However, instead of the focus being one of the relationship between Crown and Parliament, the former finding it necessary to convince the latter, it is possible to present a more complex process in which, in addition, the need to use Parliament to influence an extra-parliamentary debate over national issues is stressed.

Parliament's rôle in the debate over foreign policy increased in the last years of William III's reign because of political circumstances, specifically the royal need to win support for a contentious foreign policy, but a necessary precondition was the establishment of Parliament on a permanent basis after the Glorious Revolution. Prior to that Parliament could play a major rôle in foreign policy, not least by the negative criteria of measures taken to prevent it meeting, but the rôle was clearly episodic and generally limited to one of seeking to thwart royal policy.

The rôle of Parliament in foreign affairs from William's reign was not simply a matter of constitutional function or of the interpretation of the latter in light of the operation of the political system. It was also the case that British politics were in a state of flux, with the identity, nature and aspirations of political groupings far from constant. Hitherto, general agreement is lacking on the validity of a description in terms of defined political parties, and the terms used by contemporaries were far from uniform. However, the very existence of a government tended to produce one rough distinction, that between those who supported the government of the day and those who opposed it, however divided these two groups might be. John Ellis, an Under-Secretary of State, wrote to an English diplomat from Whitehall in December 1701 concerning 'this contentious place that peaceable men can hardly live in, without being mauled by one side, or other ' (BL Add. 7074 f. 73).

Parliament could serve as both an institution in which political groups could define their identity and express their views, and one in which ministerial schemes could be expounded and presented as national interests to both domestic and international audiences. Thus Ellis wrote in 1701: 'I hope we shall take such resolutions, when we meet in Parliament, as the present great conjuncture requires, and as may inspire our confederates with the courage that is necessary for the preservation of us all.' Two years later, Sir Rowland Gwynne, a former Whig MP, hoped that 'the resolutions of the Parliament, may give some new life to the allies' (BL Add. 7074 f. 63; BL Eg. 929 f. 51). In 1743, Carteret wrote to James Cope, the Resident in Hamburg, and, like Ellis, later an MP, concerning the debate in the Commons over the size of the army,

> That great point was then likewise settled by so great a majority as has hardly been known . . . 120. As the whole of the measures His Majesty is now pursuing, for the supporting the House of Austria according to his engagements *totis viribus*, for securing the liberties of the Empire, and re-establishing the Balance of Power, was then professedly under deliberation, you will have a convincing proof in your hands . . . how void of foundation all those malicious reports have been, which have insinuated, that the conduct of our affairs in pursuit of those great views . . . would be disapproved in Parliament, and from which very sanguine hopes have been formed by our ill wishers abroad of seeing us fall into difficulties in our domestic affairs . . . must recommend to you to make the best use in your power of this very material intelligence.

Anthony Thompson, the embassy chaplain who was left in charge of British representation in France in 1740–4 at a time of deteriorating relations, observed in a letter to an Under-Secretary of State in London in 1742, 'the vigorous resolutions of the Parliament, I have some reason to think, will encourage the King of Sardinia to exert himself more and more'. In 1753, Newcastle was concerned to dismiss reports of disputes over Jacobite sympathies in the ministry: 'I know great industry has been used to represent in foreign courts that these affairs had created such difference and uneasiness here, as would entirely engage the King's whole attention, and prevent His Majesty from concerning himself at all with affairs abroad.' Writing to Sir Charles Hanbury-Williams, then on a mission to Vienna, he did so by outlining the size of the government's parliamentary majority over the affair. Ten years later, John, 4th Earl of Sandwich, Secretary of State for the Northern Department, cited the unanimity of both addresses as evidence 'to demonstrate the stability of His Majesty's government, and to refute any ill grounded surmises that may have been conceived from that spirit of licentiousness, which has but too much manifested itself in this country' (PRO SP 82/64 f. 220, 78/227 f. 465; Newport Library, 23 March 1753; PRO SP 91 /72 f. 194).

These were the ministerial aspirations that underlay the attempt to secure obvious parliamentary support for British foreign policy. It was not surprising that Secretaries of State sometimes attended Commons debates, William, Lord Harrington, watching that on foreign subsidies in April 1746. They realised that such debates could affect foreign views of Britain. The impact of parliamentary debates and votes on foreign governments and diplomats clearly varied. Majorities could be ascribed to corruption. In 1742, for example, the French envoy François de Bussy stressed the capricious and corrupt nature of the Commons (AE CP Ang. 414 f. 91, 107), while, in 1748, Frederick II argued that George was always able through corruption to obtain a parliamentary majority (*Polit. Corresp.* VI, 148). However, what was important was that British ministers and diplomats generally believed that parliamentary debates were of influence abroad. This was not invariably the case. 1n 1708, the 1st Duke of Manchester, Ambassador at Venice, wrote to the Secretary of State, the 3rd Earl of Sunderland: 'I am glad both Houses of Parliament have taken notice of sending Prince Eugene. If anything will prevail with the Court of Vienna, I should think that should; but I am far from thinking it will.' On the other hand, in May 1743, Carteret wrote from The Hague to his fellow Secretary of State, the Duke of Newcastle, concerning 'a happy change in this country since I was here in October last. First they have a good opinion of the stability of our affairs in England, which they had not when I was here last, but the great majority which His Majesty had in Parliament all the last session had an excellent effect here, and the more because it was not expected; this they have frankly owned to me' (Huntingdon CRO DD M 36/8; PRO SP

43/31, 19 May 1743). Conversely, parliamentary weakness could be fatal. The diplomat Sir James Gray, explaining the failure of George II's attempt to create a ministry around Carteret in February 1746, claimed that the new government had forgotten 'one little point, which was to secure a majority in both houses' and that when the Earl of Bath had told George that there would be no support from the Commons, 'Bounce went all the project into shivers, like the vessels in the Alchymist when they are on the brink of the Philosopher's Stone' (BL Add. 23822 ff.243–4).

To this extent the Glorious Revolution gave England, and then Britain, a parliamentary foreign policy, a policy that was often expounded and debated in Parliament for political reasons that were not related solely to Parliament's fiscal powers. Such a definition does not assume any particular standard of knowledge of foreign policy on the part of parliamentarians (on which see pp. 59–60). The development of a parliamentary foreign policy was a process associated with Anne rather than with William III. William has been criticised on this score: 'he made no attempt to secure their support for . . . the Partition Treaties. Convinced of the desirability of this policy and relying on the undoubted treaty-making power of the crown, he ignored signs of a change in opinion' (Hatton and Bromley, 1968: 131–2). Graham Gibbs saw the episode as arising from a failure to convince Parliament that British interests were being considered 'during the period 1698–1701 when William III was made to see very clearly the serious disadvantages attached to policies inspired and conducted without regard to Parliament, and complained, seemingly unaware of his own responsibility in the matter, that indifference and parochialism' were general in Britain (1962: 20).

This political crisis is commonly regarded as having resulted in a parliamentary foreign policy as defined above. Several points should perhaps be made, not least in explanation of William's attitude. First, any discussion of relations between Crown and Parliament carries with it the danger that the position of the latter is made to appear consistent, that, in short, a sound basis existed for defining a relationship with the monarchy and for settling the ambiguities produced by the contrary pressures of constitutional convention and political exigency. This was not, of course, the case, and there is hence need to avoid exaggerating the influence of the Glorious Revolution in inhibiting the Crown's control of foreign policy.

The political history of William's reign was markedly unstable in terms both of Parliament and of his British ministers. If this instability diminished the chances of mutual trust developing, they were hindered even more by William's knowledge and suspicions concerning the Jacobite links of many leading political figures. As the possibility existed of a return to the male line of the Stuarts on the death of William or Anne, these were commonly, though not solely, developed for insurance purposes. In addition, the conspiratorial activities of numerous British politicians in 1688, when his uncle had been toppled, and subsequently, both fostered William's distrust and made him aware of the danger of trusting British politicians, whether in or out of government.

A true Stuart, and an intensely private man whose experience with representative institutions in the United Provinces was far from happy, William sought the advice of trusted intimates and his own counsel. To turn to Parliament over the Partition Treaties was to risk surrendering his political initiative, at home and abroad, over a contentious subject that would invite attempts by foreign envoys to influence parliamentarians and where there were no agreed national interests, nor any process by which such agreement could be readily elicited. There was a danger that Charles II of Spain would be angered by having his succession debated publicly and that other rulers would be offended or, worse still, become unwilling to confide in William. Immediate post-war periods were classically difficult in diplomatic and domestic political terms in an age when total victory was rare and when peace thus entailed contentious compromises. The situation was made worse in 1697 by the issue of the Spanish succession which revealed the bankruptcy of the notion of obvious, let alone agreed, national interests as a guide to policy. It was far from clear how any particular allocation of the Spanish succession could be reconciled with domestic British views on the desirable nature of international relations. The prospect of a Bourbon claim to all or part of the succession focused the contentious issues of Louis XIV's intentions and France's relative strength.

William had to manoeuvre in a difficult diplomatic situation made more volatile by the recriminations following the peace, the prospects for realignment that it offered and the opportunities presented by the Spanish succession. To take Parliament into his trust would have involved acting in public and might have entailed limitations to his room for manoeuvre. William had to convince foreign rulers that he was securely in control when it was by no means clear that a majority of parliamentary opinion would follow the tergiversations of his partition diplomacy. Arriving in London in March 1698, the French envoy Tallard reported that month that William was less powerful than was believed in France. He claimed correctly that the parliamentary opposition wished to prevent William becoming 'le maître', and he stressed William's unpopularity. Tallard presented a two-party system, the Whigs opposed to royal authority and the Tories unhappy about the Revolution, a monarch who found it difficult to find ministers whom he could rely upon and 'un mouvement perpétuel' in the political sphere (AE CP Ang. 174 f. 106: 175 ff. 37–8; 181 f. 14).

Given the sensitivity of the negotiations and the need to keep them secret from Charles II of Spain, as well as William's difficulties with British politicians, it was not surprising that he chose to confide in only a few, principally Dutch, ministers. Tallard stressed likely parliamentary opposition to William's plans and, claiming that English politics altered completely during the session, argued that as a result any agreement would have to be made before it.

Any agreement would have led to parliamentary criticism, but, in the event, Louis XIV's acceptance of Charles II's will ensured that William had the worse of both worlds. The Second Partition Treaty was ignored by Louis, and William was criticised for failing to take adequate advice before concluding it, Ellis commenting in March 1701: 'It may be supposed that when the addresses of the Houses are made intelligible to the princes abroad, they will scarce think it safe to conclude Treaties without the concurrence of the Parliament, and sure nothing can be a secret there, who will enter into negociation with us?' (BL Add. 7074 f. 7). Tallard came to a similar conclusion, telling the Portuguese envoy that the unreliability of any alliance negotiated with England should make Portugal turn to France (AE CP Ang. 191 f. 71).

It was from the session of 1701 that Thomson dated a new more open relationship between Crown and Parliament in foreign policy (Hatton and Bromley: 135), but it is necessary not to exaggerate the change that took place. Parliament was given only general details, and policies and actions were concealed from it. In 1706, for example, Victor Amadeus II of Savoy-Piedmont was given, besides his agreed subsidy, 'fifty thousand pounds sterling, for which no provision was made by Parliament' (BL Add. 7059 f. 101). Possibly the significance of 1701 has been over-emphasised as a result of the war between England and France that began the following year. This increased the need for parliamentary support, both in order to raise funds and to impress foreign powers, and, in addition, provided a relatively popular basis for co-operation, ensuring that the government was ready to turn to Parliament for help. Tallard had warned Louis in 1698 that, whatever his current domestic and parliamentary difficulties, William would be able to raise all the money he asked on the day that war began with France. Five years later, Edward Harrison, himself later an MP, noted: 'things have gone smooth in the main this session I mean as to raising money and men and that is the sinews of the war' (AE CP Ang. 175 f. 83; BL Add. 22852 f. 75).

If royal disclosure of policy to Parliament increased from 1701 it was nevertheless the case that Parliament was not told the whole truth. There had been and continued to be the working out of a process of consultation and review, whereby the monarch retained the initiative over foreign and military policy. Parliament could debate and fund proposals and investigate outcomes, but it did not make policy, and non-government MPs continued to lack access to information. The somewhat uncertain use of royal authority under William III gave way to a more managed approach under Anne and George I.

In practical terms, the reasons for monarch and ministers to remain hesitant about discussing policy remained. There was no automatic parliamentary support for governmental policy and the particular grievances of specific constituencies could cause difficulties. In 1704, Robert Harley, then Secretary of State for the Northern Department, wrote to George Stepney, the envoy in Vienna, concerning a petition from Exeter and several other West Country boroughs complaining about Austrian tariffs on their woollen cloths: 'there is the greater reason to consider the petitions, and endeavour to obtain redress herein, because, besides the general interest of the nation, the members from the West have a great influence in the resolutions of the House of Commons, and especially in the granting of money' (BL Add. 7059 f. 45). West Country towns were heavily represented in Parliament, and many MPs gave priority to the interests of their own constituency and locality, a process encouraged by the frequency of general elections. Both in 1728–9 and in 1738–9, Walpole was to be pressed in Parliament by mercantile agitation over Spanish depredations on British commerce in the West Indies.

The possible impact of domestic politics on Britain's capacity to acquire and retain foreign allies was also stressed. Indeed, it was cited in 1743 by an anonymous pamphleteer who proposed that a malleable Parliament was crucial for this very reason. Defending William Pulteney's new-found ministerial position, he asked whether

'annual or even triennial Parliaments, annual or triennial Ministers would greatly affect our weight abroad? Ignorant as other nations are, of our constitution, they yet know, supplies are granted annually: And what state would enter in any expensive engagements with us, let it be ever so necessary or pressing, when they could not be certain of our continuance in it from year's end to year's end?'

The writer went on to contrast the national need to deal with European affairs and the Opposition's parliamentary pressure for domestic reforms and to argue that the former must be stressed (*A Letter to a Great Man in France*: 16, 20–1).

Similarly, the parliamentary difficulties that might spring from foreign negotiations were frequently an issue. When, in 1745, the Bavarian envoy Count Königsfeld told Lord Harrington, the Secretary of State for the Northern Department, then attempting at Hanover to negotiate an alliance, that Bavaria would not allow her troops to be used to invade the territories of her late allies, in other words France, Harrington wrote to Newcastle: 'I see no great prospect of our being able to conclude anything with that Prince, which will be justifiable in Parliament.' The following year, Robert Trevor, British envoy at The Hague, informed Thomas Robinson, his counterpart at Vienna, that the Dutch might require more money than 'a disgusted Parliament will at length at least give ear to'. In 1747, Newcastle ordered the Earl of Sandwich to press the Dutch to declare war on France: 'if they make a difficulty in declaring war, it is in vain to think of engaging this Parliament, and Nation, in taking the necessary measures for another campaign'. In 1761, Charles III of Spain proposed to delay declaring war on Britain until the beginning of the session in order to harm the British system of public finance, an idea that revealed the importance attached to Britain's financial strength (PRO SP 43/36, 29 July 1745; BL Add. 23822 f. 47, 32810, 29 Sept. 1747; AE CP Espagne 533 f. 432).

The difficulties that Parliament could create were amply demonstrated in 1713 when the Anglo-French commercial treaty was rejected. This exposed the unpopularity of the Tory government's attempt to improve relations with France and was a significant blow against the diplomatic realignment that the ministry sought after the dissolution of the Grand Alliance. The correspondence of government officials provides an interesting indication of their perception of an absence of control in the face of parliamentary decision. On 12 June 1713, Richard Warre, one of the Under-Secretaries, wrote to Lord Lexington, the envoy in Spain:

> The Commons in a Grand Committee have for 2 or 3 days sat late in hearing what some merchants had to say upon the Treaty of Commerce, wherein some have shown they little understand trade as to the nations interests, how able so ever they may be in their private concerns, which may have misguided them, and made them lay a greater stress on some parts of trade than the thing will bear. We shall quickly see, what effect their speeches will have had with the members; the majority hitherto has appeared considerably for making good the good articles; and as little has been said that was not known before, few perhaps will be moved to change their opinion.

Four days later, Warre's colleague, Erasmus Lewis, wrote to Lexington:

> There having been no open trade between Britain and France these five and twenty years I find the treaty now made is not comprehended by the generality of people. It is natural where people are ignorant they should be diffident and that is the state of our case. The adverse party is against it, because the present Ministry made it, but the misfortune is our friends are much divided in their sentiments. Your Excellency knows the cry of Popery or woollen manufactory will raise this nation into a ferment at any time.

On 19 June, Warre wrote to Lexington's secretary to inform him of the defeat of the bill:

> 'Several voted and some spoke against the Bill of whom it was little expected, which turned the scales. Many boroughs are strangely possessed with an opinion, of great prejudice threatened by this Treaty to our woollen manufactures abroad, which others think they can prove will be advanced by it. However some may think that by voting against it, they have the better secured their interest in the next Election (BL Add. 46546 ff. 71, 22, 74)

The events of 1713 might appear to prove that the Revolution had given Britain a parliamentary foreign policy, which William III had managed to delay but not prevent. A contrast with the situation in France was readily apparent. In June 1712, the month in which Oxford's peace policy had been decisively endorsed by both Houses of Parliament, Louis XIV's foreign minister Torcy had written to Henry St John, soon to be created Viscount Bolingbroke, to inform him that Louis was opposed to the idea that his grandson Philip V's renunciation of his rights in the French succession should be ratified by an Estates General.

Nearly eighty years later, Pitt the Younger cited parliamentary difficulties as a reason for backing down from confrontation with Russia in the Ochakov Crisis of 1791, although other factors, including division within the government, were also important.

> 'I saw with certainty, in a very few days after the subject was first discussed in Parliament, the prospect of obtaining a support sufficient to carry through this line with vigour and effect was absolutely desperate. We did indeed carry our question in the House of Commons by not an inconsiderable majority; and we shall I am persuaded, continue successful in resisting all the attempts of the opposition, as long as the negotiation is depending. But, from what I know of the sentiments of the greatest part of that majority, and of many of the warmest friends of the government, I am sure, that, if in persisting in the line of the status quo, we were to come to the point of actually calling for supplies to support the war; and were to state, as would then be indispensable, the precise ground on which it arose, we should either not

carry such a question, or carry it only by so weak a division as would amount to a defeat. (Matlock, Derbyshire CRO 239 M/O 759, Pitt to Ewart, 24 May 1791)

In 1748, Sandwich complained that his defence of Britain's position in the peace negotiations at the end of the War of the Austrian Succession had been compromised by the speeches in the Commons of 'those gentlemen who are for peace without ifs' (BL Add. 32811 f. 348). Nevertheless, caution is necessary before pressing the case for a parliamentary foreign policy too far. Significant defeats for governmental policy did not begin with the Revolution Settlement. Indeed it might be suggested (not that the subject readily lends itself to quantification) that governmental initiatives in the field of foreign policy were checked more frequently prior to 1689 than after it, and, in particular, than after the consolidation of a new political order with the Hanoverian succession, Whig ministries and the Septennial Act. Naturally, it could be argued that after 1689 a measure of confidence was produced by the fact that governmental composition and policy generally, in large part, reflected that of the parliamentary majority, or, as Ellis put it in 1701, 'the Governing part of our ruling Senate' (BL Add. 7074 f. 25). That was indeed the supposition made by Whig apologists for the Revolution Settlement and for the Old Corp Whig ascendancy during the reigns of Georges I and II.

However, several criticisms of this thesis must be advanced. First, the Revolution Settlement did not prevent monarchs from following a *secret du roi*, with or without the knowledge of some of their ministers. Furthermore, suspicions that Parliament was being kept in the dark could not be disproved, and reports to that effect circulated. It was alleged, for example, that not all the Treaty of Seville (1729) was laid before Parliament, although the secret clauses attributed to the treaty did not in fact exist. In January 1744, Richard Tucker wrote from Weymouth to his brother John, one of the MPs for the constituency: 'had the opportunity to entertain our friends at the Club, with your accounts of debates on the Hanover troops . . . I find the people at the helm go on in the old way of refusing the people the satisfaction of knowing what treaties are formed and this will give the world room to conclude that the worst which is suggested of their purport is true' (Bod. MS. Don. c. 106 f. 161).

Secondly, what successive ministries told Parliament in the field of foreign policy was limited and did not appreciably increase after 1714. In January 1744, the opposition Whig George Grenville told the Commons, then meeting as a Committee of Supply to debate continuing forces in Flanders, that:

> As it is not now the fashion to let the Parliament know anything of our public measures: as our measures, or at least the motives for them, are always of late too great a secret to be communicated to such a numerous body of men, I protest I know nothing of them; nor can I, from any public appearances, comprehend the meaning of them: no man can, who has not an intimate correspondence with some of our ministers of the closet.

In the winter of 1782–3, the government refused to divulge the details of the preliminary peace articles, the *Morning Herald* noting on 23 January: 'To the utter astonishment of the peace-proclaiming politicians, who yesterday thronged the gallery of the House of Commons not a syllable fell from the lips of his Majesty's ministers.'

Thirdly, the re-evaluation of Tory popularity after 1714 and of the continued vitality of the Tory Party, which has been such a marked feature of the scholarship of the last two decades, calls into question the power that Whig majorities in Parliament could have over the king. Instead, both monarch and Whig ministries can be seen as somewhat vulnerable, neither enjoying complete freedom of public manoeuvre in face of the ever-shifting and complex mix of patronage and acceptable policies that the management of Parliament and the political nation entailed.

To a certain extent, this became a greater problem after the 1700s. War with France had been, in its early stages, a widely popular policy, although significant differences existed from the outset, both within Britain and between her and her allies, concerning war objectives and diplomatic and military strategy. The Austrian envoy for example had failed in 1702 to get an English fleet sent to Naples. The following year, Paul Methuen, the English envoy in Lisbon, complained about Leopold I: 'I see no other use that he makes of us, than as plaisters to cover all his defects and soares, to the disappointment of those designs that are for our interest and advantage.' After the Austro-Savoyard victory at Turin in 1706, Stepney wrote to Harley: 'it is to be feared the victory near Tunn may elevate the spirit of our Austrian Ministry; and we shall have much ado to keep either of these allies within bounds, who are equally incapable of bearing prosperity with moderation'. Harley criticised Austria shortly afterwards: 'unless that Court will grow more reasonable towards their allies, or in truth consult really their own interest, it is vain to labour to help those who will undoe themselves' (Maidstone, Kent Archives Office, U1590 053/10, 029/5; BL Add. 7059 ff. 199, 121).

Marlborough's successes helped to stem war-weariness, but there was no doubt of the strength of the latter by the end of the decade. The Tory determination to end the war by, if necessary, abandoning Britain's allies appears to have been very popular, and Whig newspapers, such as the *Protestant Post-Boy*, which on 2 February 1712 referred to the 'British Nation, who have been always jealous of the growing power of France', were increasingly out of touch with current views and problems. Indeed, when peace with France was proclaimed in London in May 1713, 'the joy was suitable to so great a blessing, expressed universally in the City and suburbs, by such marks as might best declare it. The mob went from street to street, and broke the windows where the houses were not illuminated, with so little distinction, as not to spare some of eminence and distinction, who it is well known, did not omit lights, for want of affection to the Peace' (BL Add. 46546 f. 62).

However, the peace was not popular with the Whigs, although they were fortunate that the Tories were to bear the responsibility for a settlement that they also knew to be necessary. War-weariness in the late 1700s destroyed the relative degree of unity concerning the desirability of fighting France that existed in the political nation; and, thereafter, such a degree was not to be revived until the days of the 'Bells of Victory' in 1759, the celebrations of the highpoint of victories over France in the Seven Years' War. In the meantime, foreign policy was generally contentious and commonly devoid of wide-spread popularity. A case could be made for war with Spain in 1718 or confrontation with Russia in 1720 and Austria in 1725, but they were not, particularly the latter two, very popular. War with Spain in 1739 was clearly entered into against the wishes of Walpole, and the charge of mismanagement was advanced with vigour. Carteret's motives in the mid 1740s were widely questioned.

Thus, the very course of foreign policy made political management more of a problem and increased the chances of parliamentary difficulties and the risks of ministerial division. Pelham wrote in February 1745 to Philip, 4th Earl of Chesterfield, then on a mission to Britain's Dutch allies, who were concerned about French advances in the Austrian Netherlands: 'whatever assistance we give to you in Holland creates for us here greater difficulties in carrying on the king's business at home. Your friends at The Hague call for ever more Hanoverians into Flanders . . . and your friends here call for sending away those that are still there' (BL microfilm 645, 13). Contentious policies led monarchs to keep some ministers in the dark or to ignore their opinion, helping to precipitate the Whig ministerial splits of 1717 and 1743–4, and led ministries to refuse parliamentary requests for papers. This did not prevent the reiterations of the constitutional conventions of co-operation, conventions that could be maintained because government majorities could defeat opposition requests for papers, while royal discretion and secrecy helped, in general, to reduce the political significance of differences between monarch and ministers. Thus on 29 August 1792 the Whig *Morning Chronicle* was able to contrast *ancien régime* French diplomacy with its British counterpart and its Revolutionary successor:

> Nothing is so manifest as that it is the interest of the English nation to prevent the re-establishment of the old tyranny in France; of that tyranny which sustained itself at home, by embroiling the nation with its neighbours, and which being in its wars subjected to no control, watched by no Parliament, thwarted by no declaration of the public voice, was able to carry on its operations with a secrecy which no free Government could enjoy, and which was most favourable to a sudden attack, and to every species of miscreant intrigue.

Reality was otherwise. Secret diplomacy was practised by British monarchs and ministers; Parliament could be ignored, particularly if peace prevailed and controversial subsidy treaties or commercial agreements were not being considered. Many speeches from the throne were, as Joseph Yorke, a government supporter and diplomat, described that of 1753, 'very guarded . . . the dexterity that is employed to say nothing' (BL Add. 35356 ff. 115, 118). A memorandum on peace treaties in the papers of Bute's supporter Sir Gilbert Elliot and presumably dating from 1763 claimed:

> The King's prerogative undoubtedly impowers him to conclude peace without laying the terms before Parliament. He may however ask their advice. Parliament unasked may interpose their advice. The question therefore merely upon usage. Anciently articles few and simple, not unusual to ask advice. In modern terms more complicated and branched into more particulars, scarce possible certainly not expedient to ask advice. Accordingly for 150 years hardly an instance Treaty of Utrecht excepted. (NLS MS 11036 f. 26)

In addition, there was the problem addressed by George Gordon in 1741 when he asked: 'how shall Gentlemen be judges of the conduct of our ministers, with regard to foreign affairs, unless they understand, as far as possible for one in a private station, the interests and views of foreign nations, and attend to every public transaction that happens in Europe?' (*Annals of Europe* II, iii). Five years later, James Oswald MP mocked a parliamentary speech that he attributed to the foolish 'high, vulgar, native English expectation of beating France by every confederacy whereof England is a part' (*Caldwell Papers* I, ii, 81).

If a parliamentary foreign policy, in the sense of a policy over which

Parliament, even if it had no executive functions, was nevertheless fully consulted, did not pertain, it might be asked whether the term is not applicable with regard to a policy that had to take note of parliamentary views and Parliament's constitutional and political rôle. In this case, the answer is clearly yes, in so far as any monarch and ministry had to respond to the political and constitutional circumstance of their state. However, the extent to which policy was affected as a consequence is open to question. In 1748, Newcastle attributed the filling of the crucial Secretaryship of State for the Northern Department by Bedford rather than Sandwich to parliamentary pressure:

> . . . the pacific party in the House of Commons, (which, by the by, as now *constituted*, is the whole House of Commons,) . . . were so alarmed at the resignation of the pacific Lord Chesterfied; and had such a dread of another warlike Secretary; that they expressed such apprehensions, and uneasiness . . . that very ugly consequences were flung out; and I really think, it was not certain, but some parliamentary attempt might have been stirred up to embarrass affairs. . . . You cannot imagine, how pacific this House of Commons is, to a degree, that, except the Solicitor General, there is hardly a man, that does not almost insinuate, more, or less, the necessity of making any peace. (BL Add. 32811 ff. 213-15)

There is no doubt that British monarchs and ministers were aware that Parliament's existence and activities were taken note of abroad. In December 1770, when, at a time of Anglo-Bourbon crisis over the Falkland Islands, George, 4th Duke of Manchester criticised the state of the British naval forces at Gibraltar, Earl Gower called for the clearing of the Lords on the grounds that the spectators might include foreign agents. In 1774, David, Viscount Stormont, Britain's ambassador in Paris, reported that D'Aiguillon, the French foreign minister, had

> spoke of what Lord North had said in Parliament, with regard to Falkland's Island, with expressions of great pleasure and satisfaction, and added that he had that morning read the account to Monsieur d'Aranda, who was much pleased, and took a particular note of it. 'Tis wonderful, added the Duke, what a stress the Spaniards laid upon the wretched Island, which is not of the smallest value. (PRO SP 78/291 f. 77)

Five years later, shortly before he became a Secretary of State, Stormont

> . . . condemned loudly the frequent indiscretions which noble lords were guilty of in mentioning matters of state in that House. While he was in a public character at Paris, he had almost daily reason to experience it . . . he believed that newspaper accounts, and other publications, in pamphlets etc. of their lordships' debates, containing angry and indiscreet expressions,

either respecting the French court or the French king, had worse effects than anything else whatever in bringing matters to their present state. He was very sorry to hear Spain brought into the present debate; the conduct of crowned heads, and the spirit and ability of great nations, were subjects of a very delicate nature, and ought to be mentioned with great caution. (Cobbett 1806-20: XX, 45–5)

In 1786, William Eden reported to William Pitt that he had been shown by a French official 'a long French despatch regularly numbered as the continuation of a weekly journal of all the proceedings of our Parliament: and it had the appearance of being executed with some ability and accuracy' (CUL Add. 6958 no. 111).

However, this state of affairs was scarcely the consequence of the Revolution. In so far as Parliament became an annual feature, the Revolution was clearly not without consequence, but Britain prior to the Revolution had a reputation abroad for political and ministerial instability that owed something to the existence of Parliament but was not dependent on Parliament's constitutional position. Indeed, it would be possible to argue that the problems of post-Revolution parliamentary management helped to produce a measure of political stability eventually by encouraging monarchs to turn to ministers who could manage, and by leading the latter to pass the Septennial Act and thus decrease the volatility of parliamentary politics. In February 1681, the Austrian minister Count Königsegg told the English envoy Middleton that the prorogation of Parliament by Charles II would probably oblige the king to 'close with France', as Charles would find no other way to support himself. A peevish Middleton replied that Charles's revenues were better than those of Leopold and that the king was able both to subsist honourably and to make his friendship very advantageous to his allies (PRO SP 80/16 f. 269). This was bluster, though the willingness to compare resources is worth noting. Charles was obliged to turn to Louis for subsidies. Without parliamentary financial support, it was impossible for him to follow an active foreign policy in a period of tense international relations. This was the case both before and after the Revolution Settlement. The latter can be seen as redefining the terms of the relationship, rather than as creating a new political world.

It is possible, when considering foreign policy for the century after the Revolution, to repeat an analysis of the century prior to it, namely to show that, in some circumstances and particular contingencies, Parliament was of considerable influence, if only through its existence, but that on other occasions this was not the case. If, for example, the history of the breach between Britain and Russia in the late 1710s and their subsequent reconciliation in the early 1730s can be written without any significant reference to Parliament, the same is not the case with regard to the failure to cement an alliance after the Seven Years' War or the collapse of the Pitt ministry's confrontation with Russia in 1791. In 1763, the Grenville ministry was concerned about the domestic, as well as the diplomatic, consequences of Russian demands, especially in terms of possible expenditure at a time when national indebtedness was a subject of political concern. In 1791, falling ministerial majorities in the face of Opposition attacks in the Commons upon foreign policy sapped the determination of the ministry.

In general, Parliament featured as a factor, active or passive, more in commercial issues and Anglo-Bourbon relations than in those with the powers of central, eastern and northern Europe. Nevertheless, a London item, reprinted in the *Newcastle Journal* of 6 February 1773, suggested that the difficulties relations with the Bourbons could present should not be exaggerated.

> The celebrated Dr. North [the First Lord of the Treasury, Lord North] . . . has lately constructed an instrument, called *The Modern Political Perspective*. It is contrived that no less than 500 persons [the House of Commons] can look through it at once, if they please. By turning one end of it, dangers of all kinds will be magnified to the greatest degree. For example, the fears of a war with France and Spain will be so magnified, that the parliament will immediately vote large sums of money for raising troops and equipping of ships. By turning the other end, dangers the most imminent will appear at a vast distance.

Impressed by the fuss that parliamentarians could create, foreign diplomats arguably exaggerated its influence. They were, of course, products of a political culture that, while often accepting the existence of representative institutions, believed that they should not debate foreign policy and that it was an essential prerogative of royal authority.

It is difficult to evaluate the quality of the debates. Conventions of behaviour and speech, standards of argument and proof were different from those of today. In addition, the nature of the surviving evidence is scanty. Nevertheless, one of the more impressive features of the debates was the knowledge of international relations displayed by some parliamentarians. Expert opinion could be presented to Parliament. Both chambers contained several diplomats or former diplomats, and some of them contributed their knowledge to the debates. Not all who had been diplomats revealed the same degree of knowledge or made an equal contribution. In the Lords in the 1730s, Lord Harrington, the Northern Secretary and an experienced former diplomat, did not take a rôle comparable to that of Lord Carteret, an ex-diplomat and ex-

Secretary, or of his colleague as Secretary of State, the Duke of Newcastle, who lacked any diplomatic experience. In the same period, Horatio Walpole played a major rôle in the Commons, unlike another former envoy at The Hague, William Finch. Many parliamentarians, especially members of the House of Lords, were quite well informed and many had travelled on the Continent or served there in war.

Much parliamentary discussion, especially on the part of opposition speakers, was simplistic and alarmist, but rhetoric is not necessarily incompatible with an intelligent assessment of the situation. The public discussion of policy, in Parliament as much as in the press, was intended to illuminate diplomatic options in terms that could be readily understood, and to provide ammunition for use in political debate. To suggest that parliamentary discussion of foreign policy was designed to serve a purely partisan political purpose does not imply that it was without standards or quality. Parliamentarians often focused on the cost of policy, in terms of both subsidy treaties and the size of the army, but this was because expenditure required parliamentary backing and provided a readily comprehensible issue.

The language employed by speakers – terms such as 'natural interests' and 'the balance of power' – might appear imprecise, but it was also the language used by ministers and diplomats. The conceptualisation of international relations and thus foreign policy created considerable problems, given the often apparently arbitrary and inconsistent nature in which rulers managed their affairs. The importance of individuals in the conduct of policy does, however, make the moralistic tone of much public debate appear less out of place.

A stress on the rôle of particular circumstances leads away from the conclusion that there was any simple relationship between parliamentary consideration of policy and a diplomacy that was largely outside parliamentary control and knowledge. It similarly precludes any simple answer to the question of why ministries, enjoying substantial parliamentary majorities, nevertheless should be concerned about the parliamentary implications of foreign policy and the debates themselves. Foreign policy certainly had a higher profile in the reporting of debates than the mass of local matters that came before Parliament. The particular issue in dispute, the natural desire of politicians to avoid trouble, the need to exercise persuasive powers, and the fiscal implications of policy, real and perceived, can all be stressed when considering the sensitivity of parliamentary discussion, but any detailed study would reveal variations and the play of contingency.

This provides a significant clue about the nature and consequences of the Revolution Settlement. Historians have argued that the latter was not simply a matter of the events and resolutions of 1688–9, but also of developments over the following years and, in particular, the political and fiscal impact of William III's war with France. This process is commonly regarded as finishing in 1701, the date of the Act of Settlement and of a shift towards the parliamentary disclosure of foreign policy. What is possibly not sufficiently stressed is that the resulting political and constitutional conventions and arrangements, summarised in terms such as the Revolution Settlement and parliamentary foreign policy, were far from fixed and were indeed very varied in their impact. Combined with an appreciation of the absence of consensus, that casts doubt on both contemporary and modern claims of eighteenth-century British national interests, this offers a vision of flexibility and debate that enables us to appreciate that issues were indeed at stake in the field of foreign policy, that political skills and management could be of great importance and that detailed research is required if the effects of Parliament's existence and prerogatives, and of parliamentary views and politics are to be appreciated. It is clear that more work is required if the nature and consequences of the Revolution Settlement are to be charted in the field of foreign policy.

CHAPTER FOUR

DIPLOMATS, SECRETARIES OF STATE AND OTHER MINISTERS

BRITISH DIPLOMATS

The art of negotiation was not in this period a taught skill. Though the foundation of the Regius Chairs of History at Cambridge and Oxford in 1724 was designed to facilitate the training of diplomats, the scheme had little practical effect. The principal school of leading diplomats continued to be the court in London, that of their less socially distinguished colleagues the households of other diplomats. A diplomat was the personal representative of the sovereign and paid from the Civil List, as those affected by George II's parsimony were all too aware, and, in a prestige-conscious age, the ability of a man to discharge an office was believed to reflect in part his social rank. Honour was a crucial concept in diplomatic representation and just as the rank of the official appointed, whether ambassador, envoy extraordinary, minister resident, secretary or a less common designation, was an expression of respect and trust, not least because representation was usually reciprocated at the same rank, so also was the social rank of the individual (Horn 1961). When George II sent an ambassador to Turin 1732, the crucial raising in status reflected a strong wish to improve and cement relations, as did the fact that the ambassador was an earl, William, 3rd Earl of Essex. Conversely the poor state of Anglo-Prussian relations in 1731–56 and of their Anglo-French counterpart in 1740–4 was reflected in the fact that George was represented at Berlin only by a Secretary from July 1730 to August 1740, in 1745 and 1747, and by no one from May 1747 until the following April, again from November 1748 until July 1750, and from March 1751 until May 1756, and at Paris by the former ambassador's chaplain from October 1740 until the French declaration of war in March 1744 (Horn 1932).

The most prestigious postings for British diplomats were Paris, Madrid, The Hague and, in the eighteenth century, Vienna. With the addition of Rome, this list was a common European one, and at these courts the diplomatic world constituted an exclusive aristocratic circle. It would be wrong to suggest that simply because most aristocratic diplomats had had no previous experience they were therefore mediocre. Several of the most impressive diplomats were aristocrats, such as James, 1st Earl Waldegrave (Vienna 1728–30, Paris 1730–40), Philip, 4th Earl of Chesterfield (The Hague 1728–32, 1745), William, 4th Earl of Rochford (Turin 1749–55, Madrid 1763-6, Paris 1766–8) and David, Viscount Stormont (Dresden 1756–63, Vienna 1763–72, Paris 1772–8). It was no accident, however, that these men, of whom all bar Waldegrave became Secretaries of State, were all long-serving. Joseph Yorke (Paris 1749–51, The Hague 1751–80) was the son of Earl Hardwicke and was promoted to the peerage.

If the survey is confined to aristocratic diplomats who served for fewer than three years, then it is harder to find diplomats of distinction, and yet the vast majority of such diplomats sought only short missions. Aside from becoming Secretary of State, there were few promotion prospects that could not be better obtained by remaining in Britain, and many diplomats complained bitterly that absence from London hindered their careers and the pursuit of other interests. Although a few embassies left plenty of time for leisure, as Sir Horace Mann at Florence (1738–86) and Sir William Hamilton at Naples (1764–1800) testified, diplomats could be criticised severely if they failed to write sufficiently often or comprehensively, or if they left their posts. Essex found London unsympathetic to his desire to attend the carnival at Venice, and many envoys complained about not being allowed to return to London when they wished.

Far from being a sinecure, diplomacy was not well paid. Most diplomats complained about expenses and their bills for extraordinaries were generally paid considerably in arrears. In 1697, the credit of John Robinson (Stockholm) came near to collapsing. In 1704, Stepney pressed for his recall from Vienna on the grounds of cost, estimating that he had personally lost £2260 (BL Eg. 929 ff. 63–4) Being out of pocket was also a problem for James Scott, appointed to Dresden in 1711, while Hugh Elliot, who was dependent on his pay, got into debt at Munich in 1775 and took leave of absence. Thomas Walpole claimed in 1784 that 'whilst the pay of our foreign ministers is so very inadequate to their situation, none but persons necessitous adventurous or of uncommon command of temper will enter into that road to fortune' (Bury St Edmunds CRO, Grafton 423/829). Cost was a particular problem at the more expensive and prestigious courts where diplomats were expected to maintain a costly state, and was an additional reason to appoint wealthy men. The Duke of Shrewsbury aroused complaints in Paris in 1713 by going to bed too soon and not having a ball on Queen Anne's birthday. In 1750, Pelham reckoned the cost of a new ambassador in Paris at £7000. Two years later, Hanbury-Williams wrote of the Habsburgs: 'there is no treating with that House unless much more able ministers are employed, there must be a Duke with a Blue Ribbon at Vienna' (BL Add. 51393 f. 110). It hardly needs stating, but the pool of available talent was drastically reduced by contemporary attitudes to women: none were appointed.

Below aristocratic rank there were a number of obviously talented diplomats including Sir George Downing (The Hague 1657–65, 1671–2), Sir William Temple (Münster 1665, Brussels 1666, The Hague 1667–70, 1674–9), George Stepney (Berlin 1692, Vienna 1693, 1701–6, The Hague 1706–7), George Whitworth (Vienna 1703–4, St Petersburg 1704–12, The Hague 1717–21, Berlin 1719–22, Cambrai 1722–5), Thomas Robinson (Paris 1723–30, Vienna 1730–48, Aix-la-Chapelle 1748), Benjamin Keene (Madrid 1727–39, 1749–57, Lisbon 1746–9), Robert Keith (Vienna 1748–57, St Petersburg 1758–62), his son Robert Murray Keith (Dresden 1769–71, Copenhagen 1771–2, Vienna 1772–92), Andrew Mitchell (Brussels 1752–5, Berlin 1756–71) and James Harris (Madrid 1768–71, Berlin 1772–6, St Petersburg 1778–83, The Hague 1784–8). Apart from a disproportionate number of Scots, benefiting from the career opportunities presented by the Union of 1707, it is difficult to see any pattern in those who followed diplomacy as a career. Many had acquired experience through posts on the staffs of envoys, such as Robert Keith with the Earl of Sandwich and Robert Trevor with Horatio Walpole, though there are examples of non-aristocratic envoys appointed to responsible posts without any such experience. Language was less of a problem than might have been expected as French increasingly became the diplomatic *lingua franca*. However, there were courts where this was not the case, or at least not until the mid eighteenth century, and German, Italian and Spanish were important diplomatic languages. It is apparent that many British diplomats were insufficiently familiar with languages other than French, though Robinson knew Swedish. German was seen as an important qualification in Copenhagen in 1764.

The choice of envoys was not always an easy one. In 1748, Newcastle complained that he needed 'some person of figure and consequence to The Hague. It is very difficult to find a proper one . . . I really know no one' (BL Add. 32811 f. 370). Various factors had to be considered. Royal approval was generally necessary and envoys who fell foul of the monarch usually lost their posts. In 1748, George II was furious with Legge's conduct in Berlin, Newcastle noting that the king 'abuses us all, for sending a man, purely because he can make a speech in the House of Commons' (NeC 694) . Many diplomats were MPs. Newcastle was also concerned that year about his brother, Henry Pelham's stress on economy:

> . . . The constant mention of the necessity of Civil List economy . . . The indifference, or rather the objection to the sending any man of rank, and experience, to The Hague, where all business that relates to foreign measures must be transacted . . . what an appearance will it have . . . how will Europe be astonished, and our old fiends alarmed, when they shall see, only Resident Keith at Vienna, and Resident Dayrolle at The Hague, and the Duke of Richmond ambassador in France, and my Lord Chancellor's son Secretary to the Embassy. (BL Add. 35410 ff. 95,98)

Connections were crucial in appointments, Lord Beauchamp complaining in 1763: 'I have just heard that Mr. Bunbury is appointed Secretary to the Embassy at Paris – what a potent counsellor! What a wise and experienced negotiator! In one word he is Mr. Fox's brother in law, and that is at present sufficient to gild a character with all the lustre it can wish' (BL Add. 34412 f. 56).

Diplomatic skill is difficult to assess, but so also is the extent to which diplomats influenced the policies they were supposed to pursue. In 1785, Sir James Harris delivered an oft-quoted opinion on the poor quality of his instructions (Horn 1961: 3). Charles, Earl of Northampton wrote from Venice in 1762: 'it is astonishing that our ministry dont take more notice of their ministers abroad, they seem to think no more of us as soon as we have left the kingdom' (BL Stowe 257 f. 66). Other envoys who felt neglected and complained, included John, Viscount Mountstuart in Turin in 1782 and Sir Robert Murray Keith in Vienna in the 1780s.

It was indeed the case that many diplomats complained about the absence or the content of their instructions. It is equally reasonable to point out that complaints were reciprocated. In 1764, Sandwich, then a Secretary of State, deplored a memorandum by the Earl of Hertford, envoy in Paris, adding, 'if any more are to be presented to that court on matters of importance it seems absolutely necessary to send them from England' (BL Stowe 259 f. 5). The following year, Sir George Macartney seriously exceeded his instructions in commercial negotiations with Russia.

In addition the understaffed Secretaries of State naturally

concentrated on pressing problems and left other diplomats to their own concerns. This was especially the case during years of domestic political instability and during periods when a non-interventionist diplomacy was stressed. In the former case, diplomatic correspondence from London often ceased altogether, bar acknowledgements of dispatches, and envoys in the midst of important negotiations were left without instructions. The fall of Carteret in 1744, for example, had a disturbing effect. When Britain was essentially adopting a reactive attitude in much of her continental diplomacy, then also there were few political topics on which to send instructions, though in some embassies, such as Lisbon, Madrid, Constantinople and St Petersburg, commercial matters were frequently raised.

Even when instructions were frequent, fast and comprehensive, as was generally the case at Paris and The Hague, there was considerable room for manoeuvre on the part of individual diplomats, though in 1774 Benjamin Langlois, the Secretary of Embassy at Vienna, pointed out to his Parisian counterpart that 'Paris and London are too near for any step not to be known' (Northumberland CRO ZBU B 3/25). Room for manoeuvre increased after 1755 when the monarch ceased to go abroad and was therefore no longer accompanied by a Secretary of State on journeys on which envoys could be asked to travel to Hanover to report and receive instructions in person, as Thomas Robinson was in 1732.

Envoys developed their own contacts and could commit themselves, and therefore their sovereign, to a particular faction or interest in the court to which they were accredited, as Hanbury-Williams did at St Petersburg in 1757, with his links to the young court of the heir, the future Peter III, and his wife Catherine. If such commitment was judged excessive the envoy could be discredited with other interests and, ultimately, his recall could be sought. The British government sought that of the Frenchman Chavigny in the 1730s and of the Prussian Michel in 1762 because of their strong links with opposition elements. Frederick II pressed for the recall of Hanbury-Williams from Berlin, because the diplomat made little attempt to conceal his animosity.

The shifting nature of court factions made the diplomatic task a difficult one, and, when mistakes and misunderstandings arose, the potential damage was made worse by the difficulty of securing supplementary lines of communication that could provide a check on diplomats. Distance and protocol kept most sovereigns from personal diplomacy. However, senior figures could be sent to supplement other diplomats, usually in Paris and The Hague, though James Stanhope went to Vienna in 1714 and in 1729 William Stanhope, who had formerly served as envoy in Spain, was sent to negotiate the Treaty of

Seville to the disappointment of the current envoy, Benjamin Keene, who had been reprimanded in late 1727 for giving a false impression of what was acceptable to London.

The extent to which diplomats influenced policy varied. A stress on impersonal structural forces or factors necessarily limits any discussion of this rôle while, conversely, attempts to piece together the process of negotiations leads to an awareness that the rôle of individual diplomats could be very important. Initiatives were not necessarily successful, Newcastle, writing of Hanbury-Williams in 1750: 'He had a mind to do something. He was absolutely tied up, as to subsidies. Therefore, he would make himself as agreeable, as he could, in other respects . . . we shall not follow any *flights* of Sir Charles Hanbury Williams' (BL Add. 35411 ff. 127–8). However, the way in which contemporary debate over the merits of foreign policy fastened on the motives and qualities of individual diplomats, such as Horatio Walpole at The Hague (1734–5), Benjamin Keene at Madrid (1738–9) or Willam Eden at Paris (1786), is striking. The activities of diplomats could be crucial both in crises, as those of Harris were at The Hague in 1787 in helping to direct British policy into an actively pro-Orangist path, and in pressing forward negotiations for alliances or arrangements arising from alliances, as were those of Joseph Ewart in the case of Anglo-Prussian relations in 1790–1. Diplomats could also play a major rôle when relations were poor in averting crises or lessening tension, as did Waldegrave at Paris in the 1730s. They were less important when relations were cool but with no major issue at stake, as with Austria in the 1780s. In these circumstances, envoys frequently sought their recall or leave, or concentrated on minor points, especially commercial disputes or the recreational possibilities of the post. Though, as the Earl of Hardwicke pointed out in 1782, diplomats were 'servants of the *state* at large, rather than of *any particular ministry*' (WW Rl-2124), they were clearly most important when they enjoyed close links with the Secretaries of State or other leading ministers, or when the Secretaries were weak. Stair's position in Paris (1715–20) was enhanced by the relative insignificance as Secretaries of State of Methuen (1716–17), Addison (1717–18) and Craggs (1718–21)

British diplomats did not enjoy the high reputation of their French counterparts and the diligence and competence of individuals were criticised. However, given the difficulties of the job and the resources available, it would be inappropriate to adopt too critical a note. Learning on the job could have unfortunate consequences, but it was a feature of the semi-professionalised nature of much British administration in the period. Hugh Elliot complained in 1776:

The Germans, Russians and French in general fix secretaries of legation at the most considerable posts, whose duty it is to give a new minister every information he requires, and this constant residence and experience in business enables them to do much more effectually than the most voluminous collection in writing. It is also common for foreigners to have resided some time without character at a post they are destined to fill.

In England the original establishment for foreign missions does not seem to have been founded with so much caution as on the continent. An English minister often arrives at his station with no better assistance than what a private secretary of his predecessors can give him, that is copying papers, cyphering etc. Information from home may be worded with the greatest clearness. It can no more convey an adequate idea of the situation of a court and of its principal inhabitants, than a map can of the high and low grounds of a country. Ten days conversation upon the spot with his predecessor would forward a newcomer at least a twelve month in his knowledge of men and things and enable him to take up the thread of intelligence where it had been left. (BL Add. 34413 ff. 62–3)

Possibly there was a certain decline in the quality of diplomats in the post-1760 period. During the period 1689–1760 interventionist policies and foreign rulers had ensured that ministers and diplomats were generally forced to take a close interest in foreign policy and in the views of other powers. Alliances helped in the development of personal links and of habits of co-operation, especially with the Dutch. The close interest of the monarchs in foreign policy led some diplomats to win favour. After 1763, most diplomats, however competent, were less close to the centre of the political storm and some envoys, such as George Pitt, absent from Turin from April 1764 until his mission was revoked in September 1768, or Sir William Lynch, similarly absent from Turin from October 1776 until September 1779, were allowed to neglect their posts. The energy of the diplomats appointed to Turin reflected the somewhat narrower range of British diplomacy. Britain played less of a rôle in Mediterranean affairs in the second half of the century. William, 2nd Earl of Shelburne, a former Secretary of State, complained in the Lords in 1779 that 'the business of the northern courts had been so ill-conducted by the ignorant persons to whom it had been entrusted of late years, that we had not a friend among them' (Cobbett 1806-20: xx, 667). However, a diplomatic corps that could boast Goodricke, Harris, Keith, Rochford, Stormont and Yorke was not without men of activity and talent.

This was important, because the 'English plan' of conducting diplomacy was for negotiations to be handled by Britain's envoys, rather than by foreign diplomats in London. This helped to lessen the dangers of foreign envoys intriguing with British opposition politicians, and it allowed the Secretaries of State to retain more control over negotiations. There were naturally examples of crucial discussions being handled by foreign diplomats or ministers in London or wherever the monarch might be when he was abroad, for example Tallard's negotiations with William III over the partition of the Spanish empire, in both London and the United Provinces, Dubois's mission to London in 1718, or Anglo-Wittelsbach negotiations at Hanover in 1729. However, although it is not possible to quantify the matter, it seems to be the case that after William's death in 1702 relatively more diplomatic negotiations were handled by British diplomats abroad, rather than being conducted with their foreign counterparts in London. This probably owed much to the determination of Charles II, James II and William III to keep the detailed conduct of diplomatic transactions, as well as the general framework of policy, under their personal control; to the importance of negotiating directly with monarchs whose relations with their ministers were known or suspected to be less than close; and to the weakness of the English diplomatic corps. There had been no corps prior to 1660 and its development in the following decades was a halting one, affected by political uncertainties and abrupt changes (Lachs 1965). There was certainly nothing comparable to the size and self-confidence of Louis XIV's diplomatic corps, but French diplomats benefited from the strength and reputation of their monarch and his willingness and ability to spend heavily in order to bolster his position.

Foreign diplomats in London were often accused of meddling in British politics, an understandable choice as these politics were so important to the conduct of British foreign policy. Thus, in 1710, Gallas, the Austrian envoy, and his Dutch and Hanoverian counterparts tried unsuccessfully to persuade Anne to retain her Whig ministers and the Austrian alliance. The French diplomat Iberville reported in 1716 that, having been close to the Tories, he could not satisfy the Whig ministry. The fall of Chesterfield in 1748 led to 'very virulent and impertinent letters' by the Dutch envoy Hop, who was close to him, while, the following year, Yorke reported from Paris his belief that the foreign minister Puysieulx was affected by 'the accounts he receives from the person they employ at London, who . . . does not content himself with only transmitting a plain narrative of matters of fact, but embellishes his dispatches with flying stories picked up in the town' (BL Add. 32811 f. 278, 35355 f. 68). In 1763, Sandwich blamed delays in the conclusion of an Anglo-Russian alliance on 'the misrepresentations of Count Woronzow, who is extremely ill-intentioned to the present administration, and seems entirely under the influence of Mr. Michel', the Prussian envoy, of whom Sandwich wrote in 1764, 'it is impossible to suppose that a friendly intercourse can be carried on, through the channel of a minister, with whom His Majesty's servants can never communicate with freedom and confidence . . . he joins in the cry of faction here in the most open and unguarded manner, and adopts their principles and practice' (PRO SP 80/199, 27 Dec. 1763; 90/83 ff. 1–2, 16 18).

A case-study of the important rôle of diplomats is provided by Anglo-Austrian relations in the 1720s and 1730s. Their significance was enhanced by the absence of a widespread sympathy for Catholic Austria to complement the general agreement on the need for a strong Austria in the international system. Compared with the widespread respect for the Dutch constitution, culture and intellectual life, there was little respect for, or interest in, things Austrian. In Austria, there was no vogue for British constitutionalism, literature, science, attitudes or fashion comparable to that which affected France. The significance of this absence of cultural empathy is difficult to evaluate, and its relationship to political links impossible to chart, but the ambiguity of the issue does not detract from its importance for the political historian. Perceptions of other states played a large rôle in shaping the policy decisions of statesmen, particularly because accurate information about other powers was difficult both to obtain and to interpret.

Given the absence of commercial, religious or cultural bonds, the Anglo-Austrian alliance was dependent upon political links. In that, it compared to the Anglo-French alliance of 1716–31, and contrasted with the Anglo-Dutch co-operation of the early eighteenth century. During 1725–40, these links were to be weakened by an Austrian failure to appreciate the British political situation: their inability to comprehend the strength and stability of the Walpole government. Johann Christoph, Baron Pentenriedter, a senior Austrian diplomat, claimed wrongly in 1727 that the parliamentary position of the Walpole ministry was secured by corruption only and that this situation could not last. Convinced that the ministry was weak and vulnerable, the Austrians had no hesitation in developing links with its opponents. Indeed, they put far more efforts into this than into any attempts to improve relations with the ministry. Whether an Austrian attempt thus to improve relations would have succeeded is unclear, but, by consistently seeking to change the ministry and co-operating with opposition elements, the Austrians made it impossible. A struggle for control within the British ministry in 1721–4 really marked the breach between Walpole and the Austrians, whose envoy, Starhemberg, chose to ally with the group termed by a French diplomat 'la cable autrichienne': Cadogan, Stair, Carteret and the Hanoverian minister

Bothmer. Starhemberg's alignment is easy to understand, as this group was powerful and readier to adopt anti-French prejudices than the Walpole connection, but the latter controlled Parliament. The Austrian response to the triumph of Walpole was an intermittent and irritating campaign to remove him that persisted until 1735. Starhemberg's successor, Karl Josef von Palm, responded to the Treaty of Hanover of 1725 by pressing George I to remove Walpole. Palm followed Starhemberg in maintaining close links with William Pulteney, the leader of the opposition Whigs, whilst attributing Walpole's parliamentary power to bribery. Palm's errors were compounded because, unaware of the excellent quality of the British postal interception and decyphering system, he allowed the ministry to obtain copies of his incriminating correspondence. In early 1727, in response to George I's speech to Parliament, Palm published a strident memorial that challenged George's claims about Austrian policy, for which he was expelled amidst uproar over his public challenge to George's honour. Palm's replacement, Count Philip Kinsky, repeated his mistakes, while a further cooling in relations was accomplished by Bishop Strickland of Namur, dispatched to Britain in 1734 to supplement Kinsky's efforts in winning Britain over to intervention in the War of the Polish Succession. His efforts to persuade George II to dismiss Walpole led the British to demand his recall.

The impact of this succession of unsatisfactory envoys was serious for Anglo-Austrian relations. Austrian intelligence concerning British policy and developments was heavily dependent on the reports of their envoys. There was nothing equivalent to the close relationship between Stanhope and Dubois in 1716–21, which more than compensated for the antagonistic views of Stair and Iberville, or the extensive correspondence between British and Dutch politicians in the 1720s, and there were few alternatives as sources of information. Unable to appreciate the strength of the Walpole ministry, the Austrians showed little interest in heeding British governmental views.

Equally, the British were poorly represented at Vienna. In this period only James, Lord, and then 1st Earl, Waldegrave (1728–30) pleased the Austrians. Much was due probably to his sympathy with and understanding of Catholic culture. He had been brought up in Europe as a Catholic, part of a Jacobite family in exile. He must have been the only British diplomat in the century who had been presented to the Pope as a young boy. Conversion to Protestantism had enabled Waldegrave to enjoy ministerial patronage, but he retained a sympathy for Catholic culture that enabled him to be a popular diplomat at both Paris and Vienna. This was true neither of his predecessor François

Louis de Pesmes, Seigneur de St Saphorin (1718–27), nor his successor, Thomas Robinson (1730–48). The rôle of individual diplomats can be exaggerated. Better Anglo-Bourbon relations in the period 1716–31 necessarily harmed those with Austria, as did Hanoverian concerns. However, there is no doubt that the nature of diplomatic representation played a major rôle among the tensions that could transform divergent interests into bad relations.

SECRETARIES OF STATE AND OTHER MINISTERS

Shortly after David, Viscount Stormont became a Secretary of State in 1779, the opposition leader, Charles, 2nd Marquis of Rockingham, wrote of him: 'His acquirements of knowledge of foreign courts by his embassies and employments abroad – will not procure him much confidence, as an able negotiator of business with foreign courts, and his having been so long absent from this country, will not naturally impress the public with an opinion, that he has much knowledge of home affairs' (WW RI-1864). The Secretaries of State faced a difficult task. In the field of foreign policy they had to consider domestic as well as diplomatic aspects, while, aside from foreign policy, they were also responsible for the conduct of government activity in a wide range of domestic and colonial spheres. There were two Secretaries of State whose field included foreign policy, the Northern and the Southern Secretary, until in 1782 the system was reorganised with the replacement of these posts by the Foreign Secretary and the Home Secretary. The Northern Secretary was responsible for relations with the United Provinces, Austria, Prussia and the other German States, Scandinavia, Poland and Russia, the Southern Secretary for France, Spain, Portugal, Switzerland, Turkey and the Italian states. This system was not always satisfactory. In 1752, Joseph Yorke, envoy at The Hague, wrote to a brother: 'I do think two Secretaries for foreign affairs is a wrong arrangement for business' (BL Add. 35363 f. 301). The Secretaries could follow different policies and could clash, as did Carteret and Townshend over negotiations with Austria in 1723, or Suffolk and Rochford over relations with France in 1772–3. British policy, for example attempts to reconcile Austro-Spanish differences over Italian questions, could involve both Secretaries in the same set of negotiations with sometimes unfortunate consequences. By European standards, the arrangement was exceptional and confusing; although there were still ministerial clashes over foreign policy after the 1782 change, for example between Fox and Shelburne in 1782.

And yet there were important advantages to the pre-1782 system which it is too easy to overlook. If one Secretary was in the Lords and the other in the Commons, government policy could be authoritatively defended in both Houses, as in George I's early years and George II's last ones, though only infrequently under George III. In 1750, Newcastle wanted Robinson as his co-Secretary but wrote of the objection to him 'as a commoner' (BL Add. 35411 ff. 100,137). When the monarch went abroad, as William III, George I and George II did frequently, it was useful if one Secretary could accompany him and one stay in London, though, at times, this arrangement was broken, as in 1723 when both Secretaries went to Hanover and Robert Walpole had to act as Secretary in London. When the monarch travelled, the division between two Secretaries facilitated the execution of policy and the conduct of routine correspondence with diplomats. However, when Secretary-at-War William Blathwayt acted as Secretary of State when he accompanied William III to the Continent, there were complaints that he and William failed to keep the ministers in London informed, rather as Carteret and George II were to be criticised in 1743. In September 1701, Sir Charles Hedges, the Northern Secretary, wrote to Blathwayt: 'The king's ministers abroad send me duplicates of the letters they write to you, but unless I have some knowledge of His Majesty's directions upon them, when he is pleased to give any, I am but half instructed and the thread of affairs is discontinued, which I desire you will please from time to time to supply me with, not only for my own satisfaction, but that I may be able to give My Lords Justices such accounts of affairs, as their Excellencies expect from me' (Beinecke, Osborn Shelves, Blathwayt Boxes 21)

Another important advantage arose from the political and personal commitments of Secretaries. If one had to leave London it was possible to have the other responsible for the conduct of all business, as in 1734 when Newcastle went electioneering. This was also very helpful when Secretaries were ill, as Harrington and Suffolk frequently were, while Townshend was seriously ill in late 1727. Aside from these conveniences, the dominance of one of the Secretaries could bring coherence to the system. This was achieved by Bolingbroke in 1710–14, Stanhope in 1718–21, Townshend in 1724–9, Newcastle in 1744–54, Sandwich in 1763–4, and Stormont in 1779–82. Once he had overcome his initial lack of confidence and his inexperience in the field, Newcastle was not prepared to have his fellow Secretaries resist his views, if he could turn the monarch against them, and he played a major rôle in the falls of Townshend (1730),Carteret (1744), Chesterfield (1748) and Bedford (1751). In 1750, he explained to his brother his opposition to George, 2nd Earl of Halifax succeeding Bedford: 'He is so conceited of his parts, that he would not be there one month, without thinking he knew as much, or more, of the business than any one man; and I am sure it would be impracticable to go on with him' (BL Add. 35411 f. 100).

Some Secretaries were experienced diplomats, as were Carteret, Robinson, Rochford, Stormont and Grantham, though such experience did not necessarily lead to success as Secretary. William Stanhope, Lord Harrington, was generally considered a very successful envoy in Spain (1717–18, '20–7, '29), but made little impact as Northern Secretary (1730–42, '44–6) because he was overshadowed by Newcastle, lacked political weight and was apparently lazy. Diplomatic experience was, however, considered by many to be an advantage. It was cited in 1750 by Newcastle when commending the choice of the Earl of Holdernesse, who had been envoy at Venice (1744–6) and The Hague (1749–51), as Bedford's successor, a post he was to hold from 1751 until in 1754 he replaced Newcastle at the Northern Department, remaining there until 1761:

> . . . he has a solid understanding; and will come out, as prudent a young man, as any of the kingdom He is good-natured, so you may tell him his faults; and he will mend them. He is universally loved and esteemed almost by all parties in Holland. He is very taciturn, dexterous enough; and most punctual in the execution of his orders. He is got into the routine of business . . . He is very diligent and exact in all his proceedings: He has great temper, mixed with proper resolution . . . the consideration of the king's having named him of his own mere motion is not an inconsiderable one' (BL Add. 35411 f. 101).

As Secretaries had both to assess reports and to negotiate with foreign envoys, diplomatic experience was clearly valuable, especially if the nature of the ministry and of the international situation did not require a proficient parliamentarian. Secretaries who were experienced diplomats were clearly affected by the domestic situation. Grantham confessed in a period of political instability in February 1783 that it was difficult to send instructions to Harris and Keith because of the international situation, adding, 'this is undoubtedly increased by the situation in which we stand at home' (BL Add. 35528 f. 22).

The burden upon the Secretaries could be lessened by the rôle of other ministers and the monarch in policy decisions. Foreign policy was not compartmentalised, but neither were there any consistent rules about the consultation of other ministers. The rôle of the council and of a smaller *ad hoc* group of ministers, the 'inner cabinet', depended on circumstances and individuals. In April 1748, Newcastle drew up a memorandum of a conversation with the Austrian and Saxon envoys and, having communicated it to Bedford (Southern Secretary), Dorset (Lord President of the Council), Gower (Lord Privy Seal), Grafton (Lord Chamberlain), Hardwicke (Lord Chancellor) and Pelham (First Lord of the Treasury), gained their approval for sending instructions to Cumberland and Sandwich. Later the same month, instructions to Sandwich were communicated to and approved by Bedford, Dorset, Hardwicke and Pelham (BL Add. 32812 ff 31, 80). Newcastle continued to take a close interest in foreign policy when he moved to the Treasury in 1754. An earlier First Lord of the Treasury, Walpole, had also played a major, though episodic, rôle in foreign policy, as later did Pitt the Younger. Walpole could write thoughtful letters on diplomatic strategy and in some periods, such as the summer of 1730, he read many of the diplomatic dispatches and played an active rôle in the drafting of instructions. On occasion, Walpole held important meetings with foreign envoys.

The major rôle of ministers not formally responsible for the conduct of foreign policy could, however, create confusion. In the negotiations at the end of the War of American Independence, there was a lack of consistency in British policy as different ministers supported different policies and used their own representatives in Paris. Fox, the Foreign Secretary, clashed with Shelburne, the Home Secretary. In 1782, Fox used Thomas Walpole to negotiate with France over Grenada, writing to Shelburne: 'I do not believe that there was consultation of a Cabinet Council upon the subject, if I took too much upon myself to act in such a business without one, I am to blame' (Bedford CRO L30/14/146/2).

Thus arrangements were informal and much dependent on the personal standing and determination of individual ministers, a situation that was both flexible and likely to produce tension if particular ministers clashed with a Secretary and wished to have their views heeded. Ministerial meetings could defuse tension between Secretaries or exacerbate their political effects. Inchoate arrangements were not restricted to foreign policy. They characterised government in its senior levels as a whole, reflecting not only the obvious interrelationships of government and politics at that level, but also the disparate nature of a political world that had to consider two distinct, though interrelated, political spheres and sources of power – Parliament and the Court. Though royal actions could lead to a measure of ministerial solidarity, as against George II and Carteret in 1744, in general relations between Crown and ministers were less tense or combative and more complex. The monarch could be kept in the dark, as Newcastle coached Sandwich to do in 1748 (BL Add. 32811 f. 239), but ministers sought royal support, and ministries that were believed to lack it appeared precarious. Relationships between Secretaries and their colleagues depended in part on the degree of royal favour for individual ministers. Whether overt or shadowy, the monarch played a major rôle in most ministerial rivalries.

Secretaries of State generally sought the efficient conduct of business. In August 1701, Hedges wrote to Blathwayt that he wanted one of his Under-Secretaries, John Tucker, to succeed the unwell Sir Joseph Williamson, who had held the post since 1661, as Keeper of State Papers:

> My aim . . . is to make that office which is the repository of the papers of state, as useful as I can to His Majesty and the public by putting it into so good order that we may find precedents of public affairs, and transactions of state without difficulty, which, in the present condition it is, cannot be done, but that it should be made easy, is, in my opinion, a thing of great importance. (Beinecke, Osborn Shelves, Blathwayt Boxes 21)

Tucker gained the post, but complaints on this score did not ease.

Seventy-one years later, the Northern Secretary, Suffolk, wrote to one of his under-secretaries, William Eden, later an important diplomat:

> The Russian business I foresee will now come seriously upon the tapis -you must attend to it very closely and accurately – and not content yourself with reading dispatches and doing nothing in consequence of them. The two proposals must be made out, examined, compared, and agitated: and the former discussions pro and con relative to each other, collected. (BL Add. 34412 f. 182)

This stress on method co-existed, and at times clashed, with the more diffuse arrangements that characterised much government in this period. Possibly diplomacy, with its diplomats, aristocratic in mien if not in person, located in the world of courts and not of officialdom, was especially prone to resist method, but allowance must be made for the difficulties of predicting international developments, the need to leave room for manoeuvre to the man on the spot, and the understaffed nature of the Secretaries' offices. The British system did not strike many British envoys as excellent, Robert Liston writing from Spain to a colleague in 1784 about the Under-Secretary of the Foreign Office:

> Perhaps the immense detail is too great for any one man, and the mechanical and higher parts ought to be more separated. I have been struck with the footing on which Count Floridablanca's office is carried on. The subalterns there are all in some degree *Under-Secretaries*. They have their different departments. One England, One France, another Portugal, and so forth. They read memorials, make their reports to the count, draw up

answers for his correction and approbation, etc. It is true they are better paid, and are people of more character and consequence than our clerks, few of whom could be made any use of in this way. But I think it gives a hint for essential reformation. (BL Add. 36806 f 58)

Geographical specialisation was also taken further in France than in Britain. How far the relatively undifferentiated nature of the administration of foreign policy affected its quality is unclear: it is not readily subject to measurement. It certainly made the situation depend heavily on the calibre and experience of the Secretaries, making the position of 'political' Secretaries, without diplomatic experience, more difficult. Newcastle was fortunate that he had the long-serving Delafaye (1717–34) and Stanyan (1715–29) as his Under-Secretaries. Continuity was also provided by Under-Secretaries such as George Tilson (1708–38) and Edward Weston (1729–46, 1761–4). The influence of such men on policy is difficult to assess, but they served as a vital fund of continuity in method.

Delafaye, who came from a family of Huguenot refugees, was described by the Sardinian envoy in 1730 as having 'a lot of credit. One could say even that he alone directs the office.' Delafaye certainly discussed matters with foreign envoys and he clearly played a major rôle in drafting instructions. In an undated letter to Newcastle of George I's reign, Delafaye also made it clear that the king played a major rôle: 'you see the King whose memory I have known to be very good in those matters does not recollect anything of it: upon which I would propose to alter that paragraph in the manner your Grace will find it in the draft; and if you approve of it, you will be pleased to sign 4 or 5 lines below the mark'. In December 1730, Delafaye wrote to Newcastle about an instruction he had drafted for Waldegrave: 'the two first pages are Milord Harrington's own, the rest mine. . . . I endeavoured to explain everything further in a long supplemental letter of my own to Lord Waldegrave' (AST. 37, 10 July; PRO SP 36/1 f. 15, 35/65 f. 324; BL Add. 32770 f. 275). Waldegrave indeed had a confidential correspondence with Delafaye, as well as with Tilson and Weston.

The British system rested on such men and on what Keith complained he lacked after the formation of the Fox-North coalition in 1783, 'personal acquaintance or connexion' (HL HM 18940 p. 245). There was no coherent 'foreign service'; rather a world of patronage and personal relationships in which individual connections, circumstances and good fortune played the major rôle, complementing the absence of system and method in the affairs of the greater world.

CHAPTER FIVE

STRATEGIC AND MILITARY CONSIDERATIONS

Britain's strategic position was central to debate over what her foreign policy should be. She faced two related strategic and military problems in the period 1660–1800. Neither was novel, though both were made more serious by dynastic and international developments. The problems were the weakness of Britain as a military power and her vulnerability to invasion. The developments were the growth in Bourbon strength and the growing British commitment to continental diplomacy, partly as a consequence of this, but, more markedly, as a result of the accession of foreign monarchs. Any stress on these points may appear misleading in light of the triumphalist note of much writing about Britain in this period with its stress on military victory and the growth of Empire. However, such a stress, though pertinent at some periods, for example immediately after the Peace of Paris in 1763 or at a time of marked Bourbon weakness in 1787–91, was generally inappropriate. Both ministers and the political nation in general were acutely concerned about the strength and intentions of other powers and about British vulnerability in the face of them.

MILITARY POWER

The essential military problem was that Britain increasingly sought to act as a major power while possessing a peace-time army which was that of a second rank state. Although the size of the peace-time army increased, from about 30,000 in the late 1720s to 45,000 after the Seven Years' War, dropping to about 36,000 at the start of 1775, it never matched that of France (110,000 in 1717), Prussia (80,000 in 1740, 190,000 after 1772), Austria (170,000 in 1775) or Russia (240,000 in 1740). In wartime, the number of British troops increased, the Army Estimates presented to the Commons in December 1779 noting a rise to 179,000, although that figure included foreign troops in pay and 42,000 militia. However, the size of possible field forces was comparatively small, while the country was poorly fortified. The navy really was the wooden walls of the country and when it failed in its task in 1688 William of Orange encountered few obstacles. When, in 1690, 1744 and 1779, the French appeared likely to seize control of the Channel there was grave concern about whether invasion could be resisted successfully. Henry Conway, an officer who was secretary to the Lord Lieutenant of Ireland, reported in October 1756 that there were only two forts worth defending in Ireland (Matlock, Derbyshire CRO Catton Hall mss). The poor state of the fortifications of Plymouth and Portsmouth was a political issue during the War of American Independence.

In part, the small size of the army was a matter of demography. Britain was not an especially populous country, at least in comparison with Austria or France, and the size of her possible forces was further reduced from 1689 by the stress on an all-Protestant army. This greatly diminished one of the greatest sources of soldiers – Ireland – which became instead a reservoir of troops for Bourbon recruiters. In part, this loss was balanced after 1746 when the 'pacified' Scottish Highlands became an important source of troops. A Highland charge, such as the Duke of Cumberland had faced at Culloden in 1746, helped to bring the royal army victory over the French on the Heights of Abraham in 1759 and thus gain Canada for Britain. However, the demographic imbalance with France persisted. In a pre-census age, it is difficult to be precise, but Louis XIV had about 20 million subjects, whereas the population of England and Wales was only about 5.5 million in 1688, 6.5 in 1760 and 8.6 in 1791.

Finance was not an important constraint on manpower, as the British willingness and ability to hire foreign soldiers indicated, though this was not the case when monarchs lacked parliamentary support, as the reign of Charles II or the last years of William III indicated. The issue of such support was crucial, and successive rulers were faced with the problem that, however much their policies might be acceptable, there was a sustained hostility to the idea of a large army. The origins of this were various, though they were essentially political, rather than being based on any analysis, informed or otherwise, of Britain's military situation. A large permanent army was regarded as an actual and potential threat to British liberties, a view that owed much to the experience of military influence and rule in 1645–60, to the interpretation of political developments abroad, and to fears aroused by Charles II's and James II's use of force and intentions. Opposition to standing garrisons under the Crown played a rôle in the 1786 defeat of the bill for financing improved fortifications for Plymouth and Portsmouth.

Criticism of the size of the army could focus both anxiety about foreign policy and concern about domestic developments, as after the Peace of Ryswick (1697), when a successful attempt was made by Parliament to reduce the size of the army, despite the opposition of William III who feared both that war might break out over the Spanish Succession and that his diplomatic efforts to arrange a satisfactory solution of the issue would be handicapped by the foreign response to British troop reductions. Conversely, a pamphlet of 1750 attacking the Mutiny Bill, a measure believed by its supporters to be essential for discipline in the army, referred to the 'terrors of a Standing Army, in such absolute subjection to the will and pleasure of their officers' (*Seasonable and Affecting Observations on the Mutiny Bill*: 66).

Because the standing army was so small, British military effectiveness was limited at the beginning of wars when large numbers of untrained troops were recruited. An obvious remedy was the hiring of foreign units. This was a policy favoured by a number of European powers, including France and Spain, but whereas the number of Swiss, Germans and Irish in the French army, though large, was not a substantial percentage of the total force, the position was different in Britain. The British ability to follow a military interventionist policy was dependent on the willingness of foreign powers to provide troops for hire. Furthermore, foreign troops had to be used both when Britain was invaded or threatened with invasion, as in 1689, 1715, 1719, 1744, 1745 and 1756, and when she confronted a serious rebellion in America. Henry Fox, Secretary of State for the Southern Department, wrote to the Duke of Devonshire on 31 January 1756, when a French invasion was threatened: '. . . if we have secured the metropolis it is all. There is not in all the west or north of England a single soldier . . . if invasion or threats of invasion from France can effect the keeping our fleets and troops at home, while they send regular troops, with their fleets to North America, the object of the war will be lost in the first year of it . . . we have required both Dutch and Hessians' (Chatsworth). Thirty-three per cent of the British strength in America in 1778–9 was provided by German auxiliaries, a percentage that rose to 37 in 1781 (Black 1999c; Brewer and Hellmuth 1999: 53–70).

However, the use, especially hiring, of foreign troops was an extremely contentious policy and it was politically dangerous as it could be interpreted as evidence and consequence of the distortion of supposedly British interests for foreign ends. This was particularly a

problem when the monarch was foreign, as with William's use of Dutch troops and the Hanoverians' of German forces. In addition, the stress in British campaigns on the rôle of Allied troops, especially in the Low Countries in the Nine Years', Spanish and Austrian Succession Wars, placed a considerable strain on good diplomatic relations with wartime allies. The general absence of any ideological bond in the alliances of the period, the disparate aims that characterised them and the frequency of unilateral negotiations with rivals made wartime alliances precarious, but disagreements over troop quotas, forage allowances or the date of arrival of troops on campaign added the continual strain of recrimination and petty dispute. They certainly sapped relations with Austria and the United Provinces in the 1700s and 1740s.

If the conduct of the Allies was commonly a theme of ministerial complaint, it could also arouse public agitation as the conviction that allies were rogues was well established in Britain. The importance of such attitudes is open to debate, but it could be suggested that they limited the options for ministers in negotiations with foreign powers and thus made the creation of alliances more difficult. And yet there was no simple division of opinion with unwilling ministers being constrained by public attitudes. Ministers instead were divided in their opinions, as the controversies over the continental policies of Carteret and Newcastle indicated.

Concern over the size of the army and over national vulnerability to invasion helped to lead to agitation over the degree of reliance that could be placed on a militia. This became a serious political issue during the Seven Years' War. The militia system established in England and Wales in 1757 was, however, adopted only with some difficulty, including major riots in Bedfordshire, Hertfordshire, Lincolnshire and Yorkshire. The 'Patriot' rhetoric of national self-reliance, centred on an active and virtuous citizenry, proved unwelcome to many when it became a matter of action and obligations. Nevertheless, the militia survived the Seven Years' War and, under an Act of 1762, was obliged to drill for four weeks in peacetime each year. The entry of France into the War of American Independence in 1778 revived concern about national defence and, that year, the militia was embodied while Parliament approved an increase in its size. In 1778–9, nearly 40,000 men were mustered. The militia, therefore, helped to bring home to many the consequences of British foreign policy.

Other than in 1757–9, when it seemed that militia service would not last for long and when there was considerable concern about the possibility of invasion, militiamen were generally neither men of wealth nor motivated by patriotic zeal. Instead they were mostly poor men who joined for the pay, and most of the officers were socially undistinguished. As a potential fighting force, the militia had severe limitations and 'for political no less than for economic and administrative reasons it was not possible to advance to a true system of national military training from the quaint simulacrum of it that was the militia' (Western 1965: 302). Compared with the cantonal systems of military recruitment of countries such as Prussia, or the extensive overlapping of the nobility and the large officer corps in countries such as France, Britain was not a militaristic society in either institutions or attitudes, at Court or in the localities. The extent to which this affected foreign policy is difficult to assess. Whatever the opposition to a standing army, the vigour of the naval tradition provided a powerful element of bellicosity.

THE NAVY

If the British army was numerically weak, dependent on foreign manpower and, with the exception of Marlborough's victories in the 1700s and Minden (1759), not conspicuously successful in Europe, the navy was strong, reliant on national resources and generally successful. It also enjoyed an established rôle in British strategic thought and public debate.

The mid seventeenth century was a period in which naval forces became more dedicated, as vessels that were not specialised warships were gradually excluded from the wartime fleet. The increasing use of line-ahead formations with their consequent artillery exchanges, in contrast to the former preference for the line-abreast formation and the tactics of boarding, led to the distinction between what were known from the 1690s as 'ships of the line' and other vessels. Comparisons of naval strength are not without their problems, especially as the size of guns varied, but it is nevertheless possible to chart a marked increase in the size of English naval forces in the late seventeenth century, although, thanks to French and Dutch shipbuilding, England declined from leading to third most important naval power. English naval strength greatly revived in the late 1670s, thanks to a major shipbuilding programme in 1677–80, although the French navy remained larger in the 1680s. In 1677, a new land tax was created 'for the speedy building of thirty men-of-war'.

Had the navy been well-positioned and united and a full-scale engagement been fought, it is extremely doubtful that William could have invaded England in 1688. Even if forces had landed, the Dutch fleet could subsequently have been defeated with serious consequences for William's momentum. Instead it was difficult to position the navy so as to cover the island from invasion, in the face of adverse winds, while opposition within the navy to James helped to incapacitate the standing force on which he and his brother had lavished so much attention.

The building up of English naval strength increased after 1688, although the French launched more warships than England in the early 1690s. As a result of an Act of 1691 sponsoring new construction, England had a definite lead in new launchings over both the Dutch and the French from 1695. By 1700, the English fleet was larger than that of France and there was also a significant improvement on the logistical side, with the creation of an entire new front-line operational yard at Plymouth. This superiority was maintained throughout the following century.

The Royal Navy 1660–1790

	Ships of the line
1660	57
1670	60
1680	89
1685	98
1690	83
1695	113
1700	127
1710	123
1720	102
1730	105
1740	101
1750	115
1760	135
1770	126
1780	117
1790	145

(Glete 1993)

However, though Britain was the largest naval power, that did not mean that she was free from anxiety about her naval strength There were problems both domestically and from abroad. There was a major difference between constructing ships and manning and maintaining them. The maintenance was both expensive and required an extensive and effective administration system that indicated the capability of the British state for successful and continuous state-directed action.

Nevertheless, the condition of the navy was a very contentious political issue during the War of American Independence.

Manning was a more serious problem. As naval forces were not kept permanently prepared for action, with the exception of a small force, crises led to naval mobilisations in which ships were prepared and crewed speedily, as in 1770 over the Falkland Islands or in 1790 over Nootka Sound. The manning was completed by impressment – forcible conscription – which led not only to individual hardship and the disruption of trade but also to problems of desertion and generally inadequate naval man-power. It was not possible to deal with the problem by hiring foreign manpower in any significant numbers. Indeed, a significant difference between British navy and army strength was that the former was essentially self-reliant, with the important exception of Baltic naval stores for ship construction and maintenance, while wartime army strength required the use of foreign troops. As a result, the government had greater control over naval operations. This was further enhanced by the decline of the naval strength of Britain's only major maritime ally, the United Provinces.

In the abortive defensive treaty of 1678, the ratio of Dutch to English capital ships had been fixed at 3:4. In 1689 this was lowered to 3:5, but during the Spanish Succession War the Dutch were generally more than half-way below their quota, and those often arrived late. The situation deteriorated further in the following decades. Though Dutch naval strength was called upon on a number of occasions, for example the naval mobilisation at Spithead in 1729 to intimidate Spain, the Dutch were of little assistance during the War of the Austrian Succession. In the Seven Years' War they were neutral and in the War of American Independence opposed to Britain, the Fourth Anglo-Dutch war breaking out in 1780.

The other major European naval powers were France and Spain. A number of countries, especially Russia in the eighteenth century, were locally powerful, but none of them was of real consequence in oceanic and colonial naval conflict. When Britain was allied with France, her naval preponderance was particularly marked. French support for the Dutch in the Second Anglo-Dutch war created considerable difficulties, but in the Third war, when Charles II was allied to Louis XIV, the English were in a far better position to take the initiative. Between 1716 and 1731, the Anglo-French alliance facilitated a wide-ranging use of British naval power in the Baltic against first Sweden and then Russia, in the Mediterranean against Spain, and then, in 1725–7, in a formidable display of power against Russia and Spain. These episodes have received insufficient attention largely because, with the exception

of the dispatch of Admiral Sir George Byng's force to the Mediterranean in 1718 and the sinking of the Spanish fleet covering the invasion of Sicily off Cape Passaro, they did not involve conflict. However, it is a mistake to consider naval power simply in terms of conflict or, even more, battles won. The simple presence of naval forces could achieve important military and political objectives (Black and Woodfine 1988). In 1726, Charles, 2nd Viscount Townshend, the Secretary of State for the Northern Department, wrote to William Stanhope, the envoy in Spain:

> It is indeed a reflection which must afford His Majesty a great deal of comfort and satisfaction, as it rebounds highly to the glory of the British nation and the honour of our navy, that whilst one of his fleets is preserving the tranquillity of the North, against the ambitious and pernicious designs of the Czarina, and another is keeping the Spanish treasure in the West Indies, and thereby preventing the Emperor and Spain from disturbing the peace of the South, the very report of a third squadron going out has caused such alarm and confusion in the Austrian Netherlands, and has put Spain, in the low and miserable condition of her finances, to the trouble and expense of marching their troops and fortifying their seaport towns. (PRO SP 94/98 11 Aug.)

This favourable position collapsed in 1731 with the disintegration of the Anglo-French alliance. The strategic consequences were so serious that, in so far as the term means anything, a mid-eighteenth-century crisis can be seen as beginning then. Britain lost the strategic edge that she had hitherto enjoyed and, exposed as she was to the Jacobite challenge, now had to face the prospect of effective intervention on their behalf. The change was immediately and dramatically signalled by the war panic of June–July 1731. Following the collapse of the alliance the governments of both Britain and France sought to win the support of Spain and each became receptive to alarmist rumours concerning the intentions of the other. As part of the agreement they negotiated with Spain, the British undertook to convoy a Spanish force to Tuscany, but the preparation of this major force led to French concern that an attack on Dunkirk was intended. The French responded by moving large forces towards Dunkirk which, in turn, led the British to fear invasion, especially as the Stuart Pretender 'James III' left Rome. Much of the British army was moved to the south coast and requests for assistance were dispatched to Britain's allies.

The panic passed, but it indicated not only the uncertainty of peace in an international system prone to suspicion and rumour, but also the marked deterioration of Britain's position. She had been threatened by action on behalf of the Jacobites during her confrontations with

Sweden, Spain, Russia and Austria between 1716 and 1727, but, although the Spaniards had actually mounted a major invasion attempt in 1719, and had managed to land a few troops in Scotland, none of these powers posed a threat comparable to that of France. France threatened Britain simply by keeping her fleet in being, for, with this, an invasion by the more numerous French army remained a serious prospect. This was more especially the case because significant French forces were kept near the frontier with the Austrian Netherlands and these could be easily moved to the Channel ports, although sufficient transports were far harder to assemble. Spying on the preparedness of the French fleet was, with interception and decyphering of diplomatic correspondence, and spying on the Jacobites, the principal activity of British espionage (Black 1987g).

With the French fleet in being, the British were obliged to keep much of their fleet in home waters and ports. This position was exacerbated when France and Spain were allies and, in 1779, during the War of American Independence, the Bourbon fleets were able to mount an invasion attempt intended for the south coast of England which, however, was abandoned as the result of lack of provisions and epidemic disease among the invading force. Even when only French warships were involved, a hostile force was able in 1744 to sail from Brest to Dunkirk in order to convoy an invasion from there that was, in the event, dispersed by storm; while Minorca was also lost in 1756 when Britain was only at war with France.

Obliged, therefore, to keep the bulk of her naval forces in a position where they could resist any possible Bourbon invasion attempt, the British had their strategic options limited until such time as they could destroy an appreciable portion of the opposing force, as at the battles of Quiberon Bay and Lagos (Portugal) in 1759. Three years earlier, Britain's ally, Frederick II of Prussia, had told the British envoy Andrew Mitchell:

> though he could not persuade himself that France really intended to invade England, yet we could not be too much upon our guard, and he hoped for that reason that neither the service of America, the defence of Minorca, nor any project whatever would induce us to dégarnir our coasts by sending out too many ships of war, that, while we had a strong fleet at home, France would hardly venture to invade, but, if we weakened ours too much, it became the interest of France, in the present conjuncture, to risk everything with an equal force. (PRO SP 90/65, 27 May)

Alternatively, a concentration of French effort on privateering, as opposed to fleet activity, as during the War of the Spanish Succession, limited the strategic threat from French naval power. However, the economic consequences were serious for Britain, with ship losses, the need for convoys, commercial disruption and higher insurance premiums, and, in addition, the political storms created by the alleged neglect of the protection of trade could be serious. In both the Nine Years' and Spanish Succession Wars there were serious losses to French privateers, and counter-measures evolved only slowly. Thus, whether the French concentrated on capital ships or on privateering, British naval policy was affected by the need to respond, in the latter case, for example, by the provision of numerous ships for convoying and guard duty. Between 1714 and 1793, the number of 5th and 6th rates, crucial for commerce protection and raiding, rose from 66 to 114.

There were often too few ships to spare for the many tasks for which the fleet was required. The nature of communications ensured that, once detached, ships were difficult to recall speedily and this was an increasing problem as more ships were sent to trans-oceanic stations. In European waters, the crucial tasks were the maintenance of the control of home waters, convoy duty, observation of the principal Bourbon ports and Baltic and Mediterranean missions. The difficulty of wooden ships maintaining all-weather stations precluded effective blockades. That was but one of the limitations of naval power; ships were very much affected by the constraints of the tide and wind. George, 2nd Earl of Bristol, envoy in Turin, reported on 22 September 1756: 'the French say that His Majesty's fleet cannot hold the sea long as the winter is approaching, and that when Sir Edward Hawke retires into port, their communication will be again opened with Minorca without their risking an engagement' (PRO SP 92/64). British naval weakness thanks to other commitments had been responsible for the loss of the island that year, while the limitations of naval power prevented it from being regained by blockade.

Nevertheless, more important, in so far as foreign policy was concerned, were the limitations of naval power, however preponderant, in affecting the political and strategic plans of other powers. Clearly in the case of major colonial powers – Britain, France, Spain, the United Provinces and Portugal – naval strength could inhibit their links with their colonies, with serious commercial and financial consequences, while such strength was an essential precondition of amphibious operations. Thus, major efforts were made to disrupt the remission of silver from the New World to Spain, a British fleet being sent to the West Indies for that purpose in 1726. Amphibious operations were an appropriate means to seize many colonial possessions, particularly those that were islands or isolated coastal trading bases, the common form of European settlement in Africa and Asia. In the Seven Years' War the

British were able to take all the major French bases in both continents (bar New Orleans) and, also, their leading West Indian islands, Martinique and Guadeloupe.

However, such amphibious operations had their military limitations, while their political effectiveness abroad was less sweeping than British proponents of 'blue water' policies might suggest. The disastrous failure of the attack on Cartagena (modern Columbia) in 1741 helped to substantiate unfounded complaints that the Walpole ministry was not seriously pursuing the war with Spain (Harding 1991). In fact, leaving aside the logistical problems the British faced and the difficulty of obtaining army-navy co-operation, the Spanish Empire was far more resilient than was appreciated in Britain, where notions of Spanish decadence were well established. Local military units, reasonably strong fortifications, and the incidence of Caribbean epidemic diseases produced in combination an effective defensive system, although it did not prevent the British taking Porto Bello in 1739 and, more impressively, Havana in 1762, the year in which Manila also fell (Tracy 1995). Gains made through local military superiority could be threatened if the arrival of hostile forces reversed the situation, and therefore naval strength was a vital prerequisite of successful colonial operations. The biggest colonial disaster of the period, the surrender of Cornwallis's army to its American and French blockaders at Yorktown in 1781, occurred as a direct result of the inability of the British to challenge French naval control of Chesapeake Bay (Rodger 1993).

British naval success certainly played a rôle in the perilous state of the French economy towards the end of the War of Austrian Succession, and in the Seven Years' War forced both France and Spain to make territorial concessions as a price of peace. It led to French fears of a British monopoly of colonial resources in and trade with North America and the Caribbean. However, the effect of British naval power on non-colonial powers was far more limited. Several rulers and ministers made contemptuous references to the idea that they could or would be affected by such power. In 1726, Frederick William I of Prussia, fearful of Russian power, told the British envoy: 'as to your fleet, it is of no manner of service to me'. The following year, the Austrian Chancellor, Count Sinzendorf, mocked the capacity of the British navy, arguing that a few houses burnt in Naples or Palermo would not settle matters. In 1728, the Duke of Parma, who had angered Britain by his Jacobite sympathies, was reported as claiming that he 'did not fear the English, for their fleet could not come to him at Parma'. In 1730, Sinzendorf doubted the capacity of the Allies of Seville, Britain, France, Spain and the United Provinces to harm the

maintained, it was not a game to play often' (C. Ross, ed., *Correspondence of Cornwallis* 1859:1, 201). Any treatment of the Seven Years' War as a strategic success for Britain that fails to place weight on the failures of 1756–7, the vulnerability of Hanover, Prussia and, in 1762, her Portuguese ally, and the threat until late 1759 of a French invasion of Britain, is misleading.

The search for Continental allies after 1763 did not centre on a desire for assistance in the event of renewed war with the Bourbons, for the war would be fought at sea and in the colonies and Austria, Prussia and Russia were unlikely to give any help. In addition, the British were likely to win. The war that eventually broke out, in the extraordinary circumstances of an American rebellion, placed wholly unexpected military burdens on Britain. In the period after the Seven Years' War, there seemed less obvious need for Continental allies, however desirable such alliances might be. The claim that the absence of a diversionary war on the Continent helped lead Britain to lose the American war underrates the difficulty of achieving victory over the Americans (which had eluded Britain *prior* to the French intervention in the conflict in 1778), and, also, British resilience in the face of Bourbon efforts in the latter conflict.

'Blue water' could not secure either the specific objectives that the Continental strategy was designed to protect, essentially the Low Countries and Hanover, or more general goals, summarised by the vague notion of the balance of power. However, in domestic political terms it was a more acceptable strategy, while it lessened the need for co-operation with allies. A shift towards 'blue water' attitudes can be detected in mid-century, especially from the latter years of the War of the Austrian Succession after the fall of the major French Canadian base of Louisbourg on Cape Breton Island in 1745. This process was facilitated in the Seven Years' War (1756–63), not least because the Austro-French alliance of 1756, the Treaty of Versailles, and Dutch neutrality removed the need to protect the Low Countries, the central purpose behind British continental intervention since 1678, with the important exception of the period of Anglo-French alliance of 1716–31. The war witnessed the commitment of British troops to Germany from 1758, in support of both Frederick II of Prussia and Hanover, and significant trans-oceanic amphibious operations.

The latter were surrounded with an aura of success, helping to set the political tone for discussion of potential British military action for the next three decades. As the War of American Independence involved no hostilities in Europe, apart from the unsuccessful Bourbon siege of

Gibraltar and their capture of Minorca, and Britain did not intervene in the Austro-Prussian War of the Bavarian Succession (1778–9), the generation of ministers and generals who faced in 1793 the problems of co-ordinating significant Continental operations against revolutionary France had no recent experience on which to look back.

CHAPTER SIX

TRADE AND COLONIES

> Her fondness for conquest as a warlike nation, her lust of dominion as an
> ambitious one, and her thirst for a gainful monopoly as a commercial one
> (none of them legitimate causes of war) will all join to hide from her eyes
> every view of her true interests; and continually goad her on in these
> ruinous distant expeditions, so destructive both of lives and treasure, that
> must prove as pernicious to her in the end as the Crusades were to most of
> the nations of Europe . . . the true and sure means of extending and securing
> commerce is the goodness and cheapness of commodities and the profits of
> no trade can ever be equal to the expense of compelling it, and of holding it
> by fleets and armies.
>
> (Benjamin Franklin, July 1776, *Papers of Benjamin Franklin* XXII, 520–1).

Commercial and colonial development were of major consequence for
Britain's ability to develop and sustain great-power status and they
played an important rôle in the public debate over policy. Between 1660
and 1793 Britain became the leading European trans-oceanic
commercial state and colonial power. Her possessions might not vie
with those of Spain but the British Empire was more dynamic and
expanding than that of Spain, and more powerful than France and the
United Provinces.

Destinations of Exports, England and Wales
(Figures in million pounds. Annual averages for each 5-year period.)

	1701–5	1726–30	1751–5	1776–80
North Europe	3.12	3.53	5.13	3.90
Baltic	0.30	0 20	0.29	0.37
Portugal and Spain	0.73	1.55	2.14	1.25
Mediterranean	0.60	0.85	1.00	0.75
Africa	0 10	0.20	0.23	0.24
East Indies	0.11	0.11	0.79	0.91
British West Indies	0.31	0.47	0.71	1.24
North America	0.27	0.52	1.30	1.30

Average annual exports rose from £4.1 million in the 1660s to £6.9

(1720), £12.7 (1750), £14.3 (1770) and £18.9 (1790), during a period of only modest inflation. Imports rose from £6 million (1700) to £6.1 (1720), £7.8 (1750), £12.2 (1770) and £17.4 (1790). More important than the numerical change was the diversification of markets and products. The relative importance both of woollen exports and of trade with nearby areas of Europe declined, while that of oceanic trade increased. Average annual exports to North America rose from £0.27 million in 1701–5 to over £2 million in 1786–90. The British Atlantic 'shrank' between 1675 and 1740 as a result of improvements such as the development of postal services and the invention of the helm wheel which dramatically increased rudder control on large ships. The number of transatlantic sailings doubled in this period. There was to be further expansion after 1740. Thanks in large part to the protective system created by the Navigation Acts, British-owned shipping tonnage grew appreciably.

Growth of English Shipping Tonnage

1629	115,000	1765	23,000
1686	340,000	1775	608,000
1702	323,000	1786	752,000
1751	421,000		

Figures for Britain

1760	609,000
1792	1,540,000

(Duffy 1980: 57; Black and Woodfine 1988: 124)

The increase in colonial possessions was also striking. Including the possessions of the trading companies and considering only acquisitions that were retained after each war, British gains in the period 1660–1700, included Bombay (1661), Fort James (West Africa) (1664), the Bahamas (1670), Accra (1672), three Sumatran bases (1684-5) and Calcutta (1698). These were added to Jamaica, Belize, the Mosquito Coast of modern Nicaragua and Barbados.

In numerical and territorial terms the expansion of the North American colonies was more impressive. Former Dutch and Swedish possessions were seized, including New Amsterdam, which became New York; Charleston (1672) and Philadelphia (1682) were founded, while the population of the colonies grew as a result of immigration (Canny 1998). By 1700 there were about 10,000 French inhabitants of French North America, but about 210,000 Europeans in British North

America. This was despite France's population being about four times as large. In Britain there was a willingness to emigrate or to act as an entrepreneur in distant areas which was much more limited in France. This contributed to the dynamic of British expansion. The disparity became more marked during the eighteenth century. Canada had about 56,000 inhabitants of French origin in 1740, British America nearly a million people of European background. Large-scale emigration encouraged the growth of trade within the British empire.

The North American colonies grew markedly in the eighteenth century. Settlement spread geographically both westward and into the gaps between the coastal enclaves. New towns included Baltimore (1728), Richmond (1733) and Charlottesville (1744). There was a significant expansion of settlement to the south, whence rice and cotton were exported to Europe. Carolina was divided into North and South in 1713, Georgetown being founded in 1735 and Charlotte in 1750. Georgia was established in 1732, Savannah being founded the following year.

Further north, the claims of the Hudson's Bay Company were recognised by the Peace of Utrecht 1713, by which Britain also gained Gibraltar, Minorca, Newfoundland and Nova Scotia. The Wars of Jenkins' Ear and the Austrian Succession (1739–48) did not bring any permanent gains, but the Seven Years' War (1756–63) brought Senegal, Grenada, Tobago, St Vincent, Dominica, Florida, French Canada and Louisiana east of the Mississippi.

Britain also became a major territorial power in India in mid-century. The perception of Britain's role and capacity changed dramatically in the 1760s and 1770s. Bengal, Bihar and Orissa were brought under British control after victories at Plassey (1757) and Buxar (1764). The army of the East India Company rose from 3,000 in 1748 to 69,000 in 1763. Bengal's resources were to be crucial to later expansion.

The American War of Independence (1775–83) led to a number of losses, including the Thirteen Colonies, Florida, Tobago, Minorca and Senegal, but Britain retained Canada and her Indian and West Indian possessions, and in the 1780s the number of overseas possessions increased with the foundation of settlements in Australia (1788) and Sierra Leone (1787). The British decision in 1786 to found the colony of New South Wales at Botany Bay in Australia was primarily taken for strategic reasons and to found a penal settlement for the convicts who could no longer be sent to North America.

The process of expansion was to take a tremendous leap forward during the French Revolutionary and Napoleonic wars which destroyed or weakened the imperial systems of the other European states and provided military and diplomatic incentives for Britain to seize their territories, so that the period 1793–1815 marked the apogee of one method of territorial gain – the acquisition of the colonies of other European powers – even though the other method, the gain of non-European-ruled territories, continued, especially in India and Australasia. The defeat of Tipu Sultan of Mysore in the war of 1790–2 led to modest gains in southern India; victory in another conflict in 1799 was followed by the acquisition of much of southern India (Marshall 1998).

The seizure of the extra-European territories of other European powers was bound up with foreign policy, understood as the formal diplomacy of the state. This was less the case with the acquisition of non-European-ruled lands, as initiatives were taken by non-governmental bodies, most importantly the East India Company (Lawson 1993), although the extent and reputation of British strength were clearly of importance. Furthermore, the willingness to allow such bodies a major role was itself an aspect of state policy.

The Hudson's Bay Company provided an example of the primarily commercial interests of a privileged company concerned to maintain and develop its privileges and profits. This produced criticism of its effectiveness in upholding national interests in the face of French competition and of its lack of interest in expanding into the interior of Canada, criticism that led in 1749 to a parliamentary enquiry, and in 1752 to an unsuccessful attempt by London merchants to obtain trading privileges in Labrador. Other privileged companies, such as the British Royal Africa Company, faced similar criticism. Their monopolies aroused anger in those excluded from their benefits, principally the merchants of secondary ports. Demands for governmental assistance, such as those from the British Royal Africa Company, were resented.

Expansion at the expense of non-Europeans is frequently not treated as an aspect of foreign policy, and possibly this leads to an underrating of the expansionist character of Britain. The process by which expansion took place, however, is controversial (Marshall 1998). Alongside an emphasis on British imperialism as a syncretic system, dependent on the co-operation of local elites, most obviously in India, there has also been a stress on its coercive character. The former approach stresses consensus and continuity, the latter force and discontinuity. A recent study of Bengal in the eighteenth century scrutinises the different attitudes of natives and the British to authority and profit, with particular reference to financial control over markets and trade. It suggests that the idea of a market economy was more important to the British, and that the entry of the East India Company into regional trade involved force: the colonial confrontation was a prolonged contest over the habits, terms and meaning of goods, markets, and people that constituted a vital link between authority, patronage and material culture in pre-modern Bengal. Once Company power was forcibly established in mid-century, a process that began in 1757 and was complete by 1765, there was an alteration in the political economy of trade as control over customs was monopolised. The authority of local landed chiefs was banished from rivers, ferries and tollways, and intermediate writs over markets were ended. As a consequence, the colonial marketplace was opened up to the freer flow of imperial commodities and investment. The gathering of information was central to this policy. Long-distance trade rose and prices became more uniform. Published lists of prices challenged the immense variety of wholesale and retail rates that had once characterised markets where trade was subject to different political authorities (Sen 1998).

It is unclear how far a similar stress is appropriate elsewhere in the empire, but much of it clearly rested on force. This was most apparent with the role of slavery, especially in the West Indies and North America. In both, the viability of the British colonial presence was directly related to an economy of force. By 1740, two-thirds of the population of South Carolina were slaves. The ratio in the British West Indies was five-sixths, and in 1789 there were 50,000 whites, 10,500 'free coloureds', and 594,000 slaves there. The slave trade and the plantation economy were both central to Britain's Atlantic economy. Although the Society for Effecting the Abolition of the Slave Trade was founded in 1787, Britain did not prohibit the slave trade until 1806–7 and slaves were not emancipated until 1833.

There is an understandable sense that colonial and commercial considerations ought to be important in the formulation and execution of foreign policy, and that the rôle of commerce and interest in its expansion and in colonial growth were 'structural' features of British policy that played a significant rôle in decisions. However, it is by no means so easy to assess the importance of these considerations.

It is possible to point to the prevalence of economic lobbying, an aspect of an integral part of British political culture and government, namely the acceptance that interested parties would lobby and that such lobbying could be a source of government policy, indeed that many activities that were subsequently to be seen as characteristic of government could be discharged by other bodies. Ministers were frequently pressed on colonial and commercial matters by interested parties. In March 1763, Sir Ellis Cunliffe, MP for Liverpool, a major centre for trans-oceanic trade, gave a firm warning to the Earl of Bute about post-war colonial arrangements.

Being informed a message from His Majesty would come to the House of Commons 'for granting seven thousand pounds for the maintenance of the forts and settlements in the River Senegal' my duty to my constituents, as well as their instructions to me engaged me to take the liberty to enquire of the Chancellor of the Exchequer how; or under whose management this money was to be employed; suggesting at the same time it was the sense of the commercial part of the nation that 'The Committee of the Company of Merchants trading to Africa' who had been appointed and approved by Parliament in the care of the other forts, were the properest persons to have the care of these. The Chancellor answered 'He did not doubt they would be the persons employed, but wished me not to make any motion, or mention anything about it in the House'. Now, My lord! as I am desirous always to concur with Government, and have the greatest confidence in your Lordship's administration, I am content to remain silent on this occasion, provided proper assurances be given that the forts and settlements in Senegal will not be put into private hands, but placed under the direction of the African Committee; But should a contrary measure be intended, this appears to me so destructive of the commerce of this nation in general, and of that of my constituents in particular, that I must think myself obliged to oppose it.

Cunliffe informed Bute that he would wait on him in order to ascertain his views 'and to give any farther information I can' (MS Cardiff 9/93). A year later, George Grenville, then First Lord of the Treasury, was warned that a change in linen tariffs would hit trade, 'and whenever that declines the wealth, power, and influence of Great Britain must proportionably be weakened' (HL STG 21, 69-70). Senior members of great chartered companies, such as the East India Company, considered it perfectly reasonable to press ministers for meetings in order to communicate their views, as the Russia Company did to Charles, 1st Lord Hawkesbury, the President of the Board of Trade, in June 1787 on Britons becoming Russian citizens.

It would, however, be inappropriate to suggest that such actions were necessarily unwelcome. Ministries sought both information and advice from mercantile and colonial representatives. This process was not restricted to Britain. In France a Council of Commerce was active in Louis XIV's latter years, while, for example, in January 1764 the foreign minister consulted deputies from St Malo about the Newfoundland fisheries over which Britain and France were in dispute. In Britain, however, the process was more marked, partly because the integration of government and economic and financial interests was much further advanced. This owed something to the dependence of government on the financial support of the City, as the state financial system ran on credit, and the ability to raise loans increased in importance as the National Debt rose substantially after each war.

National Debt

(million pounds)

1679	16.7	1763	133
1720	50.0	1775	131
1748	76.0	1783	232
1756	74.0	1790	244

The size of the debt and the relatively low rates of interest at which the government was able to borrow were both a testimony to widespread confidence in the British system. Although most credit was raised within Britain, the British also drew heavily on foreign capital, particularly from the Dutch and from a Huguenot financial international. Jewish interests were also important. (Wilson 1941; Crouzet 1996: 221-66).

Though the peerage was a relatively closed group and in much of England few new men acquired substantial landed estates, there was a significant moneyed interest based on, but not restricted to, London. This interest was neither socially nor politically distinct from the landed elite. Intermarriage, the careers of younger sons, the financial and economic affairs of the elite, and the weakness of traditions of urban political independence all combined to produce a harmony of interests. Mercantile groups were well represented in the House of Commons which, by the standards of European representative institutions, had a large urban component. Of the 2041 MPs, elected from the dissolution of 1715 to that in 1754, there were (there is some overlap of categories) 198 'merchants', 43 principal industrialists, 31 London aldermen, 27 directors of the Bank of England, 29 directors of the East India Company, 28 directors of the South Sea Company and 27 owners of estates in the West Indies. Of the 1964 MPs returned between the dissolutions of 1754 and 1790, there were 10 directors of the Bank of England, 16 of the South Sea Company, 31 London Aldermen and 9 colonial agents. Of the 558 members in the Parliament of 1784, 90 there were 45 'East Indians' (directors of the Company or 'nabobs' who had returned from India with wealth) and 9 West Indians, compared with 26 and 14 in that of 1774–80 (Sedgwick: 148–53; Namier and Brooke: 131–62). Many of the seats they sat for were rural, but the sense of a sharp urban/rural divide was stronger in literary than in political circles.

It would be inappropriate, however, to explain mercantile influence by reference to political strength and pressure. That would imply a coherence and a need for pressure, both of which were absent.

Important mercantile interests generally enjoyed easy access to ministers and officials, a process that was facilitated when they had or were given a financial stake, as happened with the Company of Royal Adventurers, whose actions played a major rôle in precipitating the Second Anglo-Dutch war. In July 1699, James Vernon, the Northern Secretary, wrote to Blathwayt, then with William III on the Continent, urging action in response to mercantile complaints about Savoyard innovations, and separately informed him that the merchants concerned in the tobacco trade with Russia had delivered a memorial to the Lords Justices, who 'thought it very reasonable they should have a Consul at Moscow and that if His Majesty pleased they should be recommended to the Czar in general terms only as to the enlargement of their trade and that they be not obliged to bring in more tobacco than the country will take nor pay duties for more than what they bring. We have accordingly prepared the draught of a letter', for which, as for the appointment of the merchants' choice as consul, William's approval was sought. Two months later, the process of consultation was still close, Vernon writing: 'We are preparing answers to the letter from the Czar and in the meantime I have spoke with some concerned in the Russia trade' (Beinecke, Osborn Shelves, Blathwayt Box 19). Similar co-operation could also be found with the East India Company. In 1782, Shelburne wrote to Grantham: 'as the sacrifices for peace and the chief risk of the war now lie with the India Company, and as the Cabinet left it to your Lordship to settle with them, would it not be prudent for your Lordship to see the Secret Committee [of the Company] without delay to know how much farther they would be inclined to go?' (Bedford CRO L30/14/306/6).

Aware of the fiscal and economic benefits of overseas trade, successive ministries sought to foster it. This was encouraged by the prevalence in Europe of economic regulation. Ideas of free trade had little currency until the end of the eighteenth century, Adam Smith's *Inquiry into the Nature and Causes of the Wealth of Nations* appearing in 1776. Even then, Smith's ideas were widely ignored.

Economic regulation promoted government protectionism and this was further encouraged by the notion that the volume of trade was essentially constant, so that an increase in that of one power would necessarily lead to a reduction elsewhere, and by the weakness of currency mechanisms which led to a stress on bullion and therefore on a favourable balance of trade that would maintain bullion inflows. The government sought to create a protected home market and to encourage a positive balance of trade in manufactured products, and, to that end, legislated for Britain, Ireland and the colonies. The export of raw materials, such as raw wool and thus sheep, was prohibited, as was that of textile machinery and the emigration of artisans. Manufactured imports were restricted or prohibited, for example silks and printed calicoes in 1700. The Irish and colonial economies were regulated in order to make them assist, not rival, that of Britain. The growing importance to Britain of colonial re-exports and of colonial markets encouraged this tendency.

English Re-exports

(million pounds)

1700	2.13	1750	3.23
1710	1.57	1760	3.71
1720	2.30	1770	4.76
1730	3.22	1780	4.32
1740	3.09	1790	4.83

(1710, 1740, 1760 and 1780 were war years.)

In 1750, the making of steel, the refining of iron and the manufacture of finished articles from iron were prohibited in the North American colonies. When, in 1785, Pitt, influenced by the ideas of Adam Smith, sought to introduce free trade between Britain and Ireland, he was defeated because of Irish political circumstances, but the plan also aroused considerable opposition in Britain. British manufacturing interests were organised into a 'Great Chamber of Manufacturers' by the pottery entrepreneur Josiah Wedgwood, a great exporter, and the Commons received over 60 petitions from manufacturing and mercantile centres. Philip Yorke MP noted the industrialists' fear of Irish rivalry in foreign markets, their conviction that lower taxes and cheaper labour and food made Ireland more competitive, and the fall in the ministerial majority on the issue (BL Add. 35534 f. 177).

Economic interests, therefore, in general supported regulation, especially protectionism. Pressure for change came from intellectuals, not merchants, and especially not manufacturers. The principal practitioners of free-market initiatives – smugglers – were a surreptitious, not a vocal group, their services used by many of the elite including Walpole but their profits dependent on protectionism and their activities widely decried on the grounds that they purveyed foreign non-essentials such as brandy and lace, and exported bullion.

More important and vocal in calling for freer trade were merchants who sought to operate in the trades controlled by the chartered companies, whose privileges were contentious and especially unpopular in ports outside London. The importance of this rift was, however, lessened by the fact that the chartered companies operated in areas where a measure of organisation was required, either because, as in Hudson's Bay, India and West Africa, fortified bases had to be supported, or, as with Turkey and Russia, trade was heavily dependent on negotiations with a foreign power. Most British trade was not controlled by chartered companies, and this was as true of areas of major expansion, such as North America and Iberia, as of those whose progress was less spectacular, especially north-west Europe.

Thus, government-backed regulation, either directly, as in protectionism and Navigation Acts, or indirectly, as in the privileges of chartered companies, was generally supported, even if particular details might arouse opposition. Ministries sought to respond to developments, especially hostile actions abroad. A long series of treaties, such as Sandwich's of 1667, Dodington's of 1715 and Keene's of 1750, attempted to protect and expand Anglo-Spanish trade, while Colbert's protectionist regulations in France in the 1660s and 1670s led to a response in England. Trumbull, envoy in Paris, described raised French tariffs in 1686 as 'in effect a total prohibition' (PRO SP 78/150 f. 74). In 1678, the import of French wine, silk, linen, cloth, salt and paper was prohibited, a measure repealed by James II's Parliament in 1685. The prohibitions were reimposed in 1689 and extended in 1695–7, and Bolingbroke's attempt to open trade with France was defeated in the Commons in 1713.

If the Anglo-French alliance of 1716–31 did not witness a liberalisation or fostering of Anglo-French trade, Britain had only mixed success with her other allies. Portugal was the great success story. The Methuen Treaty of 1703 opened the country for British cloth and gave Portuguese wines a considerable advantage in the English market. The treaty was underwritten by the alliance of the two powers in the War of the Spanish Succession and by military assistance to Portugal when she was threatened (1735) and attacked (1762) by Spain. The Portuguese possession of Brazil became Europe's principal source of gold in the early eighteenth century and the positive balance of trade with Portugal brought Britain much bullion, though the relationship deteriorated with Pombal's protectionist measures in the 1760s and 1770s and the British government was criticised for failing to maintain commercial privileges.

Elsewhere, the situation was less satisfactory. It had been hoped that alliance with Austria would lead to improved trade. In October 1705, Blathwayt wrote to Stepney: 'I shall be very glad to find out some medium that may be of certain advantage to both nations, which may be by settling a general trade between the Emperor's dominions and the rest of Germany (with the parts adjacent) and those of Her Majesty . . . so profitable a trade which must be created and nourished by signal concessions from the Emperor, and through his high office, from the lesser princes' (Beinecke, Osborn Shelves, Blathwayt Box 21).

This hope was to prove deceptive, as were subsequent plans, and commercial disputes between the two powers continued in periods of both friendship and hostility. Considerable anger was aroused in the 1720s by Austrian attempts to develop a trade with the East Indies, the Ostend Company founded for this purpose being seen as a threat to British trade. Commercial relations were hampered further by disputes over the tariffs in the Austrian Netherlands, and by quarrels over the terms of British trade to other Austrian possessions. In Sicily the Austrians refused to grant British traders the privileges they had enjoyed while the island was Spanish, and British hostility to the acquisition of Naples and Sicily by Philip V's son Don Carlos in 1734–5 was moderated by the fact that his administration was more respectful of British interests than the preceding one. British exports to the Austrian hereditary lands in the late 1720s were affected by an increase in Austrian tariffs, especially on British cloth exports. A memorandum of November 1739 noted that mercantile pressure for action against Austrian commercial legislation had been both strong and long-lasting and that Parliament would have taken measures in the session of 1739 to end the important tariff concession on Silesian linen imports, had not the government yielded to Austrian diplomatic pressure (PRO SP 80/227, 16 Nov.).

In 1739, a determined effort to improve the situation was made. The British envoy, Thomas Robinson, supported by the specialist advice of the merchant James Porter, pressed the Austrians to permit the development of trade between Britain and the hereditary lands through Trieste. This would be a direct trade carried on in British ships, and would replace the indirect trade through Hamburg and the Low Countries, and middlemen in towns such as Frankfurt, Nurnberg and Augsburg. The British sought lower tariffs on their imports at Trieste and an agreement whereby, once the tariffs had been paid there, British goods would be exempt from taxes on internal trade. The British hoped to export indigenous products, such as woollens, as well as colonial goods, such as sugar and tobacco. Had the scheme succeeded, it would have made Austria part of the 'informal empire' of British commerce, as Portugal had been since 1703. Britain would have purchased for a low price Austrian raw materials, such as copper and silver. The silver would have helped to finance British trade to areas with which there was a negative balance of trade, such as Russia and the East Indies.

Austria would have provided in turn a secure market for both colonial and manufactured products. The latter were being increasingly shut out of continental markets, for example Sweden, Denmark and Savoy-Piedmont (Kingdom of Sardinia), by protectionist legislation aimed at improving local industries. By providing a secure market for British colonial exports, British colonies would be helped against French competition.

In 1736, Robinson had written to George Tilson, an under-secretary in the Northern Department: 'Believe me you may look upon Hungary as a new world,' to which the more phlegmatic Tilson had replied pointing out that increased trade depended on Austrian willingness to accept British goods (PRO SP 80/123, 22 Sept.; BL Add. 23799 f. 176). The success of Austrian attempts to develop manufacturing industry depended to a great extent upon protectionism, and the Austrians had no intention of jeopardising these industries for the sake of increased trade with Britain. Negotiations, begun in 1739, revived in 1742–3, but British approaches did not meet with an enthusiastic response in Vienna, where there was an unwillingness to consider commercial concessions. Similarly, discussions in 1737–40 and 1749–52 concerning the situation in the Austrian Netherlands led to no agreement (Dickson 1973).

After the War of the Austrian Succession, Charles VI's plans for commercial growth, based on protectionism and economic integration, were revived, to the detriment of foreign merchants. Plans for oceanic trade under Austrian protection agitated several British diplomats, such as Robert Walpole in Lisbon in April 1776, but they were less damaging than Austrian protectionism. In 1784, the Foreign Secretary, Francis, Marquis of Carmarthen, complained about an Austrian regulation against the import of manufactured goods, writing: 'the towns of Manchester and Sheffield have taken the alarm and have applied to government on the subject'. Keith was instructed to threaten reprisals in the face of 'daily increasing' alarm in Britain (PRO FO 7/9, 26 Oct., 2 Nov.). However, British complaints were no more successful than they had been in the 1720s. In 1763, Joseph Yorke was assured by merchants that tariffs in the Austrian Netherlands amounted to 'very near a prohibition of some of our best manufacturers' (BL Add. 58213 f. 204).

Carmarthen's concern about manufacturing opinion is interesting. The same year, when the Austrian envoy sought to win British support for the opening of the Scheldt, on the grounds that it would aid British trade, Carmarthen asked Keith whether it would 'procure solid and permanent advantages to the British commerce. I cannot but think that had this proposed scheme been likely to have produced any fatal consequences to our trade, the English merchants would e'er this, have been alarmed at the mere report of the plan, and would have already communicated their apprehensions to government' (PRO FO 7/8, 11 May).

Ministers were convinced that they had done everything possible to protect trade, Hawkesbury writing in 1787: 'The navigation of this country is so well protected at present by the laws that are made to favour it, as well as by the excellence of our ships and sailors that nothing in my judgement is to be apprehended from the rivalship of the French in this respect' (BL Add. 38309 f. 146). However, there was a limit to what could be done, not least because of the competition of other trading powers. Furthermore, most protectionist legislation was not aimed specifically against Britain. Keene reported from Spain in 1749 his suspicion that 'here is more inclination to lop off as many privileges as they can, from every nation that has trade and treaties with them, than to show any partiality or predilection to them' (PRO SP 94/135 f 53). Co-operation with other commercial powers against protectionist legislation was generally implausible in light of competition and of hostility towards British commercial strength.

In the case of the Baltic, diplomats intervened on behalf of their merchants, complaining about the enlisting of their servants in Königsberg in Prussia in 1716 and about increased duties at Elsinore in Denmark in 1730. Nevertheless, commercial interests tended to be subordinate to political concerns. Complaints over Danish and Swedish protectionist legislation did not lead to the reprisals that were threatened. Trade with Russia was subordinated to political considerations in the 1710s and 1720s, and the commercial treaty of 1734 was negotiated only after political relations had improved. British envoys complained about commercial grievances, but the ministry rarely made them a central plank of policy, and most complaints were far from effective. Daniel Pulteney reported a lack of success in Copenhagen in 1715.

> I should only have prostituted myself and the service I am employed in by continuing to threaten to no purpose. I have never neglected to solicit in favour of British subjects to the utmost of my power; had I been less zealous in this respect, I might have met with more kindness from the Danes, I might say less trouble and vexation, than I have met with; but I can only solicit and not force; and these people are not to be won by reason and persuasion. (PRO SP 75/35, 29 Jan.)

Force was not to be made available to support complaints such as Pulteney's. The fleets sent to the Baltic in the late 1710s were instructed to protect trade against privateers, not protectionism, and their primary purpose was political. Swedish fears in 1742 that British mercantile complaints about Swedish privateering would lead to the dispatch of a fleet to the Baltic were misplaced.

Nevertheless, if ministries, as opposed to their frequent acceptance of mercantile advice, rarely *yielded* to commercial lobbies, especially if to do so would entail diplomatic difficulties, they were aware that trade was a potent political symbol and slogan and that it could lead to political difficulties. There was also concern about the foreign response to Britain, which was often seen abroad as being swayed by commercial considerations, rather than simply mercantile influences. The French envoy Courtin reported in 1676 that London 'gives a great impetus to the affairs of this kingdom' (AE CP Ang. 119 ff. 22-3). In 1718, Spain wrongly hoped that the importance of her trade would prevent Britain from opposing her Italian schemes, while in late 1761 Charles III of Spain argued incorrectly that mercantile opposition to the cost of war with Spain, at the same time as Britain was fighting France, would prevent the ministry from going to war (Christelow 1946: 26). In 1730, a British print included a medallion showing Britain between the Empire and Spain, taking Spain by the hand and saying 'I prefer the useful.'

The British refusal to support Austria in the War of the Polish Succession (1733–5) was blamed by some on such attitudes. Grain exports to the Continent, at a time of agrarian depression in England, were substantial during the war, though discussion of their impact is necessarily speculative due to the failure of the sources to offer adequate guidance on ministerial thinking and thus appreciation of the 'factors', 'structure' or context of British foreign policy. The 1734 general election was a major challenge for the government, and the principal electoral interests of Walpole and Newcastle were in the grain-producing and exporting counties of Norfolk and Sussex. It is possible that concern about the electoral implications of rural stagnation, which would be exacerbated if taxes rose to finance a war, was a factor in persuading the ministry, especially Walpole, to oppose the royal support for intervention in the conflict. However, judging from surviving sources, the principal issue in the election was the recent Excise scheme.

Grain was again an issue in 1748, Newcastle writing to Sandwich that January:

> There has been an unlucky accident happened in the House of Commons, relating to the exportation of corn. Some officious, designing fools had given out that, in order to prevent carrying corn to France, there must be a total prohibition of all exportation. The country gentlemen and some others were so alarmed at this that, without considering the consequences, or knowing

what had passed in Holland, they came to a resolution against prohibiting the exportation of corn; but this is only general, and can't authorise the carrying it to France; which, as all commerce is, is prohibited by the Declaration of War. This has given me a good deal of concern; but we will try, if we cannot find out some method, to get it right, by strengthening the prohibition of France.

Sandwich replied that the impact on Britain's Dutch ally was very negative. 'The Resolution of the House of Commons about the exportation of corn has done much hurt . . . absolutely necessary for you to remove the ill impression' (BL Add. 32811 ff. 125, 179). It was not surprising that Hawkesbury believed in 1787 that the Portuguese, in pursuing their commercial differences with Britain, were only waiting 'to see what will be the sense of Parliament and the disposition of the people' (BL Add. 38309 f. 137).

And yet if the ministry could be forced to give way to agitations in which commercial issues and lobbies played a rôle, as with France over the commercial treaty in 1713, war with Spain in 1739 and peace with Russia in 1791, there were other episodes in which such issues and lobbies were less important. In June 1768, Shelburne told the Sardinian envoy that the government might be forced to war by mercantile anxiety over the consequences of the French acquisition of Corsica for trade to Italy and the Levant, but conflict was avoided.

Rather than concentrating on episodes of apparent differences of view or on the extent to which diplomatic relations were not sacrificed for trade, it is more useful to consider the question as to how far the general direction of British policy affected trade. This direction could be summarised as seeking stability in Europe and growth elsewhere. Britain was a 'satisfied' European power not seeking territorial acquisitions other than the naval bases of Gibraltar and Minorca, and her continental interventions were essentially designed to resist or redress what were believed to be threatening developments -though there were exceptions, most obviously the Treaty of Dover and the Third Anglo-Dutch war. Periods of interventionist diplomacy were similarly designed to resist threats: the danger of war over the Spanish Succession (1698–1700), Peter I's apparent threat to the Baltic balance (1716–21), Philip V's attempts to overthrow the Utrecht settlement (1718–20), French successes in the early stages of the War of Austrian Succession (1741–4), the danger that France and Prussia would threaten the subsequent peace (1748–53), the challenge posed by French influence in the United Provinces (1787), and the threat of rising Russian power in eastern Europe (1789–91). There was support for British commercial growth outside Europe and colonial acquisitions, though there was no blueprint of world conquest, and the apparent dangers posed by colonies, especially the cost of defending them and the possibility that migration to them might weaken Britain, were stressed.

This combination was arguably beneficial to trade. Britain had the smallest army of the major powers and she was at war for fewer years than Austria, France and Russia. British ministries were conscious of the economic value of keeping taxes low, though the burdens of war, in the shape of the national debt (the largest item of peacetime expenditure) and military expenditure (the second-largest item) ensured that per capita taxes were higher than in more populous France. Had British policy been more aggressive, the situation would probably have been more detrimental. War finance strained the monetary system, depressed general standards of consumption and distorted trade and manufacturing, even though certain activities, such as metallurgy, benefited. When, in April 1773, the 2nd Earl of Fife wrote to his factor expressing his hope that British naval preparations should not lead to war, he observed: 'stock jobbers, Jews and contractors make by that, but you and I are out of pocket' (A. and H. Taylor (eds), *Lord Fife*, 1925: 78). He could have added to those who did not gain those merchants affected by privateers, convoying and higher insurance rates.

Given the urban context of 'patriot' opinion, with its stress on an aggressive maritime strategy (Wilson 1995), the argument that peace assisted manufacturing and mercantile interests might appear surprising, but a number of points can be made. First, the interest in European peace of the bulk of merchant interests did not preclude support for war from others, especially those who considered themselves at a disadvantage, such as the Company of Royal Adventurers towards the Dutch in the early 1660s and the West Indian interest towards Spain in the late 1730s. Secondly, urban opinion was divided. It is misleading to consider 'patriot' views as necessarily typical. The social context of political views is not easy to identify with precision, but, in general, in London such 'patriot' opinion was supported by the Common Council, not by the more socially distinguished aldermen. Henry Fox could observe that 'No Pelham, no money was the City cry' when Carteret returned briefly in 1746 (BL Add. 51417 ff. 213–14), but the Pelham ministry was to be criticised severely in some London circles over the return of Cape Breton.

Government opinion did not always favour merchants. Joseph Yorke complained in 1764 of 'the East India Companies, who seem to me to be both in the wrong and to require some superior power to interfere and keep them in order; they certainly live in Asia in a perpetual state of warfare, and are always complaining in Europe as if they were both innocent' (BL Add. 58213 f. 343). The following year, George III expressed his support for Captain Palliser, the naval officer in command at Newfoundland, 'both against the complaints that his judicious conduct will draw on him from the French and our own merchants, as impartiality will ever make a man odious in the eyes of traders' (BL Eg. 982 f 6).

In general, governments were wary about the idea of colonial conquest, aware of both the military costs and the likely diplomatic drawbacks, though towards the end of the eighteenth century there was more support for such a policy as interest increased in lands unoccupied by other European powers, largely around the Pacific. However, it would be rash to identify mercantile opinion with publicists for colonial expansion. Merchants sought profit, not factories (trading posts) that had to be protected. Indeed, the colonial disputes that exacerbated Anglo-Bourbon relations tended to arise from the actions of local colonial and military officials, whom it was often difficult to control from Europe, as in the Anglo-French disputes over Tobago in 1749 and Turks Island in 1764, or from the actions of merchants and settlers who were not members or representatives of elite trading groups, for example the interloping Caribbean traders of the 1730s or the logwood cutters of Honduras who exacerbated Anglo-Spanish relations.

Foreign policy therefore favoured trade without being the slave of traders. Colonial gains brought pride, but their acquisition was not a central theme of policy. Instead, the preservation of colonial possessions, really or apparently endangered, such as North America in the 1750s and 1770s or India in 1784–7, was a much more important objective, though this could lead to a dangerous 'forward' policy, as in North America in 1755. The bulk of colonial gains were acquired in the Seven Years', French Revolutionary and Napoleonic wars, conflicts whose initial purposes were not major colonial conquests.

Nevertheless, the Seven Years' War reflected greater sensitivity to colonial issues. The pressure for commercial and colonial gain, for what the *Westminster Journal*, on 1 April 1749, termed 'the principle of take and hold in America', was wider in its origin than a governmental shift in favour of a foreign policy of imperial mercantilism. The Seven Years' War was about not only what Voltaire termed the wastes of Canada, but also its furs, the fish of Newfoundland, and, eventually, the sugar of the West Indies, and the trade of West Africa and India. It was the war of a society that understood the politics of economic competition.

For Britain, this was a major shift in priority. From the Reformation until 1713 foreign policy, by both design and necessity, had been essentially defensive in character, motivated primarily by concern about the intentions of the two most powerful states in western Europe, France and Spain, and, specifically, by their intentions towards the overlapping questions of the survival of the Reformation, the British question (the relationship between England/Wales, Scotland and Ireland), and the succession to the throne, both in the sixteenth century and from 1688. Thus, for example, a temporary lull in Franco-Habsburg hostilities after the Truce of Nice (1538), which enabled the papacy to press for action against England, led Henry VIII to construct a chain of coastal fortresses, increase the fleet and turn to the German Lutheran princes for allies. French troops were sent to Ireland in 1689, to help James II resist William III, and to Scotland, to help Charles Edward Stuart during the 1745–6 Jacobite rising. Anglo-French rivalry reflected domestic developments within the British Isles, and also the position of the two powers with reference to other states, especially Spain. Thus Elizabeth I sent troops to assist the French Huguenot (Protestant) leader, Henry of Navarre, Henry IV, in 1589–97, in large part because he was opposed to Spain; this was the crucial factor after Henry's reconversion to Catholicism in 1593. Colonial issues played only a minor role in this period, principally in tension between England and the Dutch.

From 1716 until 1731 Britain and France were allies. In 1733–5 and 1741 the government refused to act in favour of Austria when it was attacked by France. As with Italy and Austro-Hungary at the close of the nineteenth century, two rivals maintained their rivalry and yet allied. It was in part this very willingness of the Whigs to accept a European role for France, combined with the French acceptance that Jacobite claims should not be pushed in peacetime, that led to peace and, at times, good relations between the two powers from 1713 until the early 1740s. Again, colonial issues only took a minor role.

This essentially European agreement was wrecked by the revival during the War of the Austrian Succession of French aggression (1741) and of countervailing military intervention on the Continent by a bellicose British ministry (1742), a shift that prefigured that of 1792–3, although the ideological and domestic contexts were then very different. However, the western question was settled for over forty years by the 1748 peace settlement -thereafter there were to be no territorial shifts in the Low Countries, Rhineland or Northern Italy until the 1790s. It was possible, within a context of rivalry and competing alliance systems or attempted diplomatic alignments, for Britain and France to work out a modus vivendi in western Europe, a process eased by the extent to which France no longer had to fear her Continental neighbours as she had ever since the demise of English ambitions at the end of the Hundred Years' War.

It proved impossible, however, to make comparable progress over extra-European differences, and this helped to keep Anglo-French relations volatile from the 1750s until the check the French received in the Dutch crisis of 1787, and then, again, during the nineteenth-century heyday of imperial territorialisation. In Britain, hope and anxiety, ambition and identity, were increasingly focused on imperial, colonial and maritime issues. In 1754 hostilities began over control of the Ohio River basin in North America; in 1778 over French support for the American revolutionaries. Although Britain went to war with both Revolutionary France and Napoleon over European issues, the oceanic and colonial struggle with France played a central role during the subsequent conflicts.

Growing economic strength enabled Britain to finance increasingly heavy public expenditure, ensuring that the rise in the percentage of national income appropriated as taxes from about 3.5 per cent in the 1670s to 11–12 per cent during the War of American Independence (Brewer 1989: 91) had formidable consequences, not least in terms of the massive military effort that was made to retain America. Her increasing maritime strength and pretensions made Britain appear a threat to other trading powers, inspiring the Armed Neutrality of 1780 (p. 245), and it also led some commentators to suggest that she would be able to dominate Europe. Silas Deane, an agent of the rebel Americans, warned a French sympathiser in 1777 that:

> . . . if Great Britain, by forming an accommodation of friendship with the United States, renders herself, as by that measure she easily can, mistress of that world, by taking the affairs of the East Indies into her own hands, she will be in possession of exhaustless treasure. . . . Add to all this her strict and close alliance with Russia . . . it is easy to foresee that Great Britain, America and Russia united will command not barely Europe, but the whole world united. Russia, like America, is a new state, and rises with the most astonishing rapidity. Its demand for British manufactures and its supplies of raw materials increase nearly as fast as the American; and when both come to center in Great Britain, the riches, as well as power, of that kingdom will be unparalleled in the annals of Europe, or perhaps of the world. Like a Colossus, with one foot on Russia and the East and the other on America, it will bestride . . . your poor European world. (*Diplomatic Correspondence of the United States* II, 332–3).

Such remarks were designed to encourage the Bourbons to intervene, as were suggestions that Britain might defeat the Americans. In light of

British strength the following century, they might appear prophetic, but in 1777 threats to Britain's position in North America were more striking than the then generally implausible notion that American independence would be followed by maintenance of good commercial relations. Furthermore, Anglo-Russian trade links were under increasing strain. The commercial treaty of 1766, expired in 1786, and was not renewed, despite British efforts. Instead, Catherine II signed a trade treaty with France. French trade to the West Indies rose rapidly in the 1780s and, as French interest in Egypt and the Near East and trade with Russia via the Black Sea rose in that decade, it appeared possible to see France as the forthcoming global commercial power. It was essentially political developments that led to this prospect being overturned.

CHAPTER SEVEN

PUBLIC OPINION AND THE PRESS

I cannot rest for these preparations of the Turks.
(Politic in Henry Fielding's *Coffee-House Politician* (1730; I, iii)

Any discussion of public opinion leads necessarily to the question of how this was informed and influenced. The extent to which the public was well informed about foreign affairs clearly varied. Critical notes were struck by some commentators. In 1676, the French envoy reported: 'most of the English know nothing of general affairs. They only understand their own country and when you talk to them of the interests of Denmark, Sweden and Germany they are embarrassed' (AE CP Ang. 118 ff. 209–10). That great source of information, the press, carried criticisms of the accuracy of newspaper and other printed reports. On 13 September 1764, the *St James's Chronicle* prefaced its own description with the remark: 'many inaccurate descriptions having been given of Turks Island'. The following 28 March, it printed a letter bewailing the state of geography and history. On 28 August 1773, the *Westminster Journal* carried a criticism of reports of the Russian position in the Balkans: 'your newspaper accounts indeed have intimated, that it was but crossing the Danube and Constantinople would be theirs immediately. But what if I was to tell you that Constantinople is 300 miles from the banks of the Danube.'

Other comments were less critical. In 1768, Shelburne replied to the claim by the French envoy that Londoners were not disturbed by the French acquisition of Corsica: 'the genius of our people, who for the most part appear so occupied with domestic transactions, that the interest really taken in foreign affairs naturally escapes the observation of a foreigner, who cannot have sufficient experience of this country to foresee the effect which events will have' (PRO SP 78/275 f. 34). A wealth of information was offered in the press. Much of it was fairly basic, for example the placing of countries in brackets after towns mentioned in the *Newcastle Courant* in March 1746, Paris thereby being identified as in France. Other items were more extensive, highlighting current affairs, such as the 'succinct account of the important fortress of Maastricht and of the country about it' in the *Remembrancer* of 16 April 1748 or the account and map of the Falklands in the *Gentleman's Magazine* of October 1770. Periodicals benefited from the increasing appearance of more detailed works. The Lincolnshire clergyman and historian Laurence Echard also published descriptions of Ireland and the Spanish Netherlands (1691), a *Most Compleat Compendium of Geography* (1691, 8th edn 1713), and *The Gazetteer's or Newsman's Interpreter – a Geographical Index* (3rd edn 1695, 15th 1741). In September 1770, the *Gentleman's Magazine* described *A Geographical, Historical, and Commercial Grammar; and Present State of the Several Kingdoms of the World* by William Guthrie: 'The author's principal view has been to bring a general and comprehensive knowledge of geography, history and commerce within the reach of those who have neither much leisure nor much money . . . as the Turks are now become objects of public attention in consequence of the war carried on against them by Russia . . . we have abridged this author's account of its origin.'

The question of the press's influence is a vexed one (Black 1987b), but contemporaries were struck by the knowledge or at least interest of the humble. In his *True Patriot* of 11 March 1746, Henry Fielding commented: 'in politics, every man is an adept; and the lowest mechanic delivers his opinion, at his club, upon the deepest public measures, with as much dignity and sufficiency as the highest member of the Commonwealth . . . it may frequently happen that the wisest and best measures of a ministry may not meet with the approbation of a two-penny club or a meeting of fox-hunters'. The *St James's Chronicle* of 27 September 1764, discussing whether Britain should have continued the Seven Years' War in order to retain Guadeloupe and Martinique, commented: 'even our tinkers and cobblers are politicians and the first to roar for war; as they would be the first to roar against the additional halfpenny on their pot of porter, when that war had made the levying it necessary'. The issue of 9 January 1766 carried a coffee-room dialogue in which Dunkirk, Turks Island, Newfoundland, Honduras, Canada bills and the Manila ransom were all discussed. Fielding satirised Londoners obsessed by newspaper reports of Continental developments in his play *The Coffee House Politician* (1730), while on 13 June 1724 the *Universal Journal* printed what was ostensibly a letter from a country reader attacking a neighbouring landlord, the young Mr Novel. This 'errant coxcomb' ignored his steward's accounts in order to read newspapers and indulged in incessant political speculation: 'beginning with the Persian rebels, makes the tour of the whole world, settles treaties, unhinges governments and reforms our state'.

Newspapers and pamphlets were discussed not only in coffee houses. They were referred to also by politicians and helped to link the worlds of the politically active and the politically interested. As a result, publications were actively sponsored by politicians. This was true of the second half of the seventeenth century, the Third Anglo-Dutch war, for example, leading to printed polemics, but it was more true of the following century, for the lapsing of the Licensing Act in 1695, and the consequent expansion of the press encouraged readers to turn to publications for information and analysis and thus encouraged their sponsorship. In 1718, the Lord Chancellor, the Earl of Macclesfield, allegedly ordered the printing of 7000 copies of *A Letter from a Merchant to a Member of Parliament, Relating to the danger Great Britain is in of losing her trade, by the great increase of the naval power of Spain with a chart of the Mediterranean Sea annex'd*. A further 2000 copies were apparently produced by the author Reeve Williams. In the pamphlet, Williams complained of the ignorant level of most discussion of foreign policy:

> The late action between His Majesty's fleet and that of Spain, is become entertainment of most conversations; but the misfortune is, that there is not one in five hundred of the persons who thus entertain themselves, that has any just idea of the good consequence thereof. For though the words Sicily and Sardinia, are often in their mouths, they scarce know in what part of the world those islands are situated. (CUL C(H) papers 73/4/1)

The impact of the pamphlet was increased by press coverage. The *Worcester Post-Man* of 21 November 1718 reported:

> Last Saturday a notable book was delivered to the Members of Parliament, with a chart annexed of the Mediterranean Sea, whereby it demonstrately appears of what importance it is to the trade of Great Britain, that Sicily and Sardinia should be in the hands of a faithful ally, and if possible not one formidable by sea. That these two islands lie like two nets spread to intercept not only the Italian but Turkey and Levant trade . . .. That should the naval power of Spain increase in the manner it has lately done, that kingdom may assume to herself that trade of the Mediterranean Sea, and impose what toll she pleases as the King of Denmark does at Elsinore.

Twenty-one years later, during the agitation over Spanish depredations, Newcastle wrote to Hardwicke: 'I wish we would get some prudent, impartial, dispassionate, creditable man to write upon the great question in dispute between our adversaries and us relating to the Convention and our present conduct' (BL Add. 35406 f. 162).

It was not only the ministry that sponsored propaganda. In 1739, medals were produced depicting Spanish bribery of the British envoy, Keene. It was claimed that 500 examples of one had been sold in Warwickshire (BL Add. 35586 ff. 207–8). This claim fits in with the dominant opposition bent of the provincial press in this period and with the suspicion of public opinion expressed by ministerial papers, especially the *Daily Gazetteer*, and by governmental parliamentarians. In 1731, the Earl of Chesterfield, then envoy at The Hague, urged a vigorous ministerial publicity campaign: 'They attack with invectives, and should be answered in the same manner; and we should not content ourselves with reasoning, with enemies that fight with poisoned arrows, besides that all reasoning is thrown away upon the people, they are utterly incapable of it' (PRO SP 84/311 f. 75).

That opposition agitation was of limited direct impact in 1739 (Woodfine 1998) does not mean that it was not of more intangible impact in creating or influencing a mood within which policy options were discussed. The opposition agitation in the late 1730s helped to influence national opinion in the long term by the dissemination of 'patriot' ideas on foreign policy, thus preparing a responsive audience for Pittite propaganda. Ministerial steps to extinguish opposition publications suggest that they were regarded as influential. In 1741, Walpole took steps to try to prevent the publication of an opposition pamphlet in the United Provinces.

However, it is important not to exaggerate the potency of print. Swift's *Conduct of the Allies*, a pamphlet designed to win support for governmental attempts to end the War of the Spanish Succession by criticising Britain's allies and the previous Whig ministry, appeared in November 1711 and sold 11,000 copies in two months. Swift claimed credit for the Commons' defeat of the 'No Peace without Spain' motion – his pamphlet was used as the source of Tory arguments. Nevertheless, a certain amount of scepticism is in order, just as care is required in ascribing too much influence in the parliamentary debates over the Peace of Paris of 1763 to the active newspaper and pamphlet debate. In 1711, peace was clearly coming. There had already been serious negotiations in 1709–10, the Grand Alliance was already under severe strain, war-weariness was strong, and hostility to the Tory ministry centred rather on fears concerning their views about the succession than on their determination to negotiate peace.

Criticism in print could be wearing. On 23 March 1739, at the height of the Spanish depredations controversy, Keene wrote to his Parisian counterpart, Waldegrave:

The last public papers are full of storms and petitions, and the not to be satisfied part of the nation seems to be cutting out work for a long and irksome session. I find by experience that he who cannot despise noise is not fit for a public employment. But let him despise it as much as he pleases it must disgust him at the long run and make him weary of public business. (Chewton)

Nine years later, Newcastle complained to Sandwich: 'I am pelted with pamphlets and papers every day; and God knows, if Maastricht is taken, whether some parliamentary attempt may not be made. Many are ready for it, and be assured, that the part you and I have taken is sorely against the grain of the House of Commons' (BL Add. 32812 f. 12). However, the argument should not be pushed too far. In 1739, the ministry was able to carry the Convention of the Pardo through the Commons, in 1748 to sign a peace returning Cape Breton, and in 1763 to win overwhelming parliamentary support for the peace terms. Replying, in March 1779, to an opposition motion for printing the Army Estimates, Lord North queried what was meant by the public, 'the populace, the readers of newspapers and coffee-house readers' or 'the real public, the representatives of the Commons of England', only to be told by Barré, 'those people, so termed coffee-house readers, were the identical persons who paid for the extraordinaries of the army, and that therefore they were at least entitled to know how their money was expended' (Cobbett 1806–20, xx: 328–9). The motion was nevertheless defeated. Newcastle's shift towards peace in 1748 was due to the collapse of the Dutch position, not British domestic opinion.

To limit direct impact by public opinion on policy is not, however, the same as denying it any rôle. For example, there was a strong sense in foreign policy after the Seven Years' War that Britain must be both wary of excessive Continental commitments and vigilant towards Bourbon maritime and colonial plans. This sense matched the lineaments of public debate, and it is appropriate to see that debate as framing and in part constituting the experience that politicians used to guide or explain their actions. There was no closed bureaucratic world surrounding the formulation and execution of foreign policy. Though the staff of the Secretaries of State offices were long-serving, and Under-Secretaries such as Joseph Williamson, James Vernon, Robert Yard, John Ellis, George Tilson, Charles Delafaye, Edward Weston and William Fraser were not without influence, they rarely directed policy. Few Under-Secretaries became Secretaries, though Williamson, Vernon and Joseph Addison were exceptions, the last two, however, having little impact as Secretaries. Instead, the bureaucratic mechanisms of foreign policy were dominated by Secretaries of State who were essentially politicians and heavily, though variably, influenced by other ministers and the monarch. Thus, there was little sense of bureaucratic continuity in advocating particular lines in the face of possible political opposition.

If politicians' opinions were shaped by and responded to a wider, more amorphous world of opinion, that world was neither uniform nor did it provide detailed guidance over policy. There were public opinions, rather than public opinion, which were expressed forcefully in an episodic fashion only, and it could be argued that the press, with its general themes of xenophobia and anti-Bourbon vigilance, can be misleading. Press criticism was directed not only against foreign countries, but also against their supposed British supporters. In the reigns of Charles II and James II this provided a major theme in anti-Catholic discourse, and in 1689–1746 in attacks on the Jacobites. Aside from these political and religious reverberations, which ebbed with the decline of Jacobitism and political Catholicism as threats, there was a wider sense of cultural challenge coming in particular from France and from British supporters and consumers of French cultural fashions, ranging from cooking to hairstyles, theatre to prostitutes. These preferences were criticised bitterly in the press and yet they did not disappear. There was scant public defence of them, any more than of Catholic or Jacobite views, but to discount them is to imply a homogeneity that did not exist. More pertinently, there was no simple contrast between xenophobic views, for which 'patriotism' could be regarded as the political creed, and those that they criticised. Instead, there was clearly a range of opinions, of which one source in particular, the landed interest, appears to have been poorly represented in the world of print, though issues such as the export of grain revealed its political consequence, as did the more general tendency to centre taxation on customs and excises, rather than the inadequately assessed land tax.

An obvious feature of much printed comment on foreign policy was its paranoia. Britain was presented as under threat. Governments were condemned for failing to recognise threats. Walpole, for example, was accused of appeasing Spain. In *London*, published in May 1738, Samuel Johnson used Elizabeth I's successful stand against Spain to attack Walpole:

> 'In pleasing Dreams the blissful Age renew,
> And call Britannia's Glories back to view;
> Behold her Cross triumphant on the Main,
> The Guard of Commerce, and the Dread of Spain,
> Ere Masquerades debauch'd, Excise oppress'd,
> Or English Honour grew a standing Jest.'

The sense of threat was true even of the years after the victorious Seven Years' War. An article by 'Americanus', accusing the French of inspiring attacks by Native Americans on British colonists and published in the *St. James's Chronicle* of 10 January, was typical in its paranoia, accusations and strident tone:

'The incapacity of the peace-making ministry is nowhere more evident than in the affairs of America; our conquests there seem plainly to have been the chief object of their peace; yet so poorly did they provide for their security, that we see the French are wresting from us, by mere artifice, what we have purchased with millions of men, and ten millions of treasure. How long will the British government be the dupe of French policy? How long will it suffer in fatal supineness their sly encroachment? Will it not reflect that a similar conduct gave birth to the late war, with all its expenses and horrors? Let the ministers, who slumber on the bed of down, or riot in the feast of affluence and luxury, for a moment think on the miserable state of those who fondly trusting to their protection, are now devoted to the murderous knife of savage Indians, or to the cruel perfidy of the insinuating, and yet as murderous, Frenchmen; the father and the son, the mother and the tender infant, weltering in each others blood'.

Between September 1764 and the following June, the *St James's Chronicle*, *Ipswich Chronicle* and *Lloyd's Evening Post* between them complained about French smuggling to South Wales, French naval forces off Newfoundland, French tariffs on British iron and steel goods, the import of French lace, silks and baskets and French fishing off the British coast. Typical of the note of social criticism was the article in the *St James's Chronicle* of 18 May 1765.

It is said that several French hairdressers and friseurs, French milliners and mantua-makers, have raised good fortunes since the late peace, by artfully introducing and selling the silk manufactures of their own country to the gentry etc. they did business for, which has been the principal cause of the present miserable situation of the poor Spitalfields weavers; and notwithstanding a seizure now and then has been made of French goods, the said illicit trade is daily carried on by means of the easy access they have to the gentlemen and ladies who employ them.

Though, unlike in the reigns of Charles II and James II, there was no real suggestion that such cultural preferences determined government policy, press attacks helped to sustain a sense that foreign policy was not conducted in light of national interests, a claim that was easy to advance because of the ambiguity of these interests. This was vaguer than the more pointed critiques directed at supposed pro-French policies in 1660–88 and alleged Hanoverian domination in 1714–55, and its frequent reiteration may have dulled its political edge, but a constant theme present in public discussion was that foreign policy was misguided and unsuccessful in defending national interests.

The influence of this in electoral terms, and hence on government policy, is open to question. Criticism of an alleged ministerial failure to defend national interests can be seen as an aspect of what has recently been seen as a mentality of independence that inhibited the expression of aristocratic and patronal power. However, electoral politics have been seen as centred on specific grievances rather than on any fundamental disaffection, and it has been argued that the mid-eighteenth-century decline of party divisions transformed electoral politics into an essentially local preoccupation with oligarchy and independence. Elections were certainly not decided by electoral verdicts on foreign policy. This helped limit Parliament's exposure to outside pressures when debating foreign policy,

Nevertheless, in many seats national issues were also local. Furthermore, foreign-policy issues could be cited during elections, as in the case of the Yorkshire by-election of 1742. The *York Courant*, the leading newspaper of the region, carried in its issue of 20 October 1741 a letter from 'J.S. of Leeds' attacking Cholmley Turner for standing and for having voted, while an MP, for ministerial measures. Turner's support for the Convention of the Pardo, the Anglo-Spanish agreement of 1738, was specified, as was his backing for the Septennial Act, the standing army and government financial policies. A week later, anonymous friends of Turner's, writing from York, replied, claiming that the opposition was using the Convention as 'a cantword, adopted without meaning, and echo'd out amongst the people to inflame and abuse them'. Certain aspects of the criticism of Britain's links with the Continent clearly had a popular resonance. The Swedish scholar Kalm, visiting England on his way to America in 1748, went on a trip to the countryside near Little Gaddesden and 'saw a water-mill at one place . . . there were quartered a frightful number of large rats, which they called Hanoverian rats' (*Kalm's Account of his Visit to England*, 1892: 300).

Criticism of governmental foreign policy became attenuated in the last decades of the century, although any sign of an apparent failure to stand up to the Bourbons led to attacks. The *Public Advertiser* of 17 January 1771 employed a familiar device of opposition writing, the appeal to the supposed example of Elizabeth I. The issue of 13 February carried a letter accusing the ministry of craven surrender to France. On the other hand, the government was not without press support. In the *Westminster Journal* of 1 December 1770, C.P.G. attacked popular prejudice and, in contrast to the general claim that the Bourbons could not be trusted, argued that their friendship should be cultivated, adding

'We know very well that Jack Helter-Skelter says, damn the Spaniards, we shall soon give them a belly-full, and bring home their treasure by ship-load after ship-load. Better to cultivate their friendship, and supply them with the manufactures of Great Britain'.

The absence of Continental commitments during the War of American Independence removed the basis for charges of Hanoverian influence, while initial support for the Americans was diminished by their Bourbon alliances. Adam Ferguson, Professor of Philosophy in Edinburgh, who had in 1778 been appointed secretary to the commissioners sent unsuccessfully to Philadelphia to negotiate a settlement, wrote in January 1780: 'There never was a national cause more just than ours is at present against France and Spain and all their abettors. . . . I am not fond of national animositys but I feel and indulge the indignation of the present case. . . . Every well meaning clergyman ought to stuff his sermon with it on the approaching Fast Day' (BL Add. 34417 f. 5).

Criticism of foreign policy in the post-war world was less than after 1763 and centred not on the morale-boosting intervention against France in the Dutch Crisis (1787), but on the confrontation with Russia in the Ochakov crisis (1791). The French Revolutionary War was to be more influential in rallying support for British foreign policy. Although British participation was not universally popular, the combination of ideological and national challenge from France removed the patriotic credibility of radical critics and helped to produce the potent fusion of nationalism, conservatism and government. They were to help sustain the war effort through years of defeat and heavy expenditure.

CHAPTER EIGHT

THE DEBATE OVER POLICY

In the ignorance whether we wish a foreign system in England I have not courage to launch out into politics.

(Joseph Yorke, 1778 – BL. Add. 33515 f 54)

It would be misleading to suggest that the rich complexity of international and domestic circumstances and the varied themes of British diplomacy between 1660 and 1793 can be described in terms of a common debate over policy. However, the central feature of foreign policy was that it was debated. Even though certain assumptions were axiomatic, especially the importance of national defence and naval strength, and the need to protect trade, there was no uniformity in views about how these objectives were to be realised. Nor was there agreement over the extent to which aspirations and pretensions should be supported, whether in peacetime diplomacy, by recourse to war, or in wartime objectives and diplomacy. The extent and sophistication of the debate varied, as did its political location and consequences. Foreign policy was not considered in the abstract, but in terms of a political community that was divided over the search for power and more seriously for much of 1660–1746 over the succession and religion. These divisions were closely related to questions of foreign policy, and some of these questions, such as alleged subservience to France in the 1680s and to Hanover in the 1740s, acquired a totemic significance.

The relationship between foreign policy and the related issues of succession and religion helped to politicise the first. The *History of the Peace with France and War with Holland in the Year 1672* (1712) claimed that

'until a Tory can be reconciled to liberty, and hate tyranny, the French and Dutch will always be on the same terms with him . . . neither is it strange that those who would destroy liberty at home should hate every thing that's like it abroad' (p.1).

A ready history was offered for this stance. *War, An Epic-Satyr. Setting forth the Nature of French Policy, and the True Cause of The Present Commotions in Europe* (1747) declared:

'The noble stand old England has ever made, and indeed still continues to make, in the assertion of her own liberty, and that of her neighbours, against the ambitious attempts of all the tyrants in Europe, makes a splendid figure in history; and will to latest posterity do honour to the nation. It was she conquered Philip and his invincible Armada; she, humbled Louis XIV; and we despair not but that she will in time bring down the high crest of his successor . . . keeping down French power and securing a balance. This is called the cause of man, because wherever universal monarchy is affected, there it is every one's business to assert universal freedom' (pp. 51–2).

The Protestant-centred patriotism consisted of an intense anti-French and anti-popish xenophobia; pride in English Protestantism, prosperity and personal liberty; and an opposition to foreign powers held to threaten the balance of power. This was presented, by contemporaries and historians, as the natural product of English traditions, political circumstances and national interest (Colley 1992).

The sense of nationality so often described may not in fact have been so effortlessly dominant. The Glorious Revolution was an important advance for a particular view of England, but did not secure that view instant dominance, or allow the nation to unite around it. Instead, the Revolution produced a number of competing theses of patriotism. Alongside praise for William as a Protestant and providential blessing on the nation, were Jacobite, 'Country' and Tory views of the new king as a usurper and of an England suffering depredations under his tutelage (Claydon 1996). These other views were viable, and attracted considerable support in the 1690s. They were marginalised -not because of any inherent absurdity, or necessary incompatibility with English national character -but simply because the circumstances of William III's reign allowed him a political and polemical victory over his opponents. Most importantly, William proved able to win the military struggle over the Scottish and Irish successions which followed the Glorious Revolution. He could, therefore, exclude his opponents from power, and condemn critics of his vision of nationality as disloyal.

In addition, William's military victory coincided with a dramatic expansion of public politics. In the 1690s, the advent of annual sessions of Parliament, the ending of pre-publication censorship (1695), and the development of a considerably more active press, meant that polemical politics began to produce more and different kinds of sources. As a consequence, the particular patriotic discourse associated with the victors in 1688 was widely disseminated, and gained the highest profile in the culture of print, as well as in government records. It displaced rivals, both in the respectable discussion of the time, and in the records (especially the most-consulted metropolitan and printed texts) which historians use to reconstruct that discussion.

The consequence of this victory for Williamite patriotism has been to distort, not only Georgian Britons' views of their world, but even later historical understanding of the period. Much of the scholarship dealing with the century after 1688 has been soaked in the sort of Whiggism promoted by that event, with the result that many of the ambiguities and complexities of the period have been lost. Until recently, for example, historians of the eighteenth century were almost as effective as Williamite politicians in marginalising the Jacobite and other dissonant voices which were unsuccessful in the political struggles of the late Stuart era. An influential ideology has been accepted on its own terms. Consequently, the Protestant and Whiggish vision associated with the victors has come to seem natural to the English, and the coherence and potential persuasiveness of alternative world views has been obscured. Similarly, too little attention has been paid to the exclusivity and polemical nature of the eventually dominant patriotism. Its victory has hidden the fact that it was directed against those critical of William, that it was therefore necessarily divisive, and that (far from uniting the nation in a universal ideology) it derived much of its early drive from its partisan character, i.e. the very existence of this patriotism was due to the need to defend William explicitly.

Again, and even in very recent works, William's victory in 1688–91 has been made to appear desirable because it was necessary for national development. It has been seen as the opportunity for England to move into the first rank of European powers, and as the moment when its internal political structures diverged (very fruitfully) from Continental norms. As part of this interpretation, discussion of England's national interest has shared the Williamite assumption of the need to oppose France, when in fact any notion of 'national interest' is theoretically problematic. Ideas of national interest are inseparable from ideologies which define a country's role and destiny – so, in reality, enmity with France was only 'natural' to people who had already decided that Catholicism, Bourbon absolutism, and Continental predominance were the antithesis of Englishness.

Another potentially misleading aspect of discussion of policy by commentators in this period and one again in which an influential ideology has been accepted on its own terms, is its schematic nature and the stress on natural interests and the balance of power. This emphasis is one that frequently occurs in the history of international relations, and is also one that was central to eighteenth-century culture. The impulse for order was a dominant motif of the age, but should not be regarded as a simple reflection of some political and social reliability. Rather, commentators stressed the need for order because they were profoundly aware of the precarious nature of the order and stability that existed. In international relations, this stability seemed challenged by the expansionist interests of some powers and, more generally, by the irrational, malevolent or corrupt preference by rulers and ministers for personal interests at the expense of the true interests of their states and the international system. This was but part of the more general sense of a precarious social, political, cultural, religious and personal order under threat from self-indulgence, passion and the volatility of the irrational.

Deprived of the sense of a stable international system, contemporaries debated how best Britain should respond. The direct influence of the debate over policy is difficult to gauge. It can be shown that decisions taken at crucial episodes can be explained with reference to both domestic and diplomatic criteria. The two are not incompatible. Indeed, in any episode involving foreign policy a mixture of both should be anticipated, but the virtue of suggesting different interpretations and a complex mixture of 'factors', influences whose interrelationships are difficult to pin down or gauge, is that simple explanations can be avoided. This is related to the realisation that entities and institutions like Britain and government, as well as abstractions, such as public opinion, 'patriotism' and Tory views, were not monolithic.

Britain was not unique in having domestic divisions, Joseph Yorke, commenting in 1764 on Austrian difficulties in Hungary, wrote: 'Thus we see that every court and every country has its difficulties and disagreements, whilst we are idly imagining that we alone are the object of party, faction and passion' (BL Add. 57927 f. 306). Behind the constitutional and institutional facades of absolutism, Continental government and political culture relied substantially on consensus and co-operation, as was also obviously the case with those states that had powerful representative assemblies, the most important of which were Britain, Poland, Sweden and the United Provinces. Peacetime foreign policy required consensus and co-operation far less than raising taxes or maintaining law and order, and in this sphere the implications of the term 'absolutism' are possibly most appropriate (Black 1999a). A distinction could still be drawn between Britain and the Continental absolutisms because, although peacetime diplomacy in Britain could be as much under the control of monarch and ministers as in any Continental state, they had to consider the domestic political implications, especially the likely parliamentary response, and there were occasions when options were limited or policy altered to take note of these implications.

The existence of political groupings, which can for some periods, especially 1702–54, be described as parties, further helped to sustain debate over foreign policy, though it would be misleading to suggest that party views were fixed. There were no equivalents to the modern leader, party membership and organisation, manifesto or three-line whip. There were party attitudes or tendencies, rather than consistent, coherent policies, and there was a readiness to respond both to international developments and to the exigencies of office (Harris R. 1993). The Whigs, who had played the major rôle in sustaining the War of the Spanish Succession (1702–13) and the Austrian alliance that was central to British participation in it, and in criticising the Peace of Utrecht (1713), were instrumental in negotiating and supporting an Anglo-French alliance (1716–31) that nearly led to war with Austria (1725–30), before, in 1731, they allied with Austria, only to abandon her two years later.

Such flexibility suggests that criticism of British ministerial attitudes to foreign policy from the later 1740s to the 1780s as inflexible and wedded to an outdated analysis of international relations (Roberts 1970; Scott 1989) must explain why this should be the case given earlier shifts. Indeed, as far as the 1740s and 1750s were concerned, British ministers showed considerable flexibility, as well as understanding of the strains in the Anglo-Austrian relationship. At the same time, ministers sought to describe their goals and achievements as consistent. This was understandable psychologically; it represented the need to organise and thus better understand and make meaningful the otherwise apparently inchoate nature of international developments. Furthermore, a presentation of policies in terms of the principles of William III helped politically, not least by withstanding rival claims from opposition Whigs, such as Pitt in the early 1740s, and also George II's attempts to fit British policy to the needs of Hanover.

Foreign policy could give rise to bitter disputes within ministries. It led to Townshend's resignation as Secretary of State for the Northern Department in 1730 (Black 1986d):

> The immediate cause of dispute was a foreign negotiation, which had, at Sir Robert's desire, I believe, been dropped. Lord Townshend after having given up the point, still advanced an opinion, that the design of the negotiation ought to be mentioned in the House of Commons at the same time that the measure was given up. Sir Robert took offence at this last proposal, and, I believe, thought, that Lord Townshend's reason for working for the mention of a measure, which was not to be pursued, was that it might give him a disagreeable and troublesome day in the House. (Beinecke, Osborn Files, Sydney)

In 1761, foreign policy was Pitt the Elder's downfall, just as the inability of a divided ministry to face the domestic consequences of an unsuccessful war with France had been responsible for his rise in 1757. In 1761, Pitt pressed for a pre-emptive strike against Spain, and the opposition of most of the ministry led to a display of wilfulness in which he announced that he had been called 'by His Sovereign; and he might say in some degree by the voice of the people to assist the state, when others had abdicated the service of it . . . that in his station and situation, he was responsible; and would not continue without having the direction; that this being his case nobody could be surprised, that he could go on no longer'. Carteret, now Earl Granville and Lord President of the Council, replied 'that the point Mr. Pitt went upon was too much, unless he claimed infallibility' (BL Add. 32929 ff. 21–2).

What both episodes showed was that foreign policy was not simply a matter of ministerial conduct in relationship with external pressures and opinions, but that ministries themselves could be seriously divided, precisely because general agreement within the political nation over basic objectives could not provide guidance over how to define these objectives in a complex and changing international system, let alone over how to conceive of and execute policies (and respond to subsequent difficulties) in order to obtain these objectives. Thus, in 1751, when the Commons debated the Bavarian subsidy treaty negotiated by Newcastle, all could agree with the proposer, Pelham, that they were no friends to peacetime subsidies and that their principal objective was 'the preservation of the peace', but speakers disagreed as to whether the Imperial Election Scheme would achieve that end, and over the efficacy of subsidies. Aside from the somewhat abstract points, the political dimension was not absent. Pelham replied to an opposer, Lord Egmont, who had argued that the alliance of Denmark should be sought, by noting that this had been tried unsuccessfully, 'though he doubted not, if it had been done, it would have been found fault with' (BL Add. 32724 ff.129–34).

Consistent issues can be traced, especially the extent to which Britain should intervene in Continental affairs and the question as to how far potential rivals should be trusted. Discussion of both issues included expression of reiterated general themes as well as of more specific points. Sir John Barnard, one of the MPs for London, told the Commons in November 1742 that 'in supporting the Queen of Hungary [Maria Theresa of Austria] we did not fight others' battles but our own, as we would exert ourselves to the utmost to extinguish a fire in our neighbours' house to prevent our own being burnt next. That our sending the English forces last summer into Flanders had effectually prevented the French from sending any succours to their distressed armies in the Empire (Carmarthen, Dyfed Archive Service, Cawdor Muniments, Box 138; Bod. MS Don c. 105 f. 155).

Continental interventionism, both diplomatic and military, was troublesome, costly and frequently unsuccessful. It did not deter the French from hostile steps in peacetime and could not decide the fate of the colonial and maritime struggle in wartime. British policymakers sought a stable Western Europe, but when it existed it could be at the expense of British goals and might deny British ministers and diplomats the opportunity of creating anti-French coalitions. It was especially vexing if, as in 1736–40 and 1763–87, Britain played no role in the diplomatic combinations that created and sustained stability, but, notwithstanding alarmist comments to the contrary, in neither case is it clear that Britain suffered as a consequence.

Continuity in the discussion of foreign policy owed something to the rôle of the monarchs, two of whom, George II and George III, had especially long reigns, and to the lengthy careers of many diplomats and ministers, such as Newcastle who wrote in May 1762, the month of his departure from office after 38 years of nearly continuous service in senior positions, 'in employment and out of employment, I shall be always the same; proper connections upon the continent, I will always maintain; and what those connections should be according to the circumstances of the time' (BL Add. 32938 f. 248).

There was also a topography of British foreign policy which had some constant features. The Low Countries were most important, crucial apparently to the strategic balance between Britain and France. However, the relative importance of other regions varied. The Baltic, important for commercial and political reasons in the seventeenth century, received less attention after the 1720s. The ending of the Great Northern War (1721), the death of Peter the Great (1725), the apparent settlement of the Schleswig-Holstein question by the Treaty of Copenhagen (1732), and the improvement of Anglo-Russian relations that led to the commercial treaty of 1734, lessened Russia's apparent volatility and ended Anglo-Hanoverian fears of her power, and by the 1740s Russia was a political ally and the prospect that she would dominate the Baltic welcome. Thereafter, concern about the Baltic was episodic, for example provoked by the prospect of Russian attacks on Denmark and Sweden in 1762 and 1772–3 respectively, and did not really revive until Britain reverted to an anti-Russian policy in the late 1780s.

Spain and the western Mediterranean rose in importance with the increased deployment of British naval forces in those waters from the 1690s, the issue of the Spanish succession, and Britain's involvement in Italian affairs through her guarantee of the Peace of Utrecht and subsequent settlements (Jones G.H. 1998). Britain's rôle diminished from the 1750s with the settlement of outstanding Italian disputes in 1748–52 and the Austro-French reconciliation of 1756, the Diplomatic Revolution, which ensured that Italy would not play any rôle in an anti-Bourbon strategy. The muted nature of Britain's response to the French acquisition of Corsica in 1768 reflected the situation produced by the Austro-French alliance. The collapse of that alliance and the beginning of the French Revolutionary Wars in 1792 were the necessary preconditions for a revival of Britain's rôle in the Mediterranean. Germany was most important when Britain was playing an active rôle in Continental wars against France and consequently less so in 1733–40 and 1763–93.

The most obvious shift was the rising attention devoted to the colonies. The Anglo-Dutch wars had had an important colonial dimension, but they had centred on a struggle for control of the southern North Sea. Control of home waters was also important in the Anglo-Bourbon conflicts, but they increasingly revolved around colonial rivalry. The number of British ships and soldiers sent to the colonies rose, and, whereas the Nine Years' and Spanish Succession Wars had brought no crucial colonial changes for Britain, in the Seven Years' and American Independence Wars important colonies changed hands. The impact of this on the public debate over foreign policy is complex. Whether rising interest in and concern about the colonial situation preceded, caused or merely accompanied growing governmental intervention is a subject that can be variously debated. It is not surprising that there was a shift between the mid-1740s and the mid-1750s, although, already, in the late 1730s the press had focused on commercial, colonial and maritime issues when discussing what it presented as the Bourbon threat. In 1754, when hostilities began in America, they were more closely followed and more politically important than North American operations had been in 1745-8. In 1754, Britain was involved in no other conflict, and there were no issues comparable to Hanoverian subsidies and the Jacobite threat to offer an alternative focus of political concern and debate to Britain's North American policy. Certainly there was a geographical shift. Ministers who in the 1730s had had to address the problems of Holstein, Parma and Jülich-Berg were having to consider the Ohio River and the Appalachian watershed two decades later. Before the end of the century, places very remote from any other British settlement nearly led to war: the Falklands in 1770 and Nootka Sound on Vancouver Island in 1790.

As far as the debate over foreign policy was concerned, arguably the most important consequence of this conflict was that colonial disputes tended politically and militarily to involve only Britain, France and Spain. They were therefore less complicated than Continental issues, and free of the ambiguities latent in all alliances; and more simple solutions, centering on the assertion of national pretensions through naval strength, could be advocated. It was easier, and more appropriate, for William Pitt the Elder to offer a vision of national greatness 'projected through the great drama of the struggle against the Bourbons' (Peters 1998: 246) than for him to have to focus on Continental politics.

The debate over foreign policy became more informed about trans-oceanic issues but possibly less alert to the nature of Continental affairs. Equally, it is possible that after 1763 the experts were left with a freer hand, in so far as British approaches to Austria and Prussia and Britain's rôle in eastern Europe and the Baltic were concerned, both because there was less political interest and because the rôle of Hanover was less prominent and less controversial. Constraints on total diplomatic freedom of manoeuvre still existed on the British side, especially the effective inability to pursue with France statements and suggestions of good wishes and shared interests, such as occurred in 1748–9, 1763, 1772, 1782 and 1786. Opposition to alliances that might entail cost and unwanted diplomatic or military commitments was an important constraint after 1763, especially as the definition of welcome commitments was much narrower than it had been in 1713–33 or 1741–55. A more serious constraint on the actions of the experts was the lack of interest the major Continental powers displayed in alliance with Britain from 1763 and their unwillingness to accept Britain's terms for an alliance.

In February 1765, Sir James Porter, envoy in Brussels and a veteran of Anglo-Austrian commercial negotiations (1739–45) and of the Constantinople embassy (1747-62), wrote to another veteran of the pre-George III days, Andrew Mitchell, envoy in Berlin (1756-64, '66–71): 'Lord Granville [Carteret] died [in 1763] with this political credo: We must have some one great friend on the continent.' He added: 'commercial and political ties are inseparable, and the one must ebb and flow with the other. Our island is not a single planet revolving in its own sphere,' and referred to France: 'They are I think at present not to be feared, but not to be trusted. Would to God we took proper precautions in time' (BL Add. 6561 f. 134). Porter, who sought an Austrian alliance (BL Add. 57928 f. 22), was in tune with contemporary interest in trade, but, rather than seeking to further that by diplomatic ties with other European states, it was increasingly argued that British political and military support for her commerce was crucial. The centre of public concern about foreign trade was the colonial and trans-oceanic world and, in that sphere, Continental ties appeared of little consequence.

There was little sense of deep public concern in the 1760s and 1770s that the absence of a powerful ally might preclude the defence of the British colonial position. Instead, the relationship between British and Bourbon naval strength was seen as crucial and more worthy of ministerial, parliamentary and public concern, a view that was vindicated by the course of British foreign policy between 1763 and 1787. It was not until the Dutch crisis of 1787, when a Prussian invasion defeated French protégés, that the activities of Continental powers clearly helped Britain's maritime position, for France lost the potential assistance of the Dutch navy and colonies. However, the Prussian action was fortuitous, for Prussia, like Austria, was concerned rather about eastern Europe than about opposing the Bourbons in western Europe.

Defeat at the hands of Americans and Bourbons in 1775–83 had lent new urgency to the search for allies, but the British discovered anew that a Continental strategy involved a commitment to dynamic powers who sought territorial gains. Thse powers sought to take advantage of the opportunity, opportunism, and anxiety that characterised the volatile international relations of the period and, in so doing, helped to make it more volatile. That Britain, not seeking territorial gains in Europe, had different priorities, helped to make her less attractive as an ally. In April 1791, the Foreign Secretary instructed the Earl of Elgin to press Austria for a treaty of defensive alliance with Britain, Prussia and the Dutch. He stressed that George III sought peace and 'the maintenance of the present relative situation of the principal states of Europe. And this principle you will distinctly state to the Emperor as the great and leading object of the policy of this country on every occasion which may arise' (PRO FO 7/23 f. 94).

It was not until the Bourbons were replaced by Revolutionaries, and France became an aggressive and successful power, that the other Continental powers became willing to act against her, creating the basis for an interventionist British policy at the same time as French success in the Low Countries in late 1792 produced the need for one. Discussions over how best to proceed responded to the new situation, for the debate over foreign policy could not but be responsive to such obvious and pressing international developments.

Stressing the role of contingent circumstances restores to individuals and events some of the responsibility that a systemic perspective is apt to underrate. Arguing that the international system should be seen as inherently volatile and unpredictable in its development, necessarily focuses attention on the episodic aspects of relations. These help to explain why the three states to emerge to great-power status in 1683–1725 – Austria, Britain and Russia – were far from constant in their interactions, and why foreign policies were not consistent.

PART TWO
THE COURSE OF POLICY

CHAPTER NINE

British Foreign Policy 1660–1714

INTRODUCTION

In both the 1650s and the 1700s, Britain played a major diplomatic and military role in European affairs. Though neither period was free from disappointment in both spheres, it is difficult to appreciate the contrast with the situation in many of the intervening years. Neither the Second (1665–7) nor the Third (1672–4) Anglo-Dutch war was a success and in 1688 England was invaded successfully by the Dutch. Charles II (1660–85) allowed himself to be treated as a client by Louis XIV of France (1643–1715), especially in 1671–3 and 1681–5 when English policy was shaped to French ends, though in 1678 Louis was to find that some of Charles's parliamentary opponents were also willing to serve his purposes. Other foreign rulers also found it possible and useful to meddle in English domestic politics. The willingness of English politicians to turn abroad for support was not unusual by European standards. It reflected a venality of opinion found among the rulers and ministers of second-rank powers who sought to reconcile their interests with those of more powerful counterparts; a political culture in which tendencies that would be described subsequently as nationalist were poorly developed; and a political society that was bitterly divided, in particular over religious issues and, from 1679, the succession. Such divisions were not surprising in the aftermath of a lengthy civil war in which foreign assistance, Scottish and Irish as well as Continental, had been sought and received. The porosity of English political society to foreign influences and suggestions also reflected a widespread sense that many of the issues in dispute in England were also being contested abroad and that the fates of these struggles were interrelated. This was particularly so among opponents of James II's pro-Catholic policies.

The English monarchy was also weak, certainly in comparison with that of France, because its financial and bureaucratic resources were smaller and dependent in part on parliamentary support, especially when extraordinary sums were required to finance military expenditure and war. And yet in the years 1689–1713, when a massive effort was made in both the Nine Years' (1689–97) and Spanish Succession (1702–13) Wars, England waged war with unprecedented intensity in terms of the number of fronts that were fought on, the number of men committed and the expenditure involved. The financial and economic strain was immense and has often been underrated, but the contrast is nevertheless striking both between the foreign policy and military commitments of 1660–1688 and those of the next quarter century, and between the serious political divisions of 1689–1714 and the ability of successive ministries to sustain a major war effort during the period. Chance clearly played a rôle, not only in the defeat of Jacobitism in Scotland and Ireland in 1689–91 and the subsequent thwarting of Jacobite conspiracies and invasion plans, but also in the failure of French schemes. The French were unable to follow up their naval victory over an outnumbered Anglo-Dutch fleet off Beachy Head in 1690. In neither war did France gain triumphs in the Low Countries comparable to those under Marshal Saxe in 1744–8.

Nevertheless, though consultation of ministerial correspondence from the 1690s and 1700s reveals widespread anxiety about military prospects and the strength and reliability of allies, and there is no doubt that, in the wider political nation, a profound war-weariness developed during the course of each conflict, the contrast with the previous war, the Third Anglo-Dutch war of 1672–4, is still impressive. Charles II had been unable to support a lengthy conflict, despite the fact that, compared with the wars of the 1690s and 1700s, the British military commitment was far smaller. Charles had envisaged speedy success in a short war in which he was allied to the most powerful ruler in western Europe. He did not want a long conflict; there was no political support for it and no attempt had been made to elicit such support. In contrast, long-term concern about French intentions played a rôle in facilitating the two wars with Louis XIV, although, in each case, there was considerable unhappiness about the strategy that was adopted. Arguably more important was the degree to which in 1689 politicians had little alternative to supporting William in war with Louis, unless they wished to be condemned as backers of James, who received French support when in exile. An unsympathetic English pamphlet of 1689 claimed of Louis: 'to glut his ambition, all times are seasonable and proper; times of peace, of war and truce' (*The Spirit of France*: 5).

Another, two years later, described him as 'that Monster of Monsters' (*Description . . . of the Old and New Jacobites*: 8). After 1689, political debate centred on the conduct of the war, rather than on the direction of policy, on whether France was the enemy. The problems that different political views and the rôle of Parliament could create for the conduct of foreign policy were revealed after peace was negotiated in 1697, not least when William was forced to accept the disbandment of much of the army, but he was not prevented by domestic difficulties from conducting secret negotiations with Louis for the partition of the Spanish Empire.

Apparently provocative acts on the part of Louis XIV in 1700–1 helped to undercut opposition in England to William's determination to ensure that for a second time she would play a major rôle in an anti-French coalition, and thereafter, for the rest of the decade, political debate centred on the conduct of the war, especially on the different strategic options, rather than on the anti-French direction of policy. The extent to which this should be attributed to the impact of suspicion and fear concerning French intentions or to the compromising of alternative views by real or alleged association with Jacobitism is unclear, but the situation certainly contrasted with that which had faced Charles in 1672-4. Then war did not bring any suspension of debate over the direction of foreign policy, but, instead, exacerbated it, so that consideration of military issues – funding and success – was related to questions of domestic policy and international alignment.

Foreign policy was less contentious when England was at peace and apparently not taking a significant diplomatic rôle, when international relations in western Europe were relatively quiescent, a situation that helped James II in 1685, but that was compromised, three years later, as a major European war became more threatening, and when domestic criticism was marginalised. This occurred in 1681–5, when opposition to Charles was discredited in the aftermath of the Exclusion Crisis and denied a forum by the suspension of Parliament, and to a certain extent during both the Nine Years' and Spanish Succession Wars, though less so from 1709, as the continuation of the war became a politically charged issue, to be followed by a related controversy over peace terms.

Between 1689 and 1710, policy followed lines set by William: two periods of war with France as part of an alliance entailing substantial military commitments on the Continent, separated by an attempt to settle western-European problems by negotiations with Louis. The extent to which William was able to impose his views indicated the continued constitutional authority of the monarch in the field of foreign policy, but also his political importance as the arbitrator of the ministerial struggle for influence. This rôle was not really compromised by the emergence of political parties in the 1690s and 1700s, because they lacked the structure and ethos necessary to provide clear leadership and agreed policy. The continued rôle of the monarch as arbitrator was demonstrated by Anne's importance in the struggle between Bolingbroke and Harley in 1714.

Charles and James had enjoyed greater constitutional authority and had each acted as arbitrator in ministerial quarrels, but their domestic and international situations were less propitious. William never lost the mandate he had grasped in the invasion and constitutional coup of 1688-9 to the same extent as Charles squandered that which he had gained at the Restoration, or James the favourable position created by the reaction to Exclusion and the Monmouth rising. The unpopularity of James's domestic policies removed any chance of his conducting an active foreign policy. He did not commit himself to Louis, as Charles had done in 1670 and 1681, but he was compromised domestically and internationally by the belief that he was in effect an ally of Louis and wished to emulate him. William was actually to plan the future of western Europe with Louis in 1698–1700, but there was no doubt of his anti-French credentials. In contrast, Charles was able neither to co-operate effectively with Louis nor to pose successfully as his opponent, though he sought to do the latter in 1668 and 1678. This owed something to his unwillingness to commit himself, that could be prudent or feckless according to the circumstances, and much to the difficulty of the task he faced: a rapidly changing Continental situation and a domestic position weakened by a lack of resources, an uncertain succession and a lack of confidence in his political and religious intentions. William offered a greater measure of certainty in large part because he subordinated domestic considerations to the struggle with Louis. This struggle helped to make foreign policy appear more clear-cut, though that was to be reversed in the period of new commitments and alignments that began with the accession of George I in 1714 and had been prefigured in negotiations with Louis in 1698–1700 and, more obviously, 1713–14.

THE RESTORATION

The return of monarchy, as of much else, in 1660 in the person of Charles II might seem to mark a new beginning. Readers accustomed to the historical preference for continuity *and* change will not, however, be surprised to learn that continuing themes in foreign policy can be traced across the Restoration, a term that quintessentially suggests both change and continuity. The most obvious one was provided by the unvarying interests of the other western European powers. Historians often detect a major new starting point in western European history with the Peace of the Pyrenees (1659) ending a 24-year Franco-Spanish war that had supposedly seen the culmination of the decline of Spain, while the beginning of the personal rule of Louis XIV (1661) supposedly marked the beginning of the ascendancy of France. While not devoid of truth, this analysis is limited for a number of reasons. The extent to which France did dominate western Europe has particular relevance to an assessment of English foreign policy because the response to France was to be a central topic of diplomatic activity and public debate throughout this period.

If Spain still ruled the largest empire in the world in 1660 (as in 1793), including, until 1700, Central America, South America bar Portuguese Brazil, the Philippines, Lombardy, Naples, Sicily, Sardinia and the Spanish Netherlands (Belgium and Luxemburg), there was no doubt that she had been gravely weakened by the strains of war, for she had played a central rôle in the conflicts that had involved much of western and central Europe between 1618 and 1659. However, the terms of the Peace of the Pyrenees were not those dictated by a triumphant victor to a collapsed power. The course of the war had not fulfilled French expectations, but had instead demonstrated the severe administrative limitations of Richelieu's system. Far from the peace being followed by Spanish inactivity, there was instead an effort, albeit unsuccessful, to reconquer Portugal. That the respective strengths of Spain and France and their capacity to take political initiatives were soon to alter dramatically was not easy to predict in 1660, nor were the consequences for England readily apparent. Cromwellian intervention on behalf of France had helped her in 1658 to defeat Spain at the battle of the Dunes and capture Dunkirk, an obvious contrast to major French defeats at Pavia and Valenciennes in 1655 and 1656. It appeared that England might hope to continue to enjoy a comparably decisive rôle. She had gained Dunkirk and Jamaica from the war and was recognised as a formidable naval power, though this strength proved to be far from permanent.

Poor Anglo-Spanish relations continued despite the Restoration. Philip IV had provided funds for the exiled Charles and hoped that his restoration would lead to the return of Dunkirk and Jamaica and the end of English support for Portugal, which had rebelled against him in 1640. Charles, however, took the attitude that he had no such obligations because Philip had failed to secure his return.

The central position of royal concerns was indicated by the marital diplomacy in which Charles became involved. In the absence of a suitable Spanish match, he accepted a Portuguese approach. A treaty of August 1661 was followed in April 1662 by Charles's marriage to the Portuguese princess Catherine of Braganza. As part of her dowry, she brought Bombay and Tangier to Charles, but he was obliged to send troops to help in the continuing war with Spain. As a result, the Spaniards subsidised the plots of republican opponents of Charles. The nature of the English commitment to Portugal indicated the importance of Charles's views. Whereas the eighteenth-century Anglo-Portuguese alliance stemmed from the shared commercial and geopolitical interests that led to and were sustained by the Methuen treaties of 1703, the Anglo-Portuguese alliance of 1661, which entailed substantial English commitments and prevented any improvement in relations with Spain, was negotiated as a result of Charles's personal preference, the dynastic imperative of attempting to secure an heir (ironically so as she was to be barren).

Although English merchants had gained reasonably good trading conditions as the result of a commercial treaty of 1654, they were not responsible for the new alignment. The English merchants in Lisbon did, however, see it as an opportunity to press for the redress of their grievances (PRO SP 89/5 f. 2). Tangier was also seen as a naval base that could help to protect Mediterranean trade. Therefore, although Charles's personal interests were central to Anglo-Portuguese relations, commercial considerations did play a rôle, a pattern that was to be repeated in Charles's anti-Dutch diplomacy of 1664–73. Protestant hostility towards a rigorously Catholic regime was not a major factor in relations.

The importance of Anglo-Dutch relations was another obvious sphere of continuity from the Cromwellian period. The 1651 Navigation Ordinance, which stated that goods could be imported only in English ships or those of the country of origin, thus hitting the Dutch entrepôt trade, had helped to cause the First Anglo-Dutch war of 1652–4, although a recent study both of that conflict and of the Second Anglo-Dutch War has emphasised ideological issues, specifically, in the case of the First War, the hostility of one Protestant, republican regime towards a less rigorous counterpart (Pincus 1996).

The continued challenge of Dutch commercial ascendancy, which had increased during the Anglo-Spanish conflict begun in 1655, was regarded as a serious problem by the new regime which in 1660 passed a new Navigation Act, specifically aimed at the Dutch. This was followed in 1662 and 1663 by Acts that further consolidated the creation of a restricted commercial system for the English colonies. The Acts limited the import of specified goods to English ships or those of the country of origin, that of 1662 explicitly prohibiting import from the United Provinces. Most colonial produce was reserved for English ships, while English colonies were obliged to purchase most of their European goods in England. English ships were to have largely English crews. It was laid down in 1660 that all foreign-built ships in English ownership should be registered. Two years later, the purchase of Dutch ships was hindered when an Act of that year decreed that ships of foreign build not registered by that date were to be deemed alien and to be subject to alien duties (Wilson 1957: 97–102).

To some commentators, war with the Dutch was an obvious complement to these Acts and to the sentiments they reflected. The arrest and expropriation of Dutch ships and their cargoes for breaching the new regulations raised tension and led to an increased level of violence at sea. However, this legislation did not lead immediately to another conflict and indeed an Anglo-Dutch treaty of peace and alliance of September 1662 sought to settle all disputes. It reflected the conviction of the Earl of Clarendon, the Lord Chancellor and Charles's leading minister, and the Earl of Southampton, the Lord Treasurer, that England was not in any shape domestically or internationally for war with the Dutch. Sending assistance to the Portuguese was both a policy that could be controlled and one in which Charles found himself at one with Louis XIV, who was keen to weaken Spain. War with the Dutch would involve a much greater effort, one that would have to be met entirely from English resources.

There were serious financial and political problems in England and the danger of hostile French intervention on the Dutch side. When, in July 1661, Charles submitted the draft terms of a defensive alliance to Louis, the first article included a provision for co-operation against rebellions. In 1662, Dunkirk, gained by England in 1658 during her intervention on the French side in the Franco-Spanish war, was sold to France, a retreat from what appeared to be the over-extensive aspirations of the 1650s. Suggestions that he had been bribed led to the designation of Clarendon's new house as 'the new Dunkirk'.

Both the English and the Dutch made concessions in their treaty of September 1662. They both agreed to refuse shelter or protection to exiles or rebels seeking refuge, an important point to Charles, who feared the intrigues of republican exiles. The English gave way on the contentious issue of Dutch rights of fishing in English coastal waters; the Dutch agreed to lower the flag to English ships in British waters and to yield the island of Pula Run in the East Indies to which the English had a claim. Arbitration for future disputes was proposed.

The treaty might suggest that the passage of the English Navigation Acts was compatible with the maintenance of peace with the Dutch, but this depended on the increasingly isolated Clarendon defending his position successfully. His opposition to confrontation with the Dutch separated him from his son-in-law, Charles's brother, James, Duke of York, the Lord High Admiral, who had pressed for action against them in the summer of 1662, and from a powerful court and ministerial group that included Henry Bennet, later Earl of Arlington, who became Secretary of State for the Southern Department in October 1662 and was the most influential of the two Secretaries until his resignation in 1674.

SECOND ANGLO-DUTCH WAR 1665–7

Neither Charles nor the Dutch government sought war, but in 1663–5 a deterioration in relations was both cause and consequence of the activities of political groups in both countries that believed they could obtain their ends through firmness. De Witt, the most influential Dutch leader, was unwilling to compromise Dutch commercial ascendancy by concessions that probably would not anyway bring lasting peace. In addition, once one country had obtained commercial concessions, it was common for others to seek to do likewise. Certainly, English merchants kept a close eye on the terms under which their rivals traded in, for example, Portugal and Spain. In English court circles there was considerable hostility to the Dutch both as republicans and because of their toleration of a variety of Protestant sects. Conflict with them appeared to offer chances of employment for the former Royalist and Commonwealth warrior caste that had developed since 1642 and for whom peace offered penury, diminished opportunities or insignificance. War also appeared to offer some politicians the prospect of gaining office or promotion and, indeed, of overthrowing Clarendon. There was little doubt of parliamentary hostility towards the Dutch. The Commons address of April 1664 attacked them as obstacles to English commercial activity, a major topic of recent parliamentary discussion. The Commons stated that in support of their resolution they would 'with their lives and fortunes, assist his Majesty against all opposition whatsoever' (*Journals of the House of Commons* 8,548).

The Dutch could be blamed for most problems and that was important in a political culture that was understandably prone to paranoia as a result of the recent and continuing experience of both change and intrigue. Such attitudes helped to make the more measured advice of Sir George Downing, the envoy in The Hague, who believed that a firm approach would elicit concessions from the Dutch, inappropriate. The government hoped that a forceful approach would secure peace on their own terms but they had underestimated the determination of the Dutch (Seaward 1987).

Conflict was set off by the valuable trade of West Africa, the source of slaves for the American colonies, a prize which caused a struggle for control between the Company of Royal Adventurers trading into Africa, in which many courtiers including the Duke of York, Bennet and Coventry were active, and the Dutch West India Company. From 1661, rivalry escalated into a full-scale war. The Company was chartered in December 1660 and in early 1661 sent out a small expedition using royal vessels under the command of the aggressive Captain Robert Holmes, a protégé of York's. Holmes seized two islands in the mouth of the Gambia and attacked nearby Dutch forts, but the Dutch reacted sharply seizing English ships and in June 1663 capturing the English castle at Cape Coast. In November 1663, Holmes was sent to support the Company, and to maintain the right of English subjects by force. In early 1664, he seized the major Dutch settlements on the Gold Coast. He then sailed to North America, where he captured New Amsterdam (or New York as it now came to be called) (Ollard 1969). A Dutch fleet under de Ruyter recaptured the African settlements and Dutch complaints led to Holmes being committed to the Tower.

The Dutch wished to avoid war if possible, but the English were no longer willing to restrict hostilities to distant seas, where it was easier to present violent acts as unsanctioned or irrelevant to European diplomacy. In August 1664, Thomas Allin was sent to command in the Mediterranean with instructions to seize Dutch warships and, if possible, their Smyrna fleet, a convoy of merchantment from Asia Minor whose valuable cargoes provided a major inducement in the shape of booty and goods whose sale would help to fund English activities. The opportunistic, not to say piratical, nature of English policy was amply demonstrated by Allin's attack on a Dutch merchant fleet off Gibraltar in December 1664. From then on, Dutch merchantmen were seized in large numbers and on 4 March 1665 Charles II declared war, Holmes being released two days later.

The war was not a great success for the English. It proved impossible to mount an effective blockade of the United Provinces and thus to wreck their trade. The honours at sea were divided, with English victories (North Foreland 1666) and defeats (Four Days Battle 1666). On the English side, the war revealed financial, administrative, naval and diplomatic weaknesses. Though Parliament voted the unprecedented sum of £2.5 million, there was no money for a long war and credit proved increasingly difficult to obtain. By the Restoration the Crown had no longer any land that could be used as collateral for loans. This damaged the king's creditworthiness. The navy was short of supplies and money. In 1667, because there was insufficient money to prepare a fleet, the Dutch were able in June to sail up the Medway and attack the major naval base at Chatham. England was isolated, as it had been during the First Anglo-Dutch war, but the end of the Franco-Spanish conflict made France's position more important, especially as she was allied to the Dutch and obliged by the Treaty of Paris of 22 April 1662 to declare war against the aggressor. In November 1665, the French envoys in London warned Louis that if he supported the Dutch he must prepare for Parliament enthusiastically voting men and money to sustain the conflict. The same month, the *Gazette* of Amsterdam reported links between the envoys and an opposition MP.

In January 1666, Louis declared war in support of his Dutch ally, though the French did not campaign vigorously other than in the West Indies, and Franco-Dutch relations deteriorated as Dutch fears both of Louis's intentions in the Spanish Netherlands and of his commercial plans increased. However, the prospect of French action affected English naval strategy in 1666 and hindered Charles's efforts to acquire allies elsewhere. The attempt to create an anti-Dutch alliance was unsuccessful, crucially so in the case of Denmark which declared war on England in 1666, with important consequences in terms of Baltic trade. Alliance with Spain and the Empire against France and the Dutch was sought (PRO SP 80/11 f. 74), but without success. English hopes of significant gains at the expense of France in the West Indies and Canada were misplaced.

The war was ended by the Peace of Breda in July 1667. The daring raid on the Medway the previous month had demonstrated that England needed peace, while the French invasion of the Spanish Netherlands in the War of Devolution (1667–8) was of considerable concern to the neighbouring Dutch. The peace was a compromise: de Witt had no wish to humiliate the English whose alliance he might need, and they were allowed to keep the New Netherlands (New York and New Jersey). The English accepted some of the Dutch points on contraband trade, while the Dutch retained the South American colony of Surinam, which they had captured. Charles was left with a substantial war debt and a divided ministry.

Clarendon was dismissed in August 1667, Charles telling the Commons two months later that he hoped this would lay the foundation of a greater confidence between him and Parliament.

Charles's unwillingness to stand by his minister in the face of court and public hostility to him provided a brutal lesson in the limitations of royal support in the event of a failure in policy. Clarendon was impeached with the backing of Charles, but difficulties in securing a successful show-trial gave him the opportunity of fleeing abroad. Over the following fifty years, other leading ministers, including Danby and Oxford, were to suffer imprisonment and judicial attack for policies they had pursued at the behest of the Crown. Clarendon's fate – exile in France until his death there in 1674 – and the rejection of his petitions for leave to return to England raised the stake in ministerial politics and encouraged ministers to seek solutions that they hoped would guarantee their position. For those who feared Parliament and wished to improve the position of Catholics, this suggested the need for a new political order that could possibly be secured only through an alliance with and by means of the support of Louis XIV.

FROM PEACE TO WAR 1667–72

English diplomacy in the next few years was made more than ordinarily complex by the existence of a public and a private royal policy. The weakness of his domestic political position encouraged Charles to turn to a secret foreign policy. When, in October 1667, the French envoy Ruvigny warned him of a powerful parliamentary group that would propose help to Spain at the expense of France, Charles assured him that he was 'master of all the cabals . . . and the Parliament would not meddle in anything that displeased him' (AE CP Ang. 89. f. 114). Such claims were a necessary feature of royal majesty, but they were inaccurate, and Charles himself told Ruvigny that autumn that, though he personally was willing to make as close a connection with France as Louis sought, few thought as he did in the Council or in Parliament (Haley 1986: 150).

French aggression and insensitivity, which Ruvigny claimed were exaggerated in England, led the three leading Protestant powers, England, Sweden and the United Provinces, to combine in the Triple Alliance of January 1668, an attempt to lend substance to pressure on France and Spain to end their war with a compromise peace that would include some Spanish cessions. It is unclear why Charles negotiated the treaty, and the king's habitual secrecy renders any attempt to establish the relative importance of particular factors in his foreign policy implausible. He was apparently angered by Louis's offhand treatment of him, but the Triple Alliance also served to divide Louis and the Dutch, while the determination of Sir William Temple, the envoy at The Hague, to secure improved Anglo-Dutch links as a vital feature of both English foreign policy and international relations was also important. It was feared that Louis would seek additional gains from Spain in the campaigning season of 1668. In January 1668, the powers of the Triple Alliance demanded, without success, a cease-fire until May. As part of the new alignment, and in the face of French opposition, England negotiated a settlement of the Hispano-Portuguese conflict in 1668.

However, the House of Commons did not provide the level of support that the ministry sought. Though the request of some MPs for the public reading of the Triple Alliance in the Commons was abandoned in order not to give the appearance of treaties depending on parliamentary approval, the Commons voted only £300,000 and could not agree for a while how to raise the sum. It was sufficient for some naval preparations but not enough for any conflict. The lack of realism among parliamentarians about the real cost of armaments and war suggests that even with parliamentary support an active foreign policy entailing conflict or confrontation was not possible. This doubtless encouraged Charles to try to circumvent Parliament, providing a rationale for his natural duplicity.

The Franco-Spanish war anyway did not broaden to include England. Louis seized the Spanish-ruled Franche Comté (around Besançon), but then negotiated the Treaty of Aix-la-Chapelle (May 1668) by which he returned Franche Comté but retained his Flemish conquests, including Lille and Tournai. Louis then determined to wreck Dutch strength, because he despised their republican, mercantile culture and appreciated that they would oppose French interest in the Spanish succession, especially in the disposal of the Spanish Netherlands. Charles II of Spain (1665–1700) was a weakling with little prospect of fathering an heir and both Louis and the Emperor, the Austrian Habsburg Leopold I (1658–1705), had claims on the succession. To obtain his ends, he determined to isolate the Dutch, which he had succeeded in doing by the time he attacked in 1672. Leopold agreed to be neutral, but Charles II wished to turn the crisis to his own advantage. For Charles the Triple Alliance had not been an attempt to create an anti-French coalition, but instead a move designed to increase his own importance, and his value as a possible ally. Charles had decided that he could best achieve his objectives by allying with Louis, though he was unclear as to how far such an alliance would enable him to do so. Charles' ends are difficult to assess, but appear to have comprised short-term goals and longer-term aspirations. In the short term, he wanted money and a diplomatic position in which he would not be vulnerable in a rapidly changing international situation, made volatile by French strength and activity and the weakness of Charles II of Spain. More immediate was his need to ensure that he was not isolated in the international 'sub-system' of England, France and the United Provinces – that, in short, Louis and the Dutch were kept apart.

In the longer term, Charles hoped to ameliorate the position of English Catholics and saw Louis as a possible source of assistance in this, though the value of French subsidies in improving his situation vis à vis Parliament was more obvious and predictable. In January 1669, Charles held a secret meeting in the palace of Whitehall with James, Henry Bennet (Lord Arlington), the senior Secretary of State, his protégé Sir Thomas Clifford and Lord Arundel, a Catholic peer. Charles told them that he wished to secure the re-establishment of Catholicism and to determine the best moment for declaring himself openly. It was decided 'that the best means was to ask the assistance of His Most Christian Majesty, the house of Austria being in no position to cooperate' (J. S Clarke, *Life of James II*, 1816: 441–2). As during James II's reign, the options available to a Stuart intent on following a pro-Catholic domestic policy were limited by the growth of French and decline of Habsburg power. Three months later, Arundel, on a secret mission to France, offered an offensive and defensive alliance against all other powers on condition that Louis supported Charles's decision to become a Catholic with, if necessary, troops and £200,000. Arundel insisted that the alliance was not to conflict with the Triple Alliance and that all construction of French warships must cease, and stated that Charles would place Catholics in key offices, grant liberty of conscience to Catholics and Nonconformists when Parliament met and then declare his own conversion.

Louis was more interested in co-operation against the Dutch than in the fate of British Catholics. Charles responded by writing to Louis in June 1669 and promising to begin war against the Dutch in the next eight to ten months (Sonnino 1988: 67). As yet, Louis, still negotiating with the Dutch, had not decided precisely when he would act and what he would do, but the pace of Anglo-French diplomacy increased from late 1669. Charles's sister, Henrietta Duchess of Orléans, the wife of Louis's brother, played a crucial rôle in the secret diplomacy which led to the Secret Treaty of Dover of 1670. This outlined two related objectives, the defeat of the Dutch and the restoration of Catholicism in England. Charles agreed to join Louis in his attack, in return for which he was to receive an annual subsidy of three million livres (about £250,000), less than the 9,600,000 livres (£800,000) he had demanded in December 1669, and Brill, Flushing, Sluys and Cadsand, which would provide control over the Maas and the Scheldt estuaries. Charles was to support Louis's rights to Spanish territory and, when he judged most propitious, to declare himself a Catholic, in return for which he was to receive both money and, in the event of disturbances, 6000 French troops. A second secret treaty, providing for an attack on the Dutch, was signed in December 1670 by Protestant ministers unaware of this religious provision.

Though the treaty, like for example the Austro-French secret partition treaty for the Spanish succession of 1668, contained significant long-term provisions, in practice it was the immediate ones that were of consequence and were doubtless intended as important. England was to attack the Dutch again, in partnership with and subsidised by France. It was hoped that the unsuccessful diplomatic and military experience of the Second Anglo-Dutch war would not be repeated, and the distant prospect of French support for a share of the Spanish Empire was attractive to some ministers. Between April 1671 and February 1673, Parliament was prorogued, and on 25 March 1672 the Declaration of Indulgence, suspending the execution of the penal laws and allowing Catholics to worship in their homes, was issued. Two days earlier, English warships had attacked the Dutch Smyrna convoy in the Channel, though with only modest success. This was followed by a declaration of war on the Dutch (Hutton 1986).

THIRD ANGLO-DUTCH WAR 1672–4

The war did not go according to plan. Louis's forces easily invaded the United Provinces, capturing Utrecht, and the Dutch appeared ready to accept a humiliating peace. However, Louis's obduracy, the defence of the province of Holland by inundations, an Orangist coup in Holland (July 1672) that brought the resolutely anti-French William of Orange, Charles's nephew, to power, and German opposition, successfully marshalled by William, all caused the collapse of the French position in the United Provinces. The naval war did not go particularly well for the English in 1672, the Anglo-French fleet being defeated by Ruyter at Sole Bay, and the United Provinces was not invaded from the sea, as had been planned. William rejected Charles's proposal that he accept English protection and become hereditary ruler of the United Provinces in return for yielding to English and French demands. In 1673, the English failed to defeat the Dutch fleet, while, as in 1672, the French fleet was accused of leaving the brunt of the fighting to the English. As the war expanded to include Spain and several German rulers, Louis was obliged to withdraw his forces from the United Provinces, while Charles faced the prospect of England losing her Spanish trade.

The Dutch sought to stir up opposition to the war within England. *England's Appeal from the Private Cabal at Whitehall to the Great Council of the Nation*, written by Pierre du Moulin, a Huguenot supporter of William, appeared in March 1673 and presented what was to be the major theme of anti-Stuart propaganda, namely that the policies of Charles and his advisors were designed to assist Louis's striving for universal monarchy. Criticism of Louis could thus be focused on his English acolytes, who could not be trusted when they apparently deviated from subservience to France. The pamphlet asked:

> Let those that have advised His Majesty to this war speak, they must now pull their vizard off, they must . . . tell us plainly whether they are paid for making the French King the Universal monarch, and whether, to bring down new golden showers into their laps, England must at last be made tributary to the French.

In 1673, tension was increased by the marriage of James to the Catholic Mary of Modena, a union sponsored by Louis that was given political point by Charles's lack of legitimate heirs and by the failure of James's Protestant first wife to give birth to sons. In such an atmosphere of unease, fears flourished. It was suggested that the army, whose conduct in England gave rise to concern, might be used to implement arbitrary government. When Parliament met in early 1673 it obliged Charles to take anti-Catholic legislative steps, but provided money for the fleet which, however, was unable to defeat the Dutch and thus cover the planned invasion of the United Provinces. This failure made it clear that no benefit would come from the war.

The domestic and diplomatic impetus that led to war in the early modern period commonly did not sustain conflict for long if success was not obtained. Alliances would fracture under the strain of mutual suspicion, while the general absence of strong ideological factors helped to make unilateral negotiations a constant possibility. A peace conference at Cologne in 1673 was still-born, and, as the war widened to include Leopold and Spain, it became clear both that the Dutch would not be defeated and that French ambitions had been redirected to the Spanish Netherlands. Clifford, who was closely associated with the French alliance, was replaced as Lord Treasurer by Sir Thomas Osborne in July 1673. The unsuccessful campaign of 1673 exacerbated English domestic criticism of France and led Parliament to refuse to vote money while the war continued, and to attacks on the French alliance. Charles was forced to abandon Louis and accept, by the Treaty of Westminster of February 1674, a peace that brought him the salute of the English flag in the Channel, but no real gains. The Dutch refused to pay for the right to fish off the English coast and preserved their monopoly in the East Indies (Haley 1953).

PEACE AND FRENCH PENSIONS 1674-85

Foreign policy for the remainder of the reign was totally subordinate to partisan domestic considerations, though these were in turn influenced by foreign manipulation. William of Orange, for example, sought a peaceful settlement of the Exclusion Crisis in order that England might play an active rôle against Louis. For much of the period, western Europe was at war (1674–8, 1683–4), or close to it, but England was, as in the 1630s, neutral. In part this can be explained by French pressure. Louis provided subsidies to Charles to keep Parliament dissolved (1681–5), but was also willing in 1678 to help opposition politicians attack the government and bring down Charles's leading minister, the Earl of Danby, when it appeared that English foreign policy would be maintained in an anti-French direction. However, though such interventions and manipulation were important, subsidies and bribes were generally granted in this period to enable people to do what they would anyway have wished to do.

Charles's new-found caution is an important theme in this period, but so also was mounting public concern about France, which affected attitudes towards the king, both because of his past pro-French policies and because of the French ambience of his Court. French culture and personnel were prominent at the royal Court in Whitehall, and this cosmopolitanism was distrusted by many. Charles's promiscuity and his preference for French mistresses was seen by many as dangerous. In *Britannia and Raleigh* a figure representing absolutist France advised Charles with reference to his three kingdoms:

> 'Tis royal game whole kingdoms to deflower,
> Three spotless virgins to your bed I bring,
> A sacrifice to you, their god and King.

At a less poetic level, a lampoon of 1681, 'At the Royal Coffee House', described how 24 French dancing girls had performed naked before Charles. The image of a man who was led astray by his baser desires and could not therefore be trusted to defend national views or even his own true interests was reiterated frequently.

Charles, in turn, felt that he had to defend his position against encroachments. In 1676, Louis's enemies hoped that Parliament would press Charles to declare war on France (PRO SP 80/15 f. 40) and were correspondingly disappointed the following year that Charles resisted such pressure and prorogued Parliament (PRO SP 80/15 f. 171). In the spring of 1677, the Austrian government was pleased when the Commons addressed Charles to take measures for the defence of the Spanish Netherlands, then being conquered by Louis (PRO SP 80/15 f. 106). In May 1677, however, he rejected a Commons address pressing him to inform the House of his alliances as a prerequisite for the funds he sought:

> Should I suffer this fundamental power of making peace and war to be so far invaded (though but once) as to have the manner and circumstances of leagues prescribed to me by Parliament, it is plain, that no prince or state would any longer believe, that the sovereignty of England rests in the Crown; nor could I think myself to signify any more to foreign princes, than the empty sound of a king. Wherefore you may rest assured, that no condition shall make me depart from, or lessen, so essential a part of the monarchy. (*Commons Journals* IX, 426)

This understandable position did not, however, help to create the trust necessary to unlock the parliamentary grants necessary for an active foreign policy.

French diplomatic reports stressed Louis's unpopularity in England, despite Louis's efforts to convince the opposition that he was not leagued with Charles. Charles did not consider himself a dependent of Louis and in 1677–8 Osborne, now Earl of Danby, was able to adopt an anti-French stance. In November 1677, William of Orange married James's elder daughter Mary, a Protestant, without being poisoned, as had been predicted in Vienna. In December, an Anglo-Dutch treaty stipulated the terms for a peace settlement in western Europe, echoing the Triple Alliance. A general alliance followed three months later. English troops were landed at Ostend in the Spanish Netherlands in February 1678 in order to defend it from Louis, and Parliament was asked for funds with which to increase forces. Danby argued that war with France would be a popular measure, and this was widely believed. In October 1677, the Austrian minister Count Königsegg claimed that Charles would soon be obliged to take measures favourable to Leopold (PRO SP 80/16 f. 18). The following spring, Parliament was asked to provide military bite to the new Anglo-Dutch alignment. However, Charles's sincerity in preparing for war with France was challenged and it was claimed that the troops would be used to create a stronger monarchy in England.

International tension was defused by the Peace of Nymegen (1678) which ended the war, while in England the Popish Plot and the Exclusion Crisis (1678–81) wrecked stable government on the rocks of suspicion of Catholicism and fears about the succession. Charles lacked legitimate children and his heir, James, Duke of York, was a Catholic whose intentions were widely suspected. Ruvigny reported in 1676 that it was generally believed that James's faith would lead him to seek to alter the established religion, while James in turn sought to gain French support by inspiring French fears of the hostile intentions of Parliament (AE CP. Ang. 188 ff. 66–8).

Concerned about Charles's unreliability and his willingness to negotiate with domestic and foreign opponents of Louis, the French placed increased faith in James. In February 1681, the French envoy Barrillon suggested that James's position depended on an Anglo-French treaty; that December, he argued that it would be best for Louis if James returned from Edinburgh, where he had gone in order to reduce tension during the Exclusion Crisis, in order that he could influence his brother. James supported a policy of neutrality and dispensing with Parliament in opposition to ministers, such as Halifax and Temple, who were more concerned with the fate of the Spanish Netherlands. James was in no doubt of the direct connection between domestic and foreign affairs. In January 1682, he warned that war with France would put the Stuart monarchy in danger.

A measure of stability was regained from 1681 in reaction to the Exclusion Crisis and, in part, thanks to French subsidies and to rising customs revenues as a result of the trade boom that followed Nymegen. In 1679, Louis rejected an appeal from Charles for subsidies to enable him to dispense with Parliament, because domestic turmoil in England then satisfied the French wish to prevent her from taking a major rôle in international diplomacy. However, the danger that Charles would turn to William led Louis in April 1681 to negotiate a secret agreement with him which allowed Charles to dispense with Parliament.

The last years of Charles's reign witnessed a combination of an increasingly strong domestic alliance of Crown and Tory Anglicanism and a foreign policy that, whatever his approaches to other rulers, was characterised by disengagement. When, in 1683, war broke out between France and Spain over continuing French expansion in the Low Countries, Charles refused to provide assistance despite his treaty of mutual assistance with Spain of 1680, which had been concerted with William and with ministers keen, as Danby had been earlier, to disassociate Charles from Louis. In January 1683, Charles responded very coolly to Dutch pressure for English intervention in Continental affairs (AE CP Ang. 149 ff. 12–13). The same year, Tangier, an expensive military commitment that the Moors had sought to seize, was abandoned in order to save money. England was not to gain another base for Mediterranean operations until Gibraltar was captured in 1704.

Except for the absence of Parliament from 1681, Charles's position in his last years was in some respects reminiscent of that in his first years as king. Just as Spain had then supported republican conspirators, so Louis financed Shaftesbury, Sidney and other 'Whigs' in order to weaken England, while he conducted his *réunion* policy of territorial gains along his frontier. In other respects, England was much weaker, the king unable to turn to Parliament, while the military strength and reputation of the country were far less than they had been under Cromwell. In part, Charles suffered as a result of developments that weakened his position – the growth in French power and the related religious tensions that became more prominent – but the extent to which these weakened the cohesion of English political views over foreign policy owed much to Charles's inability to inspire trust in his views, which was, in large part, due to his failure to take sufficient steps to elicit support. However, allowances must be made for the limited room for diplomatic manoeuvre Charles possessed, the rôle of foreign intervention in English politics, and the determined views of politicians unwilling to trust the king.

JAMES II 1685–8

James was a committed Catholic and therefore in the eyes of many of his subjects necessarily pro-French. The fact that, aside from William of Orange, Louis's leading opponents were themselves Catholic had little influence on English public debate. A very sinister portrayal of French governmental intentions and methods centred in England on the position of the French Protestants, the Huguenots. English newspapers had already linked the position of Catholics in England to the persecution of the Huguenots, thus helping to sustain the idea of a common battleground (*Domestick Intelligence*, 22 Aug. 1679). Government regulation of the press had collapsed during the Exclusion Crisis and by the end of 1679 more papers were being published than at any time since 1649. Three years later, a pamphlet that claimed that Louis wished to take over the world reported:

> Pamphlets, Sir You may go into a Coffee-house, and see a table of an acre long covered with nothing but tobacco-pipes and pamphlets, and all the seats full of mortals leaning upon their elbows, licking in tobacco, lyes, and lac'd

coffee, and studying for arguments to revile one another. (*A Pleasant Conference upon the Observator, and Heraclitus: together with a brief Relation of the present Posture of French Affairs;* see also Pincus 1995)

Control was reimposed, first by Charles and then by James, who in 1685 had Parliament revive the Printing Act, the basis of governmental control, which had lapsed in 1679. However, in the meantime, anti-French opinion had flourished. While criticism of Charles's domestic policies and alleged aspirations was countered by government newspapers – 'a whole kennel of Popish Yelpers' in the words of one critic -which stressed the dangers of anarchy and republicanism, there was no equivalent defence of French policy. Instead the charge that Charles was betraying national interests was rebutted or ignored.

This essentially domestic defence of Charles's position was less appropriate in his brother's reign. James sought changes in order to foster Catholicism in Britain, while, on the Continent, international tension increased. The danger of being identified, however unfairly, with Louis rose, not least because of the treatment of the Huguenots. A period of increased persecution culminated in the Edict of Fontainebleau in October 1685, by which the privileges granted to the Huguenots in 1598 by the Edict of Nantes, under which it was legal to be a Protestant, were rescinded. This led to extensive emigration, barbaric treatment of the Huguenots, and a highly charged emotional atmosphere in European Protestantism that linked France and Catholicism to tyranny. This development exacerbated distrust of Catholicism and sapped confidence in the idea that a Catholic ruler would keep his agreements.

James himself was not a French puppet (pp. 25–9), and he claimed that he had opposed English support of Louis in his attack on the Dutch in 1672 because he feared that the cost would make Charles dependent on Parliament. Furthermore, James had poor relations with the Pope. However, his domestic policies helped to create a corpus of beliefs that was to be sustained for a century whatever the actual state of Anglo-French negotiations. The apparent interrelated domestic threat of autocracy and Catholicism was to be decisively linked in the popular mind to the strategic and ideological challenge of France, which replaced Spain in the demonology of popular thinking on foreign affairs. The revocation of the Edict of Nantes appeared to justify fears about the cruelty and untrustworthiness of Catholics, and definitely heightened concern about James. It also led to a number of questions and incidents, for example concerning the status of French wives of English subjects, that created diplomatic problems (R. Clark 1938) and were followed closely in England.

Success was vital to the consensual nature of Crown-elite relations and to the respect awarded the monarch. Charles I had lost this crucial ingredient in his unsuccessful confrontation with Scottish rebels in the Bishops' Wars of 1639 and 1640, while the Irish rising of 1641 fatally weakened his position in England. In contrast, James retained firm control of both Scotland and Ireland, easily defeating the Argyll rising of 1685, while in England he had adequate forces at his disposal to suppress domestic rebellions, as the total failure of the Monmouth rising of 1685 made clear.

James's fall occurred, instead, as the result of an external invasion of England that received a measure of domestic encouragement and support. As such, it should be seen not as another episode of domestic political turmoil, the culmination of the Great Rebellion against Charles I, but as an instance of what had last been seriously attempted a century earlier. However, whereas the Spanish Armada had failed in 1588, William's invasion succeeded and thus became the Glorious Revolution. National myth-making has played a major rôle in the historical treatment of the Jacobites. The expulsion of James II and his son's failure to prevent the Hanoverian accession, events seen by contemporaries as violent ruptures and extreme developments, have been transformed into irresistible manifestations of a general aspiration by British society for progress and liberty. The seriousness of the overt crises and of the ideological, political and diplomatic tensions of the period have been underrated.

Once 1688 is seen as a violent change, then it can be presented as possibly the most important specific episode in the history of all the parts of the British Isles in this period that was a direct consequence of foreign relations. To ascribe it to foreign policy would be far-fetched. James's policy towards the United Provinces was not the cause of the invasion. It was rather dynastic circumstance – the birth in June 1688 of a son, the future 'James III' who, if he lived, would continue the Stuarts in the Catholic male line and thus exclude the Protestant female line, James's daughters by his first wife. The influence of the pro-French ministers and courtiers who looked to the queen, now the likely regent if James died, was reinforced (Proctor and Wilson 1989: 26). For William, this was an exclusion crisis that suggested that if international circumstances altered and the uneasy western European peace of 1678–88 was replaced by a major war, James's lukewarm acceptance of Louis's position might, possibly not in complete accordance with James's wishes, become full support. The invasion of 1688 was prophylactic, designed to avoid a fourth Anglo-Dutch war, a possible future repetition of the Anglo-French alliance of 1670–4. As such, although his perceived intentions were crucial, the question of James's actual intentions in the field of foreign policy was less important. Clearly domestic developments were more important to him, but there was no way in which he could, or would, consider it honourable or prudent to signal to his son-in-law, William, that a hypothetical future international situation would not lead him to support or seek the assistance of Louis (Miller 1978; Black 1989a).

In 1688, the situation in western Europe moved towards crisis as a disputed election to the strategic Rhineland Archbishopric-Electorate of Cologne raised the stakes in the rivalry between Louis and his opponents. As war became more likely, the policy that England would adopt became more important. Anti-Dutch commercial measures in France helped to rally Dutch support to William, while Louis felt it necessary to make a military demonstration in order to intimidate his opponents. His decision to do so by besieging Philippsburg on the upper Rhine, rather than by attacking the Dutch, helped to clear the way for an invasion of England, for it undercut the French warning, delivered to the (Dutch) States General on 9 September 1688, that as soon as the Dutch moved against James, Louis would declare war.

William at the head of 14,000 men landed at Brixham in Devon on 5 November 1688. James prepared to fight him at the head of his larger army of 25,000, but, on 23 November, his confidence crumpled and he decided to retreat to London. As his military position collapsed, James was no longer in a position to negotiate from strength. On 11 December he fled from London and later in the month, having been returned to London and then expelled by William's troops, escaped successfully to France. His flight undermined the position of those who had hoped to arrange a compromise under which he could retain the throne. On 18 December, William entered London (J.R. Jones 1972; Speck 1988; Proctor and Wilson 1989; Beddard 1991; Israel 1991).

DUTCH WILLIAM AND WAR 1688–97

> The true policy of England is to keep France low.
> (Anon, *The Spirit of France*, London, 1689, p. 41)

In so far as comparisons can be made, the post-Revolution monarchs 'distorted' foreign policy to serve personal interests to a greater extent than James had done. In the case of both William and the Georges, Britain's fortunes were linked to those of a foreign state with interests and problems of its own, in the person of a ruler who was willing to direct British resources to the furtherance of his conception of the interests of the other state. This was arguably as important as the growing rôle of Parliament (see pp. 44–9), and this dual development helped to account for much of the political contention over foreign policy. Until the 1760s, post-Revolution governments generally interpreted Britain's interests in light of international circumstances and possible developments in a fashion that made an active interventionist foreign policy, resulting in guarantees, confrontation and/or conflict, the central feature of Britain's position. To that extent, the Revolution represented a sharp break in foreign policy, though Charles II's diplomacy in 1668–72 and 1677–8 cannot be described as one of turning away from Europe.

William not only had a firm view of Britain as an integral part of a European system, but also had no doubt that the central feature of that system must be opposition to France and that Britain had to play a leading rôle. William's reign saw a rapid process of state formation, constitutional and governmental change, and ideological formulation, all in close association with a perception and policy not only that France was a major threat, but also that it was Britain's task and necessity to thwart her. By presenting Louis as a threat to both Britain and Europe, and as an inexorable expansionary force, William could be absolved from the charge of causing war and the burdens and problems that stemmed from it. A prospect of a Europe freed from a hegemonic threat was offered.

London was occupied by Dutch troops in 1688–90 while the Revolution Settlement was framed. William became a joint ruler with his wife, Mary, but he alone wielded power. War was declared on Louis in May 1689. As king, William in September 1689 acceded to the Grand Alliance negotiated between the Dutch and the Austrians that May. This aimed to force France back to her frontiers under the Peaces of Westphalia (1648) and the Pyrenees (1659). Support was pledged secretly to Leopold's claims to the Spanish succession, though Parliament was not informed of this undertaking. The Anglo-Dutch defensive treaty of March 1678, renewed by James in August 1685, was renewed again by William in August 1689.

William was to be swiftly disabused of his hopes that his allies, or indeed the western and central European powers, would unite against Louis. He was unable to bring either Sweden or Denmark into the anti-French alliance or to negotiate an end to the Austro-Turkish war that would free Austrian resources for the war against Louis. The problems of alliance politics were the principal topic of English diplomacy during the Nine Years' and Spanish Succession Wars. At the same time,

Williamite propaganda sought both to disguise the problems now confronting England and to vilify critics as pro-French and/or Jacobite in sympathy. Stuart foreign policy was presented as a distortion both of English national interests and of the development of English foreign policy. It was scarcely surprising that William and his supporters should seek to influence public opinion, given the importance of winning parliamentary support, both in order to further his foreign policy and to influence foreign powers, but it is understandable that William found it impossible to unify those who were ready to accept the exclusion of James, let alone the whole country, in support of his foreign policy. There was no defined sense of national interests, so that, whereas William regarded the conflict in Ireland as a dangerous diversion of resources from the Continent, many parliamentarians saw it as more important and were unwilling to consider concessions to the Irish Catholics (Troost 1983).

William has helped by Louis' support for James. Legitimism was not only an automatic attitude and ideology for Louis; it also seemed prudent, both with reference to Britain and because of Bourbon interest in the Spanish succession. William was an enemy whom Louis was convinced was not interested in compromise. It, also, did not seem impossible that William could be defeated, and a Britain under a suitably grateful and subservient James II would have been the best possible scenario for Louis, albeit a risky and long-term one that restricted his freedom of manoeuvre in the short term. In 1689, William faced serious opposition in both Scotland and Ireland that Louis could try to exploit. In 1692, Louis' plan for an invasion of southern England could have succeeded, especially if the French Brest and Toulon squadrons had united before risking battle. William, an active soldier-monarch could have been killed while on campaign, or he could have been killed in the Jacobite Assassination Plot of 1696. Louis' support for the Jacobites proved to be a central feature of the Whig account of the Glorious Revolution, helping to locate both France and Jacobitism in the past and present of the Whig imagination, and making clear their guilt by association.

The war was both unsuccessful and costly. Whereas Charles II's army had cost £283,000 in 1684 and James II's forces had cost £620,322 per annum, between 1691 and 1697 the army and the navy each cost an annual average of £2.5 million (Childs 1987: 153, 210). Pay was generally in arrears. War also hit trade, making it more difficult to finance huge external remittances. The strain was met by clipping, banking ingenuity, and a variety of other expedients. As the pace of clipping increased, domestic and international confidence in the money stock declined. The exchange rate fell significantly, making remittances more costly. Dutch loans were important. The crisis of 1693–4, caused by heavy over-borrowing, was alleviated by the foundation of the Bank of England in 1694, but, in 1696, greater over-borrowing, a run on the Bank and a recoinage in the midst of the war made the situation more serious. The Treasury defaulted on Exchequer bills, crippling foreign credit. Very little money could be sent to the forces in the Spanish Netherlands, and the crisis seriously affected operations. It was fortunate that peace was negotiated the following year (D.W. Jones 1988).

William was a poor communicator and an indifferent manager of English politics. The extent to which the war effort should involve major commitments to the defence of the Low Countries, as opposed to a maritime strategy of coastal attacks on France and colonial conquest, was controversial, and was to be increasingly so in 1702–13 when the fate of Spain and her empire was contested in the War of the Spanish Succession. In the 1690s, the so-called 'New Country Party' criticised the Continental strategy, but the public appeal of this attitude was compromised by the degree to which similar points were made by Jacobite writers. The failure of the strategy of coastal attacks on France also helped to rally increased support for the Continental strategy in the mid 1690s, but a legacy of distrust and dissatisfaction survived. It both played a major rôle in the campaign to reduce sharply the size of the army once the war ended in 1697, and ensured that, however unfocused and questionable its assumptions and applications might be, there was during the War of the Spanish Succession a persistent sense that the correct military strategy was not being followed.

The war can be divided from the perspective of Britain into two stages, the struggle for the control of the British Isles and the English Channel, which lasted until the capitulation of Limerick in October 1691 on terms that included a general indemnity for the Irish participants in the war, and the French naval defeat of Barfleur-La Hogue in May–June 1692 that ended the plan for a French invasion accompanied by James II. Thereafter, the central focus of the war for Britain switched to the Spanish Netherlands, where fighting had begun in 1689. The size of the British corps there rose from 10,972 in 1689 to 29,100, plus 27,209 foreign troops in British pay, in 1694–7 (Childs 1987: 268). In the winter of 1693, William asked the Commons for funds to pay 93,635 men.

William's commitment of British resources to the defence of the Spanish Netherlands was eased politically by the growing concern over the fate of the region that had characterised the public debate over policy since the mid 1670s. In one sense, William was translating the programme outlined in 1677–8 into action. However, there was a substantial difference between what had been largely plans supported by a military demonstration and the full-scale and mostly unsuccessful conflict of the 1690s. The war in the Spanish Netherlands was unpopular and costly. In his *Discourses on the Publick Revenues* (1698), the political economist and MP Charles Davenant complained of the costs of keeping forces there and suggested that in any future war England should restrict herself to a maritime rôle. This was a popular view, although the attack on the French naval base of Brest in 1694 had been a major failure. Fighting also occurred in northern Spain, between France and Savoy-Piedmont, in the Rhineland, and in the colonies. The last, however, was small-scale and largely inconsequential. The English failed to capture Québec in 1690. There was nothing to compare with the trans-oceanic operations that were to be mounted in 1739–62.

From the English point of view, the most important development was the dispatch of a large fleet to the Mediterranean in 1694, which was followed by its wintering at Cadiz. Thanks to the interests of Austria, France and Spain in the area, the western Mediterranean was the cockpit of European diplomacy. In the following half-century, it was to be a major sphere of British naval power and political influence. The origins of this can be traced to the 1690s, though William's Mediterranean strategy had only limited effects in the short term.

Arguably more important to Britain's long-term strength in foreign policy was the establishment of the Bank of England and a funded national debt (Dickson 1967). This did not prevent severe financial difficulties, but, in a situation where all powers were enfeebled by monetary shortages and financial administrative weaknesses, the relative strength of England was enhanced not only by the growing wealth of the country, especially its foreign trade, but also by the administrative developments of the 1690s. However, there was no doubt of war-weariness in England (Rose C. 1999). The diplomat James Cressett wrote to his colleague Richard Hill on 9 July 1697:

> I rejoice to hear you think our master is really weary of the war. I am sure he has reason to be so, and if the king of England is in that humour the people of that island do pretty well convince the world of their being in the same disposition, for though there may be some pleasure in being cheated in the beginning of things for a while, no nation can be so ridiculous as to delight in being bubbled eternally. (Beinecke, Osborn Shelves, Hill Box)

FROM PEACE TO WAR 1697–1702

The Peace of Ryswick of 1697 reflected the exhaustion of all the belligerents. Louis returned many *réunion* gains, as well as Freiburg and Luxembourg, although his position in Alsace, including Strasbourg, was recognised. Louis, who in 1696 had massed troops, joined by James II, at Calais to invade England, only to abandon his plans in the face of a major Anglo-Dutch naval presence, in 1697 recognised William as king and promised not to support Jacobite schemes: 'And since the most Christian King was never more desirous of anything, than that the peace be firm and inviolable, the said king promises and agrees for himself and his successors, that he will on no account whatsoever disturb the said king of Great Britain, in the free possession of the kingdoms, countries, lands or dominions, which he now enjoys'. The treaty was silent about Ireland. This testified to the inability of the expeditionary force sent to Ireland in 1689 to prevent Williamite conquest. France had thus failed to benefit from the War of the British Succession in 1688-9.

The peace, which was regarded as satisfactory by English commentators such as Sir John Lowther of Whitehaven, was followed by a period of intensive diplomacy and by disputes in England over the conduct of diplomacy and the size of the army. As the diplomatic groundwork was laid before the domestic crisis it has to be understood substantially in terms of William's personal views. His position was subsequently made more difficult by the crisis, the French envoy Tallard suggesting in September 1700, in terms reminiscent of foreign envoys under the later Stuarts, that Louis would have to reach an agreement with William prior to the meeting of Parliament (AE CP Ang. 188 f. 30). It is, however, unclear that the domestic crisis really did substantially affect William's foreign policy or the response to it. On 2 December 1697, at the opening of the session, William told Parliament that the maintenance of a standing force was essential. Nine days later, the Commons decided to disband all land forces that had been raised since 1680. As a result, the English establishment was cut to 10,000 men. A year later, the Commons decided to reduce the English establishment to 7000 and its Irish counterpart to 12,000, and to restrict the army to native troops, thus ensuring that Dutch regiments would have to return to the United Provinces, a blow to William which he tried without success to reverse. In contrast, the Dutch army was kept at 45,500. There was little doubt where William's views were more influential (Horwitz 1977: 226–7, 248–55; Childs 1987: 191–206). Nevertheless, Britain was to play a major rôle in the international diplomacy of 1698–1700 and in the War of the Spanish Succession (1701/2–1713/14).

The Spanish inheritance was the central international problem in western Europe. There were three principal claimants. The marriage of the daughters of Philip III of Spain to Louis XIII and the Emperor Ferdinand III, and of their sons, Louis XIV and Leopold I, to Philip IV's daughters produced important interests on the parts of the Bourbons and the Austrian Habsburgs, and there was also a Bavarian claimant through Leopold's Spanish marriage. The wish of both Louis XIV and William III to avoid another war led them in the spring of 1698 to begin negotiating a possible partition: Louis approached William. He had correctly identified Leopold as likely to be his most obdurate opponent and had appreciated that the crucial point of tension in the Grand Alliance had been the relationship between Leopold and the Maritime Powers (Britain and the Dutch). William, who told Tallard in April 1698 that he wanted close relations but feared that they might be affected by some unexpected development (AE CP Ang. 174 f. 124), essentially had three interests in mind: the specific concerns of Britain and the United Provinces; the more general desire to maintain a European system in which the preponderance of any one family or power was avoided; and the maintenance of peace.

The partition treaty agreed by Louis and William and signed in October 1698 left most of the inheritance to Joseph Ferdinand, the child heir to the Elector of Bavaria, while allocating Spanish possessions in Italy to the Austrian and French claimants. The treaty stipulated that the signatories should, in the last resort, impose it by force and thus offered the prospect of a collective security system based on an Anglo-French understanding, a policy that was to be revived in 1716. Charles II of Spain disliked the prospect of partition, but accepted the person of the Electoral prince and left his entire inheritance to him in a will drawn up in November 1698.

However, the following February, the prince died, and William and Louis were forced to resume negotiations without any prospect of a viable alternative to the Bourbon or Habsburg claimants. That August, the British ambassador in Paris, the Duke of Manchester, assured Louis XIV 'of the great esteem, the king my master had for his person, and of his firm resolution to preserve the peace and correspondence established between the two crowns' (Beinecke, Manchester Box). By the Second Partition Treaty of March 1700, Spain, the Indies and the Spanish Netherlands were to go to the Emperor's younger son, Archduke Charles, while Naples, Sicily and, by exchange, Lorraine would be acquired by the heir to the French throne, the Dauphin.

However, neither Leopold nor Charles II of Spain accepted the treaty.

In England, there was considerable agitation over the size of the army, which William was obliged to reduce against his wishes, and over the conduct of William in not consulting widely enough over foreign policy. There was wider concern over the extent of commitments to Continental affairs. In 1701, the leading Whig ministers, Halifax, Orford and Somers, were impeached for their alleged responsibility in the signing of the Partition Treaties, and the Lords criticised the agreement to allow France territorial gains. The Secretary at War, William Blathwayt, commented 'we pass most of our time in finding fault and impeaching one another' (Beinecke, Osborn Shelves, Blathwayt Box 21). When, in February 1701, William III appealed for parliamentary resolutions 'as shall be most conducing to the interest and safety of England, the preservation of the Protestant religion in general and the peace of all Europe', the Commons undertook to do so, but the clause 'and the peace of all Europe' was carried only by 181 to 163 votes. On 8 March the Commons refused to support an army big enough to fulfil their promise of troops to help the Dutch. Paul Methuen, the envoy in Lisbon, wrote in June 1701: 'I am afraid their resolutions concerning the Treaty of Partition will be very much for our discredit abroad and that all foreign princes will be very cautious how they deal with us for the future' (Kent Archive Office U1590 029/5). The traditional ministerial argument that the king could do no wrong was dismissed, and it was declared that no royal pardon should be pleadable in bar of an impeachment. Though the impeachments failed, William revealed a new attitude to Parliament by communicating to it copies of his treaties. On 18 March 1701, he sent Parliament a report on the negotiations at The Hague, giving as his reason his 'gracious intention to acquaint you, from time to time, with the state and progress of those negotiations'.

On 1 November 1700, Charles II of Spain died. His recently made will left his entire inheritance to Louis's second grandson, Philip Duke of Anjou, on condition that the crowns of France and Spain never be united in one person. If this was not accepted by the Bourbons, the whole empire was to be offered to Archduke Charles. Repudiating the Partition Treaty, Louis accepted the will, a decision that the Austrians were unwilling to agree, although Philip was recognised by the Dutch and England. He reached Madrid on 18 February 1701. Leopold, however, was determined to gain Spanish Italy, and sent a force to seize the Milanese. The first shots were exchanged on 19 June 1701, as the French sought to block the Austrian advance.

As both Austria and France prepared militarily, political opinion in

England swung away from an obsession with punishing William and his supporters for their past policies towards a willingness to accept his view that Louis's position threatened both England and Europe. In the parliamentary session of 1701, the Commons resolved to support the Dutch with the assistance specified in the Anglo-Dutch treaty of 1678, voted more money than had ever been voted in time of peace, and gave William a free hand in the negotiation of alliances. James Vernon, one of the Secretaries of State, claimed in January 1701: 'the House had great regard to what His Majesty told them in his speech that affairs abroad would be at a standstill till their resolutions were known' (Kent U1590 053/10). Blathwayt wrote to the diplomat George Stepney on 6 June 1701 that the principles of support for a war were 'now the most popular in England' (Beinecke, Osborn Shelves, Blathwayt Box 21). On 12 June, William thanked Parliament for 'repeated assurances' of support for alliances to preserve the 'liberty of Europe'. The Commons responded by promising backing for such alliances as he should negotiate 'in conjunction with the Emperor and the States-General, for the preservation of the liberties of Europe, the prosperity and peace of England, and for reducing the exorbitant power of France'. In 1702, the declaration of war was made by royal authority, but in response to the addresses and resolutions of both Houses of Parliament, a pattern in some respects matching that of the constitutional settlement of the Crown in 1689.

The relationship between this shift towards war and the transformation of the inchoate political groupings of the 1690s into a more obvious two-party system of Whigs and Tories in the 1700s is unclear. The vigour with which the demand for a reduction in the army had been pressed owed much to the widespread appeal of 'Country' attitudes hostile to government, but such attitudes provided little guidance as to how to respond to the developing international crisis of 1701; though from the assumption of office by the Junto, the leading Whigs, in 1693–4, 'the bulk of the Country interest was accommodated within the Tory party . . . when the opportunity arose Tories scrambled for place with quite as much keenness as Whigs' (Hayton 1984: 65). In 1701, it became increasingly clear that such a scramble required support for a firm attitude towards France, as political opinion turned towards William, who alone appeared to have some idea of how to deal with the crisis. The likely problems that war would create were not faced sufficiently because, by the summer, there appeared no alternative to negotiating a strong alliance against France which would include Leopold, whose forces invaded Lombardy that June, beginning the war.

Anglo-French tension was increased when French troops replaced Dutch soldiers in the Barrier fortifications in the Spanish Netherlands in February 1701; the French were granted commercial concessions in the Spanish empire, including in August the *asiento*, the monopoly to supply the empire with slaves; France prohibited the import of English manufactures; and, in September 1701, Louis recognised James II's son as king on the death of his father, which, in Manchester's words, 'shows at least this court does not intend to keep any measures with His Majesty' (Beinecke, Manchester Box). The same month, the Alliance of The Hague created the diplomatic basis for British action against France. It brought Austria and the Maritime Powers together to support a partition. The treaty stipulated an attempt to achieve its ends by negotiation. Leopold was to receive a satisfaction for his claims to the Spanish succession, though the fate of much of it was left unclear. The Maritime Powers were to retain any conquests they might make in the Spanish Indies. The crowns of France and Spain were to be kept separate, while French trade to the Spanish Indies was to be forbidden. Louis's recognition of 'James III' led William to press successfully for an additional clause to the Grand Alliance to support the Protestant succession in England as established by the Act of Settlement of June 1701, in favour, on the eventual death of his sister-in-law Anne, of the House of Hanover.

In June, the sickly William promoted a leading military commander, John Churchill, Earl of Marlborough, commander-in-chief of the forces destined for the United Provinces and ambassador in The Hague, thus encouraging continuity with the following reign. Following a fall from a horse, William died in March 1702. Louis then unsuccessfully sought to exploit the situation by opening negotiations with the Dutch, and in May, Austria, Great Britain and the Dutch simultaneously declared war on France. In April 1703, Sir Miles Wharton described the war as 'a legacy the late king left us' (BL Add. 22852 f. 63).

THE WAR OF THE SPANISH SUCCESSION 1702–13

However aggressive they may have been in intention, and this was probably exaggerated, Louis's moves in 1700–1 were judged provocative in Britain, helping to reverse the isolationist trend of the late 1690s. Blathwayt wrote to Stepney on 1 November 1701: 'now alliances are the passion of England and will be so till we come to . . . pay money for them' (Beinecke, Blathwayt Box 21). Anne's ministers were more astute communicators than William, more willing to try to influence public opinion through press and pamphlets, and more skilful in co-operating with Parliament. Possibly as important were the successes of the early stages of the war, including Blenheim (1704), an Anglo-German victory that led to the French being driven from the Empire (Germany), and Ramillies (1706) and Oudenaarde (1708), as a result of which the French were expelled from the Spanish Netherlands. In January 1703, Sir John Chardin claimed: 'the reign of the Queen [Anne] proves as successful, glorious and beloved as that of the renowned Elizabeth, and England saw nothing like since her in point of reciprocal confidence and love between the sovereign and the people and her Majesty's is like to be as fatal to the King of France as the other to the King of Spain' (BL Add. 22582 f. 115).

Victory helped to divert attention from the refusal of allies to co-operate, and to sustain both alliances and English public support for the war. However, success could not counteract indefinitely the impact of divergent interests among the Allies and of the costs of war.

English National Debt (funded and unfunded), 1691–1711

(million pounds)

1691	3.1		1709	18.9
1697	14.5		1710	21.3
1701	12.6		1711	22.4
1707	15.2			

Helped by a substantial trade surplus, British made a formidable military and financial effort. By 1710–11, when it was at its peak, Britain 'was paying for fully 171,000 officers and men (58,000 subject and 113,750 foreign) to fight abroad in Europe' (D.W. Jones 1988: 11). Portugal and Savoy-Piedmont had been given subsidies since 1703 when they abandoned France and joined the Grand Alliance. These subsidies were crucial to the survival of the alliance. In 1703–13, Anglo-Dutch subsidies provided 26.7 per cent of the budget of Victor Amadeus II of Savoy-Piedmont (Symcox 1983: 164), without whose help the Bourbons would not have been driven from Italy in 1706–7. Other subsidies were paid to Denmark, Hesse-Cassel, Prussia, Austria and the Electors of Saxony and Trier.

Victories exacerbated relations within the alliance by raising expectations and increasing demands. In September 1706, Robert Harley, the Secretary of State for the Northern Department, argued: 'it is plain if the Allies will be but true to themselves, France may be reduced to reason, but there is no security against that Crown, but taking away the power to do hurt' (BL Add. 7059 f. 110). Differences with and between allies over objectives and methods constituted an incessant theme of British diplomatic correspondence, a situation made worse by the removal of the Williamite link with the Dutch, the greater relative contribution of British resources to the war effort, the absence of a security threat comparable to that of the years immediately after 1688, and the escalation of the Allies' war aims. Charles Davenant complained in 1706 that 'none of the confederates act their parts to the utmost strength but ourselves' (BL Add. 4291 f. 64). The following year, the Duke of Manchester, then on a diplomatic mission to Italy, wrote: 'I have seen a great deal of the different views of princes, as also their ministers which nothing but the conduct of England could have kept so long together' (Huntingdon CRO DD M36/8, 19 Aug.).

By the end of 1706, France had been driven from Germany, Italy and most of the Spanish Netherlands, but the Grand Alliance was now committed to the policy of 'No Peace without Spain', the succession of Leopold's younger son, the Archduke Charles, to Spain. Charles, Earl of Halifax, on a diplomatic mission to Hanover in 1706, told the Electress Sophia, who had been declared heir to the throne by the Act of Settlement, that Parliament had 'acted so prudently, and taken such right measures, that by the blessing of God we may expect to see Her Majesty establish the kingdom of Spain in the House of Austria, and the succession of England in the House of Hanover' (New York Pub. Lib., Montague Collection, 4 June); but this Whig linkage of domestic and diplomatic objectives was to help lead to the fall of the party in 1710. Spain proved an impossible military goal, and the failure militarily to conquer the peninsula, underlined by the defeats of Almanza (1707), Brihuega (1710) and Villaviciosa (1710), was matched by the inability to produce a satisfactory solution to the war in negotiations with Louis XIV in 1709–10. Louis refused to accept the demand that he help drive his grandson from Spain by force (Hatton and Bromley 1968: 190–212), while the bloody battle of Malplaquet (1709) revealed that it would not be easy to crack France's frontier defences.

The same year, Charles XII of Sweden was decisively defeated at Poltava by Peter the Great of Russia, a battle that was followed by the Russian conquest of Sweden's Baltic provinces. Though individual battles in the War of the Spanish Succession, such as Blenheim (1704) and Turin (1706), could alter the situation decisively in a particular sphere, it proved impossible to achieve total victory. Louis XIV was able to field new armies, his frontiers had been well fortified by Vauban, and the French economy, though battered by the war and by poor harvests, continued to sustain the war effort. Indeed, in so far as a decisive blow seemed imminent, it was the Grand Alliance that had been most vulnerable. In 1703–4, a combination of Bavaria, France and Hungarian rebels appeared about to extinguish Habsburg power. This crisis was averted in large part by Marlborough's bold march at the head of an Anglo-German army to the Danube, the most decisive British military move on the Continent during the years 1660–1793, and his subsequent victory, in co-operation with the Habsburg general Prince Eugene, at Blenheim.

In 1708, another, though less threatening, attempt was made to overthrow one of the members of the Grand Alliance. A French squadron carrying 'James III' and 5000 French troops evaded a British fleet blockading Dunkirk and reached the Firth of Forth before their pursuers. Edinburgh Castle was in no state to resist a siege and the Scots army was not powerful enough to block Jacobite plans. Much of the Scottish aristocracy was prepared to rise for James: the 1707 Union with England was unpopular. However, the opportunity was lost; there was no landing (Gibson 1988). In contrast, British attempts to exploit the Huguenot rising of 1702–10 in the Cévennes mountains of southern France were half-hearted, though the Huguenots did not pose a threat that was in any way comparable to that of the Hungarians or the Jacobites. Indeed, domestic cohesion was arguably as crucial a source of strength in this period as sound governmental finances. Such cohesion was challenged most in multiple kingdoms, such as Britain and the dominions of the Austrian Habsburgs, a situation that was exacerbated when the succession was controversial, as it was in Britain for most of the period 1679–1746 and for the Habsburgs when Charles VI died in 1740. In contrast, much of France's strength was due to the relative weakness of its centrifugal tendencies.

Under the strain of an apparently unending war, both the Whig ascendancy in Britain and the Grand Alliance collapsed. Disenchantment with the ministry and the war helped respectively to lead Queen Anne to turn to the Tories and the electorate to support them in the general election of 1710. The new ministry, whose most prominent members were the Lord Treasurer, Robert Harley, soon to be Earl of Oxford, and the Secretary of State for the Northern Department, Henry St John, more famous as Viscount Bolingbroke, decided to resume unilateral negotiations with France. They felt that Britain was suffering from the determination of Marlborough, a 'monied interest', of financiers and contractors who profited from the conflict, and her allies to pursue their own interests. Tentative negotiations were begun in July 1710 through the Earl of Jersey and, until the following spring, only a small number of ministers were kept informed, St John not playing a rôle until April 1711.

Disillusionment with the Grand Alliance and the aims of British policy was encouraged by the death without sons in April 1711 of the Emperor Joseph I, who had succeeded his father, Leopold I, in 1705. Archduke Charles became ruler of the Habsburg territories and Emperor, as Charles VI, opening up the possibility of an Austro-Spanish union. Bolingbroke pointed out In July 1711 that 'if the Empire and the dominions of Spain are to unite in the person of this prince, the system of the war is essentially altered' (BL Add. 22205). This put the Whigs in a false position, as can be seen from *The Balance of Power*, a pamphlet of November 1711, which pressed for the union of the Austrian and Spanish inheritances as the means to preserve the balance of power. Whig spokesmen reiterated their defence of the policy 'No Peace without Spain', that not only could not be obtained militarily, but also threatened to create a new political leviathan that bore no relation to traditional British objectives. Indeed, when Spain and Austria were next allied, between 1725 and 1729 in the Alliance of Vienna, they were opposed by the Walpole ministry, and Whig writers presented their union as a threat both to the European system and to the balance of power, though the international system was then very different as a result of the Anglo-French alliance.

There had been serious disquiet about the war even before Charles' succession. The failure to achieve a negotiated settlement in 1709–10 suggested that terms suitable to the Grand Alliance and yet acceptable to France could not be obtained. Furthermore, the British contribution to the war effort had enabled the Austrians to concentrate not on fighting the French but on conquests in Italy and the suppression of the Hungarian rebellion. The prospect of a union between Austria and Spain was the culmination of the problems Britain had encountered with her allies. It justified Tory caution about Continental interventionism, and reflected the difficulties of adopting a planned and consistent approach to foreign policy in an international system made unstable and kaleidoscopic by the vagaries of dynastic luck.

The Present Negotiations of Peace Vindicated from the Imputation of Trifling, a pamphlet of 1712, commented:

'. . . certainly the brains of the people were never so distempered as at present: at one time Spain and the West Indies was thought too narrow a spot for empires for such capacious souls. The great hopes we had conceived of our successes abroad had heated our imaginations, and we were all bent to carry on the war with vigour until the Spanish monarchy should be restored entire to the House of Austria; but perceiving ourselves short in that reckoning, jaded with frequent miscarriages in Spain, finding the enemy recruited to a miracle . . . and exhausted with the prodigious charge [of] a war . . . the nation abated much of their former warm resolutions, and clamoured for peace' (pp. 3–4).

On 27 September/8 October 1711, preliminaries designed to serve as the basis for the full negotiations in a general peace conference were signed. The Dutch were persuaded to accept them two months later, and the congress opened in the town hall of Utrecht on 29 January 1712. The political battle had already been won in Britain. The Tory majority carried the preliminaries through the Commons on 7 December 1711 by 232 to 106. An initial defeat in the Lords, at the hands of Whigs and a Tory group under the Earl of Nottingham, who managed to pass an amendment which condemned any peace that left Spain and the West Indies to a Bourbon, was overcome when Anne gave Oxford full backing. She dismissed her Master of the Horse, the Duke of Somerset, who had sought to undermine Oxford by claiming that Anne was unhappy with the peace terms, and created twelve new peers in order to secure his majority in the Lords. By the time the terms were announced in a speech from the throne on 6 June 1712, the Tories were united and the court Whig peers who had deserted the previous December were back in line. The ministry won the divisions on the addresses of thanks and then, having had a powerful demonstration of parliamentary support (by a majority of 45 in the Lords), kept Parliament prorogued until the treaty was signed. Parliament was prorogued eleven times, not meeting again until April 1713.

The negotiations with France that produced the Peace of Utrecht of 31 March 1713 were in effect a resumption both of the partition-treaty diplomacy and also, after a period of strident demands by the Grand Alliance, of the principles of compromise, equivalents and exchanges that characterised many negotiations in this period. The Earl of Strafford, a Tory who was one of the plenipotentiaries at Utrecht, claimed with reason in 1714 that 'as for leaving France in the power they are, it was actually impossible to have left them other ways, which I think by history, example etc may be proved next to demonstration' (Bod. MS Eng. Lett. C. 144 f. 300).

The Treaty of Utrecht was not to be the definitive partition treaty; by the time of the Third Treaty of Vienna (1738) the house of Savoy-Piedmont had won Sardinia but lost Sicily, while a cadet branch of the Spanish Bourbons had gained Naples and Sicily. However, with the important exception of the continuing Austro-Spanish struggle over Italy, the Utrecht treaty settled western Europe territorially until the French Revolution. Philip V was confirmed as king of Spain, founding a new royal line of the Bourbons, and ruler of Spain's trans-oceanic possessions, while the Spanish Netherlands (Belgium) and much of

Spanish Italy became Austrian. Philip renounced his rights to the French succession, in response to British pressure. Bolingbroke had claimed in June 1712 that preventing the possible future union of the thrones of France and Spain was 'the capital point of our negotiation' (AE CP Ang. sup. 4 f. 156). Britain gained Gibraltar and Minorca, conquered during the war in 1704 and 1708 respectively, Nova Scotia, Newfoundland and Hudson's Bay, the *asiento*, the right to supply slaves to the Spanish New World, and a limited though potentially profitable right to trade there, and recognition of the Protestant succession. The peace split the Grand Alliance, Austria fighting on for another year, and helped to damn the Tories in the eyes of an Austrian supporter, George Elector of Hanover, who became George I on the death of childless Anne in 1714 (MacLachlan 1969).

The Whigs feared that the peace would be followed by a Jacobite succession in Britain when Anne died, as Louis would be able to provide support. Domestic and international affairs were thus presented as intertwined, as when the Whig Lord Cowper told Sir David Hamilton, Anne's doctor, in October 1712 that the government had 'made France triumphant over the Allies, and when he [Louis XIV] had dealt with them, he would deal with us and fix the Pretender on the throne' (P. Roberts (ed.), *Diary . . . Hamilton*, p. 43). Marlborough, who had been dismissed as Captain General in 1711, leaving England in 1712 to avoid threatened prosecution, sought Austrian and Dutch military backing for action to prevent a Jacobite succession on the death of Anne.

Utrecht was followed by a measure of Anglo-French diplomatic co-operation, as the two powers sought to establish and defend the territorial arrangements they had stipulated (McKay 1971). The terms of a commercial treaty were also negotiated. The French had pressed for reciprocal concessions, telling the British envoy, Matthew Prior, that they could 'only take off their duties as we shall take off ours . . . To which I objected that the king being absolute master of his edicts might in the meantime take away the entire prohibition of several of our commodities,' an argument that was rejected. Torcy, the French foreign minister, wisely remarked with respect to trade 'that the confusion and misunderstanding of twenty years will not be redressed without a good deal of time and labour' (PRO SP 78/154 ff. 216 17). After difficult negotiations, an agreement was reached. It was agreed that subjects of both countries should be conceded the same trading status that those of the most favoured other nations enjoyed, though with some exceptions. However, the bill was rejected by the House of Commons in June 1713 by 194 to 185, as a result of opposition by some Tories. Sir Thomas

Hanmer, MP for Suffolk, played a major rôle in this result. A 'Hanoverian Tory' who was concerned about moves that might favour France and therefore the Jacobite cause, he was also worried about the possible impact of French competition on the declining cloth industry of his county. The Whigs had inspired a press campaign against the treaty and encouraged the presentation of critical petitions. Suspicion of links with France was therefore strong on the eve of the Hanoverian accession.

CHAPTER TEN

BRITISH FOREIGN POLICY 1714–63

INTRODUCTION

The extent to which foreign policy was a subject of political division in this period varied considerably. It was most important between 1714 and 1748, and, within that period, in 1717–20, 1725–30, 1738–9 and 1742–8, and least so thereafter, though the moves towards peace from 1761 and the concomitant deterioration in Anglo-Prussian relations led to the return of foreign policy to the centre of the political arena. As a result, any discussion of British diplomacy in these years is somewhat uneven. While Townshend in 1716 and 1730 and Carteret in 1724 and 1744 lost their Secretaryships in large part because of the interrelationship between their vulnerable political positions and their particular views on foreign policy, Newcastle benefited in 1748–53 from a relative lack of political concern with Britain's diplomacy on the Continent. Though ministers disagreed over, for example, the need to approach Frederick II (the Great) of Prussia in 1748 or the value of peace-time subsidies, the wider political resonance of these differences was muted. Peacetime subsidies were controversial, but that with Bavaria, signed while George II was in Hanover in August 1750, passed the Commons very easily the following February, Horace Walpole writing: 'the majority for the subsidy appearing very great, it was given up without telling' (*Memoirs* 22 Feb.). A discussion of British diplomacy in these years necessarily centres on international developments rather than domestic constraints. Similarly, the formation of the Pitt-Newcastle ministry in 1757 was followed by four years during which there was broad political agreement on British policy.

The relative harmony of 1757–61 can be ascribed to the care with which Pitt justified British military intervention on the Continent, presented as designed to help Frederick, not Hanover; to the more limited nature of Britain's Continental strategy compared with the Nine Years', Spanish Succession and Austrian Succession Wars; and to the rising tide of maritime and colonial successes. In contrast, British policy in 1748–53 could not be explained with reference to any popular 'Patriot' agenda. In 1748, Louisbourg, the only significant gain from France in the War of the Austrian Succession and a colonial fortress that was believed to guard the approach to French-ruled Canada up the St Lawrence, was returned in the Peace of Aix-la-Chapelle. Over the next five years, the ministry, though criticised by opposition newspapers for failing to defend colonial interests against France in North America and the West Indies, centred its foreign policy on the negotiation of a Continental collective security system and on the Imperial Election Scheme, a project that meant little to the electors of Britain, who in the general election of 1754 ignored foreign policy. The ministry was not really held to account domestically for its foreign policy.

It has been claimed that, 'as the transatlantic trade rose in importance, many baulked at the government's foreign policy which seemed unnecessarily expensive, Byzantine, deferential to Hanover, and neglectful of Britain's emerging trade in the West . . . Patriotism, nationalism, and commercial expansion . . . continued to resonate into the 1750s' (Rogers 1989: 396–7). This may well be so, but what is striking about the early 1750s is how weakly they resonated. The wider public debate appears to have been most important when the government was divided, as over Baltic policy in 1716–17, relations with France in 1730, war with Spain in 1739, the nature of British strategy during the War of the Austrian Succession in 1743–4, and relations with France in 1754–5, but, even then, its importance should not be overstated. Elections were not verdicts on foreign policy, even in wartime, except in a small number of constituencies; although foreign policy-related taxation could lead to anger. Philip Yorke MP wrote to his wife about the campaign of 1747, when Britain was at war: 'As to foreign affairs, you may be sure like a true electioneer I think more of the contest in Staffordshire, than the state of Genoa, and provided the English freeholders have beef and beer enough am little concerned how their countrymen fare in Flanders' (Bedford CRO L 30/113/16). The two seats for which he had just been returned unopposed, Reigate and Cambridgeshire, were more typical than constituencies, such as Bristol and London, where there was a strongly developed and articulate mercantile consciousness.

Political developments in the period increased governmental influence over Parliament. The Septennial Act of 1716 prolonged the maximum duration of parliaments from three to seven years, while a lengthy monopoly of power by the Whigs during the reigns of George I and II helped to ensure that the House of Lords was easier to lead, thanks to peerage creations, the manipulation of the election of Scottish representative peers, and greater control over the bishops, and that most institutions were brought under Whig control. Though the stability of the political system was limited by the continued existence of Jacobitism, political management, not least in terms of the abandoning of the wide-ranging and radical Whig programme of the late 1710s, ensured that the political system was dominated by the alliance between Crown and ministerial Whigs. This was not an alliance free from tension and rifts, and in those periods, when disaffected ministers and a discontented Prince of Wales sought opposition support, as in 1717–20, the nature of political beliefs held outside the ministerial camp was of consequence, especially if they aided or inhibited this search for support (Black 1990b). However, in general, it is the limited impact of opposition political activity that is most noteworthy. Walpole survived the attempt to unite Tories and opposition Whigs in a 'Country' grouping in the late 1720s and 1730s, just as the Pelham ministry defeated the challenge mounted by Frederick, Prince of Wales in the late 1740s.

Instead, the principal battleground for foreign policy was in the royal closet, where ministers saw the king on a confidential basis, and within the ministry. It was in Court and cabinet that contentious issues, such as Baltic policy in 1716, British neutrality in the War of the Polish Succession in 1733–5, or the decision whether to fight on in the War of the Austrian Succession in 1747, were discussed and resolved. Questions of diplomatic strategy arising in large part from assessments of the positions and intentions of other powers played a central rôle in these debates. The settlement of both the succession and the party question, as far as the political establishment was concerned, and the marginalisation of those who held different views, ensured that the domestic context of foreign policy was less complex, divided and uncertain than had been the case in the period 1660–1714. This could be presented as a triumph for parliamentary monarchy, though to do so would be to overlook the problems that had been faced in trying to achieve co-operation prior to the accession of George I and the extent to which 1714 led to an oligarchic political system dominated by one party. The consequence was a foreign policy in which diplomatic considerations played a greater rôle than under Anne, especially if they had a bearing on the position of Hanover.

GEORGE I, THE ANGLO-FRENCH ALLIANCE AND CONTINENTAL INTERVENTIONALISM 1714–7

The most surprising feature of George I's policy was the negotiation in 1716 of an Anglo-French alliance that was to last until 1731. His accession and the replacement of the Tory ministry by Whigs, a process underlined by Whig success in the general election of 1715, had led to reports that Britain would resume hostilities with France (AE CP Ang. 265 f. 39). This assumption gained further credibility from disagreements over French observance of the provision in the Peace of Utrecht that they wreck the harbour and fortifications of the port of Dunkirk, from which the Pretender had sailed on his unsuccessful French-backed attempt to invade Scotland in 1708, and from apparent French support for the Jacobites, who in 1715 rose in Scotland and northern England. Louis XIV certainly feared that the new government would provoke war (AE CP Rome 538 f. 245, Ang. 259 f. 138). Initially, the Whigs sought to recreate the Grand Alliance, provoking concern from the French. An Anglo-Dutch treaty was signed in February 1716. Relations with Charles VI were more difficult, but a treaty followed in June.

The death of Louis XIV in 1715, the succession of his infant great-grandson, Louis XV, the vulnerable regency of Philip, Duke of Orléans, and severe exhaustion after two lengthy, bitter wars and the demographic disaster of 1708–11, led to French disinclination to confront new enemies. The defeat of the Jacobite rebellion made George I a more attractive ally, at the same time that the eruption of Peter the Great of Russia's power into northern Germany in 1716 created a new diplomatic and potentially military agenda for George.

It might appear inevitable that the two vulnerable leaders, George I and Orléans, should unite. The Jacobite and Spanish threats made a resolution of Anglo-French diplomatic difficulties urgent. Yet, distrust was strong in ministerial and diplomatic circles in both countries, and closer relations by either with Austria appeared at least as likely.

The negotiation of the Anglo-French alliance was conducted in a strained atmosphere, but was assisted by differences between Austria and the Maritime Powers over the Austrian Netherlands. The alliance, signed by Orléans' advisor Dubois and the Southern Secretary, James Stanhope, on 9 October 1716 and formally on 28 November, was designed to guarantee the achievements of 1713–15: the Utrecht settlement of the Anglo-French successions, George's subsequent accession and the position of Orléans. James Stuart was to be forced to leave France, while Hanover and her recent gains were also guaranteed. France promised to abandon the alliance negotiated the previous year with George's opponent, Charles XII of Sweden. Orléans wrote to Dubois in June 1718: 'Peace, from what you say, is the English system; it is also mine' (AE CP Ang. 312 f. 274). Two years later, John, 2nd Earl of Stair, the envoy in Paris, wrote to another British diplomat: 'we want a balance of power in order, by that, to maintain the peace of Europe' (New York Pub. Lib. Hardwicke papers 54).

The Anglo-French alliance, which was broadened into a Triple Alliance the following January by the inclusion of the United Provinces, had to confront potential challenges from the two most unpredictable rulers of the period, Philip V of Spain (1700–46) and Peter the Great (1689–1725), and, within five years, this had led to war with Spain (1718–20) and confrontation with Russia (1719–20). Philip's attempt to reverse the Italian provisions of the Utrecht settlement by invading first the island of Sardinia (1717) and then Sicily (1718) was, for the moment, thwarted, in part thanks to the British naval victory off Cape Passaro (1718). This ensured that Britain retained the crucial naval superiority in the western Mediterranean necessary to influence Italian affairs that she had earlier gained in the War of the Spanish Succession. Though the partnership was uneasy, Britain fought Spain in alliance with Austria and France. Spanish hopes that Britain would not risk her trade with Spain by war proved misplaced. George I and his ministers wished to resist any unilateral overturning of the Utrecht settlement, and, in order to gain the support of the Emperor for Hanoverian acquisitions from Sweden, George supported the Austrian position in Italy. Following defeat in Sicily, the failure of his 1719 attempt to invade Britain in support of the Jacobites, and the collapse of his schemes to overthrow Orléans, Philip made peace in February 1720.

The Whig ministry was relatively united over policy towards Spain, certainly in comparison with attitudes towards relations first with Sweden and then with Russia. As Elector of Hanover, George sought to gain the duchies of Bremen and Verden, German possessions of Sweden that would give Hanover a North Sea coastline, and in 1715 he declared war on Charles XII. George sought to use the British navy, ostensibly sent to the Baltic to escort merchantmen to the Russian-held ports of the east Baltic and protect them from Swedish privateers, in order to prevent the Swedes from supporting their besieged garrisons at Stralsund and Wismar, but he was obliged to rely on verbal rather than written instructions and faced opposition from Orford, the First Lord of the Admiralty.

Tensions within the government arose from a competition for office that could be regulated only by royal favour, as there was no party leadership in the modern sense. These were exacerbated by a growing rivalry between George and his son, George Prince of Wales. As a result, differences over the extent to which George's opposition as Elector first to Sweden and then, from late 1716, to Russia should be supported by British resources led to a bitter struggle within the ministry, which produced the Whig Split of 1717–20. Walpole and Townshend went into opposition (they were reconciled with the king in 1720).

During those years, opposition Whigs sought to co-operate with Tories in attacking government policy in Parliament, but conflicting views made it difficult to produce a stable alliance. However loyal or disloyal the Tories were to the house of Hanover, most were stridently anti-Hanoverian in proclaiming their support for a 'British', as opposed to a 'Hanoverian', foreign policy or what in 1716 the Earl of Sunderland termed 'the old Tory notion, that England can subsist by itself, whatever becomes of the rest of Europe, which has been so justly exploded ever since the revolution' of 1688 (W. Coxe, *Memoirs . . . Walpole* 1798:II, 128). This notion was not held only by Tories – Sunderland was complaining at Whig reluctance to get involved 'in anything that happens' in northern Europe – but it was strongly associated with them. Most Whig leaders were more sensitive to George I's views, even if not to the extent that the king would have liked.

The limitations of naval power were demonstrated in the confrontation with Russia, for, though the British could discourage Russian amphibious attacks on Sweden, as they were similarly to do in the following decade, they could not oblige Russia to restore the territories in the eastern Baltic, Ingria, Estonia and Livonia, that she had conquered earlier from Sweden. The anti-Russian agreements that George had devoted so much effort to negotiating in 1719–20 could not be translated into effective action, while British determination was also inhibited by the South Sea Bubble, a major financial crisis, in 1720. The Great Northern War (1700–21), the struggle over the fate of the Swedish Empire, did not end with a compromise peace, as that of the Spanish Succession had done. Instead, by the Peace of Nystad of 1721, Peter retained his gains. Nevertheless, the rise of Russian power was, in time, to assist Britain, when she was opposed to France and Prussia.

Having brought peace at least to western Europe, France, Britain and Spain agreeing in June 1721 to resume diplomatic relations, the Anglo-French partnership was faced in the early 1720s with the difficult task of maintaining it. The principal problem came not from changes within the alliance but from the schemes of other powers. The partnership survived the deaths of both Orléans and Dubois in 1723, and the constitution of a new ministry round the Duke of Bourbon, just as it was to survive Bourbon's replacement by Cardinal Fleury in 1726. In Britain, the deaths of George's principal ministers in his early years, Stanhope and Sunderland, in 1721 and 1722, their replacement by Walpole, First Lord of the Treasury 1721–42, and Townshend, Northern Secretary 1721–30, and the Jacobite Atterbury Plot of 1722 did not compromise the alliance. The plot was exposed with French assistance and French refusal to support the Jacobites in 1722 indicated the value of the alliance. Though the Jacobites could turn to other powers for assistance, receiving Spanish backing in 1719 and seeking help from Charles XII, Peter the Great and, in 1726, the Austrians, it was the French position that was vital, for they were best placed to intervene militarily. During the crucial period in which the Hanoverian regime was establishing and consolidating its position, the French government refused to heed widespread pro-Jacobite sympathies within France. George I was happy to follow the French lead at the international congress of Cambrai, which met finally in 1724:

> His Majesty having no other view or concern in the settlement of those affairs but the preservation of a strict and firm union between the courts of Great Britain and France and the establishing of the peace and tranquillity of Europe, whereas the court of France being more particularly interested in the several questions that are depending at Cambray are the properest to propose and suggest what should be done upon them to which His Majesty will always very readily agree. (BL Add. 32739 ff. 142–3).

George took a more active rôle in Baltic affairs, resisting French pressure to settle his differences with Russia, which arose essentially from his concern, as Elector of Hanover, with Russia's growing influence in northern Europe. Neither Austria nor Spain was keen to accept Anglo-French guidance and their disagreements, essentially over the succession to Tuscany and Parma in Italy, were not solved at Cambrai. This led to a surprising shift when Spain approached Austria in an attempt to create a new diplomatic order, a settlement of their Italian differences linked to a marriage alliance. The result was the Alliance of Vienna (April–May 1725), an apparently threatening alignment that was countered that September by the Alliance of Hanover, an alliance of Britain, France and Prussia.

The two alliances confronted each other in a cold war for two years, that of Vienna gaining the support of Prussia (1726) and Russia (1726), while that of Hanover won Denmark, Sweden and the United Provinces. That George I's last years were not, however, spent in war owed much to the unwillingness of Austria and France to fight, which was to lead to a preliminary peace settlement in May 1727, shortly before George's death, and to restraint in the face of provocations, especially British naval action in 1726 to prevent the sailing of the Spanish treasure fleet, with its much-needed bullion, from the West Indies, and the Spanish siege of Gibraltar in early 1727.

Nevertheless, even though George's reign did not close with war, it had witnessed a major expansion of British foreign policy, including significant intervention in Baltic affairs. The South Sea Bubble, however, helped to lead to more cautious diplomacy and a backing-down from confrontation with Russia (Murray 1969; Hatton 1978). During William's reign Britain had been committed to active and wide-ranging alliance diplomacy, a process that had culminated in the Grand Alliance of 1701, but the partition diplomacy of 1698-1700 had been largely personal and secret, while the Grand Alliance was addressed to the defence of apparently vital interests and was the response to apparent French provocations and to the move of western Europe towards war. In contrast, George I's wide-ranging Continental interventionism was essentially public, supported by parliamentary funds, harder to define and defend in terms of what were traditionally seen as national interests, and involved continual commitment and activity in peace-time. Fortunately for George and his ministers, this period of commitment involved only one war, which was brief (1718–20), successful and fought with a power, Spain, that was not widely popular. The confrontation with Austria in 1725–30 was not taken to the point of what might have been a long, unsuccessful and unpopular war.

In many senses, the experience of George I's foreign policy set the tone for British policy until the mid 1750s. Walpole, first minister from 1721, and more clearly 1727, to 1742, was convinced of the potential domestic political costs of Continental interventionism and lacked his predecessors' emotional and intellectual commitment to it. His more cautious attitude, which characterised British policy in the 1730s (Black 1985a), was followed in 1742–4 by energetic interventionism under the auspices of Lord Carteret, who, as an envoy in Stockholm in 1719–20, when British policy was becoming markedly anti-Russian, and Secretary of State in 1721–4, had developed his ideas during the period of earlier interventionism.

Carteret's ministry revealed the dangers of the policies of George I's reign. Britain became involved in a major war, that of the Austrian Succession (1740–8), without lasting success and in a manner that caused substantial domestic political discontent. The Duke of Newcastle, the most influential minister in the field of foreign policy from 1744 to 1755, reacted against the anti-Austrian attitude of George I's last years, writing in 1752 to his political ally, the Earl of Hardwicke: 'the dread of the politics of 1725, I have always had before me' (BL, Add. 35412 f.

18). One aspect of policy, however, in which George I's reign had little resonance was Anglo-French relations. It represented the longest period of alliance or good relations between the two powers during the eighteenth century, but the alliance failed to strike roots and, after it collapsed in 1731, few regrets were expressed about its passing, despite the fact that the result was a major deterioration in Britain's strategic position (Black 1986a).

FROM THE ACCESSION OF GEORGE II TO THE FALL OF WALPOLE, 1727–42

All alliances represent a struggle for influence between partners. In the case of the Anglo-French alliance, Britain had played the dominant rôle when the alliance was at war or under threat or confined to Britain, France and weaker powers, such as the United Provinces. This had essentially been the case in 1716–20 and 1725 to early 1727. However, France was more influential, worryingly so for the British, when the alliance system encompassed Spain and when relations with other powers were not too hostile. This was the case in the early 1720s and may have been responsible for the interest shown by some ministers, for example Carteret in 1723, in better relations with Austria.

As the cold war between the alliances of Hanover and Vienna diminished in intensity in 1727, British anxiety about French intentions increased, and this was exacerbated the following year during the Congress of Soissons when Britain found little support for her interests. The French were less than eager in their support of Britain over her retention of Gibraltar, which, in 1721, George I had promised to restore when he could win parliamentary support, and over her dispute with Spain over British rights to trade with her colonies in the West Indies. However, France proved willing to compromise better relations with Spain in the winter of 1727–8 for the sake of supporting British pressure on Spain to accept an interim settlement of their dispute over Caribbean trade; and in 1729, when the Austro-Spanish alliance collapsed, both Britain and France negotiated an alliance with Spain, the Treaty of Seville.

Although the Anglo-French alliance was maintained in 1729, a year in which secret Anglo-Austrian negotiations also failed, it was increasingly developing in a worrying fashion for the British ministry, and was facing mounting political criticism in Britain. Ready themselves to confront Charles VI earlier in the decade in order to block the Austrian attempt to found an East Indian trading company, the

Ostend Company of 1722, and to defend Hanoverian interests, the British ministry found by 1729 that the French were increasingly thinking of active steps to thwart Charles VI's policy of achieving the undivided inheritance of his territories by his eldest daughter, Maria Theresa, by means of the Pragmatic Sanction. French pressure for an alliance with Charles's principal German rival, Charles Albert, Elector of Bavaria, in the winter of 1729–30 underlined this trend, which was unwelcome to a British ministry that was unwilling to commit itself to what might lead to a permanent reduction of Austrian strength. It was one thing to seek to thwart Austro-Spanish union; quite another to destroy the only European power that might be able to balance French strength.

The British ministry clearly did not see their French alliance as a fixed entity, a sensible view in light of the unpredictability of French policy, with so much apparently dependent on chance factors of life and death, particularly those of Louis XV and Fleury. The situation was brought home when Louis's smallpox attack in late 1728 was accompanied by obvious preparations by his uncle Philip V to seize the French throne, a move that would have destroyed the Anglo-French alliance. Louis survived the attack and lived until 1774, but this was no more predictable to contemporaries than the fate of Peter II of Russia, born five years after Louis, who succumbed to smallpox in 1730 with significant consequences for Russian policy. Added weight was lent in 1730 by the greater vulnerability of Hanover that followed the failure of the Fontainebleau discussions to give teeth to the provisions in the Alliance of Seville for military pressure on Austria to satisfy Spain's Italian demands, and the consequent danger that Philip V would approach Charles VI again (Black 1987d).

Equally the British decision to approach Austria in September 1730 can be attributed to domestic pressures, in particular the fear that the ministry, which had been savaged already in the parliamentary session of 1730 for a failure to prevent the Dunkirk works of its French ally, a clear breach of Anglo-French treaties, would be attacked afresh in the 1731 session if the French refused to honour their promise to demolish the works. In Dunkirk the opposition had found an issue over which it could both unite and benefit from unease about French intentions among ministerial supporters. A clear case can be made that the decision to approach Austria in 1730 stemmed from ministerial concern over the parliamentary consequences of the failure to persuade Britain's principal ally to act in accordance with the wishes of the political nation, that, in short, domestic political exigencies dictated an end to acceptance of the tension natural to every alliance. Conversely, it can be argued that Dunkirk was doubtless important, but that the

Anglo-French alliance had faced significant domestic criticism from its inception without succumbing; only the previous years, sustained pressure for war with Spain in order to punish her for her depredations on British Caribbean commerce had been unsuccessful.

Anglo-Austrian negotiations culminated in the Second Treaty of Vienna of March 1731. Besides guaranteeing each other's possessions, George II guaranteed the Pragmatic Sanction, while Charles VI agreed to suppress the Ostend Company and to a settlement of Italian disputes that was acceptable to Spain and that therefore enabled the British in July 1731 to bring Philip V into the new alliance system, which the Dutch, in turn, were to join the following year. The treaty was generally welcomed by British politicians and it helped to 'depoliticise' foreign policy. It was not a major topic of debate in the parliamentary sessions of 1732 and 1733, in contrast with the situation in recent years. The treaty with the Landgrave of Hesse-Cassel, who since 1726 had been paid for holding 12,000 men ready for use, essentially for the defence of Hanover, a controversial measure, was not renewed in 1732.

France, however, was unwilling to accept the new diplomatic order, essentially because of the guarantee of the Pragmatic Sanction. British hopes that France would act otherwise proved naive. From 1731 onwards British politicians were fearful of war with France, and rumours of imminent hostilities circulated frequently. Indeed, within four months of the signature of the Second Treaty of Vienna, the British government moved a large portion of the army to the Channel coast, because they feared an imminent French attack. By 1733, the French envoy, Chavigny, could suggest to Paris a French invasion of Britain in support of the Jacobites. In so far as there was a mid-century crisis in eighteenth-century Britain it began in 1731 and lasted until the decisive defeat of the French navy at Lagos and Quiberon Bay scotched French invasion plans in 1759. It was a period of acute vulnerability, and of serious fears about potential invasion on a number of occasions, including 1744–6 and 1756–7. Ministries suffered domestically as a result of adverse international developments, although it would be mistaken to suggest that the entire period was characterised by anxiety, and such a suggestion is particularly inappropriate for 1749–52.

The new diplomatic order created in 1731 lasted only until 1733, a reminder of the kaleidoscopic nature of international relations that arguably posed special problems for countries like Britain where the public debate over policy obliged the government to offer a defence of policy to Parliament, which had both a defined constitutional rôle and an undefined political importance in the field of foreign policy. In 1733, a contested election to the throne of Poland that led to Russian intervention against the candidature of Louis XV's father-in-law was followed by an attack on Russia's passive ally Austria by France, Spain and Sardinia, the action of the last two occurring to the complete surprise of the British ministry. Fearing a Franco-Spanish alliance, Austria pressed, throughout 1733, for the dispatch of a British naval force to the western Mediterranean. It was felt that such a force might dissuade the Spaniards from attacking Naples or Sicily. However, the requests were refused, despite an Austrian memorandum arguing that the dispatch of a squadron was crucial to the European balance of power. In addition, when France attacked, the British refused to regard it as a cause of hostilities. The Austrians found that the Walpole ministry was prepared only to facilitate peace negotiations by means of talks held at The Hague in the winter of 1734–5 involving Walpole's influential diplomat brother Horatio. Though these talks threw up proposals that were not too dissimilar to those eventually adopted, in fact the peace owed nothing to Britain but was secured through secret Austro-French negotiations in 1735 that led to the Third Treaty of Vienna in 1738. This left France with the reversion to Lorraine, which she gained as a result in 1766, her most substantial European territorial acquisition in the pre-Revolutionary eighteenth century.

A pattern of domestic causation can be discerned in Britain's abandonment of Austria, the loss, for the second time within two and a half years, of her principal ally. In the spring of 1733, Walpole's attempts at fiscal reform met with violent, voluble and sustained opposition in the Excise Crisis. Several contemporaries ascribed British neutrality in the war to domestic turmoil and this view has found favour with some historians. Chavigny claimed repeatedly that Britain was on the verge of collapse and that this precluded any active foreign policy. An examination of the dispatches of Chavigny and of his Sardinian counterpart, Ossono, reveals a society on the brink of civil war and a ministry maintained solely by corruption. This view of British weakness was shared by the Spanish envoy, Montijo, who proclaimed his sympathies by providing free beer to those who demonstrated in London against the ministry. Reports of discontent and opposition in Britain, far from being ignored on the Continent, were exaggerated.

If Chavigny's analysis is accepted, then the problem of explaining British neutrality in the War of the Polish Succession is readily solved. A ministry weakened by the Excise Crisis, fearful of the domestic consequences of conflict, and facing the prospect of a general election in 1734, could not risk a war.

However, British neutrality can be explained also from a diplomatic perspective. The Anglo-Austrian alliance had to all intents and purposes collapsed in 1732. It had always been weak as a consequence of the failure to comprehend Austria's principal allies, Prussia and Russia, and their differences with Britain and, more particularly, Hanover. In 1732, Charles VI refused to heed British and Hanoverian wishes on a wide variety of topics, instead preferring to retain already strong links with Frederick William I of Prussia. Britain had been excluded from negotiations in which Austria was involved in 1732, both those relating to the Polish Succession and those leading to the Treaty of Copenhagen. The Austrians were held responsible for the widely reported negotiations for a marriage between the Princess of Mecklenburg, niece of the Czarina Anna and widely assumed to be her intended heir, and a Prussian prince, which the British feared would lead to an alliance between the two powers and possibly their union. Thomas Robinson, the envoy in Vienna, was ordered to prevent this marriage and was informed that if Austria supported such a scheme, friendship was impossible. This reflected the fear of Prussia held by George II, and contrasted with subsequent British attempts in 1755–6 and 1766 to found their continental strategy on an alliance with Prussia and Russia.

Austrian disinclination to enforce the prohibition of trade by Ostenders to the East Indies led to further tension. The lengthy controversy over the ship *Apollo* tried the patience of both powers and led Robinson to snap: 'If they do not think it worth while to manage the dearest interests of the Maritime Powers, the latter will not be able to manage theirs' (PRO SP 80/86, Robinson to Tilson, 8 March 1732). Over the Jülich-Berg question, a problem of the disputed inheritance of two strategic Rhenish duchies, which was widely believed to threaten war between Prussia and France in 1732, Britain refused to countenance what it saw as Austrian support for the Prussian claims to the inheritance, and, instead, urged an equitable settlement; but in practice they were disinclined to help even with this scheme, Robinson being instructed by the Secretary of State, Lord Harrington: 'you must not engage for the king's giving his guaranty to any such agreement, His Majesty looking upon it as an affair liable to many disputes, which may create various troubles, and cares not to entangle himself in new guaranties' (PRO SP 80/89, 13 Aug. 1732). The following March, when conflict again appeared imminent over Jülich-Berg, Harrington told the Palatine envoy that Britain's interest extended no further than good intentions.

It was therefore in accordance with existing policy that Britain showed little interest in the first stages of the Polish crisis. The British did not want a war, whether they were involved or not, and they gave prominence understandably to information suggesting that there would be no serious problems. An unsigned marginal note in a copy of Harrington's letter of 29 June 1733 to the envoy at Berlin commented: 'we never had any intention from the beginning, but to keep out of the squabble, at any rate' (PRO SP 90/34). Anglo-Austrian disagreements combined with the disinclination of the British ministry to become involved in a war, a course of action that had been avoided since 1720, though Bourbon success in the early stages of the conflict was to lead in 1734 to the expression of more pro-Austrian sentiment.

Irrespective of domestic consequences, there were sound reasons for Britain not intervening in the war, for it did not prove a French walkover. Instead, obvious features of the conflict were the vitality of the Austro-Russian alliance, the consequent defeat of French influence in eastern Europe, where the Russian victory over a French amphibious force near Danzig (Gdansk) in 1734 underlined the difficulty the western-European powers faced in affecting developments further east, and the resilience of the Austrian military effort in northern Italy in 1734 and 1735. It has been argued that British neutrality in 1733–5 led to an increase in French power and a decline in Austrian strength, influence and diplomatic independence, all of which would prove inimical to British interests, as was to be seen at the time of the War of the Austrian Succession (1740–8), obliging Britain to make more substantial efforts to protect Austria and the balance of power. This is overstated, and an exaggeration of Britain's significance and capabilities. Austria's principal problem in 1740–1 was the Russian failure to intimidate Prussia, as she had done in the mid-1730s, a task Britain could not have achieved. In addition, the overall impression of 1741–2 is of Austrian resilience.

Despite the claim in the *Craftsman*, the leading London opposition newspaper, of 27 March 1736 that 'Lorraine alone is sufficient to endanger the balance of power in Europe', the fate of Lorraine did not represent a fundamental alteration in the balance of power, a difficult concept to apply with precision anyway. Lorraine had been militarily vulnerable to France for a long time, having been gained without struggle by the French at the start of every major war. In hindsight, this was more a filling in than a new thrust east. Yet, that was not so obvious to contemporaries. The government was worried about the possible fate of Luxembourg and Flanders.

The territorial changes in Italy in the peace settlement were not as detrimental to Austria as had been feared. Horatio Walpole wrote to Lord Harrington, Secretary of State for the Northern Department, in

July 1735 that 'the scheme for the exchange of the Duchies of Lorraine and Tuscany', the basis of the peace settlement, 'is certainly the most eligible, and if it could be effectuated, would be, as things are circumstanced, I may say a glorious end of this war' (Farmington, Weston Mss vol. 2).

The experience of the War of the Spanish Succession suggests that had Great Britain joined in, she would have found Austria committing her energies to Italian schemes and demanding subsidies, while leaving Great Britain with the difficult task of holding the Austrian Netherlands against the principal French war effort, as was to happen in 1745–8. The negotiation in 1733 of a Franco-Dutch neutrality convention obliged Britain to follow the path of negotiation if she was to try to influence Dutch policy. Both the ministry and the opposition were divided over what course Britain should follow. The scheme for a united opposition, popularised by Bolingbroke, was never more unrealistic, for the opposition Whigs shared the views of George II and the two Secretaries of State, Newcastle and Harrington, that Austria should be supported if possible, while, like Walpole, the Tories, were wary of Continental commitments.

It could be suggested that British non-involvement encouraged France and Spain to form a low estimate of British strength, and led to Spanish intransigence in 1739 over British commercial grievances in the West Indies and the subsequent Anglo-Spanish conflict, the War of Jenkins' Ear. It could also be suggested that British isolation in this conflict – for both Austria and the United Provinces remained neutral – was due to her neutrality in the War of the Polish Succession. There is, however, little basis for such a claim. British policy in 1733–5 displayed strength, not weakness, Austria complained not about Britain's failure to mobilise her forces but about her failure to send them to the assistance of Austria. The period 1734–5 witnessed an impressive naval armament, one that the British ministry trumpeted in Parliament, the press, and to foreign envoys, whom they invited to visit the fleet at Spithead in the summer of 1735. The Bourbons were well aware of the strength of the fleet, especially when, in order to assist Portugal against a feared Spanish attack, a large squadron was dispatched to the Tagus in 1735, where it remained for over a year, proof that the British ministry was not intimidated by the Bourbon powers, was willing to assist an ally, and was able to deploy a fleet at a distance. Even so, the British were cautious about needlessly offending Spain, for example by identifying themselves with Portugal in her quarrel over South American frontiers. Horatio Walpole, as acting Secretary of State, expressed the British position: 'The king is guarantee to Portugal, and His Majesty has shewn it to all the world; and will continue to do all a faithful ally ought to do; but every one knows the nature of such treaties: complaints must be enquired into and examined, and good offices must be used, before a guarantee proceeds to such extremities, as Portugal is at every turn calling upon us for' (PRO SP 80/122, Walpole to Robinson, 23 Aug. 1736).

British complaints about Portuguese demands were to be succeeded soon by the reverse, as Britain went to war with Spain and Portugal stayed neutral, an important indication of the folly of arguing that British assistance to Austria in the 1730s would have been reciprocated in 1739. The difficulties that Britain encountered with Portugal at the very time that she was providing her with military assistance underline the disinclination of the Walpole ministry in the late 1730s to seek allies as part of any interventionist diplomatic strategy.

Far from having a weak estimate of British strength, based on the nature and number of her alliances, the Bourbons were well aware of British naval power, and in 1738–9 Spain was willing to settle her differences with Britain. These arose from Spanish attempts to preserve her commercial system in the West Indies and prevent illegal British trade, and were symbolised by the alleged cutting off by Spanish coastguards of an ear of Robert Jenkins, the captain of an English merchantman, the most prominent of a string of Spanish atrocities. The successful negotiation of an agreement that could be carried in Parliament, the Convention of the Pardo of January 1739, and the unwillingness of the French to declare war in support of Spain when disputes over the implementation of this agreement led to war with Britain, suggest that the Bourbons were neither as united nor as determined to overturn the European system as anti-Bourbon publicists claimed.

The outbreak of war with Spain has been attributed to the pressure of public opinion on the ministry, to the manner in which a popular outcry limited crucially the parameters of diplomatic manoeuvre, but Spanish inflexibility played an important part in the breakdown of negotiations, and this can be understood best in terms of Spanish concern over imperial finance. The timing of the outbreak of war should be explained by locating it in the context of diplomatic relations. If public pressure was so significant, why did not war between Britain and Spain break out in 1729 or 1738? Jenkins himself lost his ear in April 1731. Diplomatic explanations cannot be suspended by invoking a surge of domestic opinion (Woodfine 1987, 1998), though this pressure was seen as important by British commentators. William Hay MP, a placeman and a reliable dependant of the Duke of Newcastle, noted: 'the ministry kept the fleet all the last year in the Mediterranean, to be in readiness if Spain complied not with the Convention. Spain made this a pretence for breaking it; alleging a promise that the fleet should be recalled: but probably she foresaw that as the nation was universally inclined to the war, the ministry would be forced into it: And therefore was unwilling to give the money [she had agreed to pay under the Convention] to those who would so soon be their enemies' (Northampton CRO L(C) 1734).

Though the Walpole ministry cannot be described as interventionist in the late 1730s, it would be misleading to argue that British policy was characterised by isolationism. Ministerial hopes were based increasingly on the possibility of alliance with Prussia and Russia, rather than Austria. Though relations between George II and his brother-in-law and cousin, Frederick William I, were poor, it was hoped that Crown Prince Frederick of Prussia, the future Frederick II (the Great), who secretly received funds from his uncle, George II, would support Britain when he came to the throne. Robert Trevor, envoy in The Hague, replied to his Berlin counterpart on 30 May 1739 agreeing 'as to the necessity of waiting for better times; though I regret from my soul the misuse of the past' (Aylesbury CRO Trevor Mss vol. 18). Three months later, Horatio Walpole wrote to Edward Weston, under-secretary in the Northern Department: 'Your notion of saving Europe by the King of Prussia is certainly just. I have thought of it often; but the King of Prussia will not be saved by force, if he was out of the way his son would certainly do well' (Farmington Weston Mss vol. 12).

The exchange of envoys with Russia in 1732 was followed by a trade treaty in 1734 (Reading 1938) and by a British diplomatic initiative launched in 1738 to negotiate an Anglo-Russian alliance. That such a treaty was not signed until April 1741 was due to Russian, rather than British, obstinacy, and to governmental changes in St Petersburg (Lodge 1928). In the late 1730s, influential members of the British ministry grasped that Austria, aligned with France since late 1735 and weakened by war with Turkey in 1737–9, was for them a broken reed, and the government shifted their desired alignment towards Prussia and Russia, just as within the Baltic they shifted from Sweden to Russia. Sir Joseph Jekyll, the Master of the Rolls, told the Commons in 1738 that 'our hopes now were in the Czarina', while, two years later, in his project for a grand alliance Horatio Walpole wrote: 'His Prussian Majesty must be convinced, that no power is more capable to disappoint the views of France, especially in the North, and even by sending, if necessary, an army to the Rhine, than the Czarina and that her interest and views in all points, will naturally lead her to join in a proper union with His Majesty and the King of Prussia' (Beinecke, Osborn Shelves,

Stair Letters no. 19; BL Add. 9132 f. 65).

The surprise invasion of the Austrian province of Silesia by the newly acceded Frederick II (the Great) in December 1740, shortly after the death of Charles VI, was to end such hopes for a long while, though the idea of an Anglo-Prusso-Russian alignment was revived in 1755–6 when Austria proved unwilling to offer support for the defence of Hanover and the Low Countries against France and again by the Pitt ministry in 1766. Hostility to Prussian intentions led the British to seek Russian support, in 1741–55 and 1763, and Anglo-Prussian alignments reflected the failure to maintain or create good relations elsewhere, as in 1756–62 and 1787–91, periods of poor relations with Austria and Russia.

In one important respect, the Walpole ministry was very fortunate in its last years. Though Jacobitism revived both as an international issue and in Scotland, there was no serious attempt to provide the Jacobites with foreign assistance. In May 1738, Bussy, the French official who spied for the British, informed Earl Waldegrave, the envoy in Paris, that the Queen of Spain had said 'that, if we force her to a war, she can raise such troubles in England as will make us sick of it', but in February 1740 he provided another report stating that the Spanish ministers 'say, that their design in sending for the late Duke of Ormonde and Lord Marshal into Spain, and their making encampments in Galicia and Catalonia, was only to create fears in England, and to slacken their ardour for America' (BL Add. 32798 f. 6, 32820 ff. 59, 44).

If so, Spanish support for the Stuart cause was little different from the intimidation and brinkmanship that constituted such an important part of the international relations of the period. Aside from providing a surrogate force and a potentially debilitating weapon, support for the Stuart cause could also be used as a diplomatic ploy. Anxiety was expressed in 1740 about the possibility of Spanish action on behalf of James, particularly an invasion of Ireland. However, it was generally agreed that the attitude of France was crucial. Spanish action alone had been unsuccessful in 1719, and, in the late 1720s, Spain had done nothing to assist James, not least because of British naval superiority. In 1739, the Spanish navy was not large enough to confront that of Britain.

In July 1740, Arthur Villettes, the envoy in Turin, wrote to Horace Mann, his counterpart at Florence, about Charles Edward, 'Bonnie Prince Charlie', the eldest son of the Stuart Pretender.

> I am persuaded as you are that a journey was really intended, or rather that this family is a tool in the hands of some people and made to believe great things in agitation on their behalf, when those or the like bruits can serve

their ends. I am still of opinion that unless another power should join with Spain in the present war against us, little or nothing is to be apprehended from that side, however one cannot be too cautious in the present circumstances, and the trusting to outward appearances and one's own conjectures in a matter of this importance is what no prudent man and truely zealous in the service of his prince could forgive himself should things turn out contrary to his surmises. (PRO SP 105/81 f. 45)

The French position was crucial. Mann wrote to Waldegrave that 'unless France should take part in the present war, nothing will be undertaken in their favour' (Chewton, 28 Feb. 1740). However, Fleury's attitude was ambivalent. He wanted by intimidation to prevent Britain from seizing any important base in the Spanish Empire and he made threats accordingly in 1740 and 1741, but he did not want war. Willing to discuss matters with the Jacobites, Fleury would not provide support, and, from late 1740, his attention was diverted from the prospect of war with Britain by the death of Charles VI. The British government received contradictory reports about French intentions and did not trust Fleury, while Waldegrave warned in August 1740 that the French could assemble troops for an invasion relatively easily, 'certainly if the French intended to draw a body together for any attempt against us, the garrisons of Calais, Dunkirk, Gravelines, Lille, Arras, Cambray, Bethune etc. would supply in four or five days a considerable body of men' (PRO SP 78/3223 ff. 272–3).

It was easier for Fleury, however, to threaten George by sending a fleet to the West Indies in 1740 and moving troops into Westphalia and towards Hanover in 1741. An invasion of Britain was too drastic a step for Fleury in 1740, and he told Waldegrave that action in favour of the Jacobites would unite Britain. It might also call into play the defensive clauses of Britain's alliances, particularly that with the United Provinces, which Fleury wished to avoid, while he had little trust in Spanish intentions. When, in the early autumn of 1741, the British government received a false report that Charles Edward had left Rome for Paris and George II pressed the French envoy on the matter, Fleury wrote to George to deny the numerous reports of Franco-Jacobite designs.

Nevertheless, when in 1739–40 Britain faced the threat of war with both Spain and France, for the French made it clear that they would not accept British gains in the West Indies, she was unable to rely on the prospect of any assistance from other powers. In 1740–1, her hopes from Prussia and Russia were exploded, as Russia drifted into factional strife and took a smaller rôle in international affairs after the death of Czarina Anna in 1740, while Frederick II rejected British advances and unexpectedly invaded Silesia, thus beginning the War of the Austrian

Succession. Frederick's attack was the first blow to Maria Theresa, who had succeeded Charles VI in October 1740, but it was to be followed by the advancing of Bavarian, Saxon and Spanish claims to parts of the Austrian inheritance. In 1741, France also intervened to orchestrate an anti-Habsburg alliance and, by the end of 1741, with Prague fallen to the new alliance, a fundamental recasting of the European system appeared imminent. George II had sought to support Austria by organising an anti-Prussian alliance, but the movement of a French army into Westphalia led him to climb down. On 25 September 1741, a declaration of neutrality was signed by the Hanoverian ministers, in accordance with which George voted for Charles Albert in his election as Emperor Charles VII. George's vote for Charles was the high point of Anglo/Hanoverian-Wittelsbach relations in the eighteenth century, but it was as precarious as most of the achievements of France and Bavaria in 1741–2.

Nevertheless, Walpole was forced to face the first session after the finely balanced general election of 1741 against an unpropitious international background. The rising young opposition Whig William Pitt had told the Commons in March 1739 that 'Spain knows the consequence of a war in America . . . it must prove fatal to her,' but this had not proved the case. The unrealistic assumptions about the costs and prospects of conflict expressed by parliamentarians in Charles II's reign were still being voiced in the mid eighteenth century. The failure to seize the Spanish base of Cartagena in modern Colombia in 1741 appeared to justify opposition charges of the mismanagement of the war with Spain, while the deteriorating position on the Continent was blamed on the ministry. The pamphlet *The Groans of Germany* which appeared towards the end of 1741 repeated themes advanced earlier in the *Craftsman*, arguing that policy in the late 1720s had been too pro-French, criticising the treaties of Hanover and Seville as anti-Austrian and condemning the provisions of the latter by which Britain aided the introduction of Spanish garrisons into Italy. Thus, the current international system was blamed on past ministerial errors, though, as Walpole told the Commons in December 1741, he had neither killed Charles VI and Frederick William I nor been responsible for the outbreak of war in the Empire.

It is unclear whether these arguments played much rôle in Walpole's fall in February 1742. The crucial problems he faced were parliamentary arithmetic and the hostile attitude of Frederick Prince of Wales. However, the international situation contributed to the feeling that Walpolean policies and methods were redundant, and helped to ensure that foreign policy played an important part in the political debate after his fall.

THE CARTERET YEARS 1742–4

The kaleidoscopic nature of eighteenth-century international relations was illustrated amply in 1742 as France's anti-Austrian alliance disintegrated and the military balance swung towards Austria. The French forces in Linz were forced to surrender in January 1742, and Munich was occupied the following month. Just as George II had been driven the previous autumn to approach Charles-Albert of Bavaria in order to prevent a French invasion of Hanover, so in the summer of 1742 the latter, now Charles VII, sought George's assistance. However, the attitude of the new Secretary of State for the Northern Department, Lord Carteret, was unhelpful as far as any support for concessions from Austria were to be expected. In May 1742, he wrote to Earl Stair, the pugilistic anti-French commander of the British force sent to the Austrian Netherlands after Walpole's fall:

> His Majesty and this whole nation being fully convinced that it is upon the preservation of the House of Austria in a condition to resist the mischievous attempts of that of Bourbon, that the maintenance of the common liberties of Europe, the support of the Empire, the continuance of the Protestant religion, and the security and independence of both the Maritime Powers do chiefly depend. (PRO SP 87/8, 4 May)

A mood of over-optimistic hope affected British policy-makers. Stair, who spoke of invading France, was delighted by the government's success in pressing Austria to accept the loss of most of Silesia to Prussia as the price of an Austro-Prussian peace, the Peace of Breslau of June 1742, as he knew this would weaken France, and he claimed that month: 'This will make everything very easy, the king can now make the peace of Europe upon the conditions he shall think reasonable' (HL LO. 7618). Though France was not in fact attacked in 1742, the operations of the British expeditionary force in the Austrian Netherlands being hindered by bad weather, the following year the British moved into Germany and, led by George II, defeated the French under Noailles at Dettingen on 24 June 1743.

This victory appeared to open up the possibility of an invasion of eastern France and a revision of Louis XIV's gains. Far from accepting Bavarian demands that her abandonment of France be purchased by Austrian territorial losses, the British suggested that Bavaria consider gains at the expense of France (Black 1989b). Newcastle, critical of the failure of Carteret, who had accompanied George to Germany in 1743, to consult the ministers left in London, wrote to Hardwicke: 'The scheme abroad certainly is, to set ourselves at the head of the Empire;

to appear a good German; and to prefer the welfare of the Germanick body to all other considerations' (BL Add. 32700, 22 July 1743).

An active forward policy was also followed in the western Mediterranean. The war with Spain had led to an increase in the number both of British warships and of ships deployed on active service. The need to protect Gibraltar, Minorca and British trade in the Mediterranean, and the attempt to blockade Spanish ports, ensured that there were generally British naval forces in the region. They were used to great effect in Italian waters during the War of the Austrian Succession. Maritime pressure, in particular Commodore Martin's threat to bombard the city of Naples in 1742, helped to keep the kingdom of Naples out of the Bourbon camp. British warships played a major rôle in the campaigns in Corsica and on the Ligurian and Provencal coasts, and from 1742 restricted the movement of troops by sea from France and Spain to Italy. With considerable difficulty, Carteret constructed an Anglo-Austro-Sardinian alliance, based on the Treaty of Worms of September 1743, that led to the expulsion of Bourbon forces from northern Italy and the unsuccessful invasion of Provence in 1746.

However, Carteret's schemes were to fail, and it is easy to appreciate why La Ville, a French diplomat at The Hague, described them in January 1744 as founded on illusion and impudent boasting (BN NAF 14915 f. 282). Carteret's German plans collapsed in the face of ministerial opposition in London, Austrian obduracy and Charles VII's disinclination to commit himself against France. This failure was to play a significant rôle in the creation in June 1744 of the Union of Frankfurt, a league of France, Frederick II, Charles VII, William of Hesse and the Elector Palatine. Frederick feared that the European system had, thanks to British support, been tilted too far towards Austria, while the Austrians were angered by the successful British pressure on them to cede territory to Prussia and Sardinia, that had been instrumental in enabling agreements to be negotiated with those powers in 1742 and 1743 respectively.

Carteret assured Parliament in December 1743 that 'it was not his view to obtain any acquisitions for Great Britain' (Beinecke, Lee papers 10a), but that did not mean that his goals were modest. Anger about Carteret's contemptuous neglect of them, concern over the extent of his wide-ranging plans and anxiety over their parliamentary consequences, specifically financial demands and the hiring of Hanoverian troops, led the Pelhams, Newcastle and his brother Henry Pelham, First Lord of the Treasury from 1743 until his death in 1754, to resist Carteret's schemes. Pitt attacked Carteret as 'a Hanover troop minister' in Parliament in January 1744 (Gibbs 1986, Black 1986b).

The hiring of Hanoverian forces was an important element in Carteret's plans. The British army was not large, Britain's Dutch ally was unhappy about the prospect of war with France, the Austrians were more concerned about the military situation in Bavaria, Bohemia and Italy, and the easiest way to create a large army in the Austrian Netherlands appeared to be to offer subsidy treaties to friendly German rulers. This method had been followed by both William III and Anne: Marlborough's victories were very much Anglo-Dutch-German affairs. However, the decision to hire Hanoverians was contentious. Critics claimed that George II was being paid to do what he should do anyway as Elector of Hanover.

The payment of Hanoverians became the central issue in attacks on British foreign and military policies which, it was claimed, were no longer directed to the pursuit of national goals against Spain, but instead were seeking more nebulous ends and leading to intervention on the Continent, that was likely to be expensive and unsuccessful, when a naval war with Spain supposedly offered victory and profit. In December 1742, Pitt attacked what he claimed were 'unnecessary alliances' and engaging in Continental quarrels, and criticised George II for being most interested in aggrandising Hanover and for being paid by Britain to do his duty as Elector and support Maria Theresa. The same month, another opposition Whig MP wrote to his brother that 'all true Englishmen' were opposed to hiring Hanoverian troops, adding: 'Whig and Tory has been laid aside a good while and the distinction of Court and Country is now sunk into that of Englishmen and Hanoverians, which is propagated with great industry by the pamphleteers.' That was certainly the aim of opposition politicians, and the strain created for the ministerial position in the Commons led the Pelhams to regard Carteret as a liability.

The crisis, a political one that repeated the rivalry between two Secretaries of State last seen between Townshend and Newcastle in 1729–30, lasted from 1743 until November 1744 when George II was obliged in the face of Pelhamite pressure to part with Carteret. He sought to restore him to a leading position in February 1746, but the crisis was very short-lived, for Carteret was unable to muster sufficient ministerial and parliamentary support. The Earl of Dumfries noted: 'all passes like a dream so soon it was over' (HL LO. 11000). The London lawyer Nathaniel Cole thought George II the sufferer, 'as it exposes his inability of appointing what ministers he pleased and also his own inclination to schemes which the people I am acquainted with think not very popular' (BL Add. 42591 f 7). Nevertheless, as opposition critics pointed out, Carteret's legacy was a weighty one. The Pelham ministry was to continue both to concentrate on the war with France rather than Spain, and to confront France on the Continent.

THE LAST YEARS OF THE WAR OF THE AUSTRIAN SUCCESSION, 1744–8

The French response to Carteret's actively hostile policy, especially to British military operations in Germany, was support for the Jacobites and an attempted invasion of Britain in 1744. They hoped that their Brest fleet would be able to gain control of the Channel and enable an expeditionary force to sail from Dunkirk to the Essex coast, and they were successful in moving the fleet from Brest into the Channel, to the consternation of the British. The Dutch agreed to the British demand for 6000 troops under their treaty of mutual guarantee, while La Ville gloated: 'the times have really changed. Only six months ago the English proposed to conquer France, but now they fear that they will be conquered' (BN NAF 14915 f. 292). But the British sent a large fleet to sea while, following a violent storm in early March 1744 which destroyed many of the transport vessels at Dunkirk, the French abandoned the projected expedition.

The response to the French threat helped to divide an opposition whose unity had been strained already by international developments and by the clash between the exigencies of political manoeuvre and compromise and the more consistent and partisan attitude of committed opposition. In an opposition meeting at the beginning of 1744, Pitt pressed the need for supporting the army, arguing that the war made a large force necessary, a measure that clashed with traditional Tory notions. To Pitt, the Tories were failing to appreciate the need to abandon rigid views in face of changes in British policy and were unable to distinguish sufficiently between help to Hanover and a national commitment to the anti-French cause. This distinction was to be vital when Pitt defended the dispatch of British forces to Germany in 1758. In February 1744, he protested his loyalty when Parliament was informed by royal message of a plan for French action on behalf of the Pretender, and 'spoke handsomely' in support of a government motion promising parliamentary funds for an increase in the army and the navy. The French followed up their invasion attempt by declaring war on Britain (McLynn 1981; Black 1999b).

The period 1744–5 was to witness a major shift of emphasis in the War of the Austrian Succession, to the detriment of Britain. The centre of the conflict moved from Germany to the Low Countries, and the succession that was soon at stake was that of Britain, not Austria. In

January 1745, the death of Charles VII and the succession of Maximilian Joseph freed Bavarian policy from the burden of commitments and expectations associated with Charles and bound up with his French alliance and Imperial status. In April, Maximilian Joseph signed the Treaty of Füssen with Austria and abandoned France. As the Anglo-Austrian alliance lost one bargaining counter – an occupied Bavaria – France gained another with its gradual conquest of the Austrian Netherlands, which began in 1744. Responding to this was relatively uncontroversial: in January 1745, Pitt supported Pelham's proposal to increase the British force in the Austrian Netherlands, rejecting the claim of the Tory MP Sir Roger Newdigate that the new ministry was simply pursuing Carteret's policies. The following month, he also supported the ministry over a proposal to increase Maria Theresa's subsidy in order, as was generally understood, to enable her to take over the financing of the Hanoverians.

The Austrian Netherlands was an area of traditional British concern, and its loss strained relations with allies who were suspected of insufficient interest in its retention. This view was shared by government and political nation, Newcastle writing to Carteret's successor as Secretary of State, the Earl of Harrington:

'The apprehension for Flanders grows pretty general . . . it begins already to be flung out (and that by persons of consideration and such as are supposed to be the most disposed to carry on the war) that the Queen of Hungary [Maria Theresa], who is by treaty obliged to furnish 24,000 men for the defence of Flanders, has, in effect no troops at all there, at present' (PRO SP 43/47, 21 May 1745).

The following month, Newcastle calculated the annual cost of subsidies Britain was already paying or on the point of paying to Austria, Sardinia, Hesse-Cassel, Saxony, Cologne and Mainz as £1,178,753, adding, 'they have not been able to procure to His Majesty, and his allies, a superiority of force in any part of Europe' and that from the losses in the Austrian Netherlands, 'danger may be to be feared for His Majesty's dominions' (PRO SP 43/37, 14 June). Against the background of fears that, having taken Ostend, the French would invade Britain, the British ministry considered peace with France, and the capture in 1745 of the French-Canadian base of Louisbourg on Cape Breton Island did little to lift the gloom.

Given these problems, it is easy to appreciate why rumours of the landing of Bonnie Prince Charlie on the west coast of Scotland did not immediately capture ministerial attention. The '45 was initially a

Jacobite, not a Jacobite-Bourbon, enterprise. Far from landing with thousands of French troops on the English coast, Charles Edward reached Eriskay in the Western Isles of Scotland on 3 August (ns) 1745 with the 'seven men of Moidart'. And yet on 17 September the prince entered Edinburgh, four days later he defeated Sir John Cope at nearby Prestonpans, and on 18 November he entered Carlisle. Already on 3 October the *London Evening Post* had noted 'a great demand' for maps of the northern counties. As rumours spread that the Jacobites would be supported by a French invasion, panic grew and ordinary people were possibly more affected by the consequences of foreign policy than at any other time that century. Thomas White wrote from Somerset on 7 October to the Duke of Bedford, one of the aristocrats raising regiments to support the Hanoverian succession, that 'we are much concerned here with the apprehensions of a French invasion either at Lyme or Torbay', while on 25 November Thomas Anson noted: 'Marshal Wade's returning to Newcastle and the rebels continuing their march with such rapidity has struck a general terror' (Bedford CRO Russell box 769; BL Add. 15955 f. 36). On 17 December, one senior official wrote: 'we are . . . expecting every day an invasion from Dunkirk' (BL Add. 23821 f. 444).

The crisis passed. Indecision, ministerial differences, the difficulty of preparing an invasion force, bad weather and the strength of the British fleet prevented the French from invading, while at Derby, on 6 December, the still undefeated Charles Edward was obliged by his Scottish officers, influenced by an absence of English and French support, to turn back. On 20 December, the Jacobites crossed the Esk back into Scotland. On 16 April, Charles Edward was to be defeated by George II's second son, the Duke of Cumberland, at Culloden, one of the most decisive battles of the century (McLynn 1981; Black 1990c).

Though the '45 was not the knock-out blow that it very nearly might have been, and though it led to the definitive crushing of Highland strength and thus of realistic Jacobite schemes, it was of considerable value to France. The British and allied troops sent to defend Britain weakened the Austrian Netherlands, where, on 21 February 1746, Brussels surrendered, to be followed by Antwerp on 31 May. Robert Trevor, the British envoy at The Hague, thought that the fall of Brussels 'is justly to be imputed to the cursed rebellion at home', though he was also concerned about the Austrian attitude towards an area he described as 'the theatre of the common cause, the barrier of its two most natural and servicable allies, and indeed the cement of their intimate union with the House of Austria' (BL Add. 23822 ff. 183, 113).

The successful suppression of the '45 did not therefore compensate for what had been, since the summer of 1745, a serious and deteriorating position in the Austrian Netherlands. Horatio Walpole could respond to the fall of Brussels by writing to his former protégé Trevor that 'the prospect of the continuance or conclusion of this war is to me so dismal that I am resolved to think of it as little as I can' (Aylesbury CRO Trevor papers vol. 55), but the government did not have that option. The situation was clarified by the failure of peace feelers to lead to an end to the conflict between Britain and France, unlike the successful negotiation of an end to the second Silesian war between Austria and Prussia the previous December, and by the failure of George II's attempt to create a second Carteret ministry in February 1746.

Taken into office in February 1746, Pitt, two months later, spoke in favour of the motion to pay for 18,000 Hanoverians to serve in the Austrian Netherlands and was condemned for inconsistency by the opposers, but the ministry's majorities were substantial: 255 to 122 and 199 to 83. The immediacy of the French threat had more political weight than opposition themes. Following Carteret's failure to form a ministry in February 1746, the public debate over foreign and military policy became less charged. The Pelham administration maintained the main themes of Carteret's anti-French policy, though his support for George's hostility to Prussia was discarded as a needless potential diversion of resources and efforts that should be directed against France. Indeed, Frederick's backing was sought unsuccessfully in early 1746. The Pelhams were concerned about both the security of the Low Countries and the maintenance of Britain's alliances, and, on that basis, sought to defend their interventionism. Henry Fielding, in his government-sponsored newspaper the *True Patriot*, warned his readers on 25 February

> against those who make use of popular topics and endeavour to improve popular dislikes to particular measures. Such, for instance, is a war on the Continent. As we have the utmost reason to confide in our ministry . . . [we should] not violently conclude, because wasting our treasures in a unnecessary Continent war, carried on madly without allies or reasonable views, is contrary to our interest and true policy, that therefore we should tamely suffer an ambitious, inveterate, and already too powerful enemy to possess himself of all Flanders, Brabant and Holland, when, with the assistance of allies, who are jointly interested in the cause, we may have a fair probability of preventing them.

However, the next two years were to show that the last statement was inaccurate, thus undermining the entire logic of the Pelhamite position and ensuring that, once peace was negotiated, Newcastle would devote his attention to strengthening the alliance. Aside from military disadvantage and defeat, the ministry was faced with financial problems, Henry Fox, one of the Lords of the Treasury, arguing that control over Parliament was insufficient, a theme that could serve as a leitmotif of Pelhamite foreign and war policy: 'the first misfortune is the want of money, no more can be raised this year and I fear it will be very difficult to supply or get money on the Vote of Credit which vote will be easily enough had' (BL Add. 51417 f. 234). In March 1748, Newcastle informed Cumberland, who had returned to his command of the British forces in the Low Countries after Culloden: 'money is so scarce that it cannot easily be got at any rate, or for any service' (RA CP 32/245).

The ministry was buoyed up by hopes that international developments would compensate for military defeat; that, for example, the death of Philip V in July 1746 would lead to the collapse of the Franco-Spanish alliance and a separate Anglo-Spanish peace. The following year, a British-supported Orangist coup in the province of Holland led to expectations of a much more vigorous pursuit of the war by the United Provinces, while negotiations with Russia led to hopes that Russian troops would be deployed against France. However, Ferdinand VI of Spain did not abandon France, the revival of Dutch strength proved chimerical, and the Russian forces did not arrive in Germany until 1748.

In the meantime, the military situation deteriorated. The French invaded the United Provinces in 1747 and two of their leading fortresses, Bergen-op-Zoom and Maastricht, fell in 1747 and 1748 respectively. These defeats increased pressure for peace in Britain, at the same time that fears of Jacobite activity and a French invasion revived (BL Add. 32810 f. 166). The domestic situation made peace both easier and more difficult. The general election of 1747, held a year earlier than was necessary under the Septennial Act, both confirmed and fortified Pelhamite dominance of the Commons. However, the retention of Cape Breton increasingly became a popular cause and one that the opposition proved eager to foster, even though it was apparent that France would demand its return as part of the peace settlement. In August 1747, the Earl of Sandwich, British representative at the peace negotiations, wrote to John, 4th Duke of Bedford, then First Lord of the Admiralty, concerning Cape Breton:

> the clamour that will be raised in consequence of any arrangements, that may be taken about that acquisition will have very great weight in the nation, which fomented by those who we know are lying in wait for the first opportunity of doing mischief, must in the end rob the administration of

their popularity; I am clear in my opinion, that this ministry cannot stand upon any other foundation. (BL Add. 32809 f 210)

The same month, Newcastle wrote to Sandwich that 'the necessity of putting an end to the war, (if it can be done upon a tolerable foot, and with the consent of our allies) is acknowledged by every body', but the definition of tolerable terms divided the ministry, producing that month a disagreement between the two Secretaries of State in front of George which led to a display of royal authority: 'the king called for the paper and altered it' (BL Add. 32809 ff. 140, 134). Newcastle and the increasingly influential Cumberland succeeded in late 1747 in pushing through their policy of substantial military support for the Dutch, while Newcastle underlined the view that was to be a major theme of his policy for the next few years: 'the great point, either in peace, or war, is to preserve the concert, and union between the allies: with that, nothing very bad can be done; and without that, it is impossible to do any good' (BL Add. 32810 f. 307). In contrast, Newcastle's colleagues, especially Bedford, Chesterfield and Pelham, pressed for peace at once, as they were pessimistic about the prospects of fighting on successfully.

The ministry, despite its parliamentary strength and the support of George, was uneasily placed, fearful of the potential interrelationship of international and domestic developments. Though characteristically he did not explain how popular opinion could harm the ministry, Sandwich was willing to argue that a fairly technical diplomatic matter, the failure to win the alliance of Frederick II, might be a theme

'for an Opposition to work upon. That party is now at a low ebb, but a change of circumstances will change their condition; and with the successor to the throne at their head, and a supposed neglect of this nature to work up the spirit of the people they may soon again become formidable' (BL Add. 32810 f. 411).

Chesterfield resigned as Secretary of State for the Northern Department in February 1748, angry at not being consulted sufficiently and opposed to what he saw as Newcastle's determination to press on with the war. His Department was taken by Newcastle, who was to hold it until he moved to the Treasury on his brother's death in 1754, while Newcastle was replaced at the Southern Department, where he had been since 1724, by Bedford, whose partnership with Newcastle, which lasted until 1751, was to be as unhappy as Newcastle's recent ones with Carteret, Harrington and Chesterfield.

A realisation of Dutch financial and military weakness obliged Newcastle to seek peace seriously in the spring of 1748. Britain was fortunate that financial and economic problems, war-weariness, naval defeats and concern about the advance of Russia led France to approve reasonable terms. The Austrians were unwilling to accept the preliminary terms, which were accordingly signed by British, Dutch and French representatives on 30 April. Nevertheless, they were persuaded by the British to accede to the final treaty five days after it was signed on 18 October.

By the Treaty of Aix-la-Chapelle (1748), France returned the Austrian Netherlands, expelled the Stuarts, guaranteed the Protestant succession, and agreed to destroy Dunkirk's sea defences. Cape Breton was returned to France, Madras, seized by the French in 1746, to the British East India Company; Silesia was guaranteed to Frederick II, and Austria had to accept an Italian settlement entailing more Bourbon gains (Lodge 1930a). Anglo-Spanish commercial and Anglo-French colonial disputes were left to future negotiations, despite Newcastle's wish that France accept measures to secure for Britain 'the safe and unmolested possession of Nova Scotia, the West Indies and the Thirteen Colonies' (BL Add. 32811 f. 434).

Anglo-Spanish differences were to be settled in 1750, but the commissioners to whom North American problems were left lacked the political will and power to settle them, so that, as the *Monitor* pointed out on 9 July 1763, the Treaty of Aix-la-Chapelle 'was big with the spawn of another more expensive war'. It was criticised by the opposition, especially for the return of Cape Breton, but Newcastle was satisfied both with the praise of pacific politicians, such as Pelham, and with the support of the bellicose Carteret (BL Add. 32812 ff. 118, 126). However, while Pelham saw Britain's task as complete and turned to consider the reduction of the national debt, which had risen during the war from £46,900,000 to £76,100,000, Newcastle wished to consolidate the peace and 'by proper measures' to 'secure the Liberties of Europe, and preserve them from being overturned by that power, which will always have it in view' (BL Add. 32811 ff. 430–1).

NEWCASTLE AND THE ATTEMPT TO CONSOLIDATE THE 'OLD SYSTEM' 1748–55

Wars were commonly followed by periods of diplomatic realignment. The Nine Years' War had been followed by the Partition Treaties, essentially an Anglo-French device, the War of the Spanish Succession by Anglo-French co-operation (1713–14) and alliance (1716–31), and the War of the Polish Succession by Austro-French co-operation. A major realignment was to take place in the western Mediterranean after the War of the Austrian Succession, one that was to keep the peace in Italy for the rest of the *ancien régime*. By the Treaty of Aranjuez of 1752, a collective security system was created essentially based on Austria and Spain, although also including Sardinia. This formed a marked contrast to hostility between the two powers that had begun with the Bourbon succession in Spain in 1700 and lasted since, with a brief interlude of alliance in 1725–9, helping to keep Italy and western European diplomacy unsettled. The Italian settlement indicated the willingness of monarchs and ministers to consider new alignments, yet further evidence against the canard that the diplomatic thought of the period was unimaginative and essentially rested on the uncritical acceptance of past patterns of behaviour. Indeed, on 8 July 1748 a French marshal, the Duke of Richelieu, wrote to Puysieulx, the foreign minister in 1747–51, proposing an Austro-French rapprochement.

The Italian settlement also throws what happened in British foreign policy into perspective. Far from being obliged to develop a collective security system directed against France and Prussia, the British ministry had the opportunity to reconsider its international position. However, it chose, instead, to seek to maintain the alliance system that had fought the war, essentially one of Austria, Britain, Russia and the United Provinces, and to ensure that it was ready to confront any challenge that France and Prussia might mount. In essence, this system was intended to be a conservative one, designed to resist change, unlike for example the system of the partitioning powers created in 1772. This accorded with traditional British notions, for Britain neither sought territorial acquisitions in Europe nor viewed those who did with particular favour. In this, the attitude of successive British ministries matched the views of the political nation. Both offered an essentially static vision of European diplomacy at the same time as there was increased pressure within Britain for the active pursuit of trans-oceanic goals, a contrast that some contemporaries drew.

However, though a colonial clash with France over American frontiers in 1754 was to set in motion the unravelling of the British system, there is little doubt that for British ministers the basis of their diplomatic strategy in the years from 1748 was not one of freeing their hands for a forward trans-oceanic strategy, but rather the maintenance of the peace in Europe. In 1750, twenty years after Walpole had been criticised on the same head, the opposition complained that France had failed to fulfil her undertaking to destroy the defences of Dunkirk. Pitt, the Paymaster-General, replied that the sole alternative to negotiation was war, that Britain was in no state for conflict, that the motion was dangerous as it would incite popular agitation, and, in reply to Egmont's claim that Pitt had formerly adopted the same position, added:

> upon some former occasions I have been hurried by the heat of youth, and the warmth of debate, into expressions which, upon cool recollection, I have deeply regretted. . . . Nations, as well as individuals, must sometimes forbear from the rigorous exaction of what is due to them. Prudence may require them to tolerate a delay, or even a refusal of justice, especially when their right can no way suffer by such acquiescence.

The ministry won the division by 242 to 115. In the circumstances of 1750, a prudential and circumspect foreign policy, the classic theme of ministerial defences of governmental policy for much of the century, could be defended in Parliament with little difficulty.

The situation abroad was less favourable. Newcastle felt that the crisis of the Austrian Succession War, with all the problems it had posed for Britain, had arisen from Austrian weakness. This had been due to two developments: the particular problems that had affected Austria (the crisis of Maria Theresa's succession which had revealed domestic, political and military weaknesses), and, arguably more serious, the failure of the Austrian alliance system in 1740–1. The Pragmatic Sanction had been guaranteed by most European rulers, but, in the crisis following Frederick II's invasion of Silesia, Maria Theresa had been abandoned by her allies including, crucially, Russia, Britain and the United Provinces. Newcastle essentially devised his diplomatic strategy to keep the peace by avoiding the repetition of the crisis of 1740–1. This was to be achieved by two means. Most importantly, a strong collective security system was to be created that would assist any individual member if intimidated. Secondly, and this arose more slowly, the Austrian position in the Empire was to be fortified by the election of Maria Theresa's eldest son, the future Joseph II, as King of the Romans, heir to the Imperial dignity enjoyed since 1745 by Maria Theresa's husband Francis I (Browning 1967–8).

Newcastle intended to subordinate other objectives to this plan, as he made clear in response to the prospect of serious negotiations with Frederick II in 1748. He was interested in such an alliance only if, as Frederick was clearly not willing to do, Prussia was prepared to surrender her room for diplomatic manoeuvre and become a staunch supporter of the 'Old System', the organisation of Europe around an Anglo-Austrian axis. This axis, however, was not without its problems and the difficulties that Newcastle was to encounter with Vienna had already been prefigured during both the post-Utrecht years and the War of the Austrian Succession (Black 1989d). Newcastle was overly inclined to forget former Anglo-Austrian difficulties, indeed to overlook recent problems in pursuing interventionist policies, and, as a result, he failed to appreciate the point of view of British ministers and diplomats who adopted a different viewpoint.

Arguably Newcastle's active sponsorship of the 'Old System' led him to pay insufficient attention to the possibility of improved relations with France and Prussia. Puysieulx sought an Anglo-French understanding and his cautious approach helped to prevent the confrontation of 1748–50 between Austria and Russia, and Prussia and Sweden from leading to war, in which Britain and France would probably have become involved thanks to their respective alliances. It is unclear how far Newcastle should be criticised for failing to approach France. Arguably more effort could have been put into solving North American differences, but it is not clear that they were soluble. Newcastle distrusted French professions of good will, arguing that Britain should 'not be amused by' French advances 'so as to neglect or grow cool to our old allies' (BL Add. 32815 f. 289), and his attitude matched that of the diplomat Sir Charles Hanbury-Williams, who had told Augustus III of Saxony-Poland in January 1748 that 'wherever there was a French party, England was sure to have them for her enemies' (PRO SP 88/69, 6 Jan.). No real effort was made by either side to test the basis of any Anglo-French reconciliation, but an approach was made to Frederick II with the mission of Henry Legge to Berlin in the summer of 1748. Legge was certainly keen on an alliance with Prussia, though, writing to Pelham in June 1748, he foresaw difficulties from George's Hanoverian interests and from those:

> we have hitherto nicknamed with the title of our allies, if the national union can be established by disposing the spirits of the respective rulers more cordially towards each other (and without doing so there is but little prospect of any union). It is certainly better that Hanover should get a little than that England should lose a great deal. Bawds frequently bring better people together, and in that light I don't think the go-between is to be neglected. At the same time I see so much jealousy arising among those with whom we are already connected, if that can be called connectional where we pay all and suffer all; that it remains a question for abler historians than myself to decide to what degree and in what manner we should form alliances here. I make no doubt but the two families and the two nations may be brought to join cordially, whether compatibly with Russia and more especially with the House of Austria I very much doubt. (NeC 598)

Newcastle was more sensitive to the views of Britain's allies, who, with France, controlled the most powerful military forces in Europe, and more pessimistic than Legge about the chances of reconciling them to

Prussia. It is possible that 1748 may have been an opportunity lost: Britain and Prussia were to become allies in 1756, but that alliance helped to drive Austria and Russia from Britain and arguably the risk was the same in 1748. Nevertheless, the failure to improve relations with France and, especially, Prussia limited Newcastle's room for manoeuvre and made him dependent on Austria and Russia, who were to fail to match up to his expectations.

In the short term, however, Newcastle was most concerned by the opposition of ministerial colleagues, especially his brother, to the subsidies that his revival of peacetime diplomatic interventionism entailed. Lord Chancellor Hardwicke was forced to act as buffer for the two brothers' differing views. In November 1748, Pelham outlined his views, criticising his brother for seeking

> 'the new modelling, or negotiating with any of the great powers at present further than to assure them we desire peace and quietness, and that if they will not personally meddle with us, we do not desire to disturb any of them, but will abide by our treatys and perform the several engagements we have entered into, whenever we are properly and legally called upon' (BL Add. 35423 f. 79).

The same month, Newcastle, with George II in Hanover on his first trip abroad, outlined his views to Hardwicke.

> . . . my whole plan is built upon this Definitive Treaty; and the best and only means of preserving it, which, I think, Nobody can answer for, if that is to depend, purely, upon the will of France and Prussia. I put those two Powers together, not that I would do any thing either jointly or separately to provoke one, or the other, but, from my apprehension that their interests are unavoidably connected, that, when either of those two powers shall think proper to disturb the present tranquillity, the other will, sooner, or later, follow; and therefore, I would propose, that such measures should be taken, that neither of them may be tempted to do it; and that . . . can no way be so effectually done, as by collecting and connecting . . . our allies, upon the Continent, and keeping, at all events, the fleet, in such a condition as to be able to maintain our superiority at sea. For if our old allies, with the addition of such, as may be got, can be supported on the Continent, and France sees that, whenever she breaks with England, she runs the same risk for her commerce and marine, which she has so severely felt, this war, neither France, nor Prussia, will be encouraged to attempt to break the Peace. I would not be understood by supporting our allies, on the Continent, to mean, that the King should be at any expence, at least only a mere trifle, by granting subsidies, for that purpose. The great point is, that our allies, and principally the States of Holland, and the Queen of Hungary, should see, that the King is fully determined to preserve and maintain the old alliance and system. (BL Add. 35410 ff. 86–7)

Newcastle's letter displayed a measure of wishful thinking. He continued by arguing reasonably that the treaty 'should not depend, singly, upon the pacific disposition of France, which may alter upon the least change in their interior administration, or, upon any prospect they may have of procuring more advantageous conditions', but, while accepting the mutability of French policy, he was unwilling to probe the possibility of Britain's allies changing their views, once Britain had made the commitment of fostering the 'Old System'. Thus, British determination was to guarantee European peace and Pelham's worries could be dismissed as a mere trifle. Newcastle's views were in part based on an assessment of the recent history of British foreign policy that endorsed interventionism and demanded opposition to France, leading him to write that month to Hardwicke of the danger of 'that fatal indolence, and indifference, and ill will, which produced the strict union with France in 1725, which, I have so often heard your Lordship condemn, as the source of all our misfortunes' (BL Add. 35410 f. 98).

Pelham, a former protégé of Walpole, had no brief for a French alliance, but he remained faithful to Walpolean principles and did not have to wait until the collapse of the Imperial Election Scheme to feel vindicated in his scepticism about his brother's policies. The Austrians did not share Newcastle's rosy view of their relationship. They had been angered since 1741 by British pressure on them to yield territory to Prussia and Sardinia, and were not happy by the cessions they had had to make, and to confirm in 1748. In January 1749, Zöhrern, the Austrian envoy in London, was informed in his instructions that fear of Prussia created the need for a British alliance, but that Austria was bitter about British policies. Disagreements over the peace and over Austrian financial claims from the war led to much anger between the Austrian and British governments in late 1748 and early 1749, causing Newcastle to complain that Austria had 'provoked the King' and 'the nation' and that he might be the dupe of his attachment to her (BL Add. 32816 ff. t 42, 185–6).

Nevertheless, despite what Newcastle termed 'an inclination to a further concert with France' in ministerial circles (BL Add. 32816 f. 188), Puysieulx's hints in February 1749, of better relations were slighted. Puysieulx had in fact outlined a theme of co-operation in the face of the powers of central and eastern Europe to which the French were to return in 1772 and 1783. Joseph Yorke, a diplomat son of Hardwicke, wrote from Paris in March 1749 of:

'the digressions that minister made, on the superiority of Great Britain by sea, and that of France by land; which tended no farther than to explain to my understanding, in what he thought the most advantageous and pleasing light, the propriety of the two nations uniting the superior force of both elements, to keep the rest of Europe in the state of tranquility' (BL Add. 32816 f. 128).

British ministries were not to respond to this theme, and their refusal to do so throws some light on shifts in British policy during the century. In 1719–20, the two powers had co-operated in seeking to intimidate Russia, in 1725–7 in confronting Austria and her allies. However, interest in the Baltic and eastern Europe had markedly diminished after the reign of George I, as Newcastle showed in 1753 with his clear unwillingness for Britain to play a rôle when discussion about a possibly imminent Polish election developed. When the interventionism of that reign revived in 1748–53, it was firmly associated by Newcastle with his conception of the 'Old System' and given a marked anti-French orientation. Possibly if the elderly George II had been more active and influential he might have given a more marked anti-Prussian orientation to British policy, but Newcastle saw containing France as the principal goal, and eastern Europe necessarily as of limited importance. To that extent, Newcastle's views marked a transition from the interventionism of George I's reign to post-1753 policy, for he followed the earlier traditions of activity but gave them a pronounced anti-French objective.

This objective lay behind Newcastle's support for peacetime subsidies. In August 1749, he argued that such peacetime expenditure had helped France in both peace and war and that Britain must respond in kind. Defending the need for an Anglo-Austro-Russian system, Newcastle presented it not only as necessary for the Continental balance of power, but also for Britain herself, for he argued that France would seek to reduce Britain 'to a state of dependancy' if she had the power and that if Britain had fewer allies French action on behalf of the Jacobites would be more successful (BL Add. 35410 ff. 126–31).

Newcastle won backing for his schemes. The Imperial Election Scheme became the central objective of British policy and subsidies were paid to German powers to achieve that end, while his critical fellow Secretary, Bedford, was replaced by the more pliable Robert, 4th Earl of Holdernesse in June 1751. A measure of Newcastle's satisfaction with Holdernesse was his long period in office. He stayed in the Southern Department until Newcastle transferred to the Treasury in March 1754, when he succeeded him at the Northern, serving there until replaced by Bute in March 1761. Holdernesse was replaced at the Southern Department by Sir Thomas Robinson, an experienced diplomat without political ambitions who was chosen by Newcastle because he felt he could rely on him.

Newcastle won the domestic battle, Pelham complaining forlornly about the Bavarian subsidy treaty in August 1750 and two months later about the policy of buying 'a prince of the Empire to do that which England at best is but collaterally concerned in' (BL Add. 35423 ff. 103, 110). However, Newcastle's Election Scheme was defeated by Austrian half-heartedness, French and Prussian hostility and the demands of the German Electors. The failure was a cruel one for Newcastle, especially as it had seemed for much of 1751-2 that he would succeed. Indeed, in September 1751, he wrote to Hardwicke that 'if ever my doctrine and system ought to take place, it is now' (BL Add. 35412 f. 16), while, in May 1752, he wrote to Hanbury-Williams that the Austrians 'begin to see their own interest' (Newport Library, Hanbury-Williams papers, 4 May 1752), a remark that helps to explain his failure to appreciate that different Austrian policies could arise from anything other than folly or knavery. Newcastle was soon disabused about Austrian views, reacting angrily and claiming that failure would badly damage British foreign policy and the domestic position of the ministry (BL Add. 35412 ff. 120, 151). Such remarks, made while Newcastle accompanied George II to Hanover in 1752, his third visit in five years, suggest that he had far less understanding than Pelham of the domestic lack of interest in German affairs and the extent to which public concern about France increasingly centred on colonial matters.

The failure of the Election Scheme appeared to leave British Continental diplomacy somewhat vulnerable as deteriorating Anglo-Prussian relations focused concern on the security of Hanover. As both cause and consequence of the failure to push through negotiations with Prussia in 1748, suspicion of Frederick's intentions remained very strong. His sponsorship of Jacobitism, particularly the appointment of a Jacobite as Prussian envoy in Paris and support for the Elibank Plot, aroused British anger, as did a number of commercial disputes, especially the non-payment of the Silesian debt to British creditors and the Emden Company, an East Indian trading company based on the Prussian port of Emden.

Arguably more serious was the danger that Frederick would act against militarily vulnerable Hanover. Hanoverian-Prussian relations were not easy, but the principal concern was that Frederick would act against Hanover in response to British steps that he disliked. Fears of a Prussian attack in 1753 led to the offer of British subsidies to Russia in return for military assistance, and to requests for Austrian support. Austria promised help, while Russian financial demands appalled the British ministry (though in October 1753 it conceded the idea of peacetime subsidies to Russia), but, as Frederick did not attack, the crisis passed. However, it had underlined the importance of Hanover in British Continental diplomacy, an importance that was to dictate its agenda in 1755 when Britain was next involved in an international crisis.

In part, the 'Old System', more especially the Anglo-Austrian-Russian collective security system that Newcastle sponsored, suffered, like most diplomatic alignments, from different interests which could be reconciled, or more properly ignored, in peace-time, but which caused strain during crises. More generally, British policy towards Austria in the decades leading up to the Diplomatic Revolution can be seen not as the product of a generally accepted desire for an alliance widely believed to be the natural and inevitable consequence of an international system revolving around the threat from France, but rather as a sequence of fragile alignments enjoying less than universal support within the British government and political nation. The need for an alliance with Austria apparently increased both in the early 1740s and in the early and mid 1750s, and as a consequence of the deterioration in Anglo-French relations, the vulnerability of Hanover and the Low Countries, and the Franco-Prussian alliance.

One of the crucial aspects of the system, from the British point of view, was the defence of the Austrian Netherlands, a strategic cover of both the United Provinces and Britain that had been entrusted to Austria at Utrecht on conditions designed to foster this cover, while preserving Anglo-Dutch economic interests. French successes in 1745–8 increased Anglo-Dutch concern over the Barrier fortresses and in 1748 the British considered acquiring Ostend in the peace (RA CP 32/337). Unfortunately, the Austrians were disenchanted with their position in the Austrian Netherlands: angry with being asked to accept a strategic situation that essentially favoured others while unable to enjoy the economic benefits that they felt they deserved. Tripartite negotiations over the Barrier were to play a large rôle in post-1748 diplomacy. It is easy to overlook them, as they did not lead to anything constructive, but, instead, they played a rôle in the continuing process of frustration and tension that characterised the 'Old System'. In May 1752, Joseph Yorke complained from The Hague: 'the Barrier Negotiation . . . that affair is so embroiled and the conduct at Vienna so extravagant, that unless it changes, the whole system is destroyed' (BL Add. 35356 f. 30). Two summers later, Britain and Austria were still quarrelling fruitlessly about the Barrier. The 'Old System' was not alone in these disputes. The Franco-Prussian alliance was similarly affected by differences and has been seen as increasingly empty of meaning.

The support for the 'Old System' of George II, Cumberland and the leading Hanoverian minister, Gerlach Adolf von Münchhausen, suggests that the determination to pursue a particular system – alliance with Austria rather than Prussia – can be attributed in part to royal and Hanoverian interests. The association of the system with Newcastle emerges most forcefully in the British ministerial correspondence, but, in part, his personal commitment to the system reflected not only royal wishes, but also his willingness ever since the fall of Carteret to support these wishes, even in opposition to his earlier views. The 'Old System' served royal and Hanoverian ends by acting as a military deterrent to Prussia, while appearing also as an anti-French step, thus being acceptable to British political opinion. The clash between hostility to France and opposition to Prussia had created major political, diplomatic and strategic difficulties during the War of the Austrian Succession, but the coming of peace enabled the differences between these two goals to be shelved. Indeed, the position was to be eased from the point of view of the British ministry, for accusations of a subordination of national interests to Hanoverian ends, a charge pressed on and off for two decades as a result in large part of Hanoverian fear of Prussia, were less publicly convincing in the period 1748–55 as a result of an agenda of Anglo-Prussian differences, including the Emden Company, Silesian debts and maritime prizes.

In July 1754, Holdernesse wrote to Robert Keith, envoy in Vienna, concerning George II's anger about Russian demands.

> . . . it is very unfortunate indeed, if the great powers of Europe will not be brought to take the measures which the honour and interests of their kingdoms require, unless their assistance is purchased at an exorbitant rate . . . The refusal to admit an attack upon His Majesty's allies, to be one of the cases in which the troops in question are to be put in activity, if His Majesty shall require it, overturns at once, the foundation upon which the whole negotiation must stand; It was entered into solely with the great and national principle, of preserving the peace, upon the surest, and most lasting foundation, viz. the forming such an alliance as should deter other powers from venturing to break it. This is the object His Majesty has steadily pursued, and if it should be frustrated, either by the blindness of some powers to their own interest, or by the ignorance and venality of private persons, the king will have nothing to reproach himself with. (PRO SP 80/194, 5 July)

Maintaining the peace by, in Anglo-Hanoverian eyes, keeping France and Prussia in their places through a collective security system, entailed two major linked problems. It made Britain dependent on her partners and it left unclear which of France and Prussia was to be regarded as the major challenge. A similar difficulty had faced the Alliance of

Hanover in its confrontation with Austria and Spain in 1725–9, and had affected Britain during the War of the Austrian Succession. Rather than being able in some fashion to choose what should be seen as the major challenge, the British were obliged in part to act with reference to their allies. Similarly, shifts in their attitude towards France and Prussia affected relations with these allies. This was to be crucially demonstrated in 1753–5, the years when a decisive shift occurred from regarding Prussia as the major challenge to seeing France in that light. In 1753, Austrian and Russian support had been sought to intimidate or dissuade Prussia; by 1755 Britain was in effect at war with France and her concern with keeping the peace on the Continent was centred on the need to avoid the war spreading. Britain thus sought Austrian support against France, a vital difference from her earlier anti-Prussian policy which had accorded with Austrian hostility towards Frederick. As Prussia was still allied to France, the fear of the Prussian attack on Hanover in support of France remained. On 11 April 1755, Holdernesse sent secret instructions to Hanbury-Williams in St Petersburg:

> 'It is our express command, that you should not sign any treaty with Russia, wherein an attack on any of our allies or upon any part of our Electoral dominions on account, and in consequence of measures taken by us, for the support and maintenance of the rights and possessions of our crown of Great Britain, is not made a casus foederis' (Newport, Hanbury-Williams papers).

All systems for keeping the peace naturally encompass different interests and aspirations, and their success is difficult to assess. Arguably the shock of Frederick's invasion of Silesia in 1740, his betrayals of treaties and his attack on Austria in the Second Silesian war (1744–5) led Britain and Hanover to exaggerate the threat that Prussia posed to international peace and to them in the post-1748 period. Frederick was clearly not averse to further gains, but the Prussian strategic position had deteriorated markedly since 1740, for Prussia was now the principal enemy of the Continent's two largest military powers, Austria and Russia. It was not obviously the case that this made it impossible for Frederick to risk other entanglements, but Anglo-Hanoverian fear of him can appear slightly implausible in light of Prussian vulnerability. The effective ending of the Italian question in 1752 further strengthened the Austrian position.

Leaving aside the question of exaggeration, it was the case that British concern for Hanover and the Low Countries appeared to dictate alliances with Austria and Russia, but what it did not do was clarify the terms upon which such alliances should be based, nor did it suggest the direction in which they should develop. Essentially Britain-Hanover sought reactive alliances that would maintain the peace by responding to real and threatened breaches of it, but it was difficult to bind allies to what might appear an essentially passive and fruitless diplomatic strategy. Given Russian determination to influence developments in Poland and Sweden, and Austrian aspirations for the reconquest of Silesia, it might be suggested that this peace strategy was likely to collapse in the long term, even had the outbreak of hostilities in North America not led Britain to seek unilaterally a change in the direction of both her foreign policy and her understandings with other powers. The Austrians were assured in 1755 that 'His Majesty adopts the general principle laid down by the Court of Vienna; that the assistance the allies are to give each other, ought to be mutual and reciprocal, and not unilateral' (PRO SP 80/196 f. 37), but, in practice, the British request that the Austrians help them to preserve the Continental peace was a one-sided demand, for there was no real reason for an Austro-French conflict in 1755, unless Austria chose to attack France's ally Prussia.

The British ministry had been provided with plenty of warnings about Austrian concern with Prussia. In May 1755, Keith reported from Vienna:

> this Court have always their eyes upon the King of Prussia; -they are in perpetual uneasiness about him, and his motions; and their measures are, and always will be, determined by what they think their interest with regard to that Prince. Monsieur Kaunitz said the other day, that he hoped, His Majesty did not consider the Empress, as his ally only against France, but likewise against the King of Prussia, who, though not so powerful as the other was fully as dangerous. He observed that this new power had quite changed the old system of Europe; and that nothing could set it to rights, but making ourselves sure of the Russians. (PRO SP 80/196 f. 32)

The use of the phrase 'the Old System' by Kaunitz, the Austrian Chancellor, was interesting. He correctly discerned the major change that had resulted from the rise of Prussia and the consequent weakness of the 'Old System'. Britain and Hanover had essentially sought to keep the peace by retaining an alliance system that would enable them to blur the distinction between France and Prussia, but this attempt had failed as soon as the choice had to be made. Whereas, in the Nine Years', Spanish Succession and Austrian Succession wars, it had been possible to treat France's allies as essentially subordinate to her and therefore a facet of the problem posed by France, as seen for example in the treatment of Charles Albert of Bavaria during the War of the Austrian Succession, this was no longer plausible in the case of Prussia for, although Britain might still regard her thus, Austria and Russia saw her as an entirely different problem.

The question that arises is whether an attempt could have been made to keep the peace in Europe on the basis of the method used in Italy, a comprehensive settlement made by all the major powers. If only because of Austro-Prussian and Prusso-Russian tensions, this appears unlikely, and the difficulty the British had experienced in negotiating the Peace of Aix-la-Chapelle in 1748, was not an encouraging precedent for a wider-ranging diplomatic initiative. Discussions between opposing states could take place, often via intermediaries, as during the Baltic crisis and the Imperial Election Scheme, but there was little sense that the two competing alliance systems could sink their differences.

In light of the realignments of 1755–6, this might appear surprising, but it is misleading to consider the diplomacy and attempts to keep the peace of 1748-54 in light of what was to happen. The causes of the Diplomatic Revolution of 1756 are the subject of debate, but there is much to be said for a stress on the rôle of contingencies, rather than a systemic viewpoint. The former perspective emphasises the rôle of human skill and foresight, as well as of chance, and makes the explanation of war and peace more difficult and, to a certain extent, apparently random. Such a view was contrary to that of the system builders of the century, but it is clear that the complex and varying nature of court politics cannot and could not be easily fitted into a pattern of readily determined behaviour. To that extent exponents of a collective security system as a means for keeping the peace can be criticised, but it might fairly be asked what else could be done. While diplomats were employed, it did little harm to talk of shared interests as long as a flexible viewpoint was maintained. In seeking an understanding with Frederick in 1755, in order to preserve the peace of the Empire and the security of Hanover, George II and his British and Hanoverian ministers were to reveal such flexibility (Horn 1927, 1930a; Browning 1967–8).

BRITAIN, FRANCE AND THE OUTBREAK OF THE SEVEN YEARS' WAR, 1754–6

In September 1751, Newcastle outlined to Hardwicke the need for compromise in Britain's American disputes with France:

> . . . it is extremely to be wished, that they might be forthwith accommodated; and that all differences between France and us, (that is Nation, and Nation,) might be adjusted. That can be done no way, but by concessions, on both sides . . . I think we should go any reasonable lengths, (at least where our

title is, at best, but doubtful,) to get quite rid of these constant pretences for quarrel; and that, upon a foot, where we shall be engaged alone; and, perhaps, the case of our defensive alliances either not exist at all, or be very doubtful. (BL Add. 35412 f. 17)

Newcastle was correct to place the possibility of colonial conflict with France in the context of Britain's Continental alliances for it was the relationship between the two that led to the crisis of 1755–6. However, this relationship was underrated by the more bellicose group led by Cumberland, Fox, the Secretary at War, and the Earl of Halifax, head of the Board of Trade, who helped to push the ministry into confrontation with France in 1754–5. Bussy, the French envoy sent to Hanover in 1755, told Holdernesse that the subjects in dispute were 'trifles' (BL Add. 35480 f. 32), and certainly they did not have the emotional reverberations or obvious support of those that had led to war with Spain in 1739. However, since the success of the Louisbourg expedition of 1745, North American issues had risen dramatically in the agenda of public interest in the field of foreign policy. In December 1746, Newcastle had expressed his support for an attack on Canada, arguing that public *and* parliamentary support for government policy would be compromised unless the war was waged vigorously in North America.

> The nation is now universally for the war: all parties in Parliament seem to agree in it: and that, which has thus united everybody, I am convinced, is their hopes and expectations of keeping Cape Breton and distressing and making an impression upon the French in North America. Should this expedition be laid aside, I am very apprehensive that the nation might think, it proceeded from an indifference, at least, with regard to the conquests in North America, and grow uneasy, for that reason, at the continuance of the war: and many gentlemen, who are now most zealous supporters of it in the House of Commons grow cool, and think it no longer their object. (BL Add. 32806 ff. 298–9)

In fact, the defence of the Low Countries was given priority, but Newcastle's comment is an important indication of the growing political, as opposed to polemical, importance of North America. In contrast, Caribbean disputes with Spain became less politically contentious. These disputes continued, particularly over the right to cut logwood on the eastern coast of Central America, where the Spanish were acutely sensitive to the danger that Britain might establish permanent colonies in unoccupied lands claimed by Spain. In July 1749, the Duke of Bedford, Secretary of State for the Southern Department, wrote to the envoy in Madrid to complain that a Spanish ship that had searched British merchantmen in the Caribbean, the crucial issue in 1738–9, must have acted under orders. He added: 'You know how extremely jealous this nation is of the least encroachments of this nature, and the Spaniards know it too; the least spark of this sort must, if not timely prevented, kindle a flame' (PRO SP 94/136 f. 1). Nevertheless, Anglo-Spanish relations improved and the commercial treaty of October 1750 was highly successful (McLachlan 1940:139).

In January 1751, the opposition attacked the treaty in the Commons, especially the fact that the Spanish claim to a right to search British merchantmen had not been explicitly denied. Pitt defended the treaty, arguing that he had been wrong to criticise Walpole in 1739 for failing to secure the same repudiation:

> 'I have considered public affairs more coolly and am convinced that the claim of no search respecting British vessels near the coast of Spanish America can never be obtained, unless Spain were so reduced as to consent to any terms her conqueror might think proper to impose.'

Pitt defended the treaty because of the favourable terms obtained for British trade and because it would serve as a basis for better Anglo-Spanish relations, a clear contrast to the habitual opposition argument that good relations with either France or Spain were impossible. For many decades, ministers had argued not only that good relations, however difficult to obtain, were possible, but also that they were essential to prevent the development of a hostile Bourbon pact. This policy, seen in alliances with France in 1716–31 and Spain in 1729–33, was revived successfully after the War of Austrian Succession. Relations with Spain improved considerably. Carvajal, one of Ferdinand VI's leading ministers, sought co-operation with Britain. His francophile rival, Ensenada, was disgraced in 1754.

Press and popular agitation over Bourbon activity was increasingly centred on France, and because supposed weakness or connivance in the face of French demands and interests had been used as a means to criticise the Walpole ministry, its successors were sensitive to such charges. Trying to negotiate an acceptable North American frontier and proposing that lines of latitude be used, rather than disputed maps, Robinson told the French envoy Mirepoix in March 1755 that any treaty would have to be approved by Parliament and that 'the circumstances of the political system obliged the ministry to be careful of opinion' (AE CP Ang. 438 f. 264). That July, George II told Bussy that he wanted to maintain good relations and that he had no doubt that Louis XV shared this view, but that 'the actual difference between the two crowns was a national affair and that the vivacity of the British nation was especially marked in defence of their commerce' (AE CP Brunswick-Hanovre 52 f. 19).

Tension in North America sprang from the wish of the British colonists to expand west from the Atlantic seaboard, which they controlled from Maine to Georgia, and the determination of the French to extend their boundaries against what they saw as a threat to the security of their North American colonies of Canada and Louisiana from the more numerous British colonists. The treaty of Aix-la-Chapelle had left North American frontier disputes to be settled by British and French commissioners, but their meetings revealed incompatible views, which were further exacerbated by the difficulty of agreeing over the mapping of disputed areas. The boundaries of Nova Scotia were a source of dispute, but tension centred on the Ohio river valley. In 1749, the Governor of New France drew up plans to join the colonies of Canada and Louisiana in order to create a barrier against British expansion, and the same year he sent an expedition to the Ohio. In 1752–4, more troops were sent. They drove out British traders, intimidated Britain's native allies, and constructed forts. French activity was seen in London as a threat to the British colonies. The Governor of Virginia was ordered to use force to repel French acts of aggression, which were defined as attempts to build forts in the Ohio valley, or attempts to prevent the erection of the forts which the Ohio Company had been given royal permission to erect since 1749 (Clayton 1981: 584).

The following summer, hostilities began in the disputed region, the French emerging victorious. The French hoped that their success would lead the British colonists to be more cautious in their projects and to devote more attention to the preservation of peace. The British government, however, responded in September 1754 by deciding to send two regiments to America which were intended to drive the French from the Ohio. Despite Newcastle's opposition, plans soon extended to a major attack on French America. The Prussian envoy reported on 18 October that the ministry was concerned about America and the Barrier, not Germany, 'because these are more national affairs and more important for maintaining their parliamentary influence' (PRO SP 107/63).

The French were keen to negotiate and continually stressed their moderation, while also maintaining their claim to the Ohio valley. They responded to British military preparations, in turn, by preparing an expedition to reinforce French America. The British failed to achieve their ends by limited action and intimidation. The force sent to America under Braddock was defeated on 9 July 1755, while Boscawen's attack on French ships sailing to Canada on 10 June 1755 led to the breaking off of diplomatic relations without preventing the French from reinforcing Canada. British attempts to excuse Boscawen's action were rejected by the French, and the British ministry suddenly found themselves threatened with a major war they did not want. The situation in some respects repeated that of 1739–40 and prefigured that of the War of American Independence: trans-oceanic war without allies.

Nevertheless, it was more threatening than the American Independence war, because the French appeared to be in a position to attack vulnerable Hanover and the Low Countries, while, unlike in 1739–40, the enemy was powerful France, rather than apparently vulnerable Spain. In addition, it was feared that France's ally Frederick would attack Hanover. The British position was eased in the autumn of 1754 and again in 1755 by the Spanish refusal to support France, but, in turn, the British were dissatisfied with their allies. It rapidly became clear that Austria would neither defend Hanover nor provide assistance against France. The Austrian Chancellor, Count Kaunitz, wrote in late August 1755 that he was glad of the breakdown of Anglo-Austrian relations, as it would free Austria from having to take part in any Anglo-French war. The Dutch seemed a broken reed, though the prospect of Russian help was more hopeful. Concern about Hanover led to the beginning of Anglo-Prussian negotiations in August, but they did not advance sufficiently until November 1755, when Holdernesse gave the Prussian envoy a copy of the Anglo-Russian agreement signed on 30 September 1755 and offered to renew past guarantees of Prussian possessions and to respect Prussia's non-involvement in the Anglo-French conflict. Frederick, offered the chance of joining an apparently powerful diplomatic alignment, guaranteed Hanoverian neutrality by the Convention of Westminster (16 January 1756).

The new system split on the contradiction between Prussian and Russian views. The British had thought that their convention with Russia, a subsidy treaty designed to ensure that Russian troops would respond to any Prussian attack on Hanover, was defensive in character, but Czarina Elizabeth and her ministers intended it as a preliminary to a planned Austro-Russian attack on Prussia, a measure that had been considered for a decade. The Russians refused to accept the Convention of Westminster as compatible with this treaty and in 1756 began actively planning an attack on Prussia. Anger respectively with Britain and Prussia led Austria and France to sign the First Treaty of Versailles (1 May 1756), a treaty that was less important for its detailed provisions than for the new alignment it created. Concerned about the prospect of an Austro-Russian attack, Frederick ignored British advice for restraint and on 28 August 1756 his troops crossed the Saxon frontier. Meanwhile, after a period when both Britain and France committed hostile acts, French forces had landed on Minorca on 18 April. Britain declared war a month later, but the failure of Admiral Byng to defeat the French fleet of Minorca on 20 May led to the surrender of the British forces on the island on 29 June.

The loss of Minorca was a humiliating failure that brought home the vulnerable nature of Britain's position, which was further underlined by fears of a French invasion. It was not going to be possible to avoid a full-scale war with France, and she was not going to be an easy power to defeat. Britain was linked to the unpredictable Frederick II, whose forces were outnumbered by those of his enemies. Whether this disadvantage could have been avoided by foresight or more skilful diplomacy is unclear. It is important neither to exaggerate Britain's influence on the Continent nor to ignore the strategic and political problems posed by Hanover. Fearful of a French attack on Hanover, Holdernesse wrote on 6 August 1756 to Andrew Mitchell, the envoy in Berlin: 'His Majesty's forces, when joined to those the king is negotiating from other princes, will not be sufficient to answer this purpose, unless a body of 30, or at least 25 thousand Prussians contribute . . . this important point, the hinge upon which the intended alliance between England and Prussia must necessarily turn' (PRO SP 90/65). Hanover had indeed been the hinge of British diplomacy in 1755–6; it was to her defence that Newcastle's system had shrunk. However, Austria, Prussia and Russia were not prepared to subordinate their schemes to this objective and, in a Continental diplomatic situation that was more volatile than the British ministry appreciated, it was not plausible to link any essentially defensive and reactive objective to the aggressive schemes of other powers. Only Prussia, the weakest of the three eastern European powers, also sought defensive objectives, Frederick telling Mitchell in 1758: 'my situation and circumstances will not admit of my going to war every day, and making a truce instead of a peace' (PRO SP 90/71, 14 June). However, he was an ally who was unwilling to follow Britain's diplomatic lead. This was clearly to be demonstrated over the course of their alliance.

THE SEVEN YEARS' WAR, 1756–63

Anglo-French maritime and colonial conflict was more significant in the Seven Years' War than in the preceding conflict. The early stages of the war were particularly unsuccessful for Britain. It is all too easy to forget this if a general or 'systemic' perspective is adopted and a detailed narrative of events is not considered. In the long term, the conflict was a major triumph, but the setbacks of the first two years vindicated the views of those who had suggested caution in rushing into hostilities with France. Minorca was lost (1756), Hanover, defended by a German force under the Duke of Cumberland, overrun (1757), and the early stages of the Canadian conflict were far from successful, particularly in the light of the contrast in the size of the armies. Greater French interest in Canada had led to a growth in the size of the garrison of Louisbourg, increased to 2500 regulars and with a supporting naval squadron; but the British expedition intended to attack the fortress in 1757 included 12,000 troops, and a force of 13,000 seized it in the following year. A small force of French regular troops in Canada engaged much of the British army.

From late 1757, however, a new energy and determination illuminated British policy, and it met with greater success. As Secretary of State from July 1757 in what could be described as the Newcastle-Pitt coalition, Pitt played a central role in strategy. His contribution has been a matter of some controversy, and recent scholarship has been harsher than earlier judgments. Far from having a clear strategic vision, Pitt's strategy emerged as a consequence of an ad hoc process of adjustment to the unique circumstances of the conflict. The concentration on maritime and colonial war appears more a product of circumstances which all ministers largely accepted than something distinctive to Pitt. The war was extended piecemeal, planned year by year. The coastal raids on France that were his most distinctive contribution were unsuccessful in their strategic purpose of diverting French resources from Germany. British success owed much to the contribution of others. Pitt was particularly irresponsible about the unprecedented costs of war (Middleton 1985, Peters 1998).

Yet it is necessary not to push the revisionist account of Pitt too far. His undoubted energy was important to the organisation of the war effort. Furthermore, as the politician with the greatest reputation 'out of doors', Pitt played a major role in securing the image of the conflict, so that it was seen as far more in accord with British interests than the War of the Austrian Succession had been. In particular, he helped to justify the commitment of resources to the conflict in Germany (Black 1999b).

The Convention of Klosterseven, by which Cumberland had agreed to disband his army, was repudiated by George II as a result of pressure from his British ministers, and assistance was offered to Frederick II, first financial and then military as well, with the dispatch of troops to Germany in 1758. Concerned that Frederick would abandon the struggle, Holdernesse wrote to Mitchell on 23 September 1757.

The winter will give time for negotiation, and if the King of Prussia shall then think himself in a condition to continue the war, His Majesty will most readily concert the necessary measures for the future operations of it, and vigorously assist His Prussian Majesty in the execution of what shall be jointly agreed upon . . . two conditions must precede the succours His Prussian Majesty may expect from hence. First, a specific explanation of the pecuniary assistance to be furnished from hence. Secondly, that His Prussian Majesty shall promise to make no pacific overtures whatsoever, but in concert with His Majesty. . . . His Majesty relies on the signal zeal of his Parliament to provide a larger subsidy than was ever given to an ally. (PRO SP 90/70)

Frederick, presented to the British public as the Protestant Hero and a military leader to rank with Caesar, was soon a figure of considerable popularity, as a London correspondent of Mitchell noted in December 1757:

'nothing seems more sincere and confirmed than the disposition, that has arisen through all parts of this kingdom and amongst all kinds of people in favour of that great prince . . . the present disposition facilitates the intentions of those in power in the exertion of the strength and assistance of this nation.' (BL Add. 6861 f. 298)

The government turned down Prussian requests to send a fleet to the Baltic, though Frederick's advocacy of diversionary attacks on the French coast played a rôle in encouraging Pitt's support for what was on the whole a militarily insignificant strategy. However, the Anglo-German army in Westphalia under Ferdinand of Brunswick recovered the military position lost by Cumberland, Frederick avoided destruction at the hands of his numerous enemies, and the British were able to finance colonial conquests, an army in Germany and Prussian subsidies, thanks to the strength of their economy, the relative sophistication of their public finance and confidence in the stability of the ministry. Holdernesse commented in October 1759 that 'the world is well mended with us since we used to lament the convention of Closter-Seven; the efforts we have made are prodigious and yet if it were necessary we can still find some guineas for a good purpose' (BL Add. 35483 f. 10). Pitt presented German and colonial operations as complementary, declaring

'the point was to consider whether it was not possible to make the German war useful to the interests of this country as a subordinate measure, while our marine and colonies should be the principal object' (BL Add. 38334 f 33)

In 1759, the French planned an invasion of Britain. If they had succeeded, judgements of Pitt's policies and of the wisdom of Britain's war with France, might have differed radically from the praise they received that year and subsequently. However, French fleets were defeated at Lagos and Quiberon Bay, on 18-19 August and 20 November, after which in London there was 'nothing but bonfires and illuminations' (Bod. MS Lyell empt. 35 f. 56); had it been otherwise, Pitt would have been criticised for dispersing British strength outside Europe. Choiseul's plan was unrealistic, in so far as it anticipated significant Jacobite support, and it is unlikely that the regular forces intended to invade Essex from Ostend and the Clyde from Brest could have conquered Britain. But the landing of a regular force, several times greater than the Jacobite army which had invaded England from Scotland in 1745, would have posed serious problems.

The war witnessed a considerable improvement in British fortunes. By February 1759, the navy had a record strength of 71,000 men. In 1756, a good supply system for the British army in North America was established; and British forces were successful there, as well as in the West Indies, West Africa and India. Amphibious forces, singularly unimpressive in their attacks on the French coast, succeeded in capturing all the major centres of the French Empire except New Orleans: Louisbourg and Goree (1758), Guadeloupe and Québec (1759), Montréal (1760) and Martinique (1762). These gains were very popular, Henry Grenville MP noting in October 1759: 'acclamations of joy fill every mouth and every corner of this region of Surrey, for the glorious and important reduction of Quebec' (HL STG 22(16)). In Germany, British troops played the major role in the French defeat at Minden in 1759. The new king of Spain, Charles III, signed an alliance with France, the Third Family Compact, in 1761, a serious defeat for British diplomacy, and Britain and Spain fought a brief war in 1762. The British conquest of Havana and Manila, two of the leading bases in the Spanish Empire, indicated that success had not left the ministry with Pitt when he resigned in 1761 (Black 1999c).

His criticism of the terms of the Peace of Paris of 1763 had little impact in the face of widespread satisfaction with the terms and general eagerness for peace shown by a country that was finding it increasingly difficult to finance the conflict. Guadeloupe, Martinique, St Lucia and Goree were returned to France, and there were concessions over Newfoundland fishing rights, but the return of Minorca and the recognition of Britain's gains in Canada, Senegal, the West Indies (Grenada, Tobago, Dominica, St Vincent), and India amounted to an impressive British triumph. However it was to be defined, there was clearly no longer a colonial and maritime balance of power between Britain and France (Middleton 1985). It would be fanciful to argue that the war ensured that the future of North America would lie with Protestant, Anglo-Saxon culture rather than its Catholic French counterpart, in so far as the two can be distinguished, because there was no serious chance of France conquering the British colonies. However, thanks to the conflict, France was irreversibly driven from Canada, while the British were able to consolidate their position as the leading European power in India. Britain had proved able to defeat not only France, but France and Spain in alliance, and the obstacles that had hindered or delayed successful colonial operations against both powers during the 1740s had been overcome. This suggested that Britain would dominate the post-war colonial world, as she was now militarily clearly able to take initiatives, while the Seven Years' War revealed that she would not necessarily be prevented from doing so by commitments to Continental partners, whether allies, in that case Prussia, or states that were more clearly dependants, such as Hanover and Portugal.

The war was not a period of protracted diplomatic activity. Though Britain was at war only with France, and eventually Spain, diplomatic relations with Austria were broken in 1757–63 and with Sweden in 1748–63, while relations with Russia were cool. Unlike the Nine Years', Spanish Succession and Austrian Succession Wars – when Britain was a member of a large alliance, inter-alliance diplomacy was very active, and negotiations with Britain's enemies were frequent – during the Seven Years' War diplomatic activity on both scores was limited. The most important negotiations were with Spain, and there is no doubt that Spanish neutrality for most of the war played a major rôle in enabling Britain to succeed against France. Benjamin Keene, the experienced envoy in Madrid, had warned in July 1755 of the need to respect Spanish views and urged 'much circumspection and complaisance on the part of our officers towards Spaniards and Spain. Much depends upon it, and I hope they will be taught to forget the Spaniards are our enemies.' He also claimed that 'long habitudes of being slaves to France and of hearing ill of the English create prejudices not easy to be eradicated, even where there is an intention to be undeceived' (Leeds Archive Office, Vyner Mss 11842).

Keene's advice was based on the hope that such prejudices would not dictate Spanish policy, and that proved to be the case. In September 1757, the Spanish government turned down a British offer of Gibraltar and an acceptable settlement of the logwood dispute on the Honduran coast in return for assistance in regaining Minorca, as they had no wish to fight France, but relations remained correct for another two years; though the Spaniards were unhappy about the British attitude in a number of commercial and maritime disputes, especially over the question of neutral rights, an important issue when the British were trying to blockade France, and one that also harmed Anglo-Dutch relations considerably during the war. Keene's successor as ambassador, the Earl of Bristol, sought to persuade the Spanish foreign minister, Richard Wall, an Irish Catholic, to differentiate between the ministry and public opinion, offering in September 1759 an analysis that clearly sprang from his view of British politics.

> I flattered myself after the first heat of the Nation was subsided, the cool part of Attention, who composed the Administration, would not construe, as a disrespect to the Spanish flag, what, I believed, was not a clear or uncontrovertable right attached to the flag of a neutral power . . . I added, that I had no doubt but that our enemies had put every bad interpretation they could, upon this affair, and would speak to the passions, without giving their hearers time to listen to reason; that the passions of the generality were easily influenced without any plausible grounds, but much more so, when there appeared the shadow of a foundation, yet I could not but hope, that the serious attention of this court would not be diverted by a foreign inflammatory circumstance from the real object, and sole view, in which this incident ought to be considered, the Law of Nations. (PRO SP 94/160 ff. 132–3)

However, the accession of the anti-British Charles III in 1759 indicated the importance of the personal views of rulers. A memorial presented by the Spanish envoy in London in December 1759 declared that Charles could not regard with indifference the destruction by British conquests of the balance of power in the New World established by the Treaty of Utrecht. Pitt replied that it was appropriate that France should suffer as a result of her defeats and stated that there was no question of a balance between the two powers in North America (PRO SP 94/160 ff. 248, 253–4). Nevertheless, Pitt took care to avoid offending Spain, while Charles III, busy establishing himself in his new kingdom, was prepared to await the result of attempts to end the war by negotiations. They failed and Anglo-Spanish relations deteriorated in 1760 with disputes over logwood cutting and the Spanish claim to a share in the Newfoundland fishery. Spain moved closer to France, as the latter power sought in the summer of 1761 either to negotiate peace with Britain or, if war continued, to obtain Spanish support.

It was over relations with Spain that the ministry divided in 1761. Until then foreign and military policy was generally less politically and ministerially contentious than it had been during the War of the Austrian Succession. The early period of the war had been one of ministerial instability, a continuation of the situation that had arisen with the death of Pelham in 1754 and the consequent problem of finding a satisfactory leader-manager of the Commons. As a result, Robinson was succeeded as Secretary for the Southern Department (the

Secretary then in the Commons) by Henry Fox in November 1755, while he was replaced by William Pitt the following November. That month, Frederick informed Mitchell about his concern over British political divisions and his desire for the restoration of calm in London (BL Add. 6843 f. 37). In fact, the Pitt-Devonshire ministry lasted only a few months. However, the formation of the Newcastle-Pitt ministry, in which Pitt was again Southern Secretary, in June 1757 brought stability, helping to create a domestic political context in which considerable sums were voted for the war and British troops were sent to Germany without significant opposition. Pitt, who had earlier opposed this commitment, became its crucial defender in the Commons, arguing that Britain was going to the aid of her Prussian ally, rather than Hanover.

The collapse of this ministry and the political debates that accompanied the negotiation of the Peace of Paris could be blamed on George III, who succeeded his grandfather in October 1760, and on his favourite the Earl of Bute (Northern Secretary March 1761–May 1762; First Lord of the Treasury May 1762–April 1763), but it is reasonable to point out that the pressures created by a long war and the difficulties attendant upon any compromise peace made some sort of political crisis likely, as did the determination, if not egotism, of Pitt, 'a man who (in a political sense) fears neither God nor Devil' in the words of George Lyttelton (HL MO. 1295). As Prince of Wales, George had greeted good war news as making a satisfactory peace more likely, writing in 1759: 'the taking of Crown Point . . . what a providential stroke this is, it will make us certain of a good peace; if the king will but with vigour push on the war'. As king he continued to hope that success would bring peace: ' . . . I hope this will forward the expedition to Martinique which seems to be the place the French will most immediately feel the loss of, and perhaps drive them to implore such a peace of us, as we may with honor conclude' and 'I am glad the face of affairs is changed at Quebec, and I hope this will encourage the French to sue for peace' (MS, George to Bute, undated).

Pitt, in contrast, was not psychologically prepared for a peace involving unpleasant compromises, certainly not in 1761 when the expectation of Spanish support influenced France in her abortive peace negotiations with Britain. The extent to which Britain and France, if they negotiated peace, could go on assisting their allies proved a serious point of contention, as did Pitt's demand that France renounce any share in the Newfoundland fishery, which was believed to be a major source of wealth, as well as a crucial training ground for sailors and thus essential for a navy that based its wartime recruiting on impressment. Though French firmness led to a certain easing in the British position, including that of Pitt, this came too late to facilitate a settlement before the signing of the Franco-Spanish Family Compact on 15 August 1761. The former Secretary of State, the Duke of Bedford, a critic of Pitt, captured the unconciliatory tone that Pitt brought to the negotiations until near their close when he wrote of the cabinet on 25 July: 'I left them . . . hammering at a dispatch upon the middle system of civilly desiring the French to lie down quietly to let us cut their throats' (PRO 30/29/1/14 f. 528). Resigning in October 1761, when the ministry refused to take preemptive action against Spain to forestall what he claimed was a conspiracy of the two Bourbon powers, Pitt's departure helped to distance George III and the administration that negotiated the peace from wartime successes, but George Dodington, a former minister and diplomat and a supporter of the ministry, wrote to Bute in October 1761:

> I look upon the late event as an obstacle removed, and not as one added, when peace is to be treated . . . some months ago I said that I thought Mr. Pitt would never make peace, because he never could make such a peace as he had taught the nation to expect. I suppose he now sees, that we are within a year or two, of an impracticability of carrying on the war upon the present footing; and may think, by going out, upon a spirited pretence, to turn the attention and dissatisfaction of the public, upon those who at a ruinous expence are to carry on his wild measures, and whom they have been taught to dislike, by a total abandonment of the press to him and his creatures. (MS 2/85)

Opposition criticism centred on policy towards Prussia and on the terms on which the ministry was willing to settle with the Bourbons. Arguing that they, especially France, could not be trusted, opposition newspapers, such as the *Monitor*, were opposed to the return of conquests to France and unwilling to entertain the idea of concessions for the sake of good relations. Opposition writers argued that these were impossible and pressed for punitive peace terms. The view that France could not be trusted was not only held by opposition spokesmen. In December 1762, Walter Titley, the veteran envoy in Copenhagen, expressed a firm conviction of the mutability of international affairs.

> While ambition and avarice govern the world, the making of peace signifies little more than the taking of breath; and the public tranquillity will last no longer, than till some aspiring power is able to disturb it with a fair prospect of advantage. France generally lays the scheme of a new war, immediately upon the conclusion of peace; though I suppose, after such a drawback, she will not speedily be in a condition of executing any hostile project. (Farmington, Weston papers vol. 6)

In a variation on the habitual theme of opposition criticism of interventionism and of Britain's allies, the government was condemned for the deterioration in Anglo-Prussian relations in 1761–2. On 27 November 1761, Bute wrote to Mitchell that he did not intend renewing the stipulation that neither power should unilaterally undertake peace negotiations, as it would restrict British options, and on 5 January 1762 Bute informed the Prussian envoys that, in place of the subsidy agreement with its commitments, they would be offered a parliamentary grant. George III, Newcastle and Bute had decided to seek to revive the 'Old System' and this entailed distancing themselves from Prussia, though, in attempting to renew good relations with Austria and Russia, George and Bute in particular did not envisage the extensive and costly commitments of Newcastle's pre-war diplomacy. The defence of Hanover was no longer to be a central feature of Britain's Continental policy (Black 1989c: 113–34).

The collapse of the Anglo-Prussian alliance was not primarily due to the events of 1761–2 – Britain's alleged desertion of Frederick -which has generally been considered the turning point, but rather a consequence of the divergent aims and interests of the partners themselves, which had weakened relations from the outset. Prussia's declining military fortunes, growing British war-weariness, the subsidy question and the complexities of peace-making all subjected the alliance to increasing strain, minimising the scope for co-operation (Schweizer 1989). The argument that the alliance was unlikely to have survived the war throws new light on the policies of Bute, who can be seen as an intelligent and effective minister forced to deal with the commitments of war, including the Prussian alliance, and obliged to adapt policy to the peacetime exigencies of domestic political and financial constraints (Schweizer 1988). Frederick claimed that he had been betrayed, but equally the British ministry was disenchanted by Prussian support for Pitt, who criticised the government's disengagement from German affairs, and unhappy with the way that Frederick exploited the accession of the pro-Prussian Czar Peter III at the beginning of 1762.

Arguably more important was the fact that 1762 brought a revival of peace negotiations with the Bourbons, as France realised that the entry of Spain into the war had not led to success either in the colonial and maritime sphere, or in Portugal, which she had attacked. The case of Portugal is interesting because, as with the decision of the Walpole government in 1735 to send a large fleet to the Tagus to deter Spanish attack, it suggests that charges of isolationism and neglect of allies brought against a pacific ministry are misplaced. Portugal, a major trading partner, could be seen as Britain's Achilles' heel, though, as Joseph Yorke pointed out, 'the episode of Portugal was not suspected by the red hot partisans of the Spanish war' (BL Add. 58213 f. 64). In December 1761, Bute observed that 'the safety of Portugal is most essential to the interest of this country' (Farmington vol. 5, 25 Dec.), and the ministry decided to send troops to her defence.

Charles III expressed the wish that Britain would send troops to Portugal, as he would then be able to treat her as an enemy and make gains in Portugal to compensate him for losses elsewhere, presumably colonial losses to Britain. Charles also suggested that a Portuguese war would harm the British and divert their attention from the war with France in Germany. Choiseul, effectively the director of French foreign policy, commented that, however many British troops were sent, Spain would enjoy military superiority. Frederick II was concerned that British aid to Portugal would be a diversion of assistance he required, while his London envoy reported that Bute regarded the commitment to Portugal as his own work, would support it at the expense of the German war, and hoped to gain credit domestically by it. The commitments to Portugal and Germany were generally seen as alternatives, with commercial pressures pushing the ministry towards the former. At the end of April 1762, the Spaniards invaded, Ossun, the French envoy in Madrid, suggesting that the conquest of Portugal would be very useful because it would either force Britain to return her North American conquests as part of the price of peace or make Portugal dependent on the Bourbons and thus harm British trade. British commercial interests in Portugal, the weakness of the Portuguese defence and Portuguese requests for assistance speeded up the dispatch of British troops. Thanks in large part to British efforts, Portugal was not conquered.

The Portuguese war, like British disengagement from her Prussian commitments, has to be set against the background of Anglo-French negotiations. In August 1762, Choiseul informed Ossun that it would be good for Spain if peace could be negotiated and that the moment had been lost for the conquest of Portugal. The British ministry wrestled with the problem of how to relate its commitment to Frederick to the developing negotiations with France, for the Seven Years' War, unlike the War of the Austrian Succession, was not ended by a general peace congress but by separate negotiations, those between Britain and the Bourbons being conducted at Paris. Concern about Frederick was increased by the apparent imminence of a Russian attack on Denmark and the possibility that Frederick would support Czar Peter III. The Danes applied for British support, in accordance with the guarantee of the Holstein-Gottorp lands they had conquered given to them by George

I in 1720, but Bute was willing to offer the Danes only neutrality in April 1762. He told the Danish envoy that:

'the vast burden of the wars against France and Spain, in which His Majesty finds himself engaged, affected the circumstances of his own kingdoms in such a manner, as to make it impossible for him to take any part in pursuance of the guaranty' (PRO SP 75/114 f. 126).

Concerned about Prussian intentions, Bute had already informed the Prussian envoys on 26 February that the British subsidy would be paid only if Frederick revealed his military and diplomatic plans, conditions Frederick, certain of Russian support, rejected on 17 March. However, unlike in 1756 when the British had had little alternative but to accept the Prussian attack on Saxony, in 1762 Bute had no intention of accepting any involvement in Peter III's anti-Danish plans, even if this jeopardised the possibility of an Anglo-Prusso-Russian alignment, an alignment that the ministry had sought in late 1759 and that Pitt was to seek when he became first minister in 1766. George Grenville, who succeeded Bute as Northern Secretary in June 1762 when Bute replaced Newcastle at the Treasury, stressed the cost of the German war and the Prussian subsidy and pressed for the end of both. His colleague, Pitt's successor, Charles, 2nd Earl of Egremont, wrote to Bute in May 1762:

I have long thought that the cordial friendship of his Prussian Majesty for our Royal Master (if it ever existed with sincerity) was totally ceased: and that both his ministers here were more connected with my predecessor than any of his Majesty's servants. . . . I should grudge him a subsidy which may probably be used, if not against us, at least to perpetuate the war in Germany and the North. (MS 7/164)

The ministry divided over the issue of the German war and the Prussian subsidy. Newcastle pressed for a vote of credit for two million pounds, resigning when Bute sought information from Treasury officials to back his support for Grenville's successful demand for only one million. On 30 April 1762, it was decided to end the Prussian subsidy. As in 1748, when, against the wishes of Pelham, he had pressed the payment of £100,000 claimed by the Austrians, Newcastle was concerned about the post-war world, specifically the retention of wartime alliances, and on 4 May 1762 he wrote to the Marquis of Rockingham, the rising leader of his political group: 'our secret negotiation with France goes at present very well, if we have not spoiled it ourselves, by abandoning the king of Prussia . . . and disobliging the Czar' (WW R1-238).

The absence of any ally for Britain to consider on equal terms helped to ensure that the negotiations with France in 1762 were smoother than those of 1748, as did the far clearer nature of military advantage. George II had sought gains for Hanover in neighbouring Hildesheim and Osnabrück, but George III had no such objectives. There were disagreements concerning the extent to which Britain was to be allowed to retain her gains, for example over St Lucia and Cape Breton in June 1762, and the navigation rights on the Mississippi the following month. Bute wrote of seeking 'a permanent alliance' with France (MS 6/150), but he failed to carry the cabinet of 26 July with him on the cession of St Lucia or concluding a peace with Spain. Discussing the Mississippi, Bute's ally Bedford told that cabinet meeting:

> that he hoped no attention would be given in the consideration of this question to popular clamour, that he had seen for some years past with concern how unreasonable the people of this country were in their claims, that they were always endeavouring to get something farther and that in the present instance he thought there was neither justice or conscience in the demand . . . that we ought upon this occasion to follow the golden rule of doing as we would be done by.

Grenville retorted: 'we had made one concession after another' (HL STG 14(43). Bute's diplomat brother, James Mackenzie, complained about Egremont and Grenville in August: 'God help the king, who has such tools to work with!' (MS 4/21). However, supported by George III, Bute was able to regain control, Bedford being sent to conduct the negotiations in Paris, whence he quarrelled with Egremont over his instructions, while Grenville was moved from the Northern Secretaryship in October. Fostered by Bedford, the negotiations progressed, surviving the crisis caused by the issue of an equivalent from Spain for the return of Havana once it had been captured.

On 3 November 1762, the preliminaries of peace were signed by Bedford and the Bourbon representatives at Fontainebleau, and a week later the cabinet agreed that George should give his orders for their immediate ratification. Hardwicke complained in the Lords on 9 December that the preliminaries had been ratified before they were laid before Parliament for their general approval. In contrast, Lord North, an MP and a Lord of the Treasury, wrote of the peace terms to his father: 'They are better than I expected, and I should think, at first sight that they are very defensible. I do not hear that they make so great a clamour in the City as was expected' (Bod. MS North adds c4/1 f. 28).

During the parliamentary debate on the preliminaries on 9 December 1762, Pitt condemned what he presented as the desertion of Frederick II as 'insidious, tricking, base and treacherous'. He also strongly criticised the restoration to France of the right to fish the rich waters off Newfoundland and stated that he would have continued the conflict in order to gain the exclusive right to fish the waters and thus cement an economic strength that was already based on dominance in the trade of African Negroes, East Indian goods and West Indian sugar. Pitt claimed that by returning Guadeloupe, Martinique, St Lucia, Goree and the fisheries to France the ministry was 'giving to her the means of recovering her prodigious losses, and of once more becoming formidable to us at sea' (Cobbett 1806–20: XV, 1265). Other opposition speakers attacked the return of St Lucia and the treatment of Frederick II.

Nevertheless, the terms were approved by a substantial majority in the Commons, while there was no division in the Lords. Lord Sandys noted that his MP son had 'voted with the Majority being fully persuaded as I am likewise that peace was necessary, that these terms are much better than those of last year, our boundaries better fixed and nothing left to commissaries and all our disputes settled with France and Spain even the long dispute about logwood' (Worcester CRO 705: 66 BA 4221/26). The definitive treaty was signed in Paris on 10 February, ratified by George III on 22 February and copies of the treaty presented to Parliament on 18 March. Minorca was returned by France and Britain gained Canada, Grenada, Tobago, Dominica, St Vincent, Senegal and recognition of her position in India from France, and Florida from Spain (Rashed 1951).

The successful conclusion of the negotiation marked a climax of two developments, and gave way to a new scene. The active Anglo-French diplomacy of 1762 was not to lead to any subsequent co-operation, while the sustained debate about the peace terms was soon to yield to a political world dominated by contentious domestic themes. On 29 December 1762, the cabinet decided on a peacetime military establishment of slightly over 50,000, in contrast to the fighting strength of 97,000 the previous 1 July. Freed from the commitments, diplomatic, military and financial, of war, the ministry was free to consider foreign policy afresh, and that against a less concerned domestic context than for many years. Financial retrenchment and reform of imperial commercial relations were to be more pressing problems, though they were clearly related to Britain's international position. In *Great Britain's True System* (1757) Malachy Postlethwayt, a prominent writer on economic topics, had argued that 'the Balance of Trade is in fact the Balance of Power'. He had also warned that 'no sooner shall a peace be made with a perfidious enemy, but he will instantly prepare again for war' (pp. 234, 270).

CHAPTER ELEVEN

BRITISH FOREIGN POLICY 1763–83

INTRODUCTION

British foreign policy in this period has not enjoyed a good press. An influential essay by Michael Roberts castigated policy as misguided, failing to appreciate the need to make concessions in order to obtain alliances, and incompetently administered, and his themes have been substantially repeated by Hamish Scott, the leading scholar on the period, who has written about 'the persistence of outdated thinking' (Roberts 1970; Scott 1989: 85). These views can be questioned if attention is devoted to the domestic situation. The national debt almost doubled from £74 million to £133 million between 1756 and 1763, and debt charges as a percentage of tax income also rose. As scholars working on policy towards America or government finances are well aware, the political and governmental strains produced by this financial situation were considerable. Bute referred in February 1763 to the themes of 'security and economy' in the size of the military (BL Add. 36797 f. 34). Economy was stepped up under Grenville, who succeeded Bute as leading minister in April 1763 and wrote on 29 September to Edmund Waller: 'I agree entirely with you that the real difficulties lie in the exhausted state of the public revenues and not in the clamour or opposition of any individuals whatsoever' (HL ST 7 vol. 1). The following month, both Secretaries of State told Guerchy, the French envoy, that Britain was too exhausted by the recent war to send money abroad and that for that reason they would not provide subsidies to anyone (AE CP Ang. 451 g. 475). Critics of diplomacy in this period have failed to explain why foreign policy should have been immune from restraint in terms of commitments and expenditure. Given the bitter ministerial debates about the need for economy in the navy, which clearly would be crucial in any confrontation with the Bourbons, the value of subsidies must have seemed distinctly hypothetical and the purpose of new diplomatic commitments unclear.

The coming of peace was followed by the resumption or improvement of diplomatic relations with Frederick's former enemies, and the Earl of Buckinghamshire and Viscount Stormont, sent to St Petersburg and Vienna in 1762 and 1763 respectively, were instructed to foster links. Stormont was ordered to give 'proper assurances of our sincere desire to return to the ancient system of union, intimacy and communication of counsels, for our mutual benefit, and for the public good' (PRO SP 80/199, 25 May 1763), while Buckinghamshire was informed in June 1763 by the Northern Secretary, the Earl of Halifax:

> A strict union with Russia is deservedly considered as the first and best foundation. When this is once laid, we may proceed upon a wise and regular plan, conformably to our joint interests, and for the maintenance of the peace of Europe. Whilst we act in perfect concert, and hold the same language, we shall speak with dignity and weight, to the several courts, with whom we may be concerned and there can be no doubt of our being heard with attention. (PRO SP 91/71 f 253)

The significance of such language is open to debate. Did it demonstrate a foolish inability to accept the differing views of other powers and the emptiness of the 'Old System', or was it the habitual tone of diplomatic approach, the customary attempt to describe a sense of shared interest as the background for more defined negotiation? If the former is stressed then a negative portrayal of British policy is offered; if the latter, a more sympathetic and arguably sensitive perspective is possible, one that does not preclude critical judgements of particular episodes or individual Secretaries of State, but that directs attention instead to the play of circumstances and individuals. In short, a concentration on the language used may be misleading if it is both held to indicate rigidity of thought and employed as an explanatory device for policy.

The years after the Seven Years' War can be presented as a period in which a position of and reputation for strength were lost and dissipated by foolish policies, an unwillingness to make the necessary commitments to foreign powers, and the effects of domestic political strife (Scott 1990). It was certainly true that many of the ministers in the post-war period lacked a determination to win allies. However, rather than presenting this as both a consequence of folly and as the loss of a strong position, it is more appropriate to suggest that Britain had little to offer as an ally, especially to major powers such as Austria, Prussia and Russia. This had been less true when George I, George II and Newcastle had sought to intervene actively with schemes such as the anti-Russian league in 1719–20 and the Imperial Election Scheme, but it would be misleading to suggest that Britain wielded considerable influence in the first six decades of the century and lost it subsequently. Her influence had been only episodic in the earlier period, as Peter the Great showed when he defied George I. The fate of Poland was plotted by its neighbours before the death of Augustus II in 1733 with as little interest in western European views as was to be shown in 1772, when the country was first partitioned. Anti-Prussian schemes in the latter stages of the War of the Austrian Succession had to be kept secret and could not be pushed, despite George II's support, because of the opposition of the British ministry who wished to concentrate on the French threat. The views of Pelham and other ministers had limited Newcastle's room for manoeuvre in his post-1748 diplomacy of commitment and cost. As France played a lesser rôle in central and eastern Europe in the 1760s than she had done in the 1730s and 1740s, so the attraction to powers there of allying with Britain in order to counter France decreased.

Even had Britain allied with Austria, Prussia or Russia after 1763 there is little reason to believe that she would have enjoyed much influence with her ally, or even been consulted. This was suggested by her experience with Austria in 1731–3 and 1748–55 and with Prussia in 1756–63. Arguably, this was true of all alliances between major powers, but there was little reason for Britain to expose herself to the financial, diplomatic and domestic political costs of such an arrangement after the Seven Years' War. British fame in the early 1760s reflected naval and colonial successes. It did not translate readily into substantial forces in north Germany.

The best point of comparison for Britain's Continental position after 1763 was not her commitment of forces to Germany from 1758, an expensive and precarious business, but the period 1751–6. Then Britain had found it difficult to win Russia as an ally on acceptable terms; had been badly disappointed by Austria's attitude towards the Imperial Election Scheme and the need to strengthen the defence of the Austrian Netherlands, and infuriated by Austria's refusal to offer support during the confrontation with France over America; and had found British influence over her new Prussian ally limited.

The centrepiece of much British Continental diplomacy in that period had been a collective security system that would protect Hanover. When this was removed, many British ministers adopted a more circumspect approach to possible commitments, one that took greater note of the facts of British capabilities, political and financial. When a Russian minister told Buckinghamshire in July 1763 that Britain might be of use to Russia in any Turkish war, the diplomat agreed but said that Britain was unlikely to accept any engagement like that 'as it must be the ruin of our Turkey trade' (PRO SP 91/72 f. 51). The Russian terms for an alliance were unanimously rejected by the ministry (HL ST 7 vol. 1, Grenville to Mansfield, 22 Sept. 1763). That December, Sandwich informed Buckinghamshire that 'the situation of his kingdoms did not require, that the king should purchase or solicit an alliance in which the interests of Russia are at least as much connected as those of Great Britain' (PRO SP 91/72 ff. 237–8). Newcastle had in the 1750s used similar language about shared interests, but he had been obliged, because of Hanover, to provide money, which Sandwich refused. In the 1760s, the sense of a recognisably British policy can be seen in official correspondence. Explaining that the principal purpose in trying to cut Franco-Swedish links in 1765 was to prevent France from using the Swedish navy, Edward Sedgwick, an Under-Secretary, wrote 'that object is truly British' (BL Add. 57928 f. 51).

The ministers sought alliances, but with greater caution when events moved from the state of expressions of good will to actual negotiations. As the three major eastern European powers were at, or close to, war in 1768–74, 1778–9 and 1782–3, the caution of these ministers was vindicated. Not only were these conflicts in which Britain had little close interest, but also it was unlikely that these powers would have been able or willing to provide appropriate support to Britain in her confrontations with the Bourbons.

Britain after 1763 was both a 'satisfied' power and one that was not interested in organising diplomatic combinations in order to sustain the international status quo. This reflected the more cautious stance adopted by George III, who was less interested than his predecessors in Hanover, and also by his ministers. It is possible to see this as the triumph of Treasury over Secretaries of State, to argue that such a struggle had characterised relations between Walpole and Townshend, and Pelham and Newcastle, and that the principle of fiscal retrenchment and, therefore, caution in diplomatic commitment triumphed with Grenville and North and was revived in Pitt the Younger's early years as first minister. However, this caution can equally be attributed to a disengagement from the interventionist tradition epitomised by George II, who died in 1760, and Newcastle, who resigned in 1762 as a result of Bute's determination both to wind down British commitments to Prussia and to control the ministry. The incompatibilities presented by the pre-war attempt to strengthen the status quo by alliances with powers – Prussia in 1740, Austria and Russia in 1755 – that wished to overturn it were appreciated more readily in the 1760s.

There was also no domestic constituency for an interventionist diplomacy. Though there was concern about developments in eastern Europe (Horn 1945), there was no widespread or politically influential pressure for any particular course of action. Instead, public and political attention centred on relations with the Bourbons, seen essentially in a maritime, colonial and commercial light, rather than with reference to such central issues of Anglo-Bourbon relations in 1660–1752 as the fate of the Low Countries and the Italian question.

In part, there had been a shift of attention from Continental concerns, though the political consequences of this should not be exaggerated for, in the case of relations with Austria, Prussia and Russia, it is difficult to see the views of the political nation as having much direct diplomatic consequence before or after 1763. Public support for Frederick the Great, the Protestant Hero, helped to sustain the Anglo-Prussian alliance during the Seven Years' War, but it cannot be cited to explain the decision of 1758 to send British troops to Hanover to cover his western flank, or that of 1762 to settle without Frederick. Instead, the views of George II, George III and the leading ministers were crucial. This remained the case after 1763.

The bounds of possible action were suggested by the views of the political nation but these centred on Anglo-Bourbon relations. The chances that Britain would react in a hostile fashion to the First Partition of Poland were therefore limited by the fact that in order to do so she would have to co-operate with France. There had been such co-operation during the negotiations over a partition of the Spanish Empire (1698–1700) and during the Anglo-French alliance (1716–31), though much of the diplomacy of the period was secret, the Anglo-French alliance was presented as defensive and these periods of co-operation were only once pushed to the point of conflict with another power. The Ochakov crisis of 1791, when the Pitt ministry backed away from war with Russia in the face of strong domestic opposition, suggests what might have been the fate of any attempts over the previous three decades to translate intimations of shared Anglo-French views into common action. Thus, domestic opinion did not dictate any particular course of action, but it did reduce the range of diplomatic options.

ANGLO-BOURBON TENSION, 1763–71

Pressing the Earl of Buckinghamshire to accept Russian terms for an alliance with Britain, the Russian Vice Chancellor told him in September 1763 that 'England from the present situation of affairs was much more likely to be engaged in a war than this country' (PRO SP 91/72 f. 132). Tension between Britain and the Bourbons began over the implementation of the peace, Peter Morin, an Assistant Under-Secretary, writing to Under-Secretary Weston on 16 August 1763, 'I can see we don't agree about Dunkirk, and I fancy there has been some squabble at Newfoundland' (WU), but more serious was the acute sensitivity that the powers now devoted to new colonial and maritime differences. This was much more marked than in 1748–52, let alone 1713–37, but, with the extension of British trans-oceanic activity, there were also more points at issue. Colonial matters took a more prominent rôle in British diplomatic correspondence with Paris and in ministerial discussions about foreign policy. There was particular concern about the prospect of France reversing Britain's American gains, and French intrigues were suspected in hostile native actions in both America and India. In September 1763, Halifax pressed the need for the Earl of Hertford, envoy in Paris, to

> be instructed to make strict enquiry, and obtain all possible information of the plans that may have been or still be adopted for the conduct and management of the French interests in America: particularly what they have done or meditate doing to strengthen or extend their colony of Louisiana. Whether they carry on from thence a correspondence with the Indians belonging to the British territory, and whether they have been the instigator of the late massacres committed at the back of our colonies. (BL Add. 57927 f. 90)

In 1764, disputes included a row with France over Newfoundland fisheries and another with Spain over logwood cutters on the Honduran coast, but British firmness brought success in both. The French expulsion of Bermudan salt-pan workers from Turks Island led to British naval preparations and a French climbdown in September 1764, while, early the following year, a similar formula brought success in a dispute over control of the Gambia in West Africa, the fate of which had been left unclear in the Peace of Paris. The ministry was influenced by fear of the popular response, for the unwillingness of ministers to stand up to the Bourbons had been a theme of opposition writing since the Peace of Paris. Grenville wrote to Sandwich on 6 August 1764 concerning Turks Island, to urge 'some immediate step to be taken, as I am convinced that when it is known it will set everybody in a flame' (HL ST 7 vol. 1). Foreign envoys were convinced that ministerial firmness reflected their wish to avoid opposition attacks.

The contrast with Britain's refusal to play any rôle in the Polish election of that year was obvious, but the disputes also underlined the folly of any possible co-operation with France in eastern Europe and the extent to which, as a naval power, Britain was able to confront the Bourbons, still closely allied, successfully. The argument that a France divested of a Continental war would be better able to confront Britain at sea, that Britain needed Continental allies to distract her, suffers from the problems that such a transfer of resources encountered. Naval power was not simply a matter of expenditure.

Grenville fell in July 1765, to be replaced by the Marquis of Rockingham, Sandwich and Halifax as Secretaries being replaced by the Duke of Grafton and General Conway, a governmental change that owed nothing to foreign-policy considerations. During the Rockingham ministry and still more its successor, that of Pitt, now Earl of Chatham (1766–8), there was a revived attempt to win Continental allies. In July 1765, Newcastle wrote to Rockingham that 'as it is intended as far as it shall appear proper and practicable, to follow Mr. Pitt's plan, which had been approved and agreed to by the king', an approach should be made to Prussia, appropriate moves made at Copenhagen, Stockholm and St Petersburg, and the Dutch should be asked to co-operate and be told that 'His Majesty proposes to enter into such defensive alliances and establish such a connection, upon the continent, as may be most proper for preserving the peace' (WW R1 456). This policy was supported by another politician of an earlier generation, Chesterfield, who told Newcastle that governmental 'success at home and abroad depends upon our making an alliance with Russia and Prussia. That he thinks will make both France and Spain execute our treaties' (WVV R1-498). Frederick II's response was not satisfactory, leading George III to stress the importance of mutuality rather than concession as the basis of any alliance (BL Eg. 982 f. 11). Frederick, allied to Catherine II (the Great) of Russia in 1764, did not wish to weaken his influence in the alliance by extending it to encompass George.

This failure should not be over-emphasised, because it was clear from the British rejection, both of Danish and Swedish subsidy requests and of Russian demands that any treaty must include a clause pledging help against Turkey, both that the views of other powers concerning alliance terms required significant British concessions and that the ministry was not willing to offer them. A commercial treaty with Russia and a treaty of friendship with Sweden were no substitute. It is not surprising that in December 1765 Newcastle wrote critically to Rockingham about British foreign policy: 'there is little regard had to foreign affairs and the forming a system of defensive alliances' (WW R1-539). George Macartney, the envoy at St Petersburg, complained that month of 'political economy', an unwillingness to spend money in order to win alliances (Bod. MS Eng. Hist. c. 62 ff. 24–5), as if nothing had changed since Grenville, while, in January 1766, George III indicated to Rockingham his wish that Britain 'be courted not court foreign powers' (WW R1-2137).

Courting resumed under Pitt, with the attempt to create a system with Prussia and Russia to counteract that of Austria, France and Spain. The response was unsatisfactory. Frederick wished neither to dilute his influence in St Petersburg by linking Britain to the existing Prusso-Russian system nor to risk committing himself to help Britain in any conflict with the Bourbons. Catherine was unhappy about the British refusal to support her interests. Newcastle blamed the failure on a lack of British determination, writing in May 1767 of a lost opportunity (BL Add. 6832 f. 57), and two months later he wrote to Rockingham:

> As an old minister and one who has been bred up in thinking that this country could not subsist without proper alliances and connections with foreign powers, I have seen, with the utmost concern, the total neglect of foreign affairs, even by My Lord Chatham, who raised himself and his reputation, by a contrary conduct. If ever this consideration became necessary, I am sorry to say, I know, it is so now. I don't pretend to say, what, or with whom, those alliances, or those connections should be made; that must depend upon circumstances, and the condition, and disposition of the respective powers: but I mean all such connections to be formed upon the principle of preserving the peace; as Sir Robert Walpole, that enemy to foreign connections, always said, *preventive and defensive* . . . [France is] in a condition to strike. (WW R1-81 2)

He returned to the theme of neglect in June 1768. Newcastle's remedy was as inappropriate as it had been in the 1750s. Catherine was not interested in a defensive foreign policy, nor was there any reason to believe that she or Frederick was any more interested in colonial disputes than Austria had been in 1755. In August 1769, Frederick II and Maria Theresa's son Joseph II promised to refrain from joining in any Anglo-French war. Britain faced France over Corsica in 1768 and the Bourbons over the Falkland Islands two years later alone, but there is little reason to think that even had she had allies her position or the result would have been different. Lord North was not alone in the ministry in feeling, as he argued in October 1767, that in the face of the Bourbons it was necessary to consider the fleet (Grafton 423/ 301). High naval costs were a problem in peacetime.

However, the value of naval strength depended on a conviction abroad that Britain intended to use the fleet, and that was lacking in France in 1768, when the British ministry complained without success about the French purchase of Corsica from Genoa and their subsequent occupation of the island in the face of a popular insurgency. The Earl of Rochford, envoy in Paris, thought that the French had been influenced by a view that Britain was weakened by 'party divisions' (PRO SP 78/285 f. 122). It was partly because of their concern with developments that the British assisted in 1769 in the passage of a Russian fleet from the Baltic thither to fight Turkey. In other respects, the ministry devoted little attention to the Russo-Turkey conflict (1768–74), with the important exception of possible French intervention, which led in 1770 to a British warning that Britain could not be an indifferent spectator to French action in the Levant.

Concern centred on Bourbon strength and intentions. The crisis came over the Falkland Islands where on 10 June 1770 a British settlement, Port Egmont, was seized by Spain, which claimed the islands. The government responded with a substantial naval armament and with negotiations in September and October that failed to settle the matter (Tracy 1988). They were encouraged by reports from James Harris, the envoy in Spain, of Spanish weakness, irresolution and concern about British strength. Criticised by Pitt for 'supine neglect or wicked treachery' (*Catalogue of Lyttleton papers*, Sotheby's 1978, 141), and faced by the resignation of one Secretary of State, Viscount Weymouth, who considered the government insufficiently firm, the ministry was helped by French unwillingness to assist Spain, a useful demonstration of the weakness of alliances. The more bellicose French foreign minister, Choiseul, was dismissed on 24 December, and Louis XV pressed Charles III of Spain to make concessions in order to preserve the peace.

The matter was settled on 22 January 1771 by a compromise. Spain promised to restore Port Egmont to the British, while declaring that this concession did not affect its claim to sovereignty, and the British gave a secret, verbal assurance that they would evacuate Port Egmont. The opposition peer Earl Fitzwilliam found the public terms bad enough – 'no satisfaction for the expence incurred . . . and matter of right left open' (WW R1-1350), but the ministry refused Spanish requests to abandon Port Egmont, the troops not being withdrawn until 1775, and then on grounds of economy.

Lord North, who had become First Lord of the Treasury in February 1770, a post he was to hold until March 1782, played a major rôle in the crisis, helping to ensure the maintenance of peace. Like other long-serving First Lords, Walpole, Pelham and Pitt the Younger, North's views were of consequence but, unlike Walpole, whose influence on foreign policy was overshadowed until 1729 by that of Townshend, or Pelham, who found himself expected to finance Newcastle's policies,

North did not have to cope with a powerful Secretary. The Falklands crisis impressed European opinion as evidence of a revival of British strength. The fall of Choiseul and the Spanish restoration of Port Egmont both appeared signs of Bourbon weakness. However, this success could not be translated into diplomatic influence. The failure of earlier attempts to mediate in the Russo-Turkish war was followed by the Russian rejection in June 1771 of a British approach for an alliance, made the previous autumn. The Russians were affected by reports of British political instability, but, more significantly, their activity in eastern Europe had no need of British support.

BRITAIN, THE FIRST PARTITION OF POLAND AND ANGLO-FRENCH RELATIONS 1772–4

In October 1763, the French envoy in London, Guerchy, spoke to Sandwich 'concerning the reports which have lately prevailed concerning the intended dismembering of some parts of Poland and added that any such dismembering ought, if possible, to be prevented, as contrary to the interest of his court as well as ours' (PRO SP 91/72 ff. 155–6). The following month, George III told Guerchy of his desire for good relations, adding that they would be advantageous for the two nations, that other powers benefited from Anglo-French disunion and that this was a reason not to heed their insinuations (AE CP Ang. 452 f. 128). That December, Sandwich told the Russian envoy that Britain was opposed to Polish territorial losses. The agenda of Anglo-French co-operation that was to be pressed by the French in 1772 in response to the First Partition of Poland had therefore already been sketched when Poland became an important issue at the time of possible post-war realignments. However, nothing came of French proposals for co-operation in 1763, Guerchy reporting that the British ministry had assured him that the government neither wished to nor could be involved. (AE CP Ang. 452 f. 41).

Talk of co-operation in eastern Europe was to be revived in 1772 against the background of another thawing in Anglo-French relations. This thawing owed much to Choiseul's replacement, D'Aiguillon (1771–4), who believed that Britain and France must co-operate to limit Russia's rising power in eastern Europe. To woo Britain he adopted a more conciliatory attitude towards Anglo-French relations than that shown by Choiseul. The prospect of French firmness in this field was anyway weakened by Spanish resentment at French conduct during the Falklands crisis, which led in the late spring of 1771 to a British attempt to improve Anglo-Spanish relations. Though there was no marked change, the early 1770s saw a decrease in Anglo-Spanish tension, which contributed to the relative sense of ease about her diplomatic and military position that characterised British ministerial thinking at the time of the Polish crisis, an obvious contrast to the situation in 1756 when Britain had had little option in her response to the outbreak of war on the Continent but to support Frederick unenthusiastically.

The first firm news of the agreement to partition Poland was received in March 1772. Leaving aside likely domestic views, Anglo-French relations were scarcely propitious for a joint response. On 21 February, the Earl of Rochford, the Secretary of State for the Southern Department, informed Earl Harcourt, the envoy in Paris, that if Russia gained the Crimea and the navigation of the Black Sea as a result of the Turkish war, it would be good for British interests and a major blow to the French Levant trade. He wrote of Poland: 'As to the views of the King of Prussia, however His Majesty may for the sake of the free commerce of his subjects wish that they should not take place, it is certainly not with France that he will concert measures to prevent them' and that France might exploit any communications Britain made on that subject (PRO SP 78/284 f. 107). Three weeks later, Rochford expressed concern about French schemes in India, and instructed Harcourt to inform D'Aiguillon that Britain would respond to any increase in French forces there and was opposed to French action against Russia in the Mediterranean. That July, Rochford criticised the French determination to retain Corsica and argued that it harmed any good understanding. Polish appeals for help were ignored and there was considerable pleasure at French discomfiture, for Poland had played an important rôle in French plans for eastern Europe.

Although D'Aiguillon's initial approaches in February and March 1772 for co-operation were unsuccessful, from late May there were signs of a shift in at least the views of George III and Rochford. In late May, Rochford told Guines, the French envoy, that he supported Anglo-French diplomatic action against the partition, while in July George III suggested that he would be glad to facilitate an alliance. The situation was complicated on 19 August 1772 by the French-backed reimposition of monarchical authority in Sweden by Gustavus III. This brought war near, as Russia threatened to intervene and France to respond. Some British ministers hoped that the crisis would lead to a revival in Anglo-Russian relations. The diplomat Joseph Yorke wrote to the Northern Secretary, the Earl of Suffolk, that he hoped the Swedish coup would make 'some courts feel the consequence of His Majesty's friendship and alliance'. Suffolk, who denied as absurd that he was pleased with the coup, argued that this increase in French influence 'cannot be regarded with indifference by the rest of Europe' (PRO SP 78/ 323 f. 320, 84/345; BL Add. 24158 f. 133). Nevertheless, there was little wish to fight France over the matter. Russia was informed that Britain would not oppose France, while France was threatened with naval action in the event of her intervention (Roberts 1967: 286–347).

The Swedish crisis lessened but did not prevent interest in a rapprochement with France which continued to be considered by George III and by Rochford. Guines described it as the latter's 'political dream' (AE CP Ang. 498 f. 453). However, George appears to have abandoned the idea in late October 1772, while Rochford was well aware that it was impracticable for domestic reasons. The effective head of Hanoverian affairs in London told Haslang, the Wittelsbach envoy, that an Anglo-French alliance was dangerous, a view endorsed by Suffolk (Bayr. London 251, 22 Jan. 1773). A secret French mission to London in the spring of 1773 revealed the emptiness of French hopes, while relations were not helped by a British naval mobilisation in April that led the French to abandon plans for Mediterranean naval activity, including a possible attack on the Russian fleet. In May a mutual naval disarmament was arranged, Viscount Stormont, envoy in Paris, writing to his Madrid counterpart, Lord Grantham: 'we may now consider this whole business as over, and hope that there is no probability of any events arising, to endanger the public tranquillity which . . . His Majesty is solicitous to maintain' (BL Add. 24159 f. 77).

Naval power and Bourbon disunity had led to a successful conclusion to the Anglo-French crisis in the spring of 1773. There was an actuality and immediacy about French naval armaments that took precedence over talk of disturbing changes in the European system. Alliance with France was not a logical response to Britain's situation and it is misleading to argue that it was rejected simply because it was too innovative for the British ministry and political nation. Such a realignment would have committed Britain to opposition to the most powerful alliance in Europe. It was unclear what could be done to protect Poland or the Swedish territories of Finland and Pomerania from possible attack by Russia, Prussia and Austria, while Hanover would also have been exposed to attack had Britain opposed these powers. The threat of British naval action had little effect on Russia in 1720 or 1791. Thus, in the short term, an Anglo-French alliance would be implausible diplomatically and unsuccessful militarily. In the longer terms, it was reasonable to hope that the partitioning powers would split and to fear that D'Aiguillon would fall, especially as French politics were very contentious and Louis XV elderly. Both these expectations were to be realised. Indeed, Franco-Spanish relations had been adversely affected by the fall of Choiseul.

The British ministry no more wished to surrender its diplomatic independence to France than it had earlier accepted Russian efforts to commit it in eastern Europe. If distrust had not prevented an Anglo-French alliance in 1716, partially as a response to the advance of Russian power, there was in 1772–3 no impetus comparable to an endangered Protestant succession to drive Britain and France together. Similarly, there was no serious international challenge to hold an alliance together, as there had been from France for Anglo-Austrian alliances in 1689–97 and 1702–13, and was to be again from 1793.

British security now seemed to rest on naval power and that was threatened by the Bourbons, not by the Russian fleet, though relations with Russia became noticeably cooler in 1773 in response to her aggressive attitudes. Russian soundings about a treaty were rejected in May 1773. Rochford instructed Stormont in January 1774 to contradict reports of a close connection with France: 'the court of France endeavours on every occasion to make their present harmony with us subservient to purposes, to which we have not in the smallest degree given encouragement. Any measures that tend to the preservation of the public peace tally so exactly with the king's views, that they cannot but meet with His Majesty's entire approbation' (PRO 78/291 f. 19); but that could not entail a joint policy that would be unpopular, probably unsuccessful and short-term.

There were no mutual allies, no common goals, to hold the two powers together. This was not different from the situation in 1740 and 1754, but then there had also been important differences of opinion over the Continental views of the two powers to keep them apart. By 1774, such differences had become less widespread and less urgent, and it had become easier for the two governments to view each other with less concern. Yet, this did not provide a basis for co-operation. This was readily apparent before the death of Louis XV and the growing crisis in the Thirteen Colonies produced new players and a new agenda of opportunity, rivalry, confrontation, and conflict.

THE AMERICAN WAR 1775–83

From late 1773 relations between Britain and her American colonies came increasingly to dominate ministerial attention. By the late summer of 1774 it was clear that a colonial rebellion was developing, and the following summer news of major armed clashes reached London. Unlike the American crisis of 1753–4, that of 1773–5 was insulated from diplomatic negotiations because it involved subjects, and not another power. However, clearly it would affect Britain's standing and the policies of other powers. On 22 March 1774, D'Aiguillon mentioned America to Stormont for the first time. The envoy replied that the troubles were 'of such a nature as spirit, firmness and temper would certainly cure', adding for Rochford's benefit the reflection that 'on such emergencies the middle way is no way at all . . . procrastination and irresolution have produced numberless evils, but never cured one' (PRO SP 78/291 ff. 184–5).

The war in America introduced new priorities to British foreign policy: a search for powers who would hire troops to Britain and an attempt to prevent maritime powers from trading with the rebels, and otherwise supporting them. In 1775, Russia refused an approach for 20,000 men, but treaties for troops were signed with a number of German states, principally Hesse-Cassel, and their men played a crucial part in allowing British generals to adopt an active rôle in the American war. The maritime powers that were of greatest importance were France and Spain, though concern about their relations with the rebels led to a revival of British diplomatic activity at a number of courts, including Copenhagen, The Hague and Stockholm.

Anglo-French relations remained relatively good until 1776. Though the British ministry was sorry that the death of Louis XV in 1774 led to the fall of D'Aiguillon, the new administration was clearly pacific and concerned with domestic problems, while the French navy was weak. The British were careful to offend neither France nor Spain and in 1774–7 to promote a peaceful settlement of the likeliest cause of Anglo-Bourbon war, the border conflict between Portuguese Brazil and Spanish South America, which led to unsuccessful Portuguese attempts to enlist military assistance from their British ally. The American rebels were disappointed in their hope that war would break out and Britain be obliged to assist Portugal, and therefore that the Bourbon powers would offer them assistance.

French policy altered in the spring of 1776 when a ministerial debate between advocates of peace, led by the finance minister Turgot, who pressed the importance of financial reform, and those, led by the foreign minister Vergennes, who saw an opportunity to defeat Britain, was won by the latter. On 2 May 1776, Louis XVI agreed to provide one million livres in secret aid to the rebels. Turgot resigned ten days later and France began planning for war and strengthening her navy. The British were swiftly aware of the latter as a result of their excellent intelligence network, and their suspicion of France increased, fostered by the rise in French aid to the rebels, the use of French ports by American privateers and the arrival of a number of American agents in Paris. Stormont was by November 1776 convinced 'that much will depend upon the continuance of success in America' (BL Add. 24162 f. 144). Anglo-French relations continued to deteriorate, especially over the issue of French help to privateers, and in June 1777 the British navy was instructed to search any French ships encountered near America. France stepped up her naval preparations and her efforts to win Spanish support. With war apparently near, the British responded by seeking to delay French intervention until they had won in America. They switched in July 1777 from their earlier moderation to threats designed to intimidate. These succeeded in distancing France from the privateers in August-September, but French caution was designed to preserve peace until the situation was deemed ripe for war, and did not preclude increased preparations.

The news of the British surrender at Saratoga in October 1777, which marked the defeat of the plan for crushing the rebellion by isolating New England, reached Europe in early December 1777. It provided an opportune moment for France, whose navy had been considerably strengthened, to increase her support for the Americans. Vergennes overcame Louis XVI's hesitation, and formal Franco-American negotiations began. They were to lead to treaties of commerce and alliance signed on 6 February 1778. The following day, Vergennes wrote to Noailles, the envoy in London, expressing his suspicion of hostile British views on Brest and of an apparent British determination to declare war. He did not see how Britain could fight the Bourbons successfully (AE CP Ang. 528 ff. 289-90, 478). The French treaties amounted to a declaration of war as the Americans were regarded as rebels in London. On 17 March, Noailles was notified of Stormont's recall and Vergennes wrote to him ordering him to leave London, though France did not formally declare war until July 1778.

The outbreak of hostilities led to a revival in British attempts to win allies on the Continent, where the situation appeared more volatile as a result of the growing crisis over the Bavarian succession which led in 1778–9 to an Austro-Prussian conflict. In February 1778, Britain offered Russia an alliance that included a subsidy, though no provision for military assistance in the event of a Russo-Turkish war. The Russians rejected the approach, while British hopes that the French alliance with Austria would lead to her becoming entangled in a Continental war were disabused by the French refusal to support her ally. Vergennes stated in January 1778 that France would not be distracted from America by the Bavarian crisis (AE CP Ang. 528 ff. 103–4, 125). George III's opposition to any Austrian acquisition of Bavaria, combined with concern over the security of Hanover, led him to respond favourably in April 1778 to Prussian approaches. Britain offered Prussia an alliance and, in return for Prussian protection of Hanover, a subsidy. However, reassured about Russian and French attitudes, Frederick II did not respond. The attempt to improve relations with Berlin led to a certain amount of uncertainty among British diplomats. Joseph Yorke was 'sorry that we have gone so far in support of the king of Prussia which may offend Vienna', distrustful of Prussia and conscious of a difference of interests between Britain and Hanover. Hugh Elliot saw 'the king's friendly conduct in his electoral capacity' as likely to please Prussia, but not Austria (BL Add. 35514 f. 170, 35515 f. 54, 35514 f. 242).

Britain, however, was not of central concern for Austria, Prussia and Russia, any more than she had been in 1756. Her views on the Bavarian succession were regarded as of little consequence and the increased gap between the armed forces of the major and those of the minor powers helped to ensure that the views of German states such as Hanover were of less consequence than they had been earlier in the century. Replying in June 1779 to criticisms of the government for the absence of foreign allies, the Attorney General, Alexander Wedderburn, refuted the idea:

'as if it were in their power to oblige foreign courts to enter into alliances with Great Britain . . . no state would enter into an alliance with another unless it stood in need of some assistance, which the other had it in its power to afford . . . the necessity was solely on our side, and therefore it was not at all to be wondered at, that other courts were not much inclined to enter into alliance with us' (Cobbett 1806–20: XX, 945).

The relations that were to be important for Britain in 1779–80 were rather those with Spain and the United Provinces. The ministry sought through negotiations to keep Spain neutral, but the Spaniards were less concerned with British views than with what France was willing to offer in return for Spain's entry into the war. When France promised to fight on until Spain obtained Gibraltar, the Spaniards signed the Convention of Aranjuez with her in April 1779, recalled their envoy from London the following month, and began preparations for a Franco-Spanish invasion of Britain. By 16 August, the joint fleet was within sight of Plymouth. The response in Britain was 'prodigious confusion . . . we have no force to oppose such a number' (WW R1-1844). Fortunately for the British, the Bourbon fleet was affected by divisions, delays, sickness, lack of water, supplies and information, and the weather. These, rather than

British naval actions, were responsible for the failure of what had been a serious threat. The British diplomat Sir Robert Murray Keith commented: 'surely never was such a prodigious force so completely misapplied' (HL HM 18940 p. 151).

Disputes with the Dutch over their trade with Britain's enemies and over the reception of American privateers embittered relations. The once close alliance had been a casualty of the Diplomatic Revolution, which made the defence of the Low Countries against France no longer credible diplomatically or militarily, as well as of Dutch financial exhaustion, war-weariness and domestic divisions, and lack of Dutch support for Britain's colonial and maritime position. The Dutch had played no rôle in the Seven Years' War and relations thereafter had not been close, though British ministers had continued to assume that they could and should be. The British believed that, under the defensive treaty of 1678, they were entitled to Dutch help against the Bourbons in the American war, while the Dutch were angered by British treatment of their merchantmen.

The cause of neutral trade was taken up by Catherine II who saw it as a possible source of influence for Russia. Having rejected in the winter of 1779–80 the British idea of a Russian mediation, Catherine issued a Declaration of Neutral Rights in March 1780 that was designed to protect neutral shipping from British maritime pretensions which were widely disliked in Europe. Sweden and Denmark joined the Armed Neutrality that July and the British, aware of negotiations for Dutch accession, declared war on the Dutch on 20 December 1780, hoping to end their supply of naval stores to France before they could accede and thus acquire a Russian guarantee. The British ministry hoped that this Fourth Anglo-Dutch war would somehow lead to the revival of the pro-British Orangist party, as defeat in 1672 and 1747 had led to a revival of Orangist power, but these hopes were to be disappointed.

Though by 1781 Britain faced France, Spain and the Dutch, as well as the Americans, the situation was not completely bleak. The Bourbons had found the war more expensive and less successful than they had anticipated, while the British were able to go on financing their high level of war expenditure, largely through borrowing. Secret negotiations with France in the summer and December of 1780 were hampered by the British refusal to discuss the position of the Americans with a third party and the French determination to obtain American independence, while Gibraltar proved the stumbling block in Anglo-Spanish negotiations that lasted from November 1779 until March 1781. Austrian and Russian attempts to mediate were unsuccessful, as were British offers in early 1781 of support for the opening of the Scheldt and of Minorca to Austria and Russia respectively, in order to win their alliance.

The diplomatic impasse was cleared by military defeat. The North ministry could have survived the loss of West Florida and the failure to relieve Minorca in 1781, but Cornwallis's surrender to blockading American-French forces at Yorktown in October 1781 led to a collapse of political nerve in London (Conway 1995). Independent MPs, no longer convinced that success was possible, deserted North and he resigned on 20 March 1782.

PEACE NEGOTIATIONS 1782–3

The Rockingham ministry which succeeded that of North was pledged to negotiate peace. Charles James Fox occupied the new post of Foreign Secretary, replacing the former division of responsibility between two Secretaries of State. He hoped for an alliance with Prussia and Russia, but he was more concerned to obtain peace. To that end, Fox was ready to yield independence to America, as Thomas Grenville, sent to Paris as minister in May 1782, was instructed (PRO FO 27/2 f. 43). Grenville told Vergennes that, except for American independence, the peace should repeat the terms of the Peace of Paris, adding that 'the independence of America would be a point gained more essential to the interest of France in the separation of Thirteen Provinces from England, than any acquisition we had made by the last peace, had been to us'. Vergennes responded that Louis XVI could not consider American independence as a concession to France and that he sought a 'more just and durable' treaty than the Peace of Paris (PRO FO 27/ 2 ff. 60–1). Both Fox and Grenville argued that France would be more accommodating once separated from America. Negotiations were complicated by the attitude of the Earl of Shelburne, the Home and Colonial Secretary, who supported American independence only as part of a general peace, advocated co-operation with France in European diplomacy, and sent his own envoy, Richard Oswald, to Paris to negotiate. Fox found himself in a minority in the cabinet, while George III supported Shelburne.

The crisis was resolved by the death of Rockingham in July 1782. George called on Shelburne to lead the ministry and Fox resigned, to be replaced by Lord Grantham, who had been ambassador to Spain from 1771 to 1779. Shelburne played a crucial rôle in the peace negotiations until he resigned on 24 February 1783. He was well aware that he faced a difficult task. George III had to be persuaded to accept the loss of America, while the political nation would have to confront the consequences of Britain's most unsuccessful war since the 1620s. Shelburne believed that secrecy, not consultation, was the best way to achieve Britain's goals. He informed Grantham that he had told the Spanish envoy

> that we could never think of anything which was not fundamentally agreeable to Parliament, but that there was a great deal of difference between coming to Parliament for a yes or no, and Parliament's meeting while things were depending, and more or less public. Such was the case of the Gibraltar article. Such I am sure will be that of the rest of the articles, if not immediately concluded. Persons interested in East and West Florida will take the alarm some for their propertys others for their trade. The Mediterranean merchants will cry up Minorca. The Mosquito Indians will find allys in Parliament . . . you may perhaps insinuate to him that the same reasoning, which has proved applicable to Parliament applys in some degree to Council, which for the sake of all concerned had better be to say yes or no. (Bedford CRO L 30/14/306/1).

Shelburne hoped to establish a close relationship with independent America, thus ensuring that the wartime Franco-American alliance did not survive the peace. He saw America as a country of economic possibility for Britain, a valuable alternative to European markets closed by tariffs. To these ends, America was given a more favourable north-western frontier than she had expected, yielding her the 'Old North West', the area between the Great Lakes and the Ohio, though the British kept Canada. Preliminaries of an Anglo-American peace were signed in Paris in November 1782.

In certain respects Britain's position vis-à-vis the Bourbons became more favourable in 1782. Rodney's victory over the French fleet at the Saints in April restored the prestige of British naval power and saved Jamaica. Bourbon attempts to capture Gibraltar failed. Vergennes was aware that in financial and naval terms the war appeared to be going Britain's way. Her naval strength was increasing rapidly, while financially the Bourbons were succumbing to the strain of war. Though without any ally to distract the Bourbons, the British were increasingly winning the naval race, especially as their North American commitment was ebbing (Black and Woodfine 1988: 161–3). Vergennes was also increasingly concerned about developments in eastern Europe, specifically Russian designs on the Turkish Empire, and wanted France to be in a position to oppose them.

This objective was shared by Shelburne, who believed that Anglo-French co-operation could counteract the strength of Austria, Prussia and Russia, a view that George III came to support. This idea had been last discussed in the spring of 1777, when Noailles had pressed Weymouth on the need to prevent the partition of the Turkish Empire and Vergennes instructed him to press Britain to urge Russia to show restraint. However, Vergennes had not then sought negotiations on the matter (AE CP Ang. 522 ff. 117–22, 134,162–3, 401). America was then the first priority and the situation in the Balkans not as threatening as it was to become with the Austro-Russian alliance of 1781.

Despite his desire for co-operation, Shelburne defended British interests against the French desire to reverse as much of the 1763 settlement as possible. Grenville had warned Fox in May 1782 that Spain wanted Florida and Gibraltar, France alterations in the state of the Newfoundland fisheries, Caribbean gains, and 'very extensive surrenders of commerce and territory in the East Indies'. Vergennes told him, the following month, that, far from the Peace of Paris serving as the basis of a new treaty, it 'should be annulled except in certain specified articles' (PRO FO 27/2 ff. 72, 132). Shelburne, however, rejected the idea of France having more in India than the trading stations she had been left in 1763 with the argument that 'it was not to be expected that the king would cede two continents' (Bedford CRO L 30/14/306/36). The British position was helped by Bourbon defeats and difficulties, by the Anglo-American preliminaries, and by the French fear that Shelburne would fall if he could not present Parliament with acceptable terms. In December, Vergennes persuaded the Spanish envoy Aranda to drop the demand for Gibraltar, which had become the principal obstacle to peace. As a result, Anglo-Bourbon peace preliminaries were signed in Paris on 20 January 1783.

The following month, Shelburne was defeated in the Commons debates over the peace preliminaries, but these were defeats for the 'universally disliked' Shelburne (BL Add. 35528 f. 27), rather than for the peace (PRO FO 27/6 ff. 57–8), although the terms were genuinely unpopular, especially the lack of any guarantees for the Loyalists and for British debts. After defeats on 17 and 21 February, Shelburne resigned on 24 February. The Fox-North ministry that replaced Shelburne accepted the preliminaries.

On 3 September 1783, the peace with the Bourbons and with America was signed at Versailles. France won minor territorial gains, including Tobago and Senegal, and consent to the fortification of Dunkirk. Spain obtained Florida and Minorca (Scott 1998). The treaty with the Dutch, who had suffered badly in the war, was not signed until the following May. The Dutch lost Negapatam, an Indian 'Factory' (trading station), and conceded the right to 'navigate' in the Dutch East Indies, which had hitherto been maintained as a monopolistic trading preserve.

The peace settlement as a whole saw Britain lose the most important part of her empire, the Thirteen Colonies, and contemporaries suspected both that this loss would mark a fundamental weakening of the empire and that France would follow up her success by challenging British power elsewhere. In early 1783, there was concern about secret French aid to anti-British rulers in India. Such threats appeared more important than the actual losses to the Bourbons at Versailles. That these gloomy predictions were to be proved wrong owed little to Shelburne's confidence in the prospect of Anglo-French co-operation, though he was to be proved correct about the possibility of revived Anglo-American commercial links. Instead it was to be French weakness that was decisive, a weakness that owed much to the financial strains of her war with Britain. To a certain extent, the French collapse in the Dutch crisis of 1787 was the last act in the American war and a testimony to the greater potency of British resources.

CHAPTER TWELVE

BRITISH FOREIGN POLICY 1783–93

IN THE SHADOW OF FRANCE, 1783–7

In the spring of 1783 two contradictory instructions were sent to British envoys. On 22 February 1783, Grantham wrote to Keith in Vienna that war was likely in the Balkans.

> In that situation of affairs, and considering that which distinguishes this country on the restoration of peace, it is impossible to hold any precise language or indeed throw out any which should seem to encourage a renewal of war in Europe. The court of France is anxious that we should concur in some plan of neutrality. I have in general admitted the eligibility of such a system but at the same time have carefully avoided committing His Majesty in any measures which should preclude him from taking such part as may suit his interests and those of his kingdoms. (PRO FO 7/6)

Two months later, Fox wrote to the Duke of Manchester at Paris: 'An intimate connection, or if possible a strict alliance with the northern maritime powers of Europe is the obvious and rational system for this country and more especially as long as the Bourbon Family Compact continues to be in force' (PRO FO 27/6 f. 169). Differences over how committed Britain should be in Continental affairs and with whom affected British policy until the autumn of 1787 when, with the Dutch crisis, she adopted an interventionist policy based on co-operation with Prussia that was to last until the Ochakov Crisis of early 1791.

The last years of the American war had witnessed vigorous efforts to win Continental allies. In December 1780, Stormont ordered Keith to take advantage of Joseph II's accession in Vienna to propose an alliance of Britain, Austria and Russia. However, the Austrian Chancellor, Kaunitz, resisted the lure of support for the opening of the Scheldt, whose closure under the Peace of Westphalia of 1648 was blamed for the economic weakness of the Austrian Netherlands. Stormont wrote in early 1781 of Kaunitz's support for an Austro-Russian alliance and for Austria counteracting Prussian influence in St Petersburg, but when an alliance between Austria and Russia was negotiated neither power informed Britain. In early 1782, Stormont returned to the theme of using Austria to influence Russia and sought to persuade Vienna to see Europe in terms of the struggle against French influence, but he was forced to appreciate that the Austro-Russian alliance would be of no immediate benefit to Britain. However, he was hopeful that the gathering crisis in the Balkans would strain Austro-French relations, an essential precondition in his eyes to any reassessment by Joseph of his position towards Britain.

Fox (Foreign Secretary March–July 1782, April–December 1783) was more hopeful of creating an Anglo-Prusso-Russian system, an aspiration that flew in the face of the Austro-Russian realignment. In contrast, Grantham, Foreign Secretary under Shelburne July 1782–April 1783), was hopeful that Austrian support for Russia's Balkan schemes against Turkey, whose territorial integrity France traditionally sought to preserve, would lead to an end of the Austro-French alliance. In August 1783, Fitzherbert, the new envoy to Russia, was instructed to negotiate an Anglo-Russian treaty. With the exception of the Shelburne ministry, hostility to France was the central theme in this period. Fox saw an Anglo-Russian alliance as a counter-balance to Bourbon power and informed Fitzherbert on 11 October 1783 that it was not in Britain's interest to prevent Russia from having warships in the Black Sea, as the French wanted: 'we are far from acting in any concert with France or with any similar views' (PRO FO 65/11). The envoy in Constantinople, Sir Robert Ainslie, was ordered the following month to co-operate with the Russian envoy, and copies of his instructions were sent to St Petersburg.

No other power, however, shared Britain's hostility to France, and Britain's views were treated as of little consequence. Engaged in war and then complex peace negotiations, she appeared too weak to act as a credible ally and had little anyway to offer the eastern-European powers. Furthermore, British political instability, which in 1780–1 reached an apparent high point with the Gordon Riots in London, the Yorkshire Association and a political and constitutional crisis in Ireland, was followed in 1782–4 by ministerial instability, with rapid changes of government. Anyone asked at the beginning of the 1780s to state which major European power would face a revolution before the end of the decade would probably have replied Britain, not France or Austria. These problems led to reasonable ministerial fears both for Britain's foreign reputation and that she would find it difficult to acquire allies. Grantham wrote to Keith in February 1783 that he hoped 'that our civil revolutions may not destroy all confidence from abroad in our councils' (BL Add. 35528 ff 22).

The year 1783 closed with a political crisis in Britain, and Fox too busy to reply to Keith's reports. George III's opposition led to the fall of the Fox-North government. The new ministry, that of William Pitt the Younger with Francis, Marquis of Carmarthen as Foreign Secretary, sought Continental allies and attempted unsuccessfully to prevent the consolidation of the Franco-Dutch alliance, though Pitt's principal priority was financial retrenchment. The diplomat James Harris was convinced that the new government would make little difference to foreign policy and in December 1783 he sent Keith an interesting letter claiming that policy was not greatly affected by domestic changes:

> . . . the same system will be pursued . . . however fluctuating we may be at home we shall be systematick as far as relates to the continent, for I am now convinced by experience of what I have so often taken upon me to say from presumption that it is neither candid or wise in foreign courts to suppose that our sentiments relative to them alter with any change of administration here. To recover our weight on the continent by judicious alliances is the general wish of every man the least acquainted with the interests of this country, and this object will be pursued with the same assiduity whether Mr. Fox or Lord Carmarthen is the channel through which the king's sentiments are to pass. (BL Add. 35530 ff 27–7)

That month, Carmarthen sent both Ainslie and Fitzherbert instructions stressing continuity with those sent by Fox. In January 1784, Keith was pressed to dissolve the 'unnatural' Austro-French alliance. Carmarthen hoped that France could be diverted by Continental affairs from 'her plans of resentment and ambition in the East Indies' (PRO FO 7/8, 23 April 1784). Hopes of both Austria and Russia, however, proved abortive in 1784. Furthermore, Carmarthen was aware that ministerial colleagues were more concerned about domestic affairs. He noted of the cabinet in 1784: 'I found I could not prevail upon them to give that attention to foreign affairs that I thought necessary, and consequently afterwards gave them little trouble on the subject.' In May 1784, Carmarthen discussed European affairs with Pitt.

> I was very happy to find our ideas were similar on the great object of separating if possible the House of Austria from France, as likewise a degree of desire to form some system on the continent in order to counterbalance the House of Bourbon, though at the same time the strongest conviction of the necessity of avoiding, if possible, the entering into any engagements likely to embroil us in a new war. (BL Add. 27918 ff. 121–2)

The following year, Carmarthen was angered by the Austrian failure to inform Britain about her plans to exchange the Austrian Netherlands for Bavaria. As a result, it was decided to sound Joseph II's principal rival, Frederick II, and, on 14 May 1785, Carmarthen wrote to Joseph Ewart, envoy in Berlin.

> France and Austria apparently connected in the closest manner and no doubt concurring in the mutual support of each others bold and ambitious project, the most natural mode of proceeding in order to prevent the mischievous effect of their designs appears to be endeavouring to detach from their cause those powers on whose assistance they principally rely. And as such Holland as well as Russia should now be regarded. (PRO FO 64/7)

Frederick was unwilling to support Britain's antipathy to France and her desire to keep her out of the United Provinces, though the previous year the Prussian envoy in London had told Carmarthen that Frederick wanted to stop French progress there. In the autumn of 1785, Earl Cornwallis, who was going to Prussia to attend the military manoeuvres, was instructed to act in a confidential manner, without any ostensible mission, in order to probe the possibility of improved relations. His instructions from Carmarthen reveal the central rôle that France played in British concerns and the difference that was drawn between cultivating friendly conduct and committing the government, a distinction that was crucial to British diplomacy in the decades after 1763.

> The earnest desire of the King of Prussia to open a more direct and confidential intercourse with England, I am apt to believe, originates rather in a desire of sounding the intentions of this court, than from any real intention of a fair and candid communication either of future views or even of present opinions: it behoves us, however, at all events to cultivate this apparently friendly conduct on the part of that Prince, and, by not committing ourselves, to meet him precisely upon his ground . . . before any serious connexion could be entered into with Prussia, it would be absolutely necessary to know how far that power might be depended upon in respect to France, and whether the former intercourse between them was either diminished or maintained; and the only circumstance which could probably totally break that intercourse would be the King of Prussia discovering some new plan of aggrandizement, projected by the Emperor in concert with, and to be supported by, the Court of Versailles. Should such an event take place, this country must then give up all hopes of an alliance with the Emperor; at the same time Prussia could no longer reckon upon the assistance of France; and in that case it might be prudent for England and Prussia to form a more close and intimate connexion.

Frederick, however, though claiming to be impressed by the state of Britain's public finances compared with those of France, and by Pitt's 'plan of strict economy', said that there was no point in an Anglo-Prussian alliance because they were too weak.

That the balance of power, which England had so long and so strenuously supported was lost; that France, Spain, Austria, and Russia were in alliance . . . . He said France and Austria were closely connected, because France wished to be able to turn her whole force to her Marine, and against England; and that the Emperor's alliance secured her from a continental war.

Frederick also warned about French attempts to foment disaffection in Ireland, a prospect that had worried Carmarthen the previous September. (C. Ross (ed.), *Correspondence of . . . Cornwallis* I, 196–203; BL Eg. 3498).

Thus, in Frederick's analysis, growing British domestic strength did not entail a stronger international position, because Continental alignments were hostile to her. The attraction of Britain as a possible ally would depend not upon Pittite stability and financial reforms, but upon shifts in these alignments and the possibilities for action presented from 1787 by Austrian and Russian involvement in the Balkans, and increasing French and Austrian instability.

Despite a lack of warmth in Austro-French relations, the British ministry was driven to share Prussia's hostility to Austria, in large part due to George III's determination as Elector of Hanover to oppose the Bavarian Exchange Scheme, a plan to exchange the Austrian Netherlands for Bavaria, which would have greatly increased Austrian power in the Empire. Carmarthen was not apparently kept informed about Hanoverian policy, and when Hanoverian participation in the *Fürstenbund*, the anti-Austrian German League of Princes founded on 23 July 1785, led to difficulties in Britain's attempts to improve relations with Austria and especially Russia, and serious complaints from both, Carmarthen blamed Hanover. However, prior to the complaints, Carmarthen seems to have been prepared to defend what he knew of the *Fürstenbund*, treating it as a necessary response to Joseph's ambitious schemes, and to have been keen on the prospect of better Anglo-Prussian relations. It was the Russian, rather than the Austrian, complaints that aroused disquiet, as did the sense that, far from forcing Austria to adopt a more acceptable position, George's policy had restricted Britain's options.

Carmarthen might complain about the effect of the *Fürstenbund*, but Joseph and Kaunitz, conscious of Anglo-French antipathy, regarded the prospect of a British alliance without favour for the latter reason. Despite Carmarthen's hopes, Austria did not press her dispute that autumn with the United Provinces over Maastricht to the point of conflict, and France proved unwilling to support her Dutch ally conspicuously during the dispute.

Britain ended 1785 with the prospect of Russia improving her relations with France and with Prussia unwilling to confront France over the United Provinces, and it was not surprising that in early 1786 Carmarthen, justifying the *Fürstenbund* as a defensive measure, ordered Keith to approach Joseph again. Joseph, however, was not interested in turning against France, which was what Carmarthen sought, and the Austrians were suspicious of Anglo-Prussian relations. As the possibility of a Balkan conflict increased in the summer, Carmarthen returned to the old hope that French ties with the Turks would anger Austria, and therefore hesitated about any improvement of relations with Prussia. The year 1786 passed without any improvement in Anglo-Austrian relations, but also without either any negotiation of an alliance with Prussia or any major international disturbance that might lead to a realignment of the powers.

The possibility of a realignment was instead suggested by Anglo-French negotiations. The Pitt ministry launched attempts to negotiate commercial agreements with a number of Continental powers, including Naples, Portugal, Russia and Sweden (Ehrman 1962), but none was as politically important as that with France, and the initiative there lay with the French.

The Treaty of Versailles had stipulated commercial negotiations with France and Spain, but the British ministry had to be pressed by the French to begin serious negotiations. Vergennes wished to neutralise British hostility to French diplomatic predominance in western Europe by means of an agreement favourable to her. The Eden Treaty, essentially an agreement to reduce some tariffs and remove some import bans, signed on 26 September 1786, was criticised by opposition politicians, one of whom, Philip Francis, told the Commons in February 1787 that 'there may be a strict union between the two crowns though never between the two nations', while Henry Flood stated that 'the idea of rendering peace durable by entering into a commercial treaty with France was, as experience proved, a false suggestion'.

More interesting was the criticism of the apparent tenor of government policy from within the ministry. Pitt declared in the Commons debate over the treaty on 12 February 1787 that 'to suppose that any nation could be unalterably the enemy of another, was weak and childish'. Carmarthen, in contrast, was hostile to any idea that the negotiations should have a political effect. Distrust of France was deeply engrained in Britain, and it was widely believed that the French intended to follow up their success in America by undermining the British position in Canada, Ireland and India. French diplomatic, colonial and naval schemes were viewed with considerable disquiet. Typical of the attitudes of British diplomats was the view of Daniel Hailes, an envoy in Paris, in November 1785 that 'India now is the part of the world we are to look at . . . possessing so much as we do in that part of the world, we cannot desire to disturb our neighbours: If any dispute shall arise France will be the aggressor', or that of Sir James Harris, envoy at The Hague, the following month, that France never acted with sincerity and uprightness, and of the Duke of Dorset, the ambassador in Paris, best known for allowing a dancer to dance in his Garter ribbon at the Paris Opéra, who wrote, on 9 February 1786, that William Eden:

> will never make anything of a Treaty of Commerce. They will make up something to sign and quarrel about it in six month time. We never can agree long. It is quite impossible. Everything bears the appearance of tranquillity, but I believe the cabinet at Versailles is working hard in every cabinet in Europe . . . the spirit of intrigue which Vergennes is endowed with is more dangerous in my opinion to the balance of power than all the mighty armies of Louis XIV. (BL Add. 35535 ff. 265, 325; Beinecke, Osborn Files, Dorset)

It was scarcely surprising that the Eden Treaty, which was blamed in France for an increase in British manufactured exports and for French industrial problems, did not yield political benefits. It could not compensate for growing British concern about French influence in the United Provinces. The Dutch bases of Cape Town and Ceylon appeared to threaten the route to India, while the Dutch navy, though not large, would be an unwelcome addition to French power. The United Provinces were divided by a struggle for power between the Patriots, an essentially bourgeois party based mostly in the cities of the west, and the Orangists. The former were supported by France and the latter by Britain, in large part due to the pressure from Harris, the British envoy (Cobban 1954).

In the summer of 1787, the British attitude towards France hardened, largely thanks to an almost obsessive concentration on the Dutch struggle to the detriment of other aspects of Anglo-French relations. The Dutch crisis was resolved as the result of a Prussian invasion on behalf of the Orangists. Frederick II's successor, Frederick William II, had been very undecided, but British diplomatic efforts helped to secure the invasion (Matlock CRO 239 M/O 759, Ewart to Duke of York, 1 Aug.). It was supported by a demonstration of British naval strength, designed to discourage the French from acting. The French threatened to intervene, but, in face of the speed and success of the Prussian invasion, British pressure and their own domestic problems, they desisted. That November, Fox welcomed what he saw as the acknowledgement by the government:

> 'that those systems of politics, which had on former occasions been called romantic, were serious systems, and such as it was the true interest of this country to be governed by; namely, systems established on that sound and solid political maxim, that Great Britain ought to look to the situation of affairs upon the continent, and to take such measures upon every change of circumstances abroad, as should tend best to preserve the balance of power in Europe' (Cobbett XXV, 1806–20:1234).

ANGLO-FRENCH RELATIONS 1787–93

> During the whole course of the troubles which have so much distracted the kingdom of France, His Majesty has observed the most exact and scrupulous neutrality, abstaining from taking any step which might give encouragement or countenance to any of the parties which have prevailed there, or from mixing himself in any manner whatever in the internal dissensions of that country. It is His Majesty's intention still to adhere to this line of conduct, unless any new circumstances should arise by which His Majesty should be of opinion that the interests of his subjects would be affected, and even in that case any measures to be taken by His Majesty would be directed to that object only. (Foreign Secretary Lord Grenville, 19 September 1791 – PRO FO 7/28)

The crucial fact of French weakness was revealed, or possibly rather created, in 1787, and it is from that year that the 'French Revolution' may be said to have begun in so far as international relations were concerned. French weaknesses were adduced as an explanation for the French failure to act in the Dutch crisis and, to a certain extent, this view was correct. However, these weaknesses, particularly those related to financial considerations, had not prevented France from taking an active rôle in European diplomacy in recent years, nor were they to prevent revolutionary France from following an active course of action from 1792. The French government had a choice as to whether or not to act and the defeat of those ministers who pressed for an aggressive policy was very significant in affecting foreign views, and thus France's international position.

The Dutch crisis was a severe blow to French prestige, while the loss of her alliance to Britain helped to ease British fears about French plans in the Indian Ocean. In 1790–1, Britain benefited from the prospect of

Dutch naval assistance in her disputes with Russia and Spain. The Dutch crisis broke the spell of Anglo-French co-operation that Vergennes had sought to weave, and the after-effects hindered any improvement in relations. Britain determined to consolidate her position in the United Provinces by widening her relations with Prussia rather than repairing those with France. As Vergennes' successor, Montmorin, sought to exploit Austrian and Russian fears of and hostility towards Prussia, this helped to ensure that a better Anglo-Prussian understanding was associated with increased suspicion between Britain and France. The Dutch crisis had left a legacy of bitterness and suspicion on both sides, engendered by the fears, intrigues and humiliation of the confrontation. The Anglo-French convention on India, signed in August 1787, did not allay British fears. In November 1788, Barthélemy, a French diplomat in London, complained that whatever France did she could not calm British governmental anxiety about her plans for the Indian Ocean. It was not until the breakdown of order in France in 1789 that British fears eased. The Third Mysore War (1790–2) was made considerably easier for the British by the fact that their Indian enemy, Tipu Sultan, unlike the American rebels, received very little foreign assistance.

The rôle of colonial concerns in keeping Anglo-French tension high is an intangible one. There is no doubt that, in both the colonies and commerce, competition was seen as the order of the day. Both governments, concerned about the fiscal implications of commercial strength, were also pressed by mercantile groups to provide support against foreign competition. Aside from the particular points at dispute and the specific groups involved, these issues served both to encapsulate and to exacerbate more general tendencies of suspicion and fear. It is clear that mutual suspicions were based on fear. Once the balance of military and diplomatic advantage had moved against France in 1787, there were fears there of hostile British actions and intrigues. These fears preceded the events of 1789. The inter-relationship of domestic troubles and foreign policy, and an atmosphere of fear and suspicion, spanned the outbreak of the French Revolution, rather than being created by it.

For the French, the alarming perception of weakness, both domestic and foreign, brought similar fears to those that had affected Britain a decade earlier: a concern about foreign intervention in internal affairs and a fear that her colonies would be lost. Whereas Britain shared the former place in the demonology of Revolutionary France with, in particular, Austria, her naval strength and colonial presence caused the latter fear to be centred on her. Just as British ministers and diplomats worried that diplomatic isolation would make them vulnerable to French schemes in India in 1783–7, so their French counterparts expressed concern over their Caribbean colonies, which were the basis of the tremendous growth of French foreign trade in the 1780s (Duffy 1987: 5–23). The idea that the British government would seek to benefit from France's diplomatic isolation and internal disorders was axiomatic, especially when these disorders spread to the French colonies. British assurances were treated as hypocritical, doubts being expressed about the intentions of both George III and Pitt.

French diplomats were aware of British sympathy for developments in their country from 1789, indeed tended to exaggerate its scale and impact, both actual and potential, and at times suggested that members of the ministry, even including Pitt, might be sympathetic or, more commonly and realistically, opposed to hostile action. Even so, these diplomats were convinced that any positive attitudes and action were being and would be thwarted by hostile groups. The rôle of George III was seen as sinister, and it was alleged that he worked through a cabal of ministers, particularly Lord Hawkesbury, President of the Board of Trade, and Lord Chancellor Thurlow, whom he sought to promote and who shared his views. Pitt's position was presented as threatened by the royal cabal and weak or precarious, British politics as a struggle between king and minister. This view of secret cabals and intrigue fitted well with the conspiracy beliefs of the Revolutionaries, but it was no new development. Paranoia characterised the unstable world of *ancien régime* diplomacy, was indeed a natural product of the intrigue that characterised court societies, and Catherine II was not alone in attributing a *secret du roi* to George III. The accuracy of this view is difficult to assess, as George's rôle in foreign policy in the early 1790s is an obscure one, though it accords with the modem tendency to stress the continued influence of the monarchy.

Naturally suspicious both of Britain and of monarchical governments, that of Revolutionary France could only have been made more so by the reports received from French agents in London, both official and unofficial. Furthermore, the fact that the links between the Revolutionary government and the British political world were closest with a section of the British opposition exacerbated the situation, for the opposition was suspicious of royal influence, the general direction of British foreign policy and ministerial attitudes towards France. Criticism was voiced in Parliament and the press, suspicion was endemic, belief in intrigue and intrigues widespread. It was scarcely surprising that the views of the opposition were transmitted to France and influenced French assumptions.

The British ministerial attitude to the linked questions of French domestic difficulties, their effects on France's strength and foreign policy, and the consequences for Anglo-French relations was neither uniform nor constant. Attention varied. In 1787, the novelty of developments in France, the meeting of the Assembly of Notables, and the potential clash between the two countries led to great interest in French development in British political circles. By the end of 1787, the attitude towards France's internal situation that was to prevail until late 1792 was firmly established. France was seen as enfeebled, weakened by ministerial instability and encroaching civil disorder, likely to become weaker, but yet possibly on the eve of a revival in strength and unity if circumstances, policy and leadership permitted. The latter was also the view held in French governmental circles, with the additional conviction that problems were due in part to external intervention and that hostile foreign forces might seek to prevent revival, because French difficulties suited their purposes by allowing them to pursue policies in other fields and at the expense of France. Just as, in Britain, French difficulties were seen to work to the national advantage and the prospect of their removal aroused speculation and concern, so in France this situation was seen by many as explaining allegations of British interference in their concerns.

Because French instability was seen as beneficial by the British, French affairs were followed closely in the winter of 1787-8 when a French riposte to their Dutch débacle was anticipated. The possibility of reform, or at least altered circumstances, bringing renewed strength was never far from the minds of at least some British commentators but, nevertheless, by the summer of 1788 this idea was not prominent.

As if to illustrate the unpredictability of international relations in a monarchical age, the winter of 1788-9 witnessed much speculation about the possible consequences of major domestic changes in Britain. Growing fears about George III's state of health in the second half of October 1788 culminated in a general conviction by mid-November that he was insane. This suggested a new political regime, for George would either die, to be succeeded by his eldest son, George, Prince of Wales, or be judged incapacitated, in which case there would be a regency, the powers of which would probably be exercised, largely or solely, by the Prince. Prince George was a keen supporter of the opposition and close to Fox, its leader in the Commons. Pitt's position was therefore severely weakened and a ministerial revolution, akin to that which had followed George's accession, appeared imminent. The government had to face the task of coping with the immediate increase in opposition hopes in a volatile political situation that led some ministerial figures to transfer their political allegiance. In addition, it was necessary to consider how the likely change in government would affect policy. The likely recall of Fox suggested a more pro-Russian policy and the probable collapse of the Prussian alliance. Additional problems were created by the possibility that different provisions for a regency would be made in Hanover and Ireland (Blanning 1989). The failure to devise a speedy solution to the crisis and the escalation of political tension led to a growing feeling that Britain would be unable to escape from protracted difficulties. In December 1788, the French envoy reported that the new government would be both unpopular and affected by domestic disputes and fiscal weakness which would lessen the confidence of foreign powers in it, adding: 'in this internal chaos they think no more of foreign affairs than if Britain was the sole kingdom in Europe' (AE CP Ang. 567 ff. 272–5,312).

By early 1789 France did not appear to be in as poor shape relatively as she had been over the previous eighteen months. Austria was affected by growing internal disorders and committed to an unsuccessful Balkan war. Catherine II had found that the Turkish Empire did not collapse like a pack of cards and was hindered by the tenacity of her other enemy, Gustavus III of Sweden. At the same time, the possibility that the Estates General, that had been summoned to produce a political constituency for government-inspired reform, would bring renewed vigour to France was discussed. George III's illness had already led Montmorin to consider in February 1789 the prospect of an Anglo-French coalition, an instance of the extent to which the international system was seen as unstable prior to the Revolution. He suggested that such a coalition would assure the peace of Europe, but he also argued that there was no basis for confidence. Montmorin claimed that the British government was jealous of France and hated her, that any alliance would witness an attempt by Britain to dominate France and that France would be foolish to sacrifice her Continental alliances to arrange a precarious liaison with a rival (AE CP Espagne 626 f. 158, Ang. 568 f. 36).

In light of the commitment of so many British politicians to the Prussian alliance and to hostility to France, of the Franco-Spanish alliance and of conflicting British and Spanish interests, Montmorin's analysis was a reasonable one. It was not until the Revolution destroyed the reality of the Austro-French and Franco-Spanish alliances in 1789 and 1790 respectively that an Anglo-French alliance became more credible in Paris. This was due not only to a sense of ideological empathy but also to the realities of diplomatic opportunity, especially after British hopes of Anglo-Austrian reconciliation following the accession of Leopold II in 1790 had proved abortive and the Anglo-Prussian alliance had collapsed in acrimony in 1791. It was diplomatically plausible for French politicians and diplomats to suggest alliance with Britain in 1792, even at the expense of Spain's position in the Americas. In early 1789, however, an alliance was implausible, not simply because of French weakness, but also because of the diplomatic situation, in particular the Anglo-Prussian alliance.

Renewed British political stability after the Regency Crisis, which closed with George's recovery in mid February 1789, was to be cemented first by the government's success in the 1790 general election (though that had not really been in doubt) and secondly by the split in the opposition over the response to the French Revolution in 1792-3 and the eventual transfer of many opposition politicians to the government, a trend prefigured by Edmund Burke's earlier emotional and ideological break with Fox over the same issue. In contrast, France became more obviously divided as hopes that the political initiatives of 1788-9 would bring renewal receded. The disorders of 1789 were so striking precisely because they represented not only the breakdown of the *ancien régime*, but also of an attempt to reform it on which much hope had been placed. By the summer violence was as apparent a feature of the French political scene as talk to British commentators, though their response varied, the Duke of Dorset, British ambassador in Paris, writing on 23 April: 'the affairs in Provence are in much the same state, the people continue to pillage everywhere, and they have violated two nunneries and fu-k (sic) all the nuns, I think there is something jolly in that idea' (Beinecke, Osborn Files, Dorset).

The violence had a direct impact on France's standing, not solely because of the defiance of royal authority, but also because it entailed a lessening of military strength, as disorder spread to the armed forces. When, in January 1790, the Austrian envoy pressed Carmarthen, now 5th Duke of Leeds, without success on the need for an Anglo-Austrian defensive alliance, he 'observed that France might still become formidable to us'. Leeds felt able to reply that 'there would probably be sufficient time for us to consider how to act when that event should happen' (BL Add. 28065 f. 13). Charles Townshend MP wrote more bluntly in August 1790: 'the French may hang one another as much as they please' (Guildford CRO, Brodrick mss 1248/ 11 f. 176). The French political nation responded to domestic disorder by alleging British intrigues and suspecting British naval moves, the atmosphere of suspicion owing much to the British refusal in July 1789 to heed a request to permit the export of flour to France.

The disorders in France led in the short term to diplomatic nullity and extensive speculation as to the likely consequences. However, at the same time that lurid accounts of French disorders circulated in the British press, there was considerable concern about French ambitions in the Austrian Netherlands. Indeed, this contrast prefigured a series of others that was to mark Anglo-French relations over the following years. Leeds observed in April 1790: 'The French ministry at present appear little calculated (from the situation of that kingdom, I mean) to be of much importance at home. Abroad, however, they may still be active' (BL Add. 28065 f. 277). Later that year, accounts of French chaos and disorder were to be matched by concern that France would arm a powerful naval force and act in the Nootka Sound Crisis.

The fears of late 1789 were inspired by the collapse of Austrian authority in the Austrian Netherlands and the possibility that a political solution would be devised that had the unintentional effect of increasing French influence by making the territory independent and thus depriving it of the rôle within a non-French polity that Austrian rule had entailed. Furthermore, it was feared that the Austrian Netherlands might be brought under direct French influence should it pass into the possession of the Duke of Orléans. During the winter of 1789–90, Britain devoted much effort to seeking to arrange a satisfactory settlement of the issue. This entailed support for a restoration of Austrian power, Leeds telling the Austrian envoy in November 1789 'of the satisfaction with which His Majesty would embrace any opportunity of contributing to the restoration of harmony and good understanding between His Imperial Majesty and his Flemish subjects' (PRO FO 7/18 f. 110). This was a policy opposed by Prussia that placed considerable strain on the Anglo-Prussian alliance in 1790, weakening it prior to the Ochakov Crisis and possibly leading the British government to take a more assertive line in the latter.

In the spring of 1790, the issue of possible French intentions in the Austrian Netherlands was pushed into the background as another central British interest, extra-European trade, came to the fore. The seizure by Spanish warships of British vessels trading on Vancouver Island, part of the extensive American territories Spain claimed, rapidly escalated towards war (Norris 1955; Evans 1974; Webb 1975). The British Navy was well prepared (Webb 1977), 'an immense naval force ready for any contingency' in the words of an Under-Secretary at the Foreign Office (BL Add. 35542 f. 215). In June, the French envoy told Pitt that the dispute was of little significance and that it would be wrong to begin war over several merchant ships of slight value and for the possession of valueless and barren territories (AE CP Ang. 573 ff 249–50), an opinion in which humanitarian sentiment mingled with a consciousness of Bourbon weakness. The crisis could not, however, be shrugged off in this fashion and by October Anthony Storer, a former MP and diplomat, was writing, in terms that were to be echoed during the following century of imperial expansion: 'Here we are going to war and for what? A place, the name of which I can scarce pronounce, never heard of till lately, and which did not exist until the other day' (BL Add. 34433 f. 363).

The dispute indicated both the intertwining of European affairs and their separation. Prussia, Austria and Russia, close to war, devoted only a limited amount of attention to the crisis, and the latter two, though in dispute with Britain and Prussia, were singularly unresponsive to Spanish approaches for assistance. On the other hand, the crisis clearly affected Britain's ability to intervene in eastern European disputes and her attitude to them. It may be suggested that by delaying the Anglo-Prussian attempted intimidation of Russia until the spring of 1791 it helped to lead both to diplomatic failure and to the linked parliamentary storm over the issue. Though the government found it expedient to blame their decision to back down in the face of Russian opposition in 1791 largely on this storm, much was in fact due to the international developments of the previous year, including the end of the Russo-Swedish war, the increasing tergiversations of Prussian policy and the failure to pin down Leopold II. The play of contingency was of central importance, as was to be crucially illustrated in Anglo-French relations in 1792-3. In June 1791, William Eden, now Lord Auckland, suggested that 'the game of projects and discussions between nations is like many other games liable to be affected both by the chance and combination of the cards and by the manner of playing them' (Matlock CRO 239 M/O 759).

The discussion of the relationship between this play and more long-term features of international relationships, such as the division in the British political nation over poor relations with Russia, hostility towards Spanish pretensions in the Americas or concern over the possible ideological and territorial assault of Revolutionary France, is difficult and fraught with serious methodological problems. The outbreak of war with France in 1793 can be considered alongside the maintenance of the peace with both Spain in 1790 and Russia in 1791. The points at issue in the latter two cases were not as crucial to national interests, however then defined, as the territorial integrity of the United Provinces, a central concern in disagreements with France over the Low Countries in the winter of 1792–3. This 'diplomatic' difference was arguably as important as the 'ideological' one, the extent to which Revolutionary France deliberately posed an ideological challenge both to Britain and to her allies, both present and future, and was believed to do so both in Britain and in France. In contrast, though the disputes with both Spain and Russia, and in particular the latter, became a subject of political debate, part of the currency of political partisanship, they neither aroused the fears and passions that relations with France inspired, nor were a public issue for so long.

The last was important, not only in heightening tension but also in causing the British political world to be transformed by the issue of relations with France. In contrast, the disputes with Spain and Russia were of transient importance, not only because they were relatively short but also because they fitted into, rather than transformed, the existing political divisions. If the contrasting situation over relations with France owed something to Burke and his determination to change the political world in order to meet the vision of the challenge posed by France outlined in his *Reflections on the Revolution in France* which appeared on 1 November 1790, it also owed much to the combined impact of the British and French radical milieus in raising fears in Britain and to the manner in which French policies and success in late 1792 seemed to give substance to these fears.

The play of contingency and the success of the British government in resisting public demands, in this case overwhelmingly for war, played a major rôle in allowing Britain what was generally conceded to be a triumph in the Nootka Sound Crisis. If the Dutch crisis of 1787 marked the diplomatic bankruptcy of *ancien régime* France, that of Nootka Sound suggested that the subsequent changes, whether or not discerned as revolutionary, had brought no improvement and that the claims of commentators that France was weak and weakening were correct. The Family Compact allowed Spain to call for French assistance, providing France with an opportunity to escape from diplomatic nullity. Hoping that success would have significant domestic results, that it would be possible to reverse the consequences of 1787, Louis XVI announced orders on 14 May 1790 to fit out 14 ships of the line. The National Assembly intervened to state that the king could not declare war without its approval, prefiguring the problem of credibility that was to affect French envoys in London in 1792, as French diplomacy fractured under the strain of competing views, the struggle to control and execute policy and the partial breakdown of the diplomatic service in the face of other accredited and unaccredited agents. On 26 August 1790, the National Assembly accepted a Spanish request for naval assistance and agreed to arm 45 ships of the line, but the impact of the decision was lessened by a general conviction that the French could not and would not act, Earl Gower, the British envoy, writing of the 'spirit of insubordination in the fleet' (PRO 30/29/1/17). The influence of British intrigue and bribery in affecting developments within France is difficult to determine.

Spain had no other power to which she could realistically turn and the lateness and inadequacy of the French response made it clear that she would have to settle with Britain, as she did on 28 October 1790. Spain recognised the British right to navigate and fish 'in the Pacific Ocean or in the South Seas' and yielded her claims to the west coast of America north of California. With the arrival of British settlers at Botany Bay in Australia in January 1788, this represented a significant development that was pregnant with future British territorial greatness. Britain was clearly winning the race to establish European power in unoccupied parts of the Pacific rim. In light of the Spanish climbdown, it was not surprising that Portugal took care in the summer of 1791 to calm British anxiety over the treatment of her merchants in Portuguese Angola, anxiety that led to a false claim in the Lords that a British settlement, which did not in fact exist, had been attacked (PRO FO 63/14, 13, 28 July, 13 Aug.).

In the Nootka Sound Crisis, France was treated not as a revolutionary state, but as a power suffering from domestic instability, though there were fears in Spain about the contagion of French ideas. By the following year, she was increasingly regarded as a revolutionary state which represented a threat simply by her existence, irrespective of her domestic weakness. France was also seen as unpredictable. The discourses both of revolution and of counter-revolution became more assertive, and governments that had no wish to go to war with France because of her revolutionary character, nevertheless, sought to stem the influence of French ideas in their own countries. Britain was not in the forefront of this movement, to the chagrin of Burke, but diplomatic relations with France continued to be cool throughout 1791. French diplomats in London continually reiterated their suspicion of British intentions and their fear of her plans.

For the British ministry, however, relations with France took a distinct second place to the Ochakov Crisis and its diplomatic consequences. Despite French fears of British intrigues in France and hopes of colonial gains, the British ministry was essentially satisfied if France was reduced to the situation she was in in early 1791, a diplomatically isolated nullity. In so far as the government feared a revival in French strength they could rely on the increasingly apparent opposition to Revolutionary France of other powers, whether allies or not. In 1788–90, the prospect of a revived France had entailed a monarchy that was stronger because of constitutional and administrative reform and national unity. Such a France would have been a powerful challenge to Britain, because she would have been a more attractive ally for other powers. From 1791, however, it was increasingly likely that, short of a successful counter-revolution, which would probably bring chaos, a stronger France would be a politically radical power, threatening to other monarchs.

In 1791–2, ministers stressed repeatedly their determination not to take part in French domestic affairs, culminating in the decision not to take part when war broke out between France and Austria in April 1792 and their subsequent assurances of neutrality. 'England has little concern now in what is going forward on the continent,' remarked Auckland in March 1792 (BL Add. 35541 f. 485).

However, the reasons why, less than a year later, Britain was to be at war with Revolutionary France were already apparent. The declaration of neutrality given to the French envoy Chauvelin on 24 May 1792 was subject to respect for Britain's treaty obligations and rights, which Chauvelin reported entailed respecting the territory of Britain's allies. At the beginning of the month, William, Lord Grenville, Leeds' replacement, had already told Chauvelin that the ministry was unhappy about the war between Austria and France as it would bring conflict to the Austrian Netherlands. Whether expressed in terms of treaty obligations or not, the British ministry did not wish to see any increase in French influence in the Low Countries, a view that political opinion in Paris took insufficiently to heart, but, in the spring of 1792, there seemed little prospect of France overrunning the region. The French plan for a speedy conquest of the Austrian Netherlands proved a dismal failure, while Frederick William II of Prussia came to Austria's support. Chauvelin argued that the Austro-Prussian alliance menaced not only France but the whole of Europe, and sought British diplomatic assistance in getting the invaders to leave. In Britain there was concern that, though the alliance menaced only France, the re-establishment of royal authority there which it seemed likely to achieve would be on terms that were not entirely welcome.

It was military success that radically altered this position in late 1792. On 20 September, the Prussians under the Duke of Brunswick faced a cannonade at Valmy east of Rheims that led Brunswick, with all the caution that had characterised the last central European war, that of the Bavarian Succession, to fall back. The French regained the initiative, overrunning Savoy and part of the Rhineland, and defeated the Austrians on 6 November at Jemappes near Mons, a success that was to be followed by the conquest of most of the Austrian Netherlands within a month. On 26 October, Chauvelin had warned that because the British had done nothing to prevent French plans to conquer the area in the spring, that did not mean they would support them in the autumn. He pointed out that the British had then relied on Austrian strength (AE CP Ang. 583 f. 100), but he could have added that the British response was likely to be different, not only because of a marked growth of concern within Britain about French radicalism, but also because the changing nature of the French government and political nation ensured that French aspirations, even if similar in a territorial sense, had altered between the spring and the autumn.

Initial setbacks and the experience of invasion had been traumatic and had helped to lead to the suspension of the monarchy of 10 August, which was followed by the recall of the British envoy a week later, and the September Massacres in Paris. Victory also brought a strident tone abroad. On 19 November 1792, the National Convention declared that fraternity and assistance would be given to all peoples wishing to regain their liberty. Three days earlier, the Executive Council in Paris had both ordered French generals to pursue the defeated Austrians wherever they sought refuge, a decision that effectively ended Dutch territorial integrity, and proclaimed the opening of the Scheldt. If the first decision had no immediate consequence, the second was followed by the passage of French warships up the river. On 16 November, Grenville wrote to his older brother, the Marquess of Buckingham, about the Dutch: 'we are so clearly bound to exert ourselves both from policy and good faith to preserve them from the progress of French arms and French principles that we have thought it best to avow the obligation'. Ten days later, he added that if the Scheldt was opened it would 'of course involve us' (HL STG 39, 6, 7). Meanwhile the French government was being falsely informed of the strength of the British revolutionary movement and that most of the British supported neutrality (AE CP Ang. 583 f 287, 585 ff. 173–4).

It was the fact of French victory as much as their declaration about the Scheldt that led to alarm in Britain. French victory made the revolutionary threat apparent and concrete, both helping to make minds up in Britain and forcing politicians to determine and express their views, as it became increasingly apparent that the ministry would have to respond to the situation in the Low Countries, at least before the next campaigning season. On 2 December, Pitt told Hugues Maret, an official in the French foreign ministry, that 'the resolution announced respecting the Scheldt was considered as a proof of an intention to proceed to a rupture with Holland; that a rupture with Holland, on this ground, or any other injurious to their rights, must also lead to an immediate rupture with this country'. He added that Maret 'must have seen the impression made here, by the decree in France, avowing a design of endeavouring to extend their principles of government, by raising disturbances in all other countries: that, while this was professed or attempted, and till we had full security on this point, no explanation could answer its purpose; and that such a conduct must be considered as an act of hostility to neutral nations'. Maret's reply – it passed only in a moment of fermentation and went beyond what was intended – begged the question of how French intentions could be identified or relied upon (BL Add. 34446 ff. 28-30).

During the next few days, the Dutch were encouraged to take a firm line towards French demands, while Grenville pressed the Austrian envoy on the need for European co-operation against French aggression. Over the winter, as ministers conducted discussions with French agents aimed at averting conflict, domestic opinion hardened, a process in which developments within France, especially the trial of Louis XVI, played a significant rôle, but in which fear of domestic radicalism was more important. The pressure for action against France, however, was criticised by some commentators, not all of them sympathetic to the then state of the Revolution, who argued that war would not be in Britain's interest.

The question of whether there was any viable alternative to war with France has to relate not only to the negotiations of the winter of 1792–3 and the circumstances of that period, but also to the possibility that peace could have been preserved in subsequent years. The latter is implausible, unless it can be suggested that Pitt's government would have been prepared to accept French hegemony in western Europe, a hegemony more powerful, insistent and threatening than that toppled in 1787. This could have been possible only if the analysis advanced in France of a feeble Britain threatened by domestic radicalism had been accurate, but it was not. The French attitude to treaties scarcely encouraged any reliance on their assurances and, as the instability of French politics affected her diplomatic personnel and policy, conspicuously so in the case of her representation in London, it was difficult to see whose assurances were to be sought. When British pressure in December 1792 for Portuguese naval preparations led to the Portuguese response that Portugal was unwilling to fight over the navigation of the Scheldt, Grenville wrote on 9 January 1793: 'this act is considered by the King as according one instance only of the general system adopted by the present rulers in France for overturning all existing governments, for carrying their principles into all the different countries in Europe, and for extending their own dominion by acquisitions of the utmost value and importance' (PRO FO 63/16). By going to war in 1793 Britain benefited from the enmity towards France of the other leading Continental powers.

French talk about their desire for an alliance with Britain was of little assistance. It became clear that opinion was divided in Paris as to whose alliance in Britain should be sought. On 21 November 1792, the French foreign minister Pierre Lebrun ordered a French diplomat in London 'to block the hostile intentions of the British government by increasing the number of our friends among the London merchants, as it is usually they who determine opinion on peace or war' (AE CP Ang. 583 ff. 276). Furthermore, French success threatened to define any Anglo-French understanding, the likely terms of which were always unclear, especially as it would affect Britain's allies, in an unacceptable fashion.

There was little basis for any long-term Anglo-French alliance in the winter of 1792–3, and the only possible positive solution to the negotiations was the avoidance of conflict for a while. However, the likely timespan of any agreement was unclear and the British government faced the danger that it might increase domestic radicalism. In addition, any agreement would make it difficult to develop links with other European powers or to influence their views. And yet, as French constancy could not be relied on, such links would be necessary, both for the security of the United Provinces and for the guaranteeing of any Anglo-French understanding. An Anglo-French settlement would have been viable in the long term only had it been part of a larger international settlement. Distrust was as important in Anglo-French relations in 1792–3 as it had been in 1787 and 1790, but, in 1792–3, it was no longer possible to measure the French threat by assessing their naval preparations. The unpredictability and potency of French aspirations and the links between British radicals and France, both real and imagined, made the situation appear more threatening. The French declaration of war on Britain on 1 February 1793 anticipated similar action on the British part (Blanning 1986: 131–72). A month later, the Duke of Leeds observed: 'we are here up to the teeth, and the people in high spirits determined to defend the King and Country' (New York Public Library, Montague 7).

The failure to preserve the peace cannot be explained solely on ideological grounds, but these play a major rôle in explaining why the fairly constant state of Anglo-French distrust developed into a tense situation in the winter of 1792–3. However, crucial to this shift, in terms of both the fears of the British political nation and the anxieties of their government, was French resilience in 1792 and the dramatic impact of French strength in an area believed crucial to British interests, or at least vital to keep out of the hands of France. The likely consequences of a revival in French strength had been an important theme in British discussion of French developments from 1787 onwards. The possible nature of French schemes in the Low Countries had similarly been a significant aspect of the discussion of French diplomatic plans. Their combination in late 1792 was a potent one, which would have been judged dangerous prior to the radicalisation of the Revolution. Ideology played an important rôle in the British response to the Revolution, but much about the crisis of 1792–3, not least the dispute over the Low Countries and their transition into an Anglo-French battlefield, was far from novel (Black 1994).

THE RISE AND FALL OF THE ANGLO-PRUSSIAN ALLIANCE, 1787–92

> You will find no material obstacles in future even in the grand work of the pacification of Europe. I look only to the great and obvious features of our affairs, which are the elevation of England from the downfall of her rival, and the preponderance of Prussia from the depression of Austria. As long as such great advantages are maintained, the rest of the world may kick and fling, but it can never do any great mischief. (Daniel Hailes, envoy in Warsaw, 1 January 1790, Matlock CRO 239 M/O 759)

The Dutch crisis led to a period of close British involvement in the affairs of Continental Europe. Based on first co-operation, and from 1788 alliance, with Prussia, it lasted until 1791 when it was a casualty of the confrontation with Russia known as the Ochakov Crisis. This was then followed by a period when Britain had no powerful allies, which ended in 1793 when Britain joined the powers opposed to France in the First Coalition. In 1790–1, as in 1719–20, an absence of concern about French activity was a condition of hostility to Russia, but the Pitt ministry found itself unable to cope with the diplomatic and political strains of a lengthy confrontation and had abandoned their 'forward' Continental policy way before they became increasingly concerned about Revolutionary France. As a result, they did less about the second and third partitions of Poland in 1793 and 1795 than they had done about Russian gains from Turkey, but, given their failure in 1791 to intimidate Russia into returning all of these, it is unclear that they could have done much over Poland. The failure to condemn the brutal denial of national sovereignty by the partitioning powers led to charges of inconsistency when contrasted with the desire to protect the Dutch against Revolutionary France. In August 1792, Anthony Storer observed: 'Things which happen at a distance have not the same effect, as those which pass near us. I scarce have a thought for Poland. France is nearer and more interesting' (BL Add. 34444 f. 48). His words summed up the attitude of the government.

Anglo-Prussian co-operation over the United Provinces in 1787 marked the fulfilment of earlier hopes of turning Prussia against France. It was therefore seen by George III as justification against the charges that the *Fürstenbund* had harmed Britain's position, and thus buried the idea that Britain should approach Austria and offer to disregard the *Fürstenbund*. Austria's ability to act in the Low Countries had been lessened by the Turkish declaration of war on Austria's ally Russia in August 1787. Joseph II promised Catherine II support and the Austrians entered the war that winter. Despite British hopes earlier in the decade, the outbreak of a Balkan war made an Anglo-Austrian alliance less likely. The Austrian attitude to the Dutch crisis became less important, the significance of Prussian views greater, and Austrian distrust of Britain was sowed by the suspicion that Ainslie had instigated the Turkish declaration of war in order to prevent Austria from helping France, a charge the British denied (Black 1984a).

From the outset, Britain and Prussia sought different goals. The Prussians were interested in an active eastern European policy that would yield them territorial gains, while the British were primarily concerned to consolidate the Orangist revival in the United Provinces. However, fear that Frederick William II would turn to France played a major rôle in determining the British ministry to push for a defensive alliance with Prussia. A provisional treaty was signed on 13 June, a definitive version on 13 August 1788. The Prussians were committed to action in case of a British war overseas, while the British were obliged to offer Prussia land as well as financial and maritime support (Ehrman 1969: 539–41). Known as the Triple Alliance, though in fact there was no one treaty that Britain, Prussia and the United Provinces signed, the new system was weakened by the British refusal to support Frederick William II's bolder schemes, in short by the traditional British position of being a 'satisfied' European power, opposed to change on the Continent. In January 1790, the Duke of Leeds (Carmarthen's title from March 1789) sent Sir Robert Murray Keith, the envoy in Vienna, a classic summary of the position.

> In all our communications with the court of Berlin, we have been particularly careful to state to His Prussian Majesty that we consider our alliance and the system on which it is founded, as purely defensive and however desirous of affording every possible degree of assistance and protection to our allies, in case of their being attacked, it is very far indeed from our inclinations and indeed would be totally repugnant to our interests to encourage them to commence hostilities merely for purposes of aggrandizement or ambition: our object is to maintain as long as with propriety can be done that tranquillity from which this country has already derived so much advantage, and sincerely desirous as we are of the

prosperity as well as safety of our allies, it is by negotiation and not by arms, that we wish to see them obtain such acquisitions of influence or dominion as they may think important to them. (PRO FO 7/19 f 29)

To Lord Chancellor Thurlow, he was blunter the following month: 'Prussia must be narrowly watched' (BL Add. 28065 f. 105). Joseph Ewart, envoy in Berlin, was one of the few supporters of Prussian views. Leeds wrote in April 1790:

At present it really seems as if the court of England had a Prussian minister at Berlin and that of Prussia an English one in London. Alvensleben has all along stated to his court the impossibility of drawing England into those wild projects of aggrandizement and ambition, which Hertzberg is perpetually suggesting; at the same time that he does ample justice to our determination of faithfully fulfilling every engagement we have contracted with our allies. (BL Add. 28065 f 273)

However, hostility to Joseph II's attempt in the winter of 1788-9 to exploit the Regency crisis, produced by George III's apparent insanity, by creating difficulties over the regency of Hanover helped to bring warmth to Anglo-Prussian relations (Blanning 1989), while growing British concern about Russian strength led the ministry to display greater interest in a 'forward' policy in eastern Europe. In addition, the Anglo-Prussian alliance helped to keep Anglo-Austrian relations cool. Keith was soon complaining from Vienna about receiving no instructions. Carmarthen replied in September 1788 to what appeared to be a tentative enquiry concerning the possibility of British mediation in the Balkans by informing Keith that Britain would do nothing without consulting her allies.

The British attitude did not change substantially until the accession of the pacific Leopold II in 1790, when British persuasion played a rôle in getting Austria and Prussia to settle most of their differences by the Convention of Reichenbach (July 1790). Austria agreed that the *status quo ante bellum* would be the basis of her peace with Turkey, while the British hoped that, if they could secure peace on that basis, they would be able to consolidate a European system, including Turkey, Poland and Sweden in the Anglo-Prussian alliance and guaranteeing to them the terms of the peace. In February 1791, Leeds expressed British willingness to sponsor a collective security system:

. . . the disposition of this court to establish and maintain, in concert with the principal powers of Europe . . . a pacific and defensive system, which may not only prevent any occasion of misunderstanding among those powers, but may enable them to act with effect for the preservation of the general peace of Europe . . . there does not appear to be any necessary obstacle to the contracting of engagements with Russia, which shall be strictly of a defensive nature, and directed to the future preservation of the established and subsisting balance between the different powers of Europe. (PRO FO 7/23 f. 66)

However, as Russia was unwilling to accept this principle, the issue of Austrian policy in the event of war between Russia and the Triple Alliance became important. The British wanted Austrian diplomatic support and argued that Russian territorial gains would harm Austria by increasing Russia's relative power. Nevertheless, a lack of Austrian support was to prove one of the major 'diplomatic' factors behind the failure to intimidate Russia in the Ochakov Crisis of 1791.

Ochakov, a town that controlled the mouths of the Bug and Dnieper rivers, was a gain from Turkey that Russia intended to retain. The Pitt ministry argued that it would further increase Russian dominance in eastern Europe, while they feared that it would hamper the idea of developing Poland as a substitute for supplies of raw materials from Russia. In March 1791, it was decided to send squadrons to the Baltic and the Black Sea to lend support to a joint Anglo-Prussian ultimatum to Russia.

The policy had, however, to be reversed the following month. There was considerable uncertainty about the value of Ochakov and the wisdom of fighting Russia, which was not seen as a traditional enemy, and this was exploited by both the Opposition, led by the pro-Russian Fox, and by the Russian envoy, Simon Vorontsov, who mobilised opinion by supplying information. Pitt's Commons majority fell, his argument that 'confidence must be given to those in whose hands the Administration was entrusted' failing to inspire support, while the cabinet was divided (Cunningham 1964–5). Auckland complained that, in seeking the support of Sweden against Russia, the ministry had sacrificed 'our leading principle' by accepting the idea of 'a war of conquest', while Francis Jackson, Secretary of Legation at Berlin, described the conduct of the opposition in terms of 'treason and sedition' (Bod. Bland Burges 30 f. 132, 36 f. 68).

The political crisis led Pitt to back down. The Prussians were informed that for domestic reasons the government would not go to war, a climbdown that led to Leeds' resignation and his replacement by William Grenville. The Anglo-Prussian system rapidly collapsed. By July 1791, Pitt was writing to Grenville of the need to get Prussia to press Turkey to accept Russian terms (BL Add. 58906 ff. 98–9). Prussia allied with Austria that summer, while, by the Treaty of Jassy of January 1792, Turkey ceded to Russia Ochakov and the territory between the Dniester and the Bug.

The crisis can be viewed in a number of lights. Pitt was unlucky that it coincided with the parliamentary session and it was essentially this that made the domestic agitation important, as with the Dunkirk agitation of 1730 and that over Spanish depredations in 1739. However, over-confidence and miscalculation can also be discerned. Possibly his success in 1790 in the showdown with Spain over Nootka Sound led Pitt to underestimate the problems of a confrontation with Russia. Naval power was of lesser value against Russia and it was easy to overlook the possibility of an adverse domestic response to confrontation with her (Webb 1980). There were also sound strategic and diplomatic reasons for withdrawing from confrontation with Russia in 1791, not least the quixotic instability of Prussian power. Auckland, who urged prudence, did so not in response to public agitation, of which his view, stemming from his experience of the commercial negotiations with France in 1786, was poor, but for sound reasons derived from his justified views of the consequences of the hijacking of British policy by Ewart. The attempt to direct political attention to the rise of Russian power was harder than in 1719–20 when under Peter the Great it appeared a new and threatening development. By 1791, the British political nation was accustomed to thinking of Russian domination of eastern Europe, and to viewing her rivals, Sweden, Poland and Turkey, as pro-French. The novel view in 1791 was the positive assessment of an anti-Russian Poland, but this did not appear to be a convincing reason for a reinterpretation of traditional opinions, any more than the maintenance of the Prussian alliance appeared to justify war with Russia.

By abandoning the policy, Pitt rode out the political storm, but the lesson was a clear one that would not have surprised ministers who in 1733, 1753 and 1763 had displayed little interest in heeding suggestions that they involve themselves in Polish affairs. It appeared best to leave these matters to Continental allies. Direct intervention might have unpredictable results, both domestically and diplomatically.

The Ochakov Crisis appeared to indicate that Britain would not heed the implications of her alliances, and made her less credible as an ally. The Austro-Prussian reconciliation of 1791 excluded Britain, which was anyway not prepared to heed the anti-French Revolutionary schemes of these powers. On 27 August 1791, Leopold II and Frederick William II issued the Declaration of Pillnitz, which claimed that the fate of Louis XVI was of concern to all European rulers and called for common action to help him. This step had been made without consulting Britain, and her government insisted on maintaining its policy of non-interference towards France, and, as Grenville wrote to the envoy in Vienna in July 1791, of 'not holding out the expectation of assistance from this country in the Emperor's plans of interference in the affairs of France' (PRO FO 7/24 f 246).

Thanks to the French issue, Britain was unable to profit from the Austro-Prussian reconciliation by seeking to improve her relations with both. Instead, relations with both became cooler and more distant. British envoys received fewer instructions and sent less well-informed reports. Thus the collapse of the Austro-French alliance, which the British had sought since 1756, did not produce any immediate revival of the 'Old Alliance'. The Austrians criticised Britain for a lack of support, while the British discouraged the Dutch from the idea of a mutual guarantee of governmental arrangements for the Austrian Netherlands and the United Provinces, and were angered by Leopold's refusal to heed their views over the settlement of the rebellion in the Austrian Netherlands. In January 1792, Grenville made it clear that he was opposed to being drawn in to defend the Austrian position in the Austrian Netherlands. Two months later, Grenville expressed the hope that Austria and Prussia would co-operate, not against Revolutionary France, but in order to prevent a Russian invasion of Poland. Britain sought to discourage a new partition, though Grenville sensibly wrote in March 1792:

> 'in the event of such an agreement being actually concluded, I doubt whether any representations, that could be made by the Maritime Powers, would be of sufficient weight to prevent its execution, unless they were attended with circumstances of more expense and inconvenience, than the occasion would appear to justify' (BL Add. 34441 f. 508).

Given British attitudes towards war with France, it was not surprising that Austria viewed Britain with suspicion and did not keep Keith informed of her plans. It was not until November 1792 that French success led Britain to seek the views of Austria and Prussia.

As for so much of the previous 130 years, it was French power and intentions that dominated British foreign policy and thus her relations with other powers. The Austro-French alliance of 1756 and Dutch neutrality in the Seven Years' War had given British politicians the luxury of having to devote few thoughts to the security of the Low Countries for 36 years, but in 1792-3 the contradiction between concern over certain Continental interests and a disinclination to commit Britain to the views of other powers had to be resolved due to French advances. Fortunately for Britain these views were not too different in 1793: Austria and Prussia also wished to resist France, though the ministry was obliged to accept their rôle in the destruction of independent Poland with the Second Partition in 1793 and the Third Partition and final destruction of the Polish state, in 1795. However, the contradiction between British views and those of other powers remained, to complicate debate over foreign policy, as it had done for so long.

CONCLUSION

To recover our weight on the continent by judicious alliances is the general wish of every man the least acquainted with the interests of this country.

(James Harris 1783 -BL Add 35530 ff. 276-7)

He knows, I am persuaded, too well, the effect which public opinion and impressions must always have in this country (Pitt on the backdown over Ochakov, 1791 – Matlock CRO 239 M/O 759)

The end of the period witnessed a crisis for British foreign policy. In November 1792, the defence of the Austrian Netherlands collapsed and the United Provinces seemed exposed to French attack, while Britain lacked powerful allies – indeed, her leading ally was the vulnerable United Provinces – and was threatened by what appeared to be a domestic political movement looking to France for support and inspiration. This was by no means the first crisis in this period. The early 1690s, 1744–6, 1755–6 and 1779–82 had all been periods of particular difficulties and these crises demonstrate and underline the vulnerability and weakness of Britain as a player in the international system. They also took precedence over British attempts to make gains in the non-Western world, and this is one of the prime qualifications of any attempt to describe British policy in terms of a system of ambition. The relationship between concerns and commitments in the European world and those in the non-European world was to be different after 1815.

It is tempting to blame wartime problems on peacetime failures of policy, but this faces two problems: it exaggerates the room for diplomatic and domestic manoeuvre enjoyed by British politicians, and it suggests patterns of causality that are difficult to substantiate. To take the example of 1792 it is by no means clear that British support for the Austro-Prussian alliance against Revolutionary France would have averted the French invasion of the Low Countries, while it would probably have increased the domestic problems of the Pitt ministry.

British ministers sometimes appeared to be confidently redrawing the map of Europe, as Carteret sought to do in 1743 and Stanhope succeeded in doing for Italy, but, in general, a close scrutiny of ministerial correspondence reveals concern and uncertainty about both diplomatic and domestic circumstances and developments. Newcastle might have been easily flappable, but his desperation when he wrote to Sandwich in March 1748 was not inappropriate:

> If peace is not made before this campaign is ended or before the French get at the knowledge of our not being able or willing on any account to continue the war another year, France will impose whatever conditions they please upon us: for, by the best judgement I can make, no consideration will bring this House of Commons to provide for another year's war; and I really doubt, whether the nation is in a condition to do it if the King, Parliament and Ministry were so disposed. (BL Add. 32811 f 369)

Newcastle's sense of what the nation could or would accept is interesting, as he clearly realised the limits to parliamentary management. Controlling the domestic political system was not enough: there were also questions of domestic resources and international developments. Because foreign policy could pose so many problems for ministers, it is a valuable means for approaching the British political system of the period, for it was a sphere where government could be under severe pressure, forced to reconcile competing demands and unwelcome developments. Britain was not, of course, unique in facing the need to consider different diplomatic strategies, or the choice between options that were interventionist or not. Nor were British ministers alone in having to assess domestic resources and responses. Yet these were also serious problems for successive governments.

The general picture of international relations in this period, as possibly in all other ones, was of uncertainty and concern. The language of systems and methods, the apparently predictable assessments present in such theories as the balance of power and the notion of natural interests, was a misleading defence against the seemingly arbitrary nature of international developments (Black 1990d). Furthermore, Europe was no chaos waiting for the guiding hand of Britain. British ministers found other powers understandably keen to maintain their own views and interests.

It is easy to suggest that the British response was often in some way inadequate, untutored or inappropriate, and British diplomats did at times complain about inadequate instructions or a lack of direction in periods of political crisis in Britain. Yet, this cannot be extended to argue that there was something fundamentally at fault with British foreign policy, either in its conduct, or as a consequence of particular features of the domestic political system. British policy was not uniquely circumscribed by the latter (Black 1987c, 1988a), and it is more appropriate to consider individual potential problems, such as the role of Parliament, in the context of particular crises and periods. If a generalisation has to be made, it would be that, rather than seeing Britain as a uniquely distinctive player in international relations, as a result of her domestic situation, it is more appropriate to stress the problems she faced in common with other powers, especially the unpredictability of international developments, the limitations of internal resources, and the difficulty of ensuring domestic consent to changes or policies that might produce more resources.

SELECTIVE BIBLIOGRAPHY

This brief list is intended only as an introduction to the very extensive literature available. For reasons of space the list is restricted to work in English and concentrates on material published since 1960. The place of publication is London unless otherwise stated.

Adams, E. D., 1904. *The Influence of Grenville on Pitt's Foreign Policy, 1787–98*. Washington D.C.

Albion, R. G., 1926. *Forests and Sea Power: the timber problem of the Royal Navy 1652–1862*. Cambridge, Massachusetts.

Anderson, M. S., 1954. 'Great Britain, Russia and the Russo-Turkish war of 1768–74,' *EHR*

Anderson, M. S., 1958. *Britain's Discovery of Russia 1553–1815*

Anderson, M. S., l958–9. 'The great powers and Russian annexation of the Crimea, 1783–4,' *Slavonic and East European Review*

Baugh, D. A., 1965. *British Naval Administration in the Age of Walpole*. Princeton, NJ.

Baugh, D. A., 1988. 'Great Britain's "Blue-Water" policy, 1689–1815', *International History Review*

Baugh, D.A., 1998. 'Withdrawing from Europe: Anglo-French maritime geopolitics', *International History Review*

Baxter, S. B. 1966. *William III*

Baxter, S. B., 1976. 'The Myth of the Grand Alliance', in Baxter, S. B. and Sellin, P. R. (eds), *Anglo-Dutch Cross Currents in the Seventeenth and Eighteenth Centuries*. Los Angeles.

Baxter, S. B. (ed.), 1983. *England's Rise to Greatness, 1660-1763*. Berkeley.

Bayly, C.A., 1989. *Imperial Meridian. The British Empire and the World 1780–1830*. Harlow

Beddard, R. (ed.), 1991. *The Revolutions of 1688*. Oxford

Birke, A. M., and Kluxen, K. (eds), *1986. England and Hanover*. Munich.

Black, J. M., 1982. 'George II Reconsidered', *Mitteilungen des Osterreichischen Staatsarchivs*

Black, J. M., 1983a. 'An "ignoramus" in European affairs', *British Journal for Eighteenth-Century Studies*

Black, J. M., 1983b. 'The development of Anglo-Sardinian relations in the first half of the eighteenth century', *Studi Piemontesi*

Black, J. M., 1984a. 'Parliament and the political and diplomatic crisis of 1717–18', *Parliamentary History*

Black, J. M., 1984b. 'Sir Robert Ainslie: His Majesty's agent-provocateur? British foreign policy and the International Crisis of 1787', *European History Quarterly*

Black, J. M., 1985a. *British Foreign Policy in the Age of Walpole*. Edinburgh.

Black, J. M. 1985b. 'The Marquis of Carmarthen and relations with France, 1784–1787', *Francia*

Black, J. M. and Schweizer, K. (eds), 1985, *Essays in European History in Honour of Ragnhild Hatton*. Lennoxville, Quebec.

Black, J. M., 1986a. *Natural and Necessary Enemies: Anglo-French Relations in the Eighteenth Century*

Black, J. M., 1986b. 'British foreign policy and the War of the Austrian Succession', *Canadian Journal of History*

Black, J. M., 1986c. 'The Anglo-French Alliance 1716–1731', *Francia*

Black, J M., 1986d. 'Fresh light on the fall of Townshend', *HJ*

Black, J. M., 1986e. 'Anglo-Russian relations 1714–1750' in Hartley J. M. (ed.), *The Study of Russian History from British Archival Sources*

Black, J. M. (ed.), 1987a. *The Origins of War in Early Modern Europe*

Black, J. M., 1987b. *The English Press in the Eighteenth Century*

Black, J. M., 1987c. 'British foreign policy in the Eighteenth Century: a survey', *Journal of British Studies*

Black, J. M., 1987d. *The Collapse of the Anglo-French Alliance 1727–31*

Black, J. M., 1987e. 'Anglo-Russian relations after the Seven Years' War', *Scottish Slavonic Review*

Black, J. M., 1 987f. 'Anglo-French relations in the age of the French Revolution 1787–1793', *Francia*

Black, J. M., 1987g. 'British intelligence and the mid-eighteenth century crisis', *Intelligence and National Security*

Black J. M., 1988a 'Britain's foreign alliances in the Eighteenth Century', *Albion*

Black, J. M., 1988b. 'Anglo-Baltic relations 1714–1748' in Minchinton, W. (ed.), *Britain and the Northern Seas*

Black, J. M., 1988c. 'Jacobitism and British foreign policy under the first two Georges', *Royal Stuart Papers* 32

Black, J. M. and Woodfine, P. L., 1988. *The British Navy and the Use of Naval Power in the Eighteenth Century*. Leicester.

Black, J. M., 1989a. 'The Revolution and the development of English foreign policy' in Cruickshanks, E. (ed.), *By Force or By Default? The Revolution of 1688–89*. Edinburgh.

Black, J. M., 1989b. 'The problems of the small state: Bavaria and Britain in the second quarter of the Eighteenth Century', *European History Quarterly*

Black, J. M., 1989c. *Knights Errant and True Englishmen: British Foreign Policy 1660–1800*. Edinburgh.

Black, J. M., 1989d. 'Anglo-Austrian relations, 1725-1740. A study in failure', *British Journal for Eighteenth-Century Studies*

Black, J. M., (ed.) 1990a. *British Politics and Society from Walpole to Pitt, 1742–89*

Black, J. M., 1990b. *Robert Walpole and the Nature of Politics in Early Eighteenth Century Britain*

Black, J. M., 1990c. *Culloden and the '45*. Stroud.

Black, J. M., 1990d. *The Rise of the European Powers 1679–1793*

Black, J. M., 1990e. 'Anglo-French relations in the mid-eighteenth century 1740–1756', *Francia*

Black, J. M., 1990f. 'On the "Old System" and the "Diplomatic Revolution" of the Eighteenth Century', *International History Review*

Black, J.M., 1994. *British Foreign Policy in an Age of Revolutions, 1783–1793*. Cambridge.

Black, J.M., 1998. *America or Europe? British Foreign Policy, 1739–63*.

Black, J.M., 1999a. *Eighteenth Century Europe*

Black, J.M., 1999b. *Pitt the Elder*. Stroud.

Black, J.M., 1999c. *Britain as a Military Power 1688–1815*.

Black, J.M., 1999d. *From Louis XIV to Napoleon. The Fate of a Great Power*.

Blanning, T. C. W., 1977. '"That horrid Electorate" or "Ma patrie germanique"?: George III, Hanover and the Fürstenbund of 1785', *HJ*

Blanning, T. C. W., 1986. *The Origins of the French Revolutionary Wars*

Blanning, T. C. W., 1989. 'George III, Hanover and the Regency Crisis' in Black (ed.), *Knights Errant*

Bond, M. F. (ed.), 1976. *The Diaries and Papers of Sir Edward Dering*

Boxer, C., 1969. 'Some second thoughts on the third Anglo-Dutch war', *Transactions of the Royal Historical Society*

Brewer, J., 1989. *The Sinews of Power: War, money and the English state, 1688–1783*

Brewer, J. and Hellmuth, E. (eds.), 1999. *Rethinking Leviathan. The Eighteenth Century State in Britain and Germany*. Oxford.

Bromley, J. S. and Hatton, R. (eds), 1967, *William III and Louis XIV*. Liverpool.

Bromley, J.S., 1988. *Corsairs and Navies 1660–1760*

Brown, G. S., 1956. 'The Anglo-French Naval Crisis, 1778: a study of conflict in the North Cabinet', *William and Mary Quarterly*

Browning, A., 1951. *Thomas Osborne, Earl of Danby*

Browning, R., 1967–8. 'The Duke of Newcastle and the Imperial Election Plan, 1749–1754', *Journal of British Studies*

Browning, R., 1975. *The Duke of Newcastle*. New Haven.

Butterfield, H., 1963. 'British foreign policy 1762–65', *HJ*

Canny, N. (ed.), 1998. *The Oxford History of the British Empire. I The Origins of Empire. British Overseas Enterprise to the Close of the Seventeenth Century*. Oxford.

Chance, J. F., 1909. *George I and the Northern War*

Chance, J. F., 1923. *The Alliance of Hanover*

Childs, J., 1987. *The British Army of William III*

Christelow, A., 1946. 'Economic background of the Anglo-Spanish War of 1762', *Journal of Modern History*

Clapham, J. H., 1899, *The Causes of the War of 1792*. Cambridge.

Clark, G. N., 1923. *The Dutch Alliance and the War against French Trade 1688–1697*. Manchester.

Clark, J. C. D., 1985. *English Society 1688–1832*. Cambridge.

Clark, R., 1938. *Sir William Trumbull in Paris 1685–1686*

Claydon, T., 1996. *William III and the Godly Revolution*. Cambridge.

Clayton, T. R., 1981. 'The Duke of Newcastle, the Earl of Halifax, and the American origins of the Seven Years' War', *HJ*

Cobban, A., 1954. *Ambassadors and Secret Agents: The Diplomacy of the First Earl of Malmesbury at The Hague*

Cobbett, W., 1806–20. *Parliamentary History of England from 1066 to 1803*

Coleman, D. C., 1980. 'Mercantilism revisited', *HJ*

Colley, L.J., 1982. *In Defiance of Oligarchy: The Tory Party, 1714–60*. Cambridge.

Colley, L.J., 1992. *Britons: Forging the Nation 1707–1837*. New Haven.

Conn, S., 1942. *Gibraltar in British Diplomacy in the Eighteenth Century*. New Haven.

Conway, S., 1995. *The War of American Independence 1775–1783*.

Coombs, D., 1958. *The Conduct of the Dutch. British Opinion and the Dutch Alliance during the War of the Spanish Succession*. The Hague.

Crout, R. R., 1983. 'In search of a "Just and Lasting Peace": the Treaty of 1783', *International History Review*

Crouzet, F., 1996. *Britain, France and International Commerce. From Louis XIV to Victoria*. Aldershot.

Cruickshanks, E., 1979. *Political Untouchables: The Tories and the '45*

Cruickshanks, E. (ed.) 1982. *Ideology and Conspiracy: Aspects of Jacobitism 1689–1759*. Edinburgh.

Cruickshanks, E. and Black, J. M. (eds), 1988. *The Jacobite Challenge*. Edinburgh.

Cruickshanks, E. (ed.), 1989. *By Force or By Default? The Revolution of 1688–89*. Edinburgh.

Cunningham, A., 1964–5. 'The Oczakov debate', *Middle Eastern Studies*

Dickson, P., 1967. *The Financial Revolution in England*.

Dickson, P., 1973. 'English commercial negotiations with Austria 1737–1752' in Whiteman, A. et al. (eds), *Statesmen, Scholars and Merchants*

Dippel, H., 1971. 'Prussia's English policy after the Seven Years' War', *Central European History*

Doran, P. F., 1986. *Andrew Mitchell and Anglo-Prussian Relations during the Seven Years' War*. New York.

Duffy, M., 1980. 'The foundations of British naval power', in Duffy (ed.), *The Military Revolution and the State*. Exeter.

Duffy, M., 1986. *The Englishman and the Foreigner*. Cambridge.

Duffy, M., 1987. *Soldiers, Sugar and Seapower: The British Expeditions to the West Indies and the War against Revolutionary France*. Oxford.

Duffy, M., 1989. 'British diplomacy and the French Wars 1789–1815', in Dickinson, H.T. (ed.), *Britain and the French Revolution, 1789–1815*

Duffy, M. (ed.), 1992. *Parameters of British Naval Power 1650–1850*. Exeter.

Dull, J. R., 1985. *A Diplomatic History of the American Revolution*. New Haven.

Dunthorne, H., 1986. *The Maritime Powers 1721–1740: A Study of Anglo-Dutch Relations in the Age of Walpole*. New York.

Ehrman, J., 1962. *The British Government and Commercial Negotiations with Europe, 1788–93*. Cambridge.

Ehrman, J., 1969. *The Younger Pitt: The Years of Acclaim*

Ehrman, J., 1983. *The Younger Pitt: The Reluctant Transition*

Eldon, C. W., 1938, *England's Subsidy Policy towards the Continent during the Seven Years' War.* Philadelphia.

Ellis, K. L., 1958. 'British communications and diplomacy in the eighteenth century', *Bulletin of the Institute of Historical Research*

Ellis, K. L., 1969. 'The administrative connections between Britain and Hanover', *Journal of the Society of Archivists*

Evans, H. V., 1974. 'The Nootka Sound controversy in Anglo-French diplomacy', *Journal of Modern History*

Feiling, K., 1930. *British Foreign Policy 1660–1672*

Feldbaek, O., 1977. 'The Anglo-Danish convoy conflict', *Scandinavian Journal of History*

Fisher, H. E. S., 1971. *The Portugal Trade: A Study of Anglo-Portuguese Commerce 1700–1770*

Geyl, P., 1969. *Orange and Stuart*

Gibbs, G. C., 1962, 'Parliament and foreign policy in the age of Stanhope and Walpole', *EHR*

Gibbs, G. C., 1968. 'Newspapers, parliament and foreign policy in the age of Stanhope and Walpole', *Mélanges offerts à G. Jacquemyns*. Brussels.

Gibbs, G. C., 1969. 'The Revolution in foreign policy', in Holmes, G. (ed.), *Britain after the Glorious Revolution*

Gibbs, G. C., 1970. 'Laying treaties before Parliament in the Eighteenth Century', in Hatton, R. and Anderson, M. S. (eds), *Studies in Diplomatic History*

Gibbs, G. C., 1986. 'English attitudes towards Hanover and the Hanoverian Succession in the first half of the eighteenth century', in Birke, A. M. and Kluxen, K. (eds), *England and Hanover*

Gibson, J. S., 1988. *Playing the Scottish Card: The Franco-Jacobite Invasion of 1708*. Edinburgh.

Glete, J., 1993. *Navies and Nations. Warships, Navies and State Building in Europe and America, 1500–1860*. Stockholm.

Goebel, J., 1927. *The Struggle for the Falkland Islands*. New York.

Gough, B. M., 1980. *Distant Dominion: Britain and the Northwest Coast of North America*

Graham, G. S., 1958. *Empire of the North Atlantic: The Maritime Struggle for North America*

Gregg, E., 1980. *Queen Anne*

Haley, K. H. D., 1953. *William of Orange and the English Opposition, 1672–4.* Oxford.

Haley, K. H. D., 1958. 'The Anglo-Dutch rapprochement of 1677', *EHR*

Haley, K. H. D., 1986. *An English Diplomat in the Low Countries: Sir William Temple and John De Witt, 1665–72*. Oxford.

Harding, R., 1991. *Amphibious Warfare in the Eighteenth Century. The British Expedition to the West Indies, 1740–1742*. Woodbridge.

Harding, R., 1995. *The Evolution of the Sailing Navy, 1509–1815*.

Harlow, V. T. (2 vols, 1952-64). *The Founding of the Second British Empire 1763–1793*

Harris, R., 1993. *A Patriot Press: National Politics and the London Press in the 1740s*. Oxford.

Harvey, A. D., 1978. 'European attitudes to Britain during the French Revolutionary and Napoleonic Era', *History*

Hattendorf, J. B., 1983. 'English grand strategy and the Blenheim campaign of 1704', *International History Review*

Hattendorf, J. B., 1987. *England in the War of the Spanish Succession: A study of the English view and conduct of grand strategy, 1701–1712*. New York.

Hatton, R. and Bromley, J. S. (eds), 1968. *William III and Louis XIV*

Hatton, R., 1950. *Diplomatic Relations between Great Britain and the Dutch Republic 1714–1721*

Hatton, R., 1978. *George I*

Hatton, R., 1982. *The Anglo-Hanoverian Connection 1714–1760*

Hayton, D., 1984. 'The "Country" interest and the party system, 1689-c. 1720' in Jones C. (ed.), *Party and Management in Parliament 1660–1784*. Leicester.

Hertz, G. B., 1907. 'England and the Ostend Company', *EHR*

Hill, B. W., 1988. *Robert Harley*. New Haven.

Horn, D. B., 1927. 'The origins of the proposed election of a King of the Romans', *EHR*

Horn, D.B., 1930a. 'The Cabinet controversy on subsidy treaties in time of peace', *EHR*

Horn, D. B., 1930b. *Sir Charles Hanbury-Williams and European Diplomacy 1747–58*

Horn, D. B. 1932. *British Diplomatic Representatives 1689–1789*

Horn, D. B., 1945. *British Public Opinion and the First Partition of Poland*

Horn, D. B., 1956. 'The diplomatic experience of Secretaries of State, 1660–1852', *History*

Horn, D. B., 1961. *The British Diplomatic Service 1689–1789*. Oxford.

Horn, D. B., 1967. *Great Britain and Europe in the Eighteenth Century*. Oxford.

Horn, D. B., 1970. 'The Duke of Newcastle and the origins of the Diplomatic Revolution', in Elliott, J. H. and Koenigsberger, H. G. (eds), *The Diversity of History*

Horwitz, H., 1977. *Parliament, Party and Politics in the reign of William III*. Manchester.

Hotblack, K., 1908. 'The Peace of Paris, 1763', *Transactions of the Royal Historical Society*

Hutt, M., 1986. 'The 1970s and the myth of "Perfidious Albion"', *Franco-British Studies*

Hutton, R., 1986. 'The making of the Secret Treaty of Dover, 1668–1670', *HJ*

Hutton, R., 1989. *Charles II*. Oxford.

Israel, J. (ed.), 1991 *The Anglo-Dutch Moment: Essays on the Glorious Revolution and its World Impact*. Cambridge.

Jarrett, D., 1973. *The Begetters of Revolution: England's Involvement with France*

Jones, D. W., 1988. *War and Economy in the Age of William III and Marlborough.* Oxford.

Jones, G. H., 1954. *The Mainstream of Jacobitism.* Cambridge, Massachusetts.

Jones, G. H., 1967. *Charles Middleton.* Chicago.

Jones, G. H., 1998. *Great Britain and the Tuscan Succession Question, 1710–1737.* New York.

Jones, J. R., 1966. *Britain and Europe in the Seventeenth Century*

Jones, J. R., 1972. *The Revolution of 1688 in England*

Jones, J. R., 1978. *Country and Court: England 1658–1714*

Jones, J. R., 1980. *Britain and the World 1649–1815*

Kennedy, P. M., 1976. *The Rise and Fall of British Naval Mastery*

Kennedy, P. M., 1988. *The Rise and Fall of the Great Powers*

Kent, H. S. K., 1973. *War and Trade in Northern Seas: Anglo-Scandinavian Economic Relations in the Mid-Eighteenth Century.* Cambridge.

Kenyon, J. P., 1958. *Robert Spencer, Earl of Sunderland*

Konopozynski, W., 1948–9. 'England and the First Partition of Poland', *Journal of Central European Affairs*

Lachs, P. S., 1965. *The Diplomatic Corps under Charles II and James II.* New Brunswick, NJ.

Langford, P., 1976. *Modern British Foreign Policy: The Eighteenth Century, 1688–1815*

Lawson, P., 1993. *The East India Company: A History.* Harlow.

Lodge, R., 1923. *Great Britain and Prussia in the Eighteenth Century.* Oxford.

Lodge, R., 1928. 'The First Anglo-Russian Treaty, 1739–42', *EHR*

Lodge, R., 1930a. *Studies in Eighteenth Century Diplomacy, 1740 1748*

Lodge, R., 1930b. 'Russia, Prussia, and Great Britain, 1742 44', *EHR*

Lodge, R., 1933. *The Private Correspondence of Sir Benjamin Keene*

Lojek, J., 1970. 'The International Crisis of 1791', *East-Central Europe*

McCann, T.J., 1984. *The Correspondence of the Dukes of Richmond and Newcastle 1724–1750.* Lewes.

McKay, D., 1971. 'Bolingbroke, Oxford and the defence of the Utrecht settlement in southern Europe', *EHR*

McKay, D. and Scott, H.M., 1983. *The Rise of the Great Powers*

McKay, D., 1986. *Allies of Convenience: Diplomatic Relations between Great Britain and Austria 1714 1719.* New York.

Mackesy, P., 1963. 'British strategy in the War of American Independence', *Yale Review*

Mackesy, P., 1964. *The War for America 1775-1783*

Mackesy, P., 1984. *War without Victory: The Downfall of Pitt, 1799–1802.* Oxford.

MacLachlan, A. D., 1969. 'The road to peace, 1710–13', in Holmes, G. (ed.), *Britain after the Glorious Revolution 1689 1714*

McLachlan, J., 1940. *Trade and Peace with Old Spain, 1667-1750.* Cambridge.

McLynn, F. J., 1981. *France and the Jacobite Rising of 1745.* Edinburgh.

Madariaga, I. de, 1962. *Britain, Russia and the Armed Neutrality of 1780*

Marshall, P.J. (ed.), 1998. *The Oxford History of the British Empire. II The Eighteenth Century.* Oxford.

Mathias, P., 1983. *The First Industrial Nation* (2nd edn)

Mediger, W., 1970. 'Great Britain, Hanover and the rise of Prussia', in Hatton, R. and Anderson, M. S. (eds), *Studies in Diplomatic History*

Metcalf, M. F., 1977. *Russia, England and Swedish Party Politics 1762–1766.* Stockholm.

Meyer, J. and Bromley J., 1980. 'The Second Hundred Years' War (1689–1815)', in Johnson, D., Bedanda, F. and Crouzet, F. (eds), *Britain and France: Ten Centuries*

Middleton, C. R., 1977. *The Administration of British Foreign Policy 1782–1846.* Durham, North Carolina.

Middleton R., 1985. *The Bells of Victory: The Pitt-Newcastle Ministry and the Conduct of the Seven Years' War 1757–1762.* Cambridge.

Miller, D. A., 1970. *Sir Joseph Yorke and Anglo-Dutch Relations 1774–1780.* The Hague.

Miller, J., 1978. *James II.* Hove.

Mitchell, L. G., 1971. *Charles James Fox and the Disintegration of thge Whig Party 1782–1794.* Oxford.

Mori, J., 1995. *William Pitt and the French Revolution, 1785–1795.* Keele.

Morris, R. B., 1963. *The Peacemakers: The Great Powers and American Independence.* New York.

Murray, J. J., 1969. *George I, the Baltic and the Whig Split of 1717.*

Namier, L. and Brooke J., 1964. *The House of Commons 1754–1790.*

Norris, J., 1955. 'The policy of the British Cabinet in the Nootka crisis', *EHR*

Oakley, S. P., 1987. *William III and the Northern Crowns during the Nine Years ' War 1689–1697.* New York.

O'Gorman, F., 1989. *Voters, Patrons and Parties: The Unreformed Electorate of Hanoverian England, 1734–1832.* Oxford.

Ollard, R., 1969. *Man of War: Sir Robert Holmes and the Restoration Navy*

Owen, J. B., 1973. 'George II Reconsidered' in Whiteman, A. *et al.* (eds), *Statesmen, Scholars and Merchants*

Pares, R., 1936. *War and Trade in the West Indies 1739–1763.* Oxford.

Pares, R., 1936. 'American versus continental warfare 1739–1763', *EHR*

Pares, R., 1938. *Colonial Blockade and Neutral Rights 1739–1763.* Oxford.

Pares, R., 1953. *King George III and the Politicians.* Oxford.

Patterson, A. T., 1960. *The Other Armada: The Franco-Spanish Attempt to invade Britain in 1779.* Manchester.

Peters, M., 1980. *Pitt and Popularity: The Patriot Ministry and London Opinion during the Seven Years' War.* Oxford.

Peters, M., 1998. *The Elder Pitt.*

Pincus, S.C.A., 1995. '"Coffee Politicians Does Create"': Coffeehouses and Restoration Political Culture' *Journal of Modern History.*

Pincus, S. C. A., 1996. *Protestantism and Patriotism: Ideologies and the Making of English Foreign Policy, 1650–1685.* Cambridge.

Proctor, D. and Wilson, C. (ed.), 1989. *1688: The Seaborne Alliance and Diplomatic Revolution*

Rashed, Z. E., 1951. *The Peace of Paris 1763.* Liverpool.

Raven, G. J. A. and Rodger, N. A. M., 1990. *Navies and Armies. The Anglo Dutch Relationship in War and Peace 1688–1988*. Edinburgh.

Reading, D, 1938. *The Anglo-Russian Commercial Treaty of 1734*. New Haven.

Reddaway, W. F., 1932–4. 'Great Britain and Poland, 1762–72', Cambridge *Historical Journal*

Reitan, E.A., 1994. *Politics, War and Empire. The Rise of Britain to a World Power 1688–1792*.

Rice, G. W., 1980. 'Great Britain, the Manila ransom and the first Falkland Islands dispute with Spain, 1766', *International History Review*

Richmond, H., 1920. *The Navy in the War of 1739–48*

Richmond, H., 1946. *Statesmen and Sea Power*. Oxford.

Ritcheson, C. R., 1983. 'The Earl of Shelburne and peace with America, 1782–1783', *International History Review*

Ritcheson, C. R., 1969. *Aftermath of Revolution: British Policy towards the United States 1782–1795*. Dallas.

Roberts, C., 1983. 'Party and patronage in later Stuart England', in Baxter, S. B. (ed.), *England's Rise to Greatness*

Roberts, C., 1985. *Schemes and Undertakings: A Study of English Politics in the Seventeenth Century*. Columbus, Ohio.

Roberts, M., 1967. 'Great Britain and the Swedish Revolution, 1772–1773', *HJ*, reprinted in *Essays in Swedish History*

Roberts, M., 1970. *Splendid Isolation 1763–1780*. Reading.

Roberts, M., 1974. *Macartney in Russia*

Roberts, M., 1980. *British Diplomacy and Swedish Politics, 1758–1773*

Rodger, N. A. M., 1993. *The Insatiable Earl. A Life of John Montagu, 4th Earl of Sandwich*.

Rogers, N., 1989. *Whigs and Cities: Popular Politics in the Age of Walpole and Pitt*. Oxford.

Rogers, N. 1998. *Crowds, Culture and Politics in Georgian Britain*. Oxford.

Roosen, W., 1987. 'The origins of the War of the Spanish Succession', in Black (ed.), *Origins of War*

Rose, C., 1999. *England in the 1690s. Revolution, Religion and War*. Oxford.

Rose, J. H., 1911. *William Pitt and the National Revival*

Rule, J., 1992. *The Vital Century: England's Developing Economy 1714–1815*.

Schweizer, K. W., 1978. 'The non-renewal of the Anglo-Prussian subsidy treaty, 1761–1762', *Canadian Journal of History*

Schweizer, K. W., 1981. 'William Pitt, Lord Bute and the peace negotiations with France, 1761', *Albion*

Schweizer, K. W. (ed.), 1988. *Lord Bute: Essays in Re-interpretation*. Leicester.

Schweizer, K. W., 1989. *England, Prussia and the Seven Years' War*. Lewiston, New York.

Scott, H. M., 1989. '"The true principles of the revolution": The Duke of Newcastle and the idea of the Old System', in Black (ed.), *Knights Errant*

Scott, H. M., 1990. *British Foreign Policy in the Age of the American Revolution*. Oxford.

Scott, H. M., 1992. 'The Second "Hundred Years War", 1689–1815', *HJ*

Scott, H. M., 1998. 'Britain as a European Great Power in the Age of the American Revolution', in H. T. Dickinson (ed.), *Britain and the American Revolution*. Harlow.

Seaward, P., 1987. 'The House of Commons Committee of Trade and the origins of the Second Anglo-Dutch war, 1664', *HJ*

Sedgwick, R., 1970. *The House of Commons 1715–54*.

Sen, S., 1998. *Empire of Free Trade. The East India Company and the Making of the Colonial Marketplace*. Philadelphia.

Sonnino, P., 1988. *Louis XIV and the Origins of the Dutch War*. Cambridge.

Speck, W. A., 1988. *Reluctant Revolutionaries: Englishmen and the Revolution of 1688*. Oxford.

Spencer, F., 1956. 'The Anglo-Prussian breach of 1762: an historical revision', *History*

Spencer, F. (ed.), 1961. *The Fourth Earl of Sandwich: Diplomatic Correspondence 1763–1765*. Manchester.

Stone, L. (ed.), 1994. *An Imperial State at War: Britain from 1689 to 1815*.

Stuart, C., 1981. 'Lord Shelburne', in Lloyd-Jones, H., Pearl, V. and Worden, B. (eds), *History and Imagination*

Sutherland, L. S., 1952. *The East India Company in Eighteenth-Century Politics*. Oxford.

Symcox, G., 1983. 'Britain and Victor Amadeus II: or, the use and abuse of allies', in Baxter S. (ed), *England's Rise to Greatness*

Szechi, D., 1994. *The Jacobites: Britain and Europe 1688–1788*. Manchester.

Tarling, P. N., 1962. *Anglo-Dutch Rivalry in the Malay World 1780–1824*. St. Lucia, Queensland.

Taylor, S. and others (eds.), 1998. *Hanoverian Britain and Empire* Woodbridge.

Thomas, P. D. G., 1985. 'George III and the American Revolution', *History*

Thomson, M. A., 1932. *The Secretaries of State, 1681–1782*. Oxford.

Tracy, N., 1988. *Navies, Deterrence, and American Independence: Britain and Sea Power in the 1760s and 1770s*. Vancouver.

Tracy, N., 1995. *Manila Ransomed. The British Assault on Manila in the Seven Years War*. Exeter.

Troost, W., 1983. *William III and the Treaty of Limerick*

Van Alstyne, R. W., 1964. 'Great Britain, the War for Independence and the "Gathering Storm" in Europe 1775–1778', *Huntington Library Quarterly*

Viner, J., 1948. 'Power versus plenty as objectives of foreign policy in the seventeenth and eighteenth centuries', *World Politics*

Ward, A. W., 1899. *Great Britain and Hanover: Some Aspects of the Personal Union*. Oxford.

Ward, A. W. and Gooch, G. P., 1922. *Cambridge History of British Foreign Policy 1787–1919. 1: 1783–1815*. Cambridge.

Webb, P., 1975. 'The naval aspects of the Nootka Sound crisis', *Mariner's Mirror*

Webb, P., 1977. 'The rebuilding and repair of the fleet, 1783–93', *Bulletin of the Institute of Historical Research*

Webb, P., 1980. 'Seapower in the Ochakov affair', *International History Review*

Western, J. R., 1965. *The English Militia in the Eighteenth Century*

Williams, B., 1932. *Stanhope*

Williams, B., 1943. *Carteret and Newcastle.* Cambridge.

Williams, G., 1966. *The Expansion of Europe in the Eighteenth Century*

Williams, J. B., 1972. *British Commercial Policy and Trade Expansion, 1750–1850*

Wilson, C., 1941. *Anglo-Dutch Commerce and Finance in the Eighteenth Century.* Cambridge.

Wilson, C., 1957. *Profit and Power: A Study of England and the Dutch Wars*

Wilson, C., 1965. *England's Apprenticeship 1603–1763*

Wilson, K., 1995. *The Sense of the People. Politics, Culture and Imperialism in England, 1715–1785.* Cambridge.

Woodfine, P., 1987. 'The Anglo-Spanish War in 1739', in Black, J.M. (ed.), *The Origins of War in Early Modern Europe*

Woodfine, P., 1998. *Britannia's Glories. The Walpole Ministry and the 1739 War with Spain*

INDEX